Play the 2 c3 Sicilian

Eduardas Rozentalis and
Andrew Harley

First published in the UK by Gambit Publications Ltd 2002

A copy of the British Library Cataloguing in Publication data is available from the British Library.

ISBN 1 901983 56 0

DISTRIBUTION:
Worldwide (except USA): Central Books Ltd, 99 Wallis Rd, London E9 5LN.
Tel +44 (0)20 8986 4854 Fax +44 (0)20 8533 5821.
E-mail: orders@Centralbooks.com
USA: BHB International, Inc., 302 West North 2nd Street, Seneca, SC 2967, USA.

For all other enquiries (including a full list of all Gambit chess titles) please contact the publishers, Gambit Publications Ltd, P.O. Box 32640, London W14 0JN.
E-mail Murray@gambitchess.freeserve.co.uk
Or visit the GAMBIT web site at http://www.gambitbooks.com

Edited by Graham Burgess
Typeset by John Nunn
Printed in Great Britain by The Cromwell Press, Trowbridge, Wilts.

10 9 8 7 6 5 4 3 2 1

Gambit Publications Ltd
Managing Director: GM Murray Chandler
Chess Director: GM John Nunn
Editorial Director: FM Graham Burgess
German Editor: WFM Petra Nunn

Contents

Symbols

+	check		Wch	world championship
++	double check		Wcht	world team championship
#	checkmate		Ech	European championship
!!	brilliant move		Echt	European team championship
!	good move		ECC	European Clubs Cup
!?	interesting move		Ct	candidates event
?!	dubious move		IZ	interzonal event
?	bad move		Z	zonal event
??	blunder		OL	olympiad
+−	White is winning		jr	junior event
±	White is much better		wom	women's event
⩲	White is slightly better		rpd	rapidplay game
=	equal position		sim	game from simultaneous display
∞	unclear position		corr.	correspondence game
∓	Black is slightly better		1-0	the game ends in a win for White
∓	Black is much better		½-½	the game ends in a draw
−+	Black is winning		0-1	the game ends in a win for Black
Ch	championship		(n)	nth match game
Cht	team championship		(D)	see next diagram

Transpositions are displayed by a dash followed by the moves (in *italic*) of the variation to which the transposition occurs. The moves start with the first one that deviates from the line under discussion. All the moves to bring about the transposition are given. Thus, after 1 e4 c5 2 c3 d5 3 exd5 ♕xd5 4 d4 ♘c6 5 ♘f3 ♘f6 6 ♗e3 ♗g4 the comment "7 dxc5 ♕xd1+ 8 ♔xd1 e5 − *4...♘f6 5 ♘f3 ♗g4 6 dxc5 ♕xd1+ 7 ♔xd1 e5 8 ♗e3 ♘c6 ±*" signifies that the reader should locate material on 1 e4 c5 2 c3 d5 3 exd5 ♕xd5 4 d4 ♘f6 5 ♘f3 ♗g4 6 dxc5 ♕xd1+ 7 ♔xd1 e5 8 ♗e3 ♘c6, to which play has transposed. The '±' sign indicates the overall assessment of that line; such signs are only given when it is meaningful to do so.

Bibliography

Rosenberg, "Sicilian/Sizilianisch, Alapin", *Chess Player 5*, 1973.

Chandler, *Sicilian 2 c3*, Batsford, 1981.

Burgess, *Winning with the Smith-Morra Gambit*, Batsford, 1994.

Palkovi, *Sizilianische Verteidigung mit 2 c3*, Caissa, 1995.

Chandler, *The Complete c3 Sicilian*, Batsford, 1996.

Sveshnikov, *B22*, Šahovski Informator, 1997.

Nunn, Burgess, Emms and Gallagher, *Nunn's Chess Openings (NCO)*, Gambit/Everyman, 1999.

Gallagher, *c3 Sicilian*, Everyman, 1999.

Bosch, "Spice up your Alapin", *New in Chess*, 1999, no. 2.

Chess Base Magazine 1 to 84.

Informator 1 to 83.

The Week in Chess 1 to 394.

Introduction – *Eduardas Rozentalis*

I started to play 2 c3 against the Sicilian Defence in my childhood, as the main lines seemed to be too sharp and forcing. For many years this line was considered a 'lazy' variation. It was partly true, as there was not so much theory; top players used it very rarely and only a few grandmasters played it frequently. However, practical experience and the use of computers have brought a lot of theory to the line. These days, you need to know forced variations and main ideas, like in any other Sicilian line. Today, chess-players of all levels like to play 2 c3 against the Sicilian Defence. Many games are played in every tournament. Grandmasters Sveshnikov, Smagin, Blatny and yours truly never forget 'the old love'. You can even see current and former world champions Anand, Ponomariov and Kramnik playing the 'Alapin Variation'.

It was also considered that this line leads to monotonous positions. I believe the opposite – the line can lead to a variety of very different situations, from very sharp to purely strategic positions. It often transposes to other openings, including the French Defence, Caro-Kann Defence, Alekhine Defence and others. From my own practice I know that some players are quite happy to meet 2 c3, as they see life then as easier than in the main Sicilian lines. However, quite a lot of Sicilian lovers feel very uncomfortable, as they have to play something that is absolutely different from the types of position that they are accustomed to having on the board.

As with the whole of modern opening theory, the 2 c3 line is developing. Evaluations and recommendations are changing constantly. A lot of books have been written about it already. We try to show our view of modern theory and practice. We give our evaluations, which can be relative and different from the evaluations of the other specialists. There are still plenty of new discoveries to be made; see, for example, my game against Lutz from early 2002 at the end of Chapter 6. I wish you a lot of interesting games and nice victories, playing the 2 c3 Sicilian – with either side!

Introduction – *Andrew Harley*

I was struck at an early age by Bent Larsen's comment that the main line Sicilian with 2 ♘f3 and 3 d4 was nothing more than a cheap trap: White gives Black a central pawn-majority in return for a few tactical chances. Analysis by Rosenberg in an old 1973 copy of *Chess Player* inspired me to take up the then rather obscure line 2 c3. As an improving young player, I found it easy to get an advantage with White as the theory was then so little known by Black, and also to score wins against strong players as they overpressed in worse positions. The peak of my 2 c3 Sicilian career came at the 1994 British Championship with a 'hat-trick' of consecutive wins against Cummings, Hennigan and McDonald.

Things then started to go downhill – both for my chess performances and for the 2 c3 Sicilian! The 2 c3 Sicilian had become very fashionable and been played by many top grandmasters in the early 1990s, and this had led to the discovery of a number of apparently equalizing options for Black. Fashion moved on, and the 2 c3 Sicilian was left devastated in its wake. I, along with other 2 c3 Sicilian players, found it difficult to prove any advantage. When reviewing Gallagher's 1999 book on the 2 c3 Sicilian, John Watson wondered if the variation even deserved a book at all, commenting that it is "giving Black effortless, often sterile, equality (or more than equality, in those complex lines where White tries to keep the play alive)", "consistently leading to prospectless play (at best) from White's point of view", and that "White is having a hard time making it even interesting".

The outlook looks brighter now, as a number of new ideas have emerged for White, some during the writing of this book! I would point particularly to our analysis of the critical variations 2...d5 3 exd5 ♕xd5 4 d4 ♘f6 5 ♘f3 ♗g4 6 dxc5 (in Chapter 6) and 2...♘f6 3 e5 ♘d5 4 ♘f3 (in Chapter 10). A frequent 2 c3 Sicilian player, Ponomariov, has become FIDE World Champion. Other top grandmasters still essaying it with confidence include Adams, Morozevich, Smirin, Kharlov, Smagin, Sermek, Pavasović, Vysochin, my co-author Rozentalis, and of course Sveshnikov. In fact, I have always thought it a great pity that the rather long-winded name 'Alapin-Sveshnikov Variation' never managed to stick in popular usage. Alapin is referenced once in this book (a test for an eagle-eyed reader!) but his contribution to this line is as nothing by comparison. The problem of course is that there is already one other Sveshnikov Variation of the Sicilian: 1 e4 c5 2 ♘f3 ♘c6 3 d4 cxd4 4 ♘xd4 ♘f6 5 ♘c3 e5 6 ♘db5 d6 7 ♗g5 a6 8 ♘a3 b5.

I have also recently added the Sicilian Defence to my repertoire for Black and would wish to reassure the Sicilian players reading this book that there are plenty of new ideas here for Black too. This is intended as an objective and comprehensive work detailing the current theoretical state of this opening as we see it. However, things change: when I reread Rosenberg's 1973 *Chess Player* article, and even Chandler's 1981 first edition of his 2 c3 Sicilian book, I notice that our Chapters 9 and 10 (besides many other main lines embedded within the other chapters) didn't even exist as subnotes then. In more recent times, the development of established systems with, for example, ...g6 or even ...g5 for Black or with dxc5 or g3 for White, have indicated how many new ideas must be lying dormant waiting to be discovered. Happy playing, and happy inventing!

Summary of Ideas

Any repertoire is a matter of personal taste, and will be dependent on the type of pawn-structures you feel comfortable with and whether you prefer to take risks to avoid a draw or to play more solidly. We have ordered the variations with those we consider to be most theoretically accurate given last, and we hope this is helpful as you try to select your own personal repertoire.

Alternatives to 2...d5 and 2...♘f6

Chapter 1 is devoted to the less played variations. Often they transpose to other openings, and often deviate from well-known paths, allowing the players to create something new.

Chapter 2 analyses 2...e6, a line often used by players whose repertoire also includes the French Defence. White can either transpose to the Advance French or choose to play against an isolated queen's pawn.

The 2...d5 Line

Chapters 3 to 6 analyse 2...d5, which is one of Black's two main options. Play generally continues 3 exd5 ♕xd5 4 d4 *(D)*:

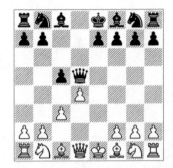

B

Like in the Scandinavian Defence, Black is willing to move his queen to the centre. Here, the c3-square is already occupied by the pawn, so the queen can't be attacked by the knight immediately. However, the centre is not the best place for the queen when all the pieces are still on the board. Black chooses 2...d5 if he wants to fight, as the play is not as forcing as in the case of 2...♘f6. It also gives White more chances to seek an advantage.

If Black plays 2...d5, he must be prepared to defend against an isolated queen's pawn. Black does well to delay ...cxd4 as long as possible, as the c3-pawn sits on White's queen's knight's natural development square. White can eventually force the exchange if he so wishes either by the prosaic ♗e3, threatening dxc5, or by the threat of the pawn advances c4 and d5. It is possible for Black to exchange off the isolated queen's pawn immediately with a very early ...e5, but this can leave him dangerously behind in development. More usually, a position with the following pawn-structure arises:

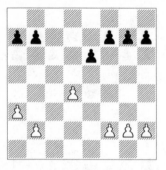

White has a space advantage, an outpost for his knight on e5 and good chances of launching a kingside attack with his pieces. A typical plan for White is to line up the light-squared bishop (on b1, c2 or d3) and queen (on c2, d3, or e4) on the b1-h7 diagonal to threaten mate on h7. This will eventually force Black to play ...g6, when White will try to use his knights, dark-squared bishop and queen to exploit Black's dark-squared weaknesses, and his h-pawn to soften up Black's kingside pawns further, while his light-squared bishop would typically move to the a2-g8 diagonal (on a2, b3 or c4) to control d5 and help support possible sacrifices on e6 and f7. White's rooks typically go to e1 and d1; or sometimes c1 for tactical reasons, though in general White doesn't want to exchange rooks. White will also always be on the lookout for playing d5. If things

are starting to become uncomfortable, White may play this to liquidate and draw, but at an appropriate moment, d5 can also be a devastating attacking breakthrough.

Black, meanwhile, will seek to take control of the d5-square using his knights. White almost always plays his pawn to a3 to stop Black playing ...♘b4 and ...♘bd5, but Black can also get the queen's knight to d5 via c6 and e7 (or, rarely, d7 and b6; the knight is much more actively situated on c6 than d7). Black can sometimes generate counterplay on the queenside with ...♘a5 and ...♘c4, exploiting the weaknesses created by a3, but Black rarely has time for this in the 2 c3 Sicilian. His rooks are often best placed defensively on d8 and e8, with his queen on d6 (or on b8 or even a8) and his dark-squared bishop fulfilling defensive duties on e7, f8 or sometimes d6 or g7, as required. If Black has managed to develop his light-squared bishop before playing ...e6, for example to g4, he can usually equalize with ease, as White's d-pawn is then more vulnerable (because the bishop attacks the defending f3-knight) and also as it is very difficult for White then to force Black to weaken himself with ...g6. The next best situation for that bishop is to be fianchettoed on b7, where it adds some support to d5 and can help Black initiate some counter-attacking ideas against White's kingside. Sometimes Black chooses to, or has to, develop the bishop to d7 (and then e8) instead, and while this offers more protection to the kingside, it is more passive. Black's ultimate aim is of course to withstand any attack, exchange pieces, and then reach an endgame where White's isolated queen's pawn proves a fatal weakness.

Some players have a paranoid fear of such an endgame, and this has been enough to put some players off the 2 c3 Sicilian altogether, as traditionally it has been thought that White must be prepared to play with an isolated queen's pawn. However, this is no longer the case – by playing 6 dxc5 against 4...♘c6 5 ♘f3 ♗g4, 4...♘c6 5 ♘f3 ♘f6, and 4...♘f6 5 ♘f3 ♗g4, and 6 ♘a3 against 4...♘f6 5 ♘f3 e6, all very respectable systems, White can avoid isolated queen's pawn positions altogether. (True, Black can continue 4...cxd4 but then White gets a particularly good isolated queen's pawn with an early ♘c3 and the possibility of developing the king's bishop straight to c4.) Instead, we reach another typical situation from 2...d5, where White has three pawns against two black pawns on the queenside, while Black has four against three on the kingside. In fact in a lot of the modern lines with 6 dxc5, White has, at least temporarily, four pawns against two on the queenside *(D)*:

If Black recaptures the pawn with his queen, White can get an initiative by chasing the queen with moves like ♗e3 and ♘a3 followed by ♘b5 or ♘c4. Therefore, Black sometimes prefers to gambit the pawn; as compensation White's king is stuck in the centre of the board. Recent practice seems to show that White can hang on by

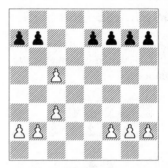

playing a plan such as b4, ♗e3, ♔c2 (or ♔c1) and ♔b2, and a3, when the king is not only safely tucked away but also defends the a1-rook in case Black plays ...a5 and then captures on b4. The precise tactical details of course vary from position to position. The reader would be advised to undertake a careful comparative study of the systems 4...♘c6 5 dxc5 ♕xd1+, 4...♘c6 5 ♘f3 ♗g4 6 dxc5 ♕xd1+, 4...♘c6 5 ♘f3 ♘f6 6 dxc5 ♕xd1+ (all in Chapter 4), and 4...♘f6 5 ♘f3 ♗g4 6 dxc5 ♕xd1+ (in Chapter 6).

When Black does recapture the pawn on c5 (be it with his queen, bishop or knight), the assessment of the resulting positions can depend on very subtle differences in piece placement. If Black is sufficiently active, the positions can just be dead equal, but if White can safely start his queenside pawn-majority advancing, he can have an advantage. Compare, for example, the two lines 4...♘f6 5 ♘f3 e6 6 ♗d3 ♗e7 7 0-0 0-0 8 c4 ♕h5 9 dxc5 ♖d8 10 ♗f4 ♕xc5 = and 4...♘f6 5 ♘f3 e6 6 ♗e2 ♘c6 7 0-0 ♗e7 8 c4 ♕d8 9 dxc5 ♕xd1 10 ♖xd1 ♗xc5 ± in Chapter 5.

The 2...♘f6 Line

Chapters 7 to 10 analyse 2...♘f6 3 e5 ♘d5 *(D)*, which is probably the main variation.

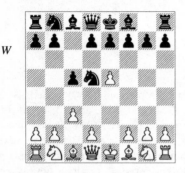

W

Like in the Alekhine Defence, Black has attacked White's e-pawn with his knight, luring it forward. The difference is the included moves c3 and ...c5, which make the position relatively better for Black. This doesn't mean that anything is wrong, however, as White can still fight for the centre. The play is more forcing than in the case of 2...d5 – a lot of far-reaching analysis has been devoted to these lines. It is considered that the variations where Black plays ...♘c6, ...d6 and develops his queen's bishop before playing ...e6 are the safest for Black if he is well prepared. This renders White's task of seeking an advantage more difficult, but he can still try for a small advantage. According to current theory and practice, neither 4 d4 cxd4 5 cxd4 d6 (in Chapter 7) nor 4 d4 cxd4 5 ♘f3 ♘c6 6 ♗c4 ♘b6 7 ♗b3 d6 (in Chapter 9) offers White any advantage against best play by Black. White's

best chances lie in deferring d4 and playing 4 ♘f3. This variation is analysed in detail in Chapter 10.

If Black is willing to endure a space disadvantage and defend for a while, the systems with 4 d4 cxd4 5 ♘f3 e6 (or 4 ♘f3 e6 5 d4 cxd4), as analysed in Chapter 8, may offer him more fighting chances. This pawn-structure then often arises:

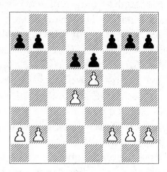

White's core plan is often almost exactly the same as with an isolated queen's pawn: he attacks on the kingside with his pieces, lining up his bishop and queen on the b1-h7 diagonal to induce the weakening ...g6 and then tries to exploit the dark-squared weaknesses on Black's kingside. By comparison to the isolated queen's pawn position, White has additional trumps here: the e5-pawn prevents Black from retreating his king's knight to the natural defensive square f6, and by controlling d6 also cramps Black's other pieces; his central pawns are not an endgame risk in the way that an isolated queen's pawn is.

However, White also has slightly less freedom. It is not so easy to develop his queenside pieces, since developing his knight to its natural square c3 can be met by ...♘xc3, when after bxc3, the pawn-structure is not so pleasant for White. While this capture is fine with an isolated queen's pawn, here White would have to fear Black resolving the tension with ...d5 or ...dxe5 (assuming Black can at some point force White to recapture with the pawn and not just pieces). Therefore, White often develops his knight to d2 instead and from there to e4 or c4. The black knight on d5 can also make it awkward for White to develop his queen's bishop; g5 and f4 are *en prise*, and its safe waiting square in the isolated queen's pawn structure, e3, blocks the e1-rook's defence of the e5-pawn. Therefore, the bishop often stays on c1 or d2, or sometimes heads to b2 after the pawn advances a3 and b4. You can see how the white pieces are starting to tread on each other's toes.

The central tension can be resolved in a number of ways. By playing exd6 at an appropriate moment, White can reach an isolated queen's pawn position; typically White would only usually consider doing so when Black has retreated his knight from d5 to b6, another move further away from the kingside. Black can resolve the tension by playing ...d5, reaching an Advance French structure (though Black's king's knight, typically having retreated to b6, is often not best placed for such a structure), or occasionally by the tactical break ...f5 hitting a piece on e4, but most typically by playing ...dxe5. Then ♘xe5 leads to an isolated queen's

pawn structure, while dxe5 leads to this pawn-structure:

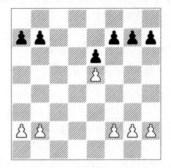

It is quite clear that White has a space advantage, and his attacking plans are much the same as before. Additionally, he can try to get a knight to the d6-outpost and can seek to make use of the third and fourth ranks to bring other pieces over to help in the kingside attack. Black, however, has chances for counterplay down the open files, and can put pressure on the e-pawn by ...♕c7, and by ...g6 followed by ...♗g7. In an endgame, while the e5-pawn is nowhere near as weak as the d4-pawn in an isolated queen's pawn structure, it is still potentially vulnerable if White is not careful. Note also that if the b2-pawn were instead on c3 (after an exchange ...♘xc3), the white pawns would be very weak indeed.

Lines with ...g6

Finally, a note on the trendy ...g6 systems for Black: 2...g6 (in Chapter 1), 2...d5 3 exd5 ♕xd5 4 d4 g6 (in Chapter 3) and 2...♘f6 3 e5 ♘d5 4 d4 cxd4

5 ♘f3 ♘c6 6 ♗c4 ♘b6 7 ♗b3 g6 (in Chapter 9). Black hopes to reach this pawn-structure (which can also occur in other variations):

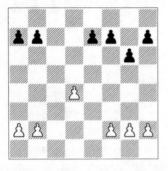

By comparison to the normal isolated queen's pawn structure discussed earlier, Black can here develop both his bishops more actively: the light-squared bishop on e6, f5 or g4, and the dark-squared bishop on g7, where it attacks d4. The king's knight can sometimes even go to f5 via h6, adding to the pressure on d4. While the e7- and f7-pawns are more vulnerable here, it is not easy for White to take advantage of this once Black is developed. Therefore, White typically tries to avoid this pawn-structure, by one of two methods:

1) By not having an isolated queen's pawn at all (e.g., capturing on c5 or advancing c4 and d5), or by forcing ...exd6 (e.g. by playing d5-d6 or by playing ♗f4 before exd6) to give Black an isolated queen's pawn too and a slight space disadvantage.

2) By forcing ...e6 (typically by pressure on f7; e.g., ♗b3 and ♘g5 or ♗c4 and ♕b3), when we have a normal isolated queen's pawn structure with the ...g6 weakness and consequent dark-squared weaknesses already provoked.

1 Alternatives to 2...e6, 2...d5 and 2...♞f6

If Black wants to avoid well-known lines, he can play one of the variations discussed in this chapter. Quite often, the game can transpose to other openings, such as the Pirc, Caro-Kann or Owen's Defence. Although quite a lot of games have already been played in these lines, there are no clear-cut conclusions about many of the original positions that can arise. Therefore there is much more room for both players to demonstrate their playing skills and imagination.

1 e4 c5 2 c3

Many players choose 2 ♞f3 first before trying to transpose to a c3 Sicilian:

a) 2...g6 (the Hyper-Accelerated Dragon) 3 c3 (3 d4 is probably stronger) is discussed under the continuation *2 c3 g6 3 ♞f3*.

b) 2...a6 (the O'Kelly Variation) 3 c3 ± leaves White practically a tempo up on most lines of the 2 c3 Sicilian.

c) 2...e6 3 c3 is discussed under *2 c3 e6 3 ♞f3*.

d) 2...♞c6 3 c3 and then:

d1) 3...♛a5 – *2 c3 ♛a5 3 ♞f3 ♞c6*.

d2) 3...e5 – *2 c3 e5 3 ♞f3 ♞c6*.

d3) 3...e6 4 d4 d5 5 exd5 (5 e5 is the Advance French) 5...exd5 – *2 c3*

e6 3 d4 d5 4 exd5 exd5 5 ♞f3 ♞c6. Note that Black has had to play ...♞c6 before ...♝d6, which gives White the additional option 6 g3!?.

d4) 3...d5 4 exd5 ♛xd5 5 d4 – *2 c3 d5 3 exd5 ♛xd5 4 d4 ♞c6 5 ♞f3*. It is generally considered that it is more accurate to play ...♞f6 before ...♞c6 so White has avoided some important lines after *4...♞f6*.

d5) 3...♞f6 4 e5 ♞d5 – *2 c3 ♞f6 3 e5 ♞d5 4 ♞f3 ♞c6*. Note that Black can no longer try many nuances of the move-orders *4 ♞f3 d6!?* or *4 ♞f3 e6* (including, for example, the system *5 d4 cxd4 6 cxd4 b6*).

e) The problem is of course 2...d6, when 3 c3!? is a quite distinct system not covered by this book.

If White is happy to prepare something else (be it 3 d4, 3 ♝b5+, 3 ♝c4, 3 d3 or 3 c3!?) against 2...d6, then playing 2 ♞f3 before 3 c3 does have the advantage of forcing Black to declare his hand (and inevitably rule out some options) before he knows White's intentions.

We now return to the position after 2 c3 *(D)*:

2...e6, 2...d5 and 2...♞f6 are analysed in other chapters. Here we consider the other five main replies:

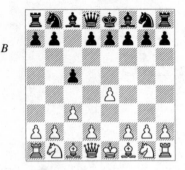

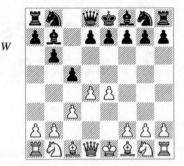

A: 2...b6	16
B: 2...♛a5	17
C: 2...g6	18
D: 2...e5	24
E: 2...d6	27

Two minor alternatives:

a) 2...a6 3 d4 cxd4 4 cxd4 d5 5 exd5 ♘f6 6 ♘c3 ♘xd5 7 ♗c4 ♘xc3 8 bxc3 (8 ♕f3? ♘b5! ∓ shows a small advantage of ...a6) 8...e6 9 ♘f3 ♗e7 10 0-0 ♘c6 11 ♖e1 0-0 12 ♗d3 g6?! (12...b5 can be met by 13 h4!? ♗xh4 14 ♘xh4 ♕xh4 15 ♖e3 f5 16 ♖g3 with an attack, or 13 ♕c2 g6 14 ♗h6 ±) 13 ♗h6 ♖e8 14 ♕d2 b5 15 h4! is much better for White, Harley-Cummings, British Ch (Norwich) 1994.

b) 2...♘c6 3 d4 d5 (otherwise White plays 4 d5) 4 exd5 (not 4 e5? ♗f5, when Black has a very good version of a Caro-Kann) 4...♕xd5 – *2...d5 3 exd5 ♕xd5 4 d4 ♘c6*.

A)

2...b6
Black doesn't try to fight in the centre, leaving it for the future.
3 d4 ♗b7 *(D)*
4 ♗d3

4 f3 is another good move: 4...e6 5 ♗e3 ♘f6 6 ♘d2 ♘c6 7 a3 (avoiding 7 ♗d3 cxd4 8 cxd4 ♘b4) 7...♗e7 8 ♗d3 a5 9 ♘e2 ♗a6 10 ♗xa6 (10 ♗c2 is probably even better: when one has more space, it is always useful to keep more pieces on the board) 10...♖xa6 11 0-0 0-0 12 ♘f4 and White has slightly better chances, Rozentalis-Tyomkin, Montreal 2000.

4...♘f6
4...e6 makes it easier for White to develop simply and naturally: 5 ♘f3 ♘f6 (5...d6 6 0-0 ♘d7 7 ♕e2 and White has a pleasant position, Klinger-Ballmann, Gausdal jr Wch 1986) 6 ♕e2 cxd4 7 cxd4 and then:

a) 7...♘c6 8 a3 ♗e7 9 ♘c3 ♘a5 10 ♗g5 h6 11 ♗f4 d6 12 b4 ♘c6 13 d5 exd5 14 exd5 ♘b8 15 ♘d4 ± Timman-Hübner, Jerusalem jr Wch 1967.

b) 7...♗b4+ 8 ♘bd2 d5 9 e5 ♘fd7 10 0-0 a5 11 ♖d1 ♗a6 12 ♘f1 ♗xd3 13 ♖xd3 ♘c6 14 ♘g5 ♗e7 15 ♕g4 h5 16 ♕g3 ± Hübner-Larsen, Bugojno 1978.

5 ♘d2
More complex is 5 ♕e2 cxd4 6 cxd4 ♘c6 7 d5 (7 ♘f3 ♘b4! =) 7...♘b4 (7...♘e5 8 ♗c2 d6?! 9 f4 ♘ed7 10 e5!

♘xd5 11 e6 ± Dubiel-Quinn, Duis-
burg jr Wch 1992) 8 ♗b5 a6 9 ♗a4 a5
10 ♘c3 ♗a6 11 ♗b5 ♗xb5 12 ♘xb5
♕c8 13 ♘c3 e6 14 ♗g5 ± Novoselski-
Veličković, Yugoslav Cht (Cetinje)
1992.

5...cxd4 6 cxd4 ♘c6 7 ♘e2
The best move. Instead, 7 ♘gf3 ♘b4
8 ♗b1 ♗a6 9 e5 ♘fd5 10 ♘e4 e6 11
a3 ♘c6 12 ♗d3 ♗xd3 13 ♕xd3 ♗e7
(Afek-Romero, Wijk aan Zee 2000)
leaves White a tempo up (thanks to
Black playing ...♗b7 followed by
...♗a6) on a line like 2...♘f6 3 e5 ♘d5
4 d4 cxd4 5 ♘f3 e6 6 cxd4 b6 7 ♗d3
♗a6 8 a3 ♗xd3 9 ♕xd3 ♘c6 10 ♘bd2
♗e7 11 ♘e4, though such a line is of
no theoretical significance (after 7 ♗d3
♗a6, White would play 8 0-0 not 8 a3)
and the position is equal.

7...e5
Or:
a) 7...g6 8 0-0 ♗g7 9 a3 0-0 10 ♖e1
d6 11 ♖b1 ± Smagin-Miles, Århus
1993.
b) The active move 7...♘b4 doesn't
achieve anything, since after 8 ♗b1
♗a6 9 ♘f3 White regroups his pieces
with a pleasant advantage, Schmitt-
diel-Grooten, Wijk aan Zee 1993.

8 d5 ♘b4 9 ♗b1 ♗c5 10 ♘c3!
A smart move. Instead:
a) 10 a3? ♘g4! with a strong attack.
b) 10 0-0 a5 11 a3 ♘a6 12 ♘g3 h5
and Black has good counterplay on the
kingside, Kharlov-Minasian, Kherson
1991.

10...0-0
10...a5 11 ♘b3 ♘a6 12 0-0 ±.

11 a3 ♘a6 12 0-0 ♘c7 13 ♗d3

White has a clear advantage, Sma-
gin-V.Milov, Iraklion 1993.

B)
2...♕a5 *(D)*

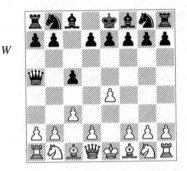

This strange move tries to prevent
White from playing an immediate d4,
as after ...cxd4 the white c-pawn would
be pinned. However, White can delay
this advance and develop his kingside
first.

3 ♘f3
Instead:
a) If White tries to push the queen
away by 3 ♘a3, Black obtains counter-chances: 3...e6 4 e5 (4 ♘c4 ♕c7
followed by 5...d5) 4...♘c6 5 ♘f3 ♕c7
6 d4 cxd4 7 cxd4 ♗xa3 8 bxa3 ♘ge7
and the position is very unclear, Roz-
entalis-Kupreichik, Minsk 1983.
b) Interesting is 3 g3 ♘c6 4 ♗g2
♘f6 5 ♘e2 (not blocking the bishop's
control of d5) 5...h5!? 6 h3 h4 7 g4
♘e5 8 d4 cxd4 9 f4 d3 (Kacheishvili-
Movsesian, Pula open 1997) and now
10 ♘d4 favours White – Gallagher.

3...♘c6 4 ♗c4
The most natural and the best. Otherwise:

a) 4 d4 cxd4 5 b4 (5 ♗c4?! ♘f6! exploits the fact that the black queen now controls e5; then 6 ♕e2 d6 7 0-0 ♗g4 ∓) 5...♕c7 6 b5 ♘e5 7 ♘xe5 ♕xe5 8 ♕xd4 gives White only a slight end-game advantage, Makropoulos-Ljubo-jević, Athens 1981.

b) 4 a3 e6 5 d4 ♘xd4 6 ♘xd4 cxd4 7 b4 ♕e5 8 cxd4 ♕xe4+ 9 ♗e3 ♕c6 gives White good compensation for the pawn, but this line has never been tested in practice, so it's difficult to make any conclusion.

c) 4 g3 is too slow in this position: 4...♘f6 5 ♕e2 d5 6 exd5 (not 6 e5? ♘d7 7 ♗g2 ♕c7 ∓) 6...♘xd5 and Black equalized easily in Rozentalis-Movsesian, Hastings 1996/7.

4...d6

4...b5 5 ♗d5! ♘f6 6 0-0 e6 7 ♗xc6 dxc6 8 ♖e1 followed by 9 d4 gives White the better position.

5 0-0 ♘f6 6 ♖e1 b5

Black can't pin the knight by means of 6...♗g4, because after 7 ♕b3 ♘d8 8 e5 he is in big trouble.

7 ♗d5! ♗d7 8 d4!

It is the right time to advance! 8 b4 cxb4 9 cxb4 ♕b6 = Keitlinghaus-Movsesian, Lazne Bohdanec 1996.

8...e6

8...cxd4 9 cxd4 ♘xd5 10 exd5 ♘b4? loses to 11 ♗d2.

9 ♗b3

White has achieved his goal. His pawn-centre is excellent, he has threats of d5 or e5, while the black queen's lo-cation on a5 is not justified.

C)

2...g6 *(D)*

This move is often used by those players who like to play the Pirc De-fence or King's Indian, in which they develop the dark-squared bishop to g7.

3 d4

Or:

a) 3 ♘f3 (a position often reached via 2 ♘f3 g6 3 c3) commits the knight prematurely and gains White nothing. Black can just proceed in the same manner: 3...♗g7 4 d4 cxd4 5 cxd4 (5 ♗c4 – 3 ♗c4 ♗g7 4 d4 cxd4 5 ♘f3) 5...d5! 6 exd5 ♘f6 7 ♗b5+ ♘bd7 8 d6 exd6 9 ♕e2+ ♕e7 10 ♗f4 ♕xe2+ 11 ♔xe2 ♔e7 = NCO.

b) 3 ♗c4 is a more interesting al-ternative – the idea is to discourage Black from playing ...d5. Then:

b1) 3...e6 seems a sound response: 4 ♕e2 ♘c6 5 ♘f3 ♗g7 6 0-0 ♘ge7 7 ♗b3 (7 d4!? cxd4 8 cxd4, Morgan-Binks, British Ch (Millfield) 2000, 8...d5 =) 7...d5 8 d3 0-0 = Slapikas-Blatny, Istanbul OL 2000.

b2) 3...♗g7 4 d4 cxd4 and here:

b21) 5 ♘f3 offers Black a transpo-sition to a Morra. Then:

b211) Black has the safe options 5...e6 and 5...d3, which work well here, where White has already developed his bishop to c4.

b212) 5...dxc3 6 ♘xc3 ♘c6 transposes to the Fianchetto Defence of the Morra Gambit (*1 e4 c5 2 d4 cxd4 3 c3 dxc3 4 ♘xc3 ♘c6 5 ♘f3 g6 6 ♗c4 ♗g7*), which, while probably viable for Black, is not considered the safest defence against the Morra, and is outside the scope of this book. However, it is worth mentioning that the critical lines are 7 0-0 d6!, when White has had difficulties proving that his compensation is fully worth the pawn, and 7 e5 ♕a5! 8 0-0 ♘xe5 9 ♘xe5 ♗xe5 10 ♖e1 (or 10 ♘d5 e6! 11 ♖e1 d6!) 10...d6! 11 ♘d5 e6! 12 ♗b5+ ♔f8, when White's attack doesn't constitute enough compensation for the material. However, it would be unwise for Black to venture into these sharp lines without some preparation.

b22) 5 cxd4 and now Black can try to deny White's move-order its point by playing 5...d5!? (5...♘c6 6 ♘f3 ♕b6 7 ♘c3!?, Mikac-Osmanbegović, Austrian Cht 1993/4) 6 ♗xd5 ♘f6 ∞.

We now return to 3 d4 (*D*):

3...cxd4

Or:

a) 3...♗g7?! 4 dxc5! ♘a6 5 ♗e3 ♕c7 6 ♘a3 (6 ♗xa6 bxa6 7 f3 ♗b7 followed by 8...f5 gives Black good counterplay) 6...♘xc5 7 ♘b5 ♕c6 8 ♕d5 and White wins the a7-pawn (analysis by Blatny).

b) 3...d6?! 4 dxc5 dxc5 5 ♕xd8+ ♔xd8 6 ♗c4 gives White a big advantage due to his better development.

c) 3...♕a5 attempts to improve on 2...♕a5 by playing this move after White has played d4. Then 4 d5 is unconvincing, while 4 dxc5 only gives White a slight edge, but the best try may well be 4 ♗e3 d6 5 ♘d2 ♘d7 6 ♘gf3 ♗g7 7 h3 ♘gf6 8 dxc5 dxc5 (8...♘xc5 9 b4) 9 ♘c4 ♕c7 10 e5 ± Pavasović-Denk, Vienna 1994.

4 cxd4

If White is unhappy with the fact that Black can meet this move with 4...d5, then he could experiment with the idea of a transposition to a line of the Morra Gambit, starting with 4 ♘f3 or 4 ♗c4. If Black stubbornly declines the pawn, then White will eventually recapture on d4, having stopped ...d5. Again, while it is outside the scope of this book to provide full coverage of Morra lines, we have tried to give some useful pointers as to which lines are safe, and which are not, and also how Black can avoid the Morra altogether. Specifically:

a) 4 ♘f3 dxc3 (4...♗g7 – *3 ♘f3 ♗g7 4 d4 cxd4*) 5 ♘xc3 and now:

a1) 5...♘c6 transposes to the Fianchetto Morra, where White can choose between the standard 6 ♗c4 and the interesting 6 h4!?.

a2) 5...♗g7 is a position not normally reached via a Morra move-order, where Black has some extra options if White goes for the 6 h4 approach (instead, 6 ♗c4 – 3 ♗c4 ♗g7 4 d4 cxd4 5 ♘f3 dxc3 6 ♘xc3).

b) 4 ♗c4 and now:

b1) 4...dxc3 5 ♘xc3 (White has some additional possibilities here, such as 5 ♕b3!?) 5...♘c6 6 ♘f3 ♗g7 – 3 ♗c4 ♗g7 4 d4 cxd4 5 ♘f3 dxc3 6 ♘xc3 ♘c6.

b2) 4...♗g7 – 3 ♗c4 ♗g7 4 d4 cxd4.

4...d5 (D)

4...♗g7 5 ♘c3 d6 gives play much more similar to some 2...d6 3 d4 ♘f6 lines; in fact, 6 ♗d3 ♘f6 transposes to 2...d6 3 d4 ♘f6 4 ♗d3 cxd4 5 cxd4 g6 6 ♘c3 ♗g7 and 6 ♗e3 ♘f6 7 f3 transposes to 2...d6 3 d4 ♘f6 4 f3 cxd4 5 cxd4 g6 6 ♘c3 ♗g7 7 ♗e3. This particular move-order gives White more options: 6 ♗b5+, 6 ♗c4, 6 ♗e2 and 6 h4!? have all been tried; the choice is very much a matter of taste and there have not been enough games played yet to draw any clear theoretical conclusions.

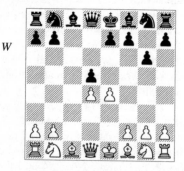

Now White has two main options:

C1: 5 exd5   20
C2: 5 e5   23

The active 5 ♘c3!? dxe4 6 ♗c4 ♘f6 7 ♕b3 e6 8 d5 can be answered by 8...exd5 9 ♘xd5 ♘xd5 10 ♗xd5 ♕e7! 11 ♕c3 (11 ♗d2 ♘d7 and White can't take the pawn: 12 ♗xb7? ♖b8) 11...♕b4, when White regains the pawn, but the ending is equal.

C1)

5 exd5

This move is the most common choice here by White. Many 2 c3 Sicilian players prefer this move as it leads to pawn-structures that they are more familiar with, and can also often transpose directly to the Panov Attack against the Caro-Kann Defence (which 2 c3 Sicilian players often play, for the same reasons).

5...♘f6 (D)

Interesting is 5...♕xd5 (reaching a position that can also arise via 2...d5 3 exd5 ♕xd5 4 d4 cxd4 5 cxd4 g6) 6 ♘c3 ♕d8 7 ♗c4 ♗g7 8 ♕b3 e6 9 ♘f3 ♘e7 10 ♗g5 0-0 11 d5!? with a slight advantage for White, Jonkman-Potapov, Korinthos 2000.

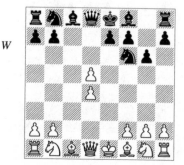

6 ♗b5+

6 ♘c3 leads to a position from the Caro-Kann Defence, Panov Attack (*1 e4 c6 2 d4 d5 3 exd5 cxd5 4 c4 ♘f6 5 ♘c3 g6 6 cxd5*, though it should be noted that White usually prefers *6 ♕b3 ♗g7 7 cxd5 ±*, when *7...♘xd5* is not possible). After 6...♘xd5 (6...♗g7 7 ♕b3 ±), we shall give just a few important theoretical examples:

a) 7 ♗c4 ♘b6 (7...♘xc3 8 ♕b3! e6 9 bxc3 ±) 8 ♗b3 ♗g7 9 ♘f3 0-0 10 0-0 ♘c6 11 d5 ♘a5 12 ♖e1 ♗g4 13 h3 ♗xf3 14 ♕xf3 ♖e8 15 ♗e3 ½-½ Kavalek-Seirawan, USA Ch (Berkeley) 1984.

b) 7 ♕b3 ♘b6 8 d5 ♗g7 9 ♗e3 0-0 10 ♖d1 ♘a6 and then:

b1) 11 ♗e2 ♕d6 12 ♘f3 ♘c5 13 ♕b5 ♘ca4 14 ♘e4 ♕d7 15 ♕b3 ♘xb2 16 ♘c5 ♕f5 17 ♖d2 ♕b1+ 18 ♖d1 ♕f5 19 ♖d2 ♕b1+ ½-½ Timofeev-Evseev, Kazan 2001.

b2) 11 ♗xa6 bxa6 12 ♘ge2 a5 13 ♕b5 ♕d7 14 ♕xa5 ♘c4 15 ♕b4 ♗a6 16 ♗f4 ♘xb2 17 ♕xb2 ♗xe2 18 ♕xe2 ♗xc3+ 19 ♗d2 ♗g7 20 ♗e3 ♗c3+ 21 ♗d2 ♗g7 ½-½ Pavasović-Slipak, Pinamar 2002.

6...♘bd7 (D)

Interesting is 6...♗d7 7 ♗c4 b5 8 ♗b3 ♗g7 9 ♘f3 0-0 10 0-0 ♗c8 11 ♗g5 ♗b7 12 ♖e1 ♖e8 13 ♘c3 b4 14 ♘e4 ♘xe4 (14...♘xd5 15 ♘c5 ♗c6 16 ♘e5 ±) 15 ♖xe4 ♗xd5 16 ♖xe7 ± Sariego-Martin del Campo, Linares 1992. Black has many other options here, but note the general principle that White does not try to hang on to the d5-pawn at all costs, which is impossible anyway, but instead uses the time it takes

Black to regain the pawn to try to create another advantage, in this case successfully applying pressure on Black's weak e7-pawn.

7 ♘c3

This move transposes to another Caro-Kann position, more commonly reached via *1 e4 c6 2 c4 d5 3 exd5 cxd5 4 cxd5 ♘f6 5 ♗b5+ ♘bd7 6 ♘c3 g6 7 d4*.

If White fears the reply 7...a6, he can instead try an immediate 7 d6 exd6 8 ♘c3, but Black can interpose 8...a6 (8...♗g7 – *7 ♘c3 ♗g7 8 d6 exd6*) 9 ♗c4, and then:

a) 9...♗g7 10 ♕e2+ ♕e7 11 ♗f4 ♕xe2+ 12 ♗xe2! ♔e7 (12...d5?! 13 ♗f3 0-0 14 ♘ge2 ♖e8 15 ♗xd5 ♘b6 16 ♗f3 ♗g4, Harley-Lamont, Huntingdon 2002, 17 ♗xb7! ♖a7 18 ♗c6 ♖e6 19 f3 ±) 13 ♗f3 ♘b6 14 ♘ge2 h6 15 h3 ♖b8 (here 15...♗e6 is less clear, as after 16 ♗xb7 the weak a6-pawn means Black has to play the less active 16...♖a7 instead of 16...♖ab8, so in this particular instance the extra tempo ...a6 has actually hindered Black) 16 ♖d1 ♗e6 17 d5!? ±.

b) 9...b5!?.

c) 9...♘b6 10 ♗b3 ♗g7 11 ♕e2+ ♕e7 12 ♗f4 ♗e6 13 ♗xe6 fxe6 14 ♘f3 0-0 15 0-0 ♘fd5 16 ♗g3 ♖ae8 17 ♖fe1 ♘f4 = Ekström-Kobaliya, Ohrid Ech 2001.

7...♗g7

7...a6 is best met by 8 ♗xd7+. Then:

a) 8...♗xd7 9 ♕b3 b5 10 ♘f3 ♗g7 11 0-0 0-0 12 ♖e1 a5 (12...♗c8!? 13 a4 ♗b7 14 axb5 a5 15 ♗g5 ± Yusupov) 13 ♘e5 b4 14 ♘e4 ♖c8 15 ♗g5 (± Yusupov) 15...♗e8? 16 d6! ♘xe4 (16...exd6 17 ♘g4 +−) 17 ♗xe7 ♕b6 18 ♖xe4 +− Ashley-Blatny, Bad Wiessee 1997.

b) 8...♕xd7 9 ♘f3 (9 ♕b3 ♕g4! ∓ Rahls-Schwamberger, Berlin 1984) 9...♘xd5 10 ♘e5 ♕e6 11 0-0 ♘xc3 12 bxc3 ♗g7 13 ♖e1 0-0 14 a4 a5 15 ♗a3 ± Miezis-Kaunas, Riga Z 1995.

8 d6! *(D)*

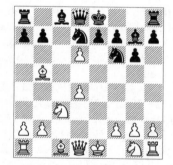

White cannot hold on to the pawn, and this pawn break gives the best chance of an initiative.

8...exd6 9 ♕e2+

Shirov suggests 9 ♗f4!? ♕b6 (or 9...♕e7+ 10 ♕e2 − 9 ♕e2+ ♕e7 10 ♗f4) 10 ♕e2+ ♔d8!? ±.

9...♕e7

Or 9...♔f8 10 ♘f3 h6 11 0-0 ♘b6 12 ♗d3 ♔g8 13 ♗f4 ♔h7 14 h3 ♖e8 15 ♕d2 ♘fd5 16 ♗g3 ♘xc3 17 bxc3 ♗e6 18 ♖ab1 with a slight advantage for White, Lautier-Yusupov, Baden-Baden 1992.

10 ♗f4 ♕xe2+ 11 ♗xe2!

Only this clever retreat gives White chances of fighting for an advantage. White plans to redirect this bishop onto the long diagonal at f3, where it will attack b7 and control d5. Instead, 11 ♘gxe2 ♔e7 12 0-0-0 ♘b6 13 ♖he1 ♗e6 14 ♗g5 h6 15 ♗h4 g5 16 ♗g3 a6 17 ♗d3 ♘bd5 is equal, Potkin-Krishilovsky, St Petersburg 1997.

11...♔e7 12 ♗f3 ♘b6 *(D)*

13 ♘ge2

Alternatively:

a) 13 b3 ♖b8?! (13...h6 is better, with the points 14 ♘b5 ♖d8 and 14 h4 ♗e6!) 14 ♘b5 ♘e8 15 ♘e2 a6 16 ♘bc3 ♘c7 17 0-0-0 ± Miles-Beliavsky, Biel 1992.

b) 13 0-0-0 ♗e6! 14 ♗xb7 ♖ab8 15 d5!? ♖xb7 16 dxe6 ♖c8! 17 ♗xd6+ ♔xe6 18 ♘ge2 (Scavo-Hoffmann, Lugano 1999) 18...♘c4 favours Black.

13...h6 14 h4

White wishes to stop the threat of 14...g5 and 15...g4, when White would have to exchange off his good bishop for a knight, though 14 0-0-0 g5 15 ♗g3 g4 16 ♗e4 ♘xe4 17 ♘xe4 ∞ has never been tested. White can also play 14 h3, when Black's best response is still 14...♗e6! with very similar play.

14...♗e6!

This pawn sacrifice has been championed by Ian Rogers on a number of occasions in this and similar positions.

White has a slight advantage after 14...♖d8 15 0-0:

a) 15...a6 16 a4 ♖b8 17 ♖fe1 ♔f8 18 a5 ♘a8 19 ♖ac1 ± Varga-Douven, Bad Wörishofen 1993.

b) 15...♖b8 16 ♖fe1 ♗e6 17 ♖ad1 ♔f8 18 ♘b5 ♘c8 19 ♘ec3 ♘e8 (not 19...a6?! 20 ♘c7 ♗g4 21 ♗xg4 ♘xg4 22 ♘3d5 ± Bagirov) 20 d5 ♗d7 21 ♘d4 ± Stohl-Bagirov, Gausdal 1991.

15 ♗xb7

15 ♖c1 ♘fd5 16 ♘xd5+ ♘xd5 17 0-0 ♔d7 = Smerdon-I.Rogers, Canberra 2002.

15...♖ab8 16 ♗f3 ♘fd5

Better than 16...♘bd5 17 b3! ±, when Black's pieces are more clogged up.

17 ♖d1!?

White is a pawn up, but Black has active pieces as compensation and good chances of eventually regaining the pawn on the queenside.

C2)
5 e5

This is considered to be theoretically the best move here, but it is not the most popular choice as it leads to pawn-structures not usually faced in

the 2 c3 Sicilian. The position after 5 e5 does score well for Black, so it would appear that those players who choose to play 5 e5 do perhaps not play the resulting positions as well as they might, and therefore that the majority playing 5 exd5 are probably making a wise practical decision.

5...♘c6 6 ♘c3 ♗g7 (D)

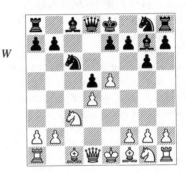

7 ♗b5

Or:

a) 7 ♘f3?! ♗g4. It is good for Black to exchange the light-squared bishop, which is why White does better to develop his knight to e2.

b) 7 h3 is possible, but probably too slow. It also creates a potential weakness which Black can later attack with ...g5, as for example in Adams-Dzindzichashvili, New York 1994, which continued 7...f6 8 exf6 exf6 9 ♘f3 ♘ge7 10 ♗e2 0-0 11 0-0 g5 with an unclear position.

c) After 7 g3!? (Gallagher suggests this might be White's best here) 7...♘h6 8 ♗g2 e6, a French-like pawn-structure arises where Black intends quick counterplay by ...♘f5 and ...f6, but more tests are needed. Then:

c1) 9 ♗xh6 ♗xh6 10 ♘ge2 f6 11 exf6 ♕xf6 12 0-0 0-0 13 ♕d3 ♗g7 ∓ Lyell-Bosch, Copenhagen 1999.

c2) 9 ♘ge2 ♘f5 10 0-0 f6 11 f4 ∞ Karlik-Siepelt, Bavaria 1994/5.

c3) 9 ♘f3 ♘f5 10 0-0 0-0 11 g4 ♘h4 12 ♘xh4 ♕xh4 13 f4 f6 14 exf6 ½-½ Langner-Szymczak, Litomerice 1990.

c4) 9 f4!? ♘f5 10 ♘f3 0-0 11 0-0 ♕b6 (11...f6 12 g4!) 12 ♘e2 with a slight advantage for White.

7...♘h6

An alternative plan is the immediate 7...f6 8 exf6 exf6 9 ♘ge2 ♗e6 10 0-0 ♘ge7. The game Pirrot-Borriss, Bundesliga 1997/8 continued 11 ♘f4 ♗f7 12 ♗xc6+ bxc6 13 ♘a4 0-0 14 b3 ♖e8 15 ♗b2 ♘f5 16 ♕f3?! (16 ♘c5 ±) 16...♕d6 17 ♘d3 ♖e4 winning a pawn.

8 ♘ge2 0-0 9 0-0

Van de Oudeweetering-Ftačnik, Dutch Cht 2000. White stands better due to his pawn-centre. Black will try to attack it by ...f6, but White can protect it with f4. Even if White gives up the pawn-centre after exf6 exf6, he keeps the better chances, as the central squares e6 and e5 (after Black plays ...f5 to reopen his g7-bishop's diagonal) will be weakened.

D)

2...e5

The main idea of this interesting move is to establish a grip on the e5-square immediately. However, Black has weakened the d5- and f7-squares, and White can exploit this.

3 ♘f3 ♘c6 4 ♗c4 *(D)*

The most natural move, since the bishop takes control of the sensitive a2-g8 diagonal.

The immediate 4 d4 is not good: 4...exd4 5 cxd4 (5 ♗c4 ♘f6 6 ♘g5 ♘e5!) 5...cxd4 6 ♗c4!? (6 ♘xd4 ♘f6 7 ♘c3 ♗b4 8 ♘xc6 dxc6 9 ♕xd8+ ♔xd8 is equal, Spangenberg-Krasenkow, Buenos Aires 1998) 6...♘f6 7 0-0 ♗c5 (7...♘xe4 8 ♖e1 d5 9 ♗xd5 ♕xd5 10 ♘c3 ♕d8 11 ♖xe4+ ♗e7 12 ♘xd4 0-0 13 ♗f4 ± Filipović-Pavlović, Kladovo 1994) 8 e5 d5 9 exf6 dxc4 10 ♖e1+ ♗e6 11 ♘g5 ♕d5 12 ♘c3 ♕f5 ∞ Vorotnikov-Filipenko, USSR 1987. These moves are identical to those played in the Max Lange Attack but with the difference that both c-pawns are missing. We would agree with Gallagher that this probably favours Black because it means that his advanced d-pawn is a passed pawn.

Now Black has:

D1: 4...♗e7 25
D2: 4...♕c7 26

Alternatively:

a) 4...♕b6 5 0-0 ♘f6 6 d4! cxd4 7 cxd4 exd4 8 e5 d5 9 ♗b3 ♘g8 10

♗xd5 ± Sveshnikov-Khenkin, Moscow 1989.

b) 4...♘f6 5 ♘g5 d5 6 exd5 ♘xd5 7 d4 cxd4 8 ♕f3 (many experts, including Sveshnikov, recommend the knight sacrifice 8 ♘xf7 ♔xf7 9 ♕f3+ ♔e6 10 0-0 ♘a5 11 ♗d3, but this is rather unclear and we prefer the positional option) 8...♗e6 9 ♘xe6 fxe6 10 0-0 ♗c5 11 ♘d2, Baev-Radjabov, Moscow 1996. Black's extra pawn doesn't mean too much, while White controls the light squares, first of all e4, with his knight. White has an advantage.

D1)
4...♗e7 *(D)*

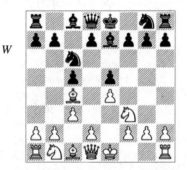

This natural developing move has been dismissed as 'passive' in the past, but has started to gain some popularity as the older main line 4...♕c7 has faced troubles of its own. 4...♗e7 stops 5 ♘g5 but doesn't stop 5 d4.

5 d4
This is the critical test. White can of course play in Closed Lopez fashion with 5 0-0 ♘f6 6 d3 0-0 7 ♖e1 but Black then has a perfectly playable position (if this were the best that

White could do, then 4...♗e7 would be a better choice than 4...♕c7 as the bishop is always going to e7 but the queen does not have to go to c7). Two recent examples illustrate some distinct plans for both players:

a) 7...d6 8 h3 ♗e6 9 a4 ♕d7 10 ♘bd2 ♖ad8 11 a5 ∞ Vajda-Munoz Pantoja, Budapest 2001.

b) 7...♕c7 8 a3 b6 9 b4 ♗b7 10 ♘bd2 is unclear, Sharma-Rahman, Calcutta 1999.

5...exd4
Most games continue routinely with 5...cxd4, but no one has tested out Sveshnikov's suggestion 6 ♕b3! ♘a5 7 ♗xf7+ ♔f8 8 ♕b5:

a) 8...♔xf7? 9 ♘xe5+ ♔e8 10 ♕d5 ♕b6 11 ♕f7+ ♔d8 12 ♕xg7 ♗f6 13 ♕f8+ ♔c7 14 ♘f7 ♕e6 15 ♗f4+ ♔c6 16 ♗e5! +-.

b) 8...a6 9 ♕xe5 d6 (after 9...♔xf7? 10 ♕d5+ ♔e8 11 ♘e5, the play is the same as after *8...♔xf7? 9 ♘xe5+ ♔e8 10 ♕d5*; the extra move ...a6 makes no difference) 10 ♕f4 g5 11 ♘xg5 ♗xg5 12 ♕xg5 ♕xg5 13 ♗xg5 ♔xf7 (or 13...dxc3 14 b4 ± Sveshnikov) 14 cxd4 ±. White has three pawns for a piece.

6 cxd4 cxd4 7 0-0 *(D)*

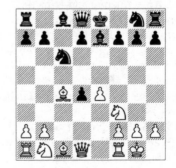

7...♘f6

Not 7...♛b6?! 8 e5! ♛c5 9 ♛b3 and White is much better, Motylev-Beltugov, Ekaterinburg 1997.

8 ♘xd4

8 e5!? leads to unclear play:

a) 8...♘g4 9 ♗f4 d6 10 exd6 ♗xd6 11 ♗xd6 ♛xd6 12 ♖e1+ ♚f8 13 ♘bd2 ∞ Liang-Beltugov, Pskov 1998.

b) 8...♘e4 9 ♗d5 ♘c5 10 ♘xd4 was played in Porper-Haist, Baden-weil 1990, and now 10...♘xe5!? is unclear.

8...0-0

Not 8...d5? 9 exd5 ♘xd5 10 ♘b5!, and then:

a) Bae-Reefat, Gausdal 2002 continued 10...a6? and both players missed 11 ♛xd5! ♛xd5 (11...axb5 12 ♛xf7+ ♚d7 13 ♖d1+ wins the queen) 12 ♘c7+, winning a piece.

b) 10...♘db4 11 ♛xd8+ ♚xd8 12 ♖d1+ ♗d7 13 ♗xf7 ♘c2 14 ♗e6 ♘b8 15 ♗f4 ♘xa1 16 ♗xb8 ♖xb8 17 ♘1c3 +−.

9 ♖e1

This is more accurate than 9 ♘c3, which allows Black to play 9...♘xe4 10 ♘xe4 d5 11 ♗b5 (11 ♘xc6 bxc6 12 ♗d3 dxe4 13 ♗xe4 ♗a6 was given as ± by A.Kuzmin and Kimelfeld, but they should have looked a move further: after 14 ♖e1, 14...♗b4 wins the exchange) 11...dxe4 12 ♘xc6 bxc6 13 ♛xd8 ♖xd8 14 ♗xc6 ♗a6 15 ♗xa8 ♗xf1 16 ♚xf1 ♖xa8 17 ♗e3 f5 18 ♖c1 a5 ½-½ Sareen-Rahman, Calcutta 1998.

9...d6 10 ♘c3 a6 11 a4

White has a slight advantage, Jacek-Hlavnicka, Czech Cht 1995.

D2)

4...♛c7 *(D)*

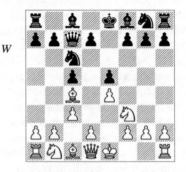

This strange-looking move is played to dissuade White from 5 d4 because the c4-bishop would then be loose, and prepares to defend against 5 ♘g5 by 5...♘d8!.

5 ♛b3!?

Or:

a) Another interesting possibility is to employ a purely positional plan: 5 d3 ♘f6 6 ♗g5 (the sharp variation 6 0-0 ♗e7 7 ♗g5 0-0 8 f4 h6 9 ♘xf7 ♖xf7 10 ♗xf7+ ♚xf7 11 fxe5 ♛xe5 yields some compensation for the lost material, but no more than that) 6...♗e7 7 ♘bd2 d6 8 ♘f1 ♗e6 9 ♘e3 0-0 10 ♗xf6 ♗xf6 11 h4. White controls the light squares and seeks to attack the black king. This plan was successfully used in several games by Schmittdiel.

b) The tactical continuation 5 0-0 followed by 6 ♘g5 is more unclear than our main line but nonetheless is currently looking good for White. Black has two ways to defend:

b1) 5...♘f6 6 ♘g5 ♘d8 7 f4 h6 8 ♘f3 d6 (8...exf4 9 e5 d5 10 ♗b3 c4 11 exf6 cxb3 12 fxg7 ♗xg7 13 ♛xb3 ±

Wach-Klundt, Passau 1998) 9 d3 a6 10 a4 ♘e6 11 fxe5 dxe5 12 ♘a3 ♗e7 13 ♘c2 0-0 14 ♕e1 ♗d7 15 ♘e3 ± Vysochin-Prokhorov, Voronezh 2001.

b2) 5...♗e7 6 ♘g5 ♘d8 (6...♗xg5 7 ♕h5 d5! 8 exd5 ♗f4! 9 dxc6 ♘f6 10 ♕e2 0-0 11 cxb7 ♗xb7 12 d3 e4! with some compensation for the pawn, Smagin-Brendel, Dortmund 1993) 7 f4 exf4 8 ♘f3 (8 ♘h3? g5 ∓ Magem-Krasenkow, Pula Echt 1997) 8...♘h6 (there may be other plans here for Black but they are not easy to find) 9 ♕e2 0-0 10 d4 ♘g4 11 e5 ♘e3 12 ♗xe3 fxe3 13 b3 d6 14 ♕xe3 ♘c6 15 ♕e4 cxd4 16 cxd4 dxe5 17 dxe5 with a slight advantage for White, Sermek-Markowski, Cannes 1997.

5...d6

5...♘a5? loses to 6 ♗xf7+ ♔e7 7 ♕d5 ♘f6 8 ♕xe5+ ♕xe5 9 ♘xe5 d6 10 ♘c4 +−.

6 ♘g5 ♘h6

The knight goes to an awkward location, as 6...♘d8 allows 7 d4 exd4 (or 7...h6 8 ♘f3 ♘f6 9 0-0 ♗g4 10 ♘bd2) 8 cxd4 cxd4 9 0-0, when White is better.

7 d3 g6

Black can't play 7...♗e7 because that cuts off the queen's defence of f7. Perhaps the best try for Black is 7...♘a5, though White still has the advantage after 8 ♗b5+ ♗d7 9 ♕a4 ♘c6 10 ♕d1.

8 0-0 ♗g7 9 f4 0-0 10 ♕d1

White has a strong initiative on the kingside.

E)

2...d6 3 d4 ♘f6 *(D)*

Black attacks the pawn, having first played ...d6 to prevent White's e5 advance. This line is very similar to variations of the Pirc and King's Indian.

4 ♗d3

Or:

a) 4 dxc5 (opening the centre like this gives White no advantage) 4...♘c6! (not 4...dxc5?! 5 ♕xd8+ ♔xd8 6 f3, when White has the better endgame):

a1) 5 cxd6 ♘xe4 6 ♗e3 (6 dxe7? ♕xd1+ 7 ♔xd1 ♘xf2+ 8 ♔e1 ♘xh1 9 exf8♕+ ♔xf8 10 g3 ♗f5 wins for Black) 6...♘xd6 =.

a2) 5 ♗d3 d5 6 ♘d2 e5 =.

a3) 5 ♕c2 d5 6 ♘d2 e5 gives Black a good position.

a4) 5 ♗c4 ♘xe4 6 ♗xf7+ ♔xf7 7 ♕h5+ (7 ♕d5+ e6 8 ♕xe4 d5 9 ♕f3+ ♕f6 10 ♗e3 b6 11 cxb6 axb6 12 ♗d4 ♘xd4 13 cxd4 ♖a4 = Azmaiparashvili-Topalov, Burgas 1995) 7...♔g8 8 ♕d5+ e6 9 ♕xe4 d5 10 ♕e3 b6 11 cxb6 axb6 12 ♘f3 ♗c5 13 ♕g5 ♕xg5 14 ♗xg5 ♗a6 gives Black sufficient compensation for the pawn, Daniliuk-Fedorov, Krasnodar 1997.

a5) 5 f3 d5 (again not 5...dxc5?! 6 ♕xd8+ ±) 6 exd5 and then:

a51) 6...♘xd5 is a good but sharp continuation, which can be played if Black wants to fight. For example: 7 ♗c4 e6 8 ♗xd5 exd5 (8...♕xd5 9 ♕xd5 exd5 is possible, transposing to the line 6...♕xd5 7 ♕xd5 ♘xd5 8 ♗c4 e6 9 ♗xd5 exd5) 9 ♗e3 ♗e7 10 ♘e2 0-0 11 0-0 ♖e8 12 ♕d2?! (12 ♗f2 ♗g5 is unclear – Gallagher) 12...♘e5 13 ♘a3 b6! and Black obtains an advantage due to the vulnerable location of White's pieces, Thorhallsson-Fedorowicz, London Lloyds Bank 1987.

a52) 6...♕xd5 is a more solid line. 7 ♕xd5 (7 ♗e3 ♕xd1+ 8 ♔xd1 ♗f5 9 ♘d2 0-0-0 10 ♘e2 ♘d5 and Black has a strong initiative, Gorelov-Ubilava, Volgodonsk 1981) 7...♘xd5 8 ♗c4 e6 9 ♗xd5 exd5 10 ♗e3 ♘e5 11 b3 (11 b4?! a5 12 ♗d4 ♘c6 13 b5 ♘d8 14 ♘d2 ♘e6 15 ♘b3 a4 Sveshnikov) 11...♘d3+ 12 ♔d2 ♘xc5 13 ♘a3 ♗d7 and the endgame is equal, Manca-Gelfand, Arnhem jr Ech 1988/9.

b) 4 f3 is a solid move by which White protects his centre. However, Black can obtain a good position by using his development advantage:

b1) With 4...♘bd7 5 ♗e3 e5, Black blocks the centre. However, the d5- and d6-squares are weakened, so White can expect a slight positional advantage. After 6 dxc5 dxc5 7 a4 ♗e7 8 ♘a3 0-0 9 ♕c2 ♘b8 10 ♗c4 ♘c6 11 ♖d1 White stands better according to Sveshnikov and Blatny.

b2) 4...♘c6 5 ♗e3 d5. White has wasted time playing f3, so it is viable for Black to spend two moves playing ...d6-d5. The plan is good in this position: 6 e5 ♘d7 7 f4 cxd4 8 cxd4 ♘b6 9

♘c3 ♗f5 10 ♘f3 e6 11 ♗d3 ♘c4! = (11...♗xd3 is worse: 12 ♕xd3 ♘c4 13 ♗c1 ± Smagin-Arnason, Sochi 1988).

b3) 4...cxd4 5 cxd4 g6 (5...e5 6 dxe5 dxe5 7 ♕xd8+ ♔xd8 ± Gallagher) 6 ♘c3 ♗g7 7 ♗e3 0-0 8 ♕d2 ♘c6 9 0-0-0 ♗d7 10 ♔b1 b5 11 ♗xb5 ♖b8 12 ♗xc6 ♗xc6 13 ♘ge2 ♖b7 14 ♗h6 ♗xh6 15 ♕xh6 ♕a5 gives Black a strong attack which compensates for the pawn, Sveshnikov-Egiazarian, Minsk 2000. The game ended in a draw.

We now return to 4 ♗d3 (D):

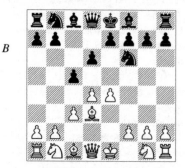

4...cxd4

Releasing the tension in the centre, but other possibilities give White an advantage:

a) After 4...e5 5 ♘f3 ♘c6 6 d5 ♘e7 7 ♗g5!, the black pieces are constrained and White can exploit this: 7...♘g6 8 ♗b5+ ♗d7 9 ♗xf6 gxf6 and Black's pawn-structure is spoiled, Rizouk-Movsesian, Shenyang FIDE WCup 2000.

b) 4...♘c6 5 ♘f3 ♗g4 6 d5 ♗xf3 (6...♘e5? 7 ♘xe5 ♗xd1?? 8 ♗b5+ +−) 7 ♕xf3 ♘e5 8 ♗b5+ (White keeps the bishop-pair, which, together with his strong centre, assures him a small but lasting advantage) 8...♘ed7 (alternatively, 8...♘fd7 9 ♕e2 a6 10 ♗a4 b5 11 ♗c2 ♘b6 12 0-0 ♕d7 13 h3 g6 14 a4, Smagin-Kofidis, Iraklion 1993) 9 a4 g6 10 a5 a6 11 ♗a4 ♗g7 12 ♘d2 0-0 13 ♘c4 ♘e5 14 ♘xe5 dxe5 15 ♗e3 and White can successfully play on the queenside, Schandorff-Mortensen, Aalborg 1994.

c) 4...g6 is a natural move, but it leads to an inferior endgame after 5 dxc5 dxc5 6 e5!:

c1) 6...♘d5 7 ♗e4 ♘b6 8 ♕xd8+ ♔xd8 9 ♘a3 ♗g7 (9...♘c6 10 ♘f3 ♗f5 11 ♗xc6 {11 ♗xf5?!, Lautier-J.Polgar, Dos Hermanas 1994} 11...bxc6 12 ♗e3 ♖b8 13 0-0-0+ ±) 10 ♘f3 ♘8d7 11 ♗e3 a6 12 e6! fxe6 13 ♘g5 ♘f6 14 ♗c2 ♔c7 15 ♗xc5 ± *Junior*-J.Polgar, Budapest (6) 1996.

c2) 6...♘g4 doesn't work either: 7 ♗b5+ ♘c6 8 ♕xd8+ ♔xd8 9 ♗xc6 bxc6 10 f4 ±.

c3) 6...c4!? 7 ♕a4+ ♗d7 8 ♕xc4 ♘g4 9 f4 ♘c6 10 ♗e4 ♖c8 11 ♕e2 ♘d4 12 ♕d2 ♗f5 13 ♗xf5 ♘xf5 14 ♕xd8+ ♖xd8 15 ♔e2 ± Ponomariov-Zozulia, Alushta 1998.

d) 4...♕c7 5 ♘f3 g6 avoids the above, but White is still better after 6 0-0 ♗g7 7 ♗f4 0-0 8 ♘bd2 ♘bd7 9 ♖e1 e5 10 dxe5 dxe5 11 ♗g3 ♘h5 12 a4 ± Karpov-J.Polgar, Dos Hermanas 1994.

5 cxd4 g6 *(D)*

Black can also try:

a) 5...♘c6 6 ♘f3 (6 ♘e2 g6 7 ♘bc3 ♗g7 8 0-0 0-0 – *5...g6 6 ♘e2 ♗g7 7 0-0 0-0 8 ♘bc3 ♘c6*) 6...♘g4 7 d5 ♗xf3 8 ♕xf3 ♘e5 9 ♗b5+ ± Chandler.

b) 5...e5 and then:

b1) 6 ♘f3 (or 6 ♘e2) 6...exd4 7 ♘xd4 ♗e7 8 0-0 0-0 (by comparison to the line *2...e5 3 ♘f3 ♘c6 4 ♗c4 ♗e7 5 d4 exd4 6 cxd4 cxd4 7 0-0 ♘f6 8 ♘xd4 0-0*, White's bishop is here less actively placed on d3) 9 ♘c3 ♘c6 10 ♘xc6 bxc6 11 ♗f4 ♗e6 12 ♕c2 (12 ♕a4 ♕b6 = Rogozenko) 12...h6 13 ♖ad1 ♕a5 14 ♘a4 ♖fd8 15 b3 c5 16 ♗c4 d5 = Jonkman-Bosboom, Rotterdam 2000.

b2) 6 d5 ♗e7 7 ♘e2 0-0 (Shaked-Yermolinsky, San Francisco 1995) 8 f3 ♘e8 9 ♗e3 ♗g5 10 ♗f2 (Yermolinsky) ±.

W

6 ♘c3

6 ♘e2 is another interesting possibility, leaving the f3-square for the pawn: 6...♗g7 7 0-0 0-0 8 ♘bc3 ♘c6 9 f3 (the modest 9 a3 allows Black to equalize: 9...e5 10 d5 ♘d4! 11 f3 ♗d7 12 ♘xd4 exd4 13 ♘e2 ♕b6 14 b3 ♗b5 15 ♗b2 ♘d7 16 ♗xb5 d3+ 17 ♘d4 ♗xd4+ 18 ♗xd4 ♕xd4+ 19 ♔h1 ♘e5 = Rozentalis-Gelfand, Uzhgorod 1987) 9...e5 10 d5 and then:

a) 10...♘e7? would be a standard move in a King's Indian, but there is a difference in that the c-file is already open, so White can start to attack on the queenside immediately: 11 ♗e3 ♘e8 12 ♕b3 f5 13 ♘b5 with a large advantage, Rozentalis-Smirin, Vilnius 1988.

b) After 10...♘d4 11 ♗e3 ♘d7 12 ♘b5 Black can't preserve the knight on d4 and has to exchange it, which leads to an inferior position.

c) 10...♘b4! makes use of the fact that the bishop can't retreat to e2. Black wins some precious time to gain sufficient activity. 11 ♗c4 ♕b6+ 12 ♔h1 ♗d7 13 a3 ♖fc8 14 b3 ♘a6 15 ♗g5 ♘h5 16 ♕d2 ♘c5 with a very complicated position, Rozentalis-Kempinski, Bydgoszcz 2000.

6...♗g7 7 h3 0-0 8 ♘f3 ♘c6 9 0-0 e5 10 dxe5

Other continuations don't promise anything for White: 10 d5 ♘d4! and 10 ♗e3 exd4 11 ♘xd4 d5 both lead to equality.

10...dxe5 *(D)*

11 ♗e3

This is better than 11 ♗c4, when Black has two active responses:

a) 11...♘a5 12 ♕xd8 (12 ♗e2 ♗e6 13 ♗e3 ♘c4 14 ♗c5 ♕xd1 15 ♖fxd1 ♘xb2! with an equal position, B.Andersson-Engqvist, Stockholm 1987) 12...♖xd8 13 ♘xe5 ♘xc4 14 ♘xc4 b5! 15 ♘xb5 ♘xe4 and Black's active pieces provide good compensation for the pawn, Jahn-Cholushkina, Debrecen wom Echt 1992.

b) 11...♗e6 12 ♗d5!? (12 ♗xe6 fxe6 13 ♕b3 ♕e7 14 ♗g5 ∞ Gallagher; the doubled pawns give Black good possibilities along the d- and f-files) 12...♘h5 (12...♗xd5 13 exd5 ♘e7 seems fine for Black) 13 ♗g5 ♗f6 14 ♗xf6 ♕xf6 15 ♗xc6 bxc6 16 ♕d6 ♘f4 17 ♕xe5 ♘xh3+ 18 ♔h2 ♕f4+ 19 ♕xf4 ♘xf4 20 ♘e5 ± Rogovskoi-Sabaev, Karvina 1998.

11...♗e6 12 ♗b5 ♘a5

12...♕a5 13 ♗xc6 bxc6 14 ♕c2 h6 15 ♘a4 ♘d7 16 ♖fd1 ± Smirin-Kempinski, Groningen 1996.

13 ♕e2 a6 14 ♗d3 ♘c6 15 ♖fd1 ♕a5

Or:

a) 15...♕c8? 16 ♖ac1 ± Adams-Gelfand, Wijk an Zee 1994.

b) 15...♘d4 16 ♗xd4 exd4 17 ♗c4 ♘h5 18 e5 ♘f4 19 ♕e4! and White wins a pawn.

16 ♗c4!

With the light-squared bishops exchanged, White can try to exploit his more active pieces and the vulnerable d5-square. He is better.

2 2...e6

1 e4 c5 2 c3 e6 (D)

This line is often used by players whose repertoire also includes the French Defence.

3 d4

3 ♘f3 is of no independent significance but often arises from the move-order *2 ♘f3 e6 3 c3*, which is popular amongst those who play *2 ♘f3 ♘c6 3 ♗b5* and *2 ♘f3 d6 3 ♗b5+*, and by some Open Sicilian players who quite reasonably consider the 2 c3 Sicilian to be more effective when Black has already committed himself to ...e6. After 3 ♘f3 we have:

a) 3...♘f6 4 e5 ♘d5 – *2...♘f6 3 e5 ♘d5 4 ♘f3 e6*.

b) 3...d5 and then:

b1) 4 exd5 ♕xd5 (4...exd5 5 d4 – *3 d4 d5 4 exd5 exd5 5 ♘f3*) 5 d4 ♘f6 – *2...d5 3 exd5 ♕xd5 4 d4 ♘f6 5 ♘f3 e6*.

b2) 4 e5 d4!? (4...♘c6 5 d4 transposes to an Advance French – *1 e4 e6 2 d4 d5 3 e5 c5 4 c3 ♘c6 5 ♘f3*) 5 ♗d3! ♘c6 6 0-0 ♘ge7 7 ♖e1 ♘g6 8 g3 ♗e7 9 h4 f6 10 exf6 ♗xf6 11 ♗e4 ♗d7 12 d3 0-0 13 ♘g5 ♗xg5 14 ♗xg5 ♕e8 15 ♘d2 ♕f7 16 ♕e2 h6 17 h5 ♘ge7 18 ♗xe7 ♕xe7 19 ♘f3 ± Torre-Illescas, Novi Sad OL 1990.

3...d5

Seldom played are:

a) 3...cxd4 4 cxd4 and then:

a1) 4...♘f6 5 ♘c3 (5 e5 ♘d5 {not 5...♘e4? 6 ♕c2! ♗b4+ 7 ♔d1! d5 8 f3 costing Black his knight} – *2...♘f6 3 e5 ♘d5 4 d4 cxd4 5 cxd4 e6*) 5...♗b4 6 ♗d3 d5 7 e5 ♘e4 8 ♘ge2 ♗d7 9 0-0 ♗c6 10 f3 ♘xc3 11 bxc3 ♗e7 12 f4 ± Nurkić-Kalajzić, Bosnjaci 2002.

a2) 4...d5 gives White a choice:

a21) 5 e5 ♘c6 transposes to a form of Advance French where Black has already exchanged on d4. White might be able to exploit this with 6 ♘f3 ♕b6 7 a3 followed by ♘c3.

a22) With 5 exd5 exd5 White opts for a symmetrical position with slightly better chances; for example: 6 ♘c3 ♘c6 7 ♘ge2 ♘f6 8 g3 ♗g4 9 ♗g2 ♗b4 10 0-0 0-0 11 ♗g5 and White has some pressure on the d5-pawn, Palkovi-C.Bauer, Austrian Cht 1999/00.

b) 3...♘f6 and then:

b1) 4 f3 d5!?.

b2) 4 ♗d3 cxd4 5 cxd4 ♘c6 6 ♘f3
♘b4 (6...♕b6 7 0-0 ♘xd4 8 ♘xd4
♕xd4 9 ♘c3 a6 10 ♗e3 ♕e5 11 ♖c1
with compensation, Podinić-Szabo,
Bucharest 2001) 7 0-0 ♘xd3 8 ♕xd3
d5 9 e5 ♘d7 ∞ Frost-S.Buckley, British Ch (Millfield) 2000.

b3) 4 e5 ♘d5 (4...♘e4 5 ♗d3 ±)
transposes to 2...♘f6 3 e5 ♘d5 4 d4
e6.

We now return to 3...d5 (D):

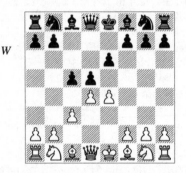

4 exd5

4 e5 leads to one of the main lines
of the French Defence (1 e4 e6 2 d4 d5
3 e5 c5 4 c3), and this probably gives
White more chances to fight for an advantage. As this is a major opening in
its own right, it does not seem appropriate to try to offer a brief analysis
here; we would instead refer the reader
to other opening books on the subject.
We will, however, give a complete
coverage here of the possibilities after
4 exd5 so that at least one option for
White is covered in full.

The text-move also leads to French-
like positions, this time from the variation 1 e4 e6 2 d4 d5 3 ♘d2 c5 4 exd5
exd5. The only difference is that there

the white knight is already developed,
while here the white pawn has moved
to c3. The move c3 is useful for White,
but the queenside pieces have to be
developed first. Therefore, this detail
can be in Black's favour. On the other
hand, White can play a solid position
without much risk. Often, Black must
be ready to have an isolated pawn, and
White – to play against it.

If White is desperate to have the
isolated queen's pawn himself, he
could try 4 ♘d2!?, transposing to another French line, this time the rare 1
e4 e6 2 d4 d5 3 ♘d2 c5 4 c3!?. Black
has two good responses:

a) 4...♘c6 5 ♘gf3 cxd4 (5...♘f6 6
e5 ♘d7 7 ♗d3 transposes to the potentially dangerous Korchnoi Gambit,
1 e4 e6 2 d4 d5 3 ♘d2 ♘f6 4 e5 ♘fd7 5
♗d3 c5 6 c3 ♘c6 7 ♘gf3!?) 6 cxd4
dxe4 (6...♕b6!?) 7 ♘xe4 ♗b4+ 8
♗d2!? (8 ♘c3 may be better) 8...♗e7
9 ♗c3 ♘f6 10 ♗d3 0-0 ∞ Papapos-
tolou-Baswedan, Leipzig OL 1960.

b) 4...cxd4 5 cxd4 dxe4 6 ♘xe4
♗b4+ 7 ♘c3 ♘f6 8 ♘f3 0-0 seems
simplest, as it leaves Black a tempo up
on a major line of the Nimzo-Indian
and Caro-Kann Panov (e.g. 1 e4 c6 2
d4 d5 3 exd5 cxd5 4 c4 ♘f6 5 ♘c3 e6 6
♘f3 ♗b4 7 ♗d3 dxc4 8 ♗xc4 0-0). In
this line with the bishop on b4, Black
often chooses to develop the queen's
knight to d7 and later to capture on c3
with the bishop, so Black probably
does well to delay the development of
his queen's knight.

4...exd5 (D)

4...♕xd5 – 2...d5 3 exd5 ♕xd5 4 d4
e6.

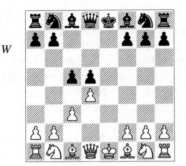

5 ♘f3

Or:

a) 5 ♗b5+, as in the French, doesn't bring White anything: 5...♗d7 6 ♕e2+ (6 ♗xd7+ ♘xd7 7 ♘f3 ♘gf6 8 0-0 ♗e7 9 dxc5 ♘xc5 10 ♘d4 ♕d7 11 ♕f3 0-0 12 ♘f5 ♗d8 and Black is fine, as his king is safe: 13 ♗h6 ♘e6) 6...♗e7 7 dxc5 ♘f6 8 ♗e3 0-0 9 ♘d2 ♖e8 10 ♘b3 a6 11 ♗xd7 (or 11 ♗d3 ♗a4) 11...♘bxd7 and Black recaptures the pawn.

b) 5 ♗e3 makes Black decide what to do with c-pawn:

b1) 5...c4 blocks the centre, but White can exchange this pawn and develop his pieces in a convenient way, obtaining a small advantage: 6 b3 cxb3 7 axb3 ♘c6 8 ♗d3 ♗d6 9 ♕f3! (the white queen will take part in the events on the kingside as well as in the centre, while the knight can be developed to e2 and then moved to f4 or g3) 9...♘f6 10 h3 h6 (10...0-0 11 ♘e2 ♖e8 12 ♗g5 ♗e7 13 0-0 h6 14 ♗xf6 ♗xf6 15 ♘f4 ± Ftačnik) 11 ♘e2 ♘e7 12 ♘g3 (12 ♗f4 is also good, as Black's dark-squared bishop is the most active piece and it is useful to exchange it) 12...♗e6 13 0-0 ♘g6 (not 13...0-0? 14 ♗xh6)

14 ♘f5 ♗xf5 15 ♕xf5 and White has the bishop-pair and a better position, Kramnik-Gelfand, Sanghi Nagar FIDE Ct (5) 1994.

b2) 5...♕b6!? 6 ♕e2 (6 dxc5 ♕xb2 7 ♕b3 ♕xa1 8 ♘f3 ♘c6 – *5 ♘f3 ♘c6 6 ♗e3 ♕b6 7 dxc5 ♕xb2 8 ♕b3 ♕xa1* ∓) 6...c4 7 b3 cxb3 8 ♕b5+ ♗d7 9 ♕xb3 ♘f6 10 ♘f3 ♗d6 = Dzindzichashvili-Benjamin, Philadelphia 1993.

b3) 5...cxd4! 6 ♗xd4 (normally, the knight should be on this square; here, the bishop comes to d4, where it will be exchanged for a knight) 6...♘c6 7 ♘f3 (7 ♗b5 a6 8 ♗a4 b5 9 ♗b3 ♘xd4 10 ♕xd4 ♘f6 11 ♘f3 ♗d6 12 0-0 0-0 13 ♘bd2 ♕c7 gives Black a useful initiative on the dark squares, which compensates for the weakness of the isolated pawn, Ponomariov-Shariyazdanov, Siofok jr Ech 1996) 7...♘xd4 8 ♕xd4 (8 ♘xd4 ♗c5 9 ♗b5+ ♔f8 10 0-0 ♘f6 11 ♘d2 a6 12 ♗e2 g6 13 ♗f3 ♔g7 is fine for Black, A.Tzermiadianos-Kr.Georgiev, Iraklion 1995) 8...a6 (8...♘f6 is also possible, but when one has an isolated pawn, it is always better to have as many pieces on the board as possible – and conversely, the side fighting against an isolated pawn should try to exchange more pieces in order to reach an endgame, where this pawn can be the most vulnerable) 9 ♗d3 ♘f6 10 0-0 ♗e7 11 ♘a3 0-0 12 ♘c2 ♕a5 13 ♕h4 h6 14 ♘e3 ♕b6 15 ♖ab1 ♗c5 16 ♘d4 ♖e8 = Smagin-I.Sokolov, Belgrade 1987.

We return to 5 ♘f3 *(D)*:

Now:

A: 5...♘c6   34

B: 5...♗d6   37

Or:

a) 5...♗g4 6 ♗b5+ ♘c6 – 5...♘c6 6 ♗b5 ♗g4.

b) 5...c4 is premature. This move is viable after White plays ♗e3, but not before. Black's control over the d3-square doesn't bother White, as the best place for the light-squared bishop is g2, to attack the d5-pawn. 6 g3 ♗d6 7 ♗g2 ♘e7 8 0-0 ♘bc6 9 b3 cxb3 10 axb3 0-0 11 ♘a3 (the knight will go to b5 or else to e3 via c2; instead, 11 c4? weakens the b4-square) 11...a6 12 ♘c2 ♗f5 13 ♘h4 ♗e4 14 f3 ♗xc2 15 ♕xc2 ♕d7 16 f4 and White gets a strong attack on the kingside, Rozentalis-Timoshenko, Tbilisi 1989.

c) 5...a6 is often just a waste of time, as White still plays 6 g3.

d) 5...♘f6 discourages 6 g3 because of 6...♕e7+, but allows 6 ♗g5!, when White threatens to win a pawn by ♗xf6, dxc5 and ♕xd5. So:

d1) 6...cxd4 7 ♕e2+! ♕e7 8 ♗xf6 gxf6 9 ♘xd4 and the weak black pawns assure White a small but pleasant advantage in the endgame.

d2) 6...♗e7 7 dxc5 ♗xc5 8 ♗b5+ ♘c6 9 0-0 – 5...♗d6 6 ♗b5+ ♘c6 7 dxc5 ♗xc5 8 0-0 ♘f6 9 ♗g5 ±.

d3) 6...♘bd7 7 ♘bd2 ♗e7 8 g3 gives White comfortable development.

d4) 6...c4 7 ♘bd2 ♗e7 8 g3 and now, if Black tries to prevent White's plan, he can find himself in trouble: 8...♕b6 9 b3 cxb3 10 axb3 ♗f5 11 ♗g2 ♕e6+ 12 ♘e5 ♘fd7 13 ♗xe7 ♘xe5 14 0-0 ♔xe7 15 ♖e1 ♘bc6 16 b4 ♔f8 17 b5 with an immense initiative, Anand-Malishauskas, Lyons ECC 1994.

A)

5...♘c6 (D)

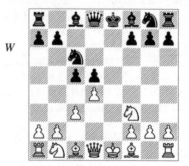

Now we consider:
A1: 6 ♗e3   35
A2: 6 g3!?   36

Instead:

a) After 6 ♗e2 ♗d6 7 dxc5 ♗xc5 8 0-0 ♘ge7 9 ♘bd2 0-0 10 ♘b3 ♗b6 Black is comfortable, as his pieces are located perfectly, while White has problems with his bishops: 11 ♗g5 h6 12 ♗xe7 (this is necessary, because after 12 ♗h4 g5 13 ♗g3 f5 White's bishop is in danger, Schoffstoll-Gulko, Los Angeles 1991) 12...♕xe7 13 ♖e1 ♗e6 = Salov-Kasparov, Linares 1993.

b) 6 ♗b5 is probably the most commonly played move here. Then:

b1) 6...♗g4 7 0-0 cxd4 8 ♖e1+ ♗e7 9 ♕xd4 (attacking g7) 9...♘f6 10 ♗g5 ♗e6 ±.

b2) 6...a6 7 ♗xc6+ bxc6 8 c4!? ♘f6 9 0-0 ♗e7 10 dxc5 0-0 11 ♘c3 dxc4 12 ♕a4 ♗g4 13 ♘e5 ± Harley-Rudd, Cambridge 1998.

b3) 6...c4 7 ♘e5! ♕b6 (7...♗d7 8 ♗xc6 ♗xc6 9 0-0 ♗d6 10 ♕g4! ± Karpov) 8 ♗xc6+ bxc6 9 0-0 ♗d6 10 b3! cxb3 11 axb3 ♘e7 12 ♗a3 (Karpov-J.Polgar, Linares 1994) and now best is 12...c5! ± Anand.

b4) 6...♘f6 7 0-0 cxd4 8 ♖e1+ ♗e7 9 ♘xd4 ± Alapin-Schiffers, Vienna 1898.

b5) 6...♗d6 – *5...♗d6 6 ♗b5+ ♘c6*.

A1)

6 ♗e3 c4

Unlike after *5 ♗e3*, it is now better not to take on an isolated d-pawn (though exchanging on d4 is possible), but instead to advance the c-pawn.

Otherwise:

a) After 6...cxd4, the knight can take on d4. After 7 ♘xd4 a typical position with an isolated pawn arises; it is playable for both sides. For example: 7...♘f6 8 ♗e2 ♗d6 9 0-0 0-0 10 ♘d2 h6 11 h3 ♖e8 12 ♘2f3 a6 13 ♘xc6 bxc6 14 c4, when White is slightly better, but Black is quite solid.

b) 6...♕b6!? is interesting and still unresolved:

b1) 7 dxc5 ♕xb2 8 ♕b3 ♕xa1 9 ♗d3 ♘f6 10 0-0 ♗e7 (Friedrich-Shulman, Pardubice 1996) and now White should win the queen while he has the

chance, by 11 ♘bd2 ♕xf1+ 12 ♘xf1 0-0, but Black has two rooks for the queen and is somewhat better.

b2) After 7 ♕c1 c4 8 ♘bd2 ♕c7 9 b3 cxb3 10 axb3 (Skytte-Schmittdiel, Deizisau 2002) we have similar play to that after *6...c4* but with the queens on different squares.

7 b3 cxb3

7...b5 can be met by 8 a4! as Black cannot respond 8...a6.

8 axb3 ♗d6 9 ♗d3 ♘ge7 *(D)*

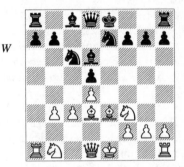

W

10 0-0

By comparison to the play after *5 ♗e3 c4*, the white knight is already located on f3, so his queen can't go to f3 itself. This makes it more difficult for White to exert pressure on Black's kingside.

Instead of castling immediately, White can try:

a) 10 ♕c2 h6 11 0-0-0 0-0 12 b4 ♗g4 13 ♘bd2 ♖c8 14 ♕b1 a6 15 h3 ♗h5 16 ♘h4 ♘a7 17 ♖c1 ♘b5 ∞ Adams-Nunn, Hastings 1996/7.

b) 10 ♘h4 ♗e6!? (10...0-0 11 0-0 – *10 0-0 0-0 11 ♘h4*) 11 ♘d2 ♕d7 12 ♕b1 h6 13 b4 g5 ½-½ Kantsler-Greenfeld, Beersheba 1996.

10...♗g4
Or:

a) White gets more chances after 10...0-0 11 ♘h4! (11 ♖e1 ♗f5 12 b4 a6 13 ♗g5 ♕d7 14 ♗xe7 ♘xe7 15 ♖a2 ♖ac8 16 ♖ae2 ½-½ Vajda-Varga, Budapest 2002), and then:

a1) 11...f5 12 f4 ± and the knight relocates from h4 to e5.

a2) 11...♗e6 12 ♕h5 g6 13 ♕f3 f6 14 ♗f4 ♗xf4 15 ♕xf4 g5 16 ♕g3 ± Petschar-Topakian, Austrian Ch (Finkenstein) 1990.

a3) 11...♕c7 12 ♔h1!? ♘g6 13 ♕h5! (13 ♘f5?! ♗xf5 14 ♗xf5 ♘ce7 15 ♗d3 f5 with counterplay – Finkel) 13...♗e6 (13...♘ce7 14 c4! ♗e6 15 c5 ♗f4 16 ♘c3 ♖fe8 17 ♘xg6 ± Finkel) 14 ♘d2 ♘ce7 (Finkel-Roiz, Ramat Aviv 1999) and now Finkel gives 15 c4! ♖fe8 16 c5 ♗f4 17 ♘xg6 ♘xg6 18 g3 ♗xe3 19 fxe3 with a significant positional advantage for White.

a4) 11...♘g6 12 ♘f5 ♗xf5 13 ♗xf5 ♘ce7 14 ♗d3 ♕c7 15 ♕h5 a6 16 c4 f5 (De Kleuver-Gausel, Reykjavik 1996) and now maybe 17 c5!? ±.

b) 10...♗f5 is just as effective as our main line: 11 c4 0-0 12 ♘c3 ♘b4 13 ♗xf5 ♘xf5 14 c5 ♗c7 15 ♗g5 ♕d7 16 ♕d2 b6 17 cxb6 ½-½ Hertneck-K.Müller, Austrian Cht 2001/2.

11 c4

11 ♖e1 ♕d7 12 ♘bd2 0-0 13 h3 ♗f5 14 ♗xf5 ♘xf5 15 ♘f1 ♘xe3 16 ♘xe3 ♗f4 was nothing for White in Brynell-Szabolcsi, Eger 1988.

11...h6 12 h3 ♗h5 13 ♘c3 0-0

In spite of White's pawn-centre and pressure on the d5-pawn, White is not better, as Black has a good square on

b4, which will be occupied by a knight or a bishop, Rozentalis-Eingorn, USSR Ch (Leningrad) 1990.

A2)

6 g3!? *(D)*

This is not the most common move here but has a very logical basis: to develop the bishop on g2, from where it can attack the d5-pawn, which can no longer be defended by pawns.

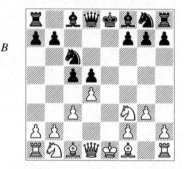

B

6...♗g4
Or:

a) 6...♕e7+ is critical but should not be dangerous for White, as Black falls behind in development: 7 ♗e3 ♘f6 8 ♗g2 ♘g4 9 0-0 ♘xe3 10 fxe3 ♕xe3+ 11 ♔h1 ♗e6 and now 12 c4! seems good: 12...0-0-0 13 cxd5 ♗xd5 14 ♘c3 ♗xf3 15 ♖xf3 ♕xd4 16 ♕b3! and White has a strong attack.

b) 6...♘f6 7 ♗g2 ♗e7 8 0-0 0-0 9 dxc5 (9 ♖e1!?) 9...♗xc5 10 ♗g5 (10 ♘bd2 ♗b6 11 ♘b3 ♗e6, Harley-Morgan, Cambridge 2002, 12 ♖fe1 ♘g4 13 ♘fd4 ♕f6 14 ♗f4 ±) 10...♗e6 11 ♘bd2 h6 12 ♗xf6 ♕xf6 13 ♘b3 ♗b6 14 a4 a6 15 a5 ♗a7 16 ♖a4 ♖ab8?! 17 ♘bd4 ♘xd4 18 ♘xd4 ♗d7 19 ♖a1,

Rozentalis-White, Linares 2002. White is only slightly better, but it is an enduring edge, since when Black takes on d4 he will have the worse bishop.

7 ♗g2 ♗d6

7...cxd4 8 0-0! (not 8 cxd4 ♗b4+, when Black is fine) 8...♗d6 and now:

a) 9 ♕b3 doesn't work: 9...♘ge7 10 ♘xd4 (after 10 ♕xb7?! ♖b8 11 ♕a6 dxc3 12 ♘xc3 ♕d7 Black's pieces are very active) 10...♕d7 11 ♗g5 0-0 12 ♗xe7 ♘xe7 13 ♘a3 ♖ad8 14 ♘ac2 ♗c5 = Rozentalis-Christiansen, Groningen 1992.

b) 9 cxd4 ♘ge7 10 ♘c3 0-0 11 h3 ♗h5 12 ♗e3 h6 13 ♕d2 ♘a5, Rozentalis-Movsesian, Batumi Echt 1999. After 14 b3 the position is rather complicated, but we think White has some advantage, since his pieces are better placed.

8 0-0 ♘ge7 9 dxc5

After the inaccurate 9 h3?! Black plays 9...♗f5! (the bishop goes to one of the key squares in such positions) 10 dxc5 ♗xc5 11 ♘bd2 (after 11 b4 ♗b6 12 b5 ♘a5 13 ♗a3 0-0 14 ♗xe7 ♕xe7 15 ♕xd5 ♕f6, Black has enough compensation for the pawn) 11...♗b6 12 ♘b3 ♕d7 13 ♔h2 0-0 = Rozentalis-Ehlvest, Rakvere 1993.

9...♗xc5 10 ♘bd2 0-0 11 ♘b3 ♗b6 12 ♖e1

Followed by ♗e3. White's chances are slightly better, but the position provides scope for a full-blooded fight.

B)

5...♗d6 *(D)*
6 ♗b5+

Instead:

a) Now 6 g3 ♕e7+ 7 ♗e3 ♘f6 8 ♗g2 ♘g4 9 0-0 ♘xe3 10 fxe3 ♕xe3+ 11 ♔h1 0-0 is fine for Black.

b) 6 ♗e3 c4 7 b3 cxb3 8 axb3 ♘c6 – 5...♘c6 6 ♗e3 c4 7 b3 cxb3 8 axb3 ♗d6.

c) 6 ♗e2 ♘c6 – 5...♘c6 6 ♗e2 ♗d6.

d) 6 dxc5 ♗xc5 7 ♗d3 (7 ♗b5+ ♘c6 – 6 ♗b5+ ♘c6 7 dxc5 ♗xc5) seems logical since in the main line below, White retreats the bishop to d3 later. Now:

d1) 7...♕e7+ is best answered by 8 ♗e2!?, when the black queen might be uncomfortable on e7. Instead after 8 ♕e2 ♘c6, Black is going to play ...d4 quickly.

d2) 7...♘e7 8 ♘bd2 ♘bc6 9 ♘b3 ♗b6 10 0-0 ♗g4 11 ♖e1 h6 12 h3 ♗h5 13 ♗e3 ± Filipović-Ekström, Banja Luka 1987. White is a tempo up on a main line here.

d3) 7...♘f6! (Black alters his plan appropriately) 8 0-0 0-0 9 h3 ♘c6 10 ♘bd2 ♗b6 11 ♘b3 ♘e4 12 ♘bd4 ♕f6 = Garner-Kasparov, Oakham simul 1997.

e) 6 ♗d3 c4 (6...♘f6!? suggests itself) 7 ♗c2 ♘e7 8 0-0 0-0 9 ♘h4 ♘d7

with an unclear position, Haba-Cvi-
tan, Haifa Echt 1989.

6...♘c6

6...♗d7?! is not good because of 7
dxc5!. Then:

a) 7...♗xc5 8 ♕xd5 ♕e7+ (White
wins after 8...♗xf2+ 9 ♔xf2 ♕b6+ 10
♘d4) 9 ♔d1! (9 ♗e2 may also be possible) and the threats of 10 ♖e1 and 10
♕xb7 cause Black severe difficulty.

b) 7...♗xb5 8 cxd6 ♕xd6 9 a4!
♗d7 (9...♗a6 10 b4) 10 0-0 ♘e7 11
♘a3 0-0 12 ♘b5 and White has the
better position, Smagin-Emms, Bundesliga 1996/7.

7 dxc5

7 ♗e3 is met by the natural 7...c4 8
b3 cxb3 9 axb3 ♘e7 10 0-0-0-0 11 ♖e1
h6 12 h3 ♗f5 = Adams-Lautier, Dos
Hermanas 1995.

7...♗xc5 8 0-0 ♘e7

The natural-looking 8...♘f6 is well
met by 9 ♗g5 ♗e6 10 ♘d4 0-0 11
♘xc6 bxc6 12 ♗xc6, when Black does
not have enough compensation for the
pawn, Smagin-R.Hernandez, Palma de
Mallorca 1989.

9 ♘bd2 0-0

In the main lines below, White attempts to stop Black playing ...♗g4,
so it is interesting for Black to try to
play it here. However, after 9...♗g4!?,
White can get 'compensation' by de-
ploying his queen more actively: 10
♕a4 ♗h5 11 ♕h4 ♗g6 12 ♘b3 ± Ivan-
chuk-Shirov, Dortmund 1992. More
tests are needed.

10 ♘b3 (D)

A standard isolated queen's pawn
position has arisen. The reader would
be advised to compare and contrast

B

with the isolated queen's pawn positions that arise in Chapter 5 of this
book. In this particular position, White,
here playing against Black's isolated
queen's pawn, is slightly ahead in development (mainly by virtue of being
White) and already has good control
of the critical d4-square. Furthermore,
the fact that White has a c-pawn rather
than an e-pawn (which Black has in
the positions of Chapter 5) increases
the scope of his dark-squared bishop,
which often comes to e3 and sometimes c5 in this line. Black's knight is
less well placed on e7 for generating
play against h2 or f2 (weaker here as
White has no e-pawn) than it would be
on f6, but from the f5-square it can
point at d4 and in some lines start
kingside play with ...♘h4. Black's two
main plans are to liquidate with ...d4
or to attack on the kingside, particularly with the plan of ...♗c7 and
...♕d6 (the same core plans as White
has in Chapter 5). White can actually
often respond in kind with ♗c2 and
♕d3; both sides are seeking to weaken
the other's kingside pawn-structure.
White's main plan of course is to seek
exchanges and try to reach an endgame

where Black's isolated queen's pawn could prove fatally weak.

Now Black has two equally popular options:

B1: 10...♗b6 39
B2: 10...♗d6 41

B1)

10...♗b6

This retreat is less common in the Tarrasch French because after *1 e4 e6 2 d4 d5 3 ♘d2 c5 4 exd5 exd5 5 ♘gf3 ♘c6 6 ♗b5 ♗d6 7 dxc5 ♗xc5 8 0-0 ♘e7 9 ♘b3 ♗b6*, White has not spent a tempo playing c3 and Black has thus not castled, so White can play an immediate *10 ♖e1 0-0* (10...♘f5 is of course illegal) *11 ♗e3*, challenging the dark-squared bishop, with a slight advantage. The exchange of dark-squared bishops would be particularly favourable for White.

11 ♖e1

11 ♘bd4 ♗g4 = Salai-Fominykh, Stary Smokovec 1990.

11...♘f5 *(D)*

This is the most active response, lining up for an eventual ...d4 or kingside play with ...♘h4. It also stops 12 ♗e3, and furthermore sets a subtle trap – can you see it?

The main alternative is 11...♗g4 12 ♗e3, and then:

a) 12...♗xe3 13 ♖xe3 ♘f5 14 ♖e1 (14 ♖d3 ♘h4 15 ♖xd5 ♕f6 with compensation) 14...♕b6!? 15 ♕xd5 (15 ♗d3 ♘h4 16 ♗e2 ♗xf3 17 ♗xf3 ♘xf3+ 18 ♕xf3 ♖ad8 19 ♖ad1 ♕a6 20 ♘c1 d4 ½-½ Pierrot-An.Rodriguez, Mar del Plata Z 2001) 15...♘ce7 16 ♕c5 ♕xc5 17 ♘xc5 ♗xf3 18 gxf3 is

slightly better for White, Marciano-Vaïsser, Bastia 1998.

b) 12...♖e8 13 h3 ♗h5 14 a4! ♗c7 (14...a6 15 ♗xb6 ♕xb6 16 ♗e2 followed by a5 ± Smagin) 15 ♗c5 a6 16 ♗xc6! and White wins a pawn; for example, 16...♘xc6 (16...bxc6 17 ♘bd4! ♗d6 18 ♘xc6! ♘xc6 19 ♖xe8+ ♕xe8 20 ♗xd6 ± Smagin) 17 ♖xe8+ ♕xe8 18 ♕xd5 ± Smagin-Cvitan, Biel 1995.

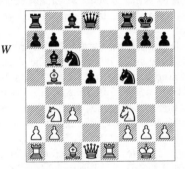

12 ♗d3

Black's last move actually threatened White's b5-bishop in a very subtle way. He threatened 12...♗xf2+ 13 ♔xf2 ♕b6+ and 14...♕xb5 winning a pawn, as 14 ♘bd4 is answered by 14...♘cxd4 15 ♘xd4 ♘xd4, removing the last defender. Rather than bolster the bishop with 12 a4, White is quite happy to relocate it to a more active square. At an appropriate moment, White would be quite happy to exchange this good bishop for one of Black's knights, and ♗xf5 is a better way to do this, as ♗xc6 bxc6 would improve Black's pawn-structure.

12...h6

Black has a number of options here. He would like to play ...d4 but can't

yet because of the simple response
♗xf5. The simplest way to add another piece to the support of the ...d4
break is to play either ...♕d6 or ...♕f6
followed by ...♖d8. The text-move prepares ...♕f6, which would otherwise
be met by ♗g5; it also stops White
answering ...♗e6 with ♘g5. Another
plan for Black is to go for mate with
...♗c7, ...♕d6 and ...♘h4 in a similar
vein to White's plans in Chapter 5 of
this book. Thus, the main alternatives
are:

a) 12...♕d6 13 ♗xf5! (White plays
this now since it forces off the dark-
squared bishops too; 13 ♗c2 ♖d8 14
♕d3 g6 15 ♗g5 f6 16 ♗d2 ♘e5 with
an unclear position, Harley-Morgan,
Cambridge 2001) 13...♗xf5 14 ♗e3
♗xe3 (14...♗c7 15 ♗c5 costs Black
the exchange) 15 ♖xe3 ♖fe8 16 ♕e2
♔f8 17 ♖e1 ± Filipović-Micalizzi,
Mendrisio 1989.

b) 12...♗c7 (note that this position
could also arise via *10...♗d6 11 ♗d3
♗c7 12 ♖e1 ♘f5*) and then:

b1) 13 ♗g5 f6! (13...♕d6 14 g3 ±)
14 ♗h4 (14 ♗d2 ♘e5 ∞ Kovaliov)
14...♘xh4 15 ♘xh4 g6! ∞ Smagin.

b2) 13 ♕c2 ♘h4!? 14 ♘bd4 (14
♗xh7+ ♔h8 15 ♘g5 f6 16 ♘e6 {16
♗g8 ♗f5!} 16...♖e8! is given as −+
by Kovaliov, though White can actually rescue his piece by both 17 ♘bc5
♗xe6 18 ♘xe6 ♕d7 19 ♗f4! ∞ and 17
♗g5!? ♘f3+ 18 gxf3 ♗xe6 ∞) 14...♗g4
15 ♘xh4 ♕xh4 16 g3 ♕h5 17 ♘xc6
bxc6 18 ♗e3 f5 with a good attack,
Yandemirov-Kovaliov, Minsk 1995.

b3) 13 g3!? (this would be more
logical after ...♕d6 since ♗f4 then

gains a tempo) 13...h6 14 ♗c2 ♗b6 15
♕d3 g6 16 ♗f4 ♔g7 17 ♘e5 ± Emms-
Mortensen, Hastings 1995/6.

b4) With 13 ♗c2 White responds
in similar fashion: both sides are playing to induce kingside weaknesses by
threats against h2/h7. Then:

b41) 13...g6 14 ♗xf5 ♗xf5 15 ♗h6
♖e8 16 ♖xe8+ ♕xe8 17 ♕xd5 ♗e4 18
♕d1 ♘e5 19 ♘fd4 ± V.Ivanov-Bala-
shov, Moscow 1999.

b42) 13...♕d6 14 ♕d3 g6 15 g3
♗b6 16 ♗f4 ♕d8 17 ♖ad1 ♗e6 18 ♘e5
♖c8 19 ♕f3 ♘cd4 20 ♘xd4 ♘xd4 21
cxd4 ♖xc2 22 ♗h6 ♖e8 23 ♘xf7 ♕d7
(23...♗xf7 24 ♖xe8+ ♕xe8 25 ♕f6
+−) 24 ♘g5 ± Striković-Arsović, Vrnjačka Banja 1999.

13 ♗c2 (D)

13...♗e6
Black defends the d-pawn so that he
can play ...♕f6. Other tries:

a) 13...♕d6 14 ♗xf5! (again this
forces off the dark-squared bishops too;
14 ♕d3 ♖d8 15 g4 ♕g6!) 14...♗xf5
15 ♗e3 ♗g4!? 16 ♗xb6 axb6 ± Tiviakov-Lautier, Groningen 1995.

b) 13...d4 14 ♗xf5 (14 c4!? ♘b4
15 ♗b1 goes for attack rather than

material) 14...♗xf5 15 ♘fxd4 ♘xd4 16 ♘xd4 ♗xd4 17 cxd4 ± Dolmatov.

c) 13...a5 14 ♕d3 (Dolmatov considers Black to have good compensation for the pawn after 14 a4 d4!? since by comparison to *13...d4*, White's a4-pawn is now stuck on a light square) 14...a4 15 ♘bd4 g6 (15...♘cxd4?! 16 ♘xd4 ♗xd4 17 cxd4 ♕b6 {17...♕h4 18 ♖e5 ±} 18 g4 ♕g6 19 ♕d1! h5 20 h3 ± Dolmatov) 16 ♘xf5 ♗xf5 17 ♕d1 ♗xc2 18 ♕xc2 ♔g7 19 ♗f4 ♕f6 20 ♕d2 g5 21 ♗e3 ± Dolmatov-Lobron, Dortmund 1993.

14 ♕d3 ♕f6 15 ♗e3 *(D)*

15 g4 ♕g6! is a common trick in such positions: 16 ♗g5 (16 h3 ♖ae8 ∞) 16...♘d6 17 ♕xg6 fxg6 18 ♖xe6 ♖xf3 19 ♗h4 ♘c4 ∓ Marciano-Belkhodja, French Cht 1998/9.

B

15...♗xe3 16 fxe3!?

This recapture controls the d4-square and thus stops the freeing break ...d4. It also gives White more active piece-play and the option of breaking with e4 when he chooses. White also has an advantage after 16 ♖xe3 g6 17 ♖e2 (Black equalized after 17 ♖ee1 ♖ad8 18 ♘c5 ♗c8 19 ♖ad1 d4 in the game

Pavasović-Smetankin, Leon Echt 2001) 17...♖ad8 18 ♖d1 ♘d6 19 ♘fd4 ±.

16...g6

16...♖fe8 17 ♘c5 ♖e7 might be superior, but White still has an annoying initiative.

17 ♘c5 ♘e5

Alternatives:

a) 17...b6 18 ♘xe6 fxe6 (18...♕xe6 allows 19 ♘d4 or 19 ♗b3 ♘ce7 20 e4) 19 e4 ±.

b) 17...♘d6 18 ♗b3 ♘c4 19 e4 (19 ♘xe6 ♕xe6 20 ♘d4 ♕d6 21 ♗xc4 ♘e5 is equal) 19...♘xb2 20 ♕d2 ♘c4 21 ♕xh6 with a slight advantage for White.

18 ♘xe5 ♕xe5 19 ♗b3 ♘h4 20 e4 dxe4 21 ♘xe6 ♕xe6 22 ♖xe4 ♕b6+ 23 ♕d4 ♕xd4+ 24 ♖xd4 ♘f5 25 ♖d7

White has a clear advantage, Godena-Salmensuu, Batumi Echt 1999.

B2)

10...♗d6 *(D)*

W

Play has now transposed to a line of the Tarrasch French, viz. *1 e4 e6 2 d4 d5 3 ♘d2 c5 4 exd5 exd5 5 ♘gf3 ♘c6 6 ♗b5 ♗d6 7 dxc5 ♗xc5 8 0-0 ♘e7 9 ♘b3 ♗d6 10 c3 0-0*, though nowadays

White would often prefer *10 ♖e1 0-0 11 ♗g5 ±* and Black *5...♘f6*.

11 ♗d3

The best try for an advantage. The point of this move is to stop 11...♗g4, which would now be answered by 12 ♗xh7+ ♔xh7 13 ♘g5+ ♔g8 14 ♕xg4 winning a pawn. Other lines have been analysed out over the years; two examples:

a) 11 ♘bd4 ♗g4 12 ♕a4 ♗h5! 13 ♗d3 h6 14 ♗e3 a6 15 ♖fe1 ♕c7 16 h3 ♘a5 = Karpov-Korchnoi, Moscow Ct (10) 1974.

b) 11 ♗g5 ♗g4 12 ♗e2 h6 13 ♗h4 ♖e8 14 ♖e1 ♕b6 with an equal position, Dolmatov-Tiller, Groningen jr Wch 1976/7.

11...h6

Black renews the 'threat' of ...♗g4. Alternatively:

a) 11...♘g6 12 ♗g5 ♘ce7 (12...f6? 13 ♗xg6 hxg6 14 ♕xd5+ ♔h8 15 ♖ad1 +− Ochsner-P.Olsen, Copenhagen 1997) 13 ♖e1 h6 14 ♗e3 ♖e8 15 ♗c5 ± Godena-Efimov, Saint Vincent 1998.

b) 11...♗c7 12 ♖e1 ♘f5 – *10...♗b6 11 ♖e1 ♘f5 12 ♗d3 ♗c7*.

12 h3 (D)

White stops ...♗g4. Note how by comparison to the systems arising after *10...♗b6*, both sides have weakened their kingsides slightly by moving their h-pawns. As Black often needs to play ...h6 anyway, this detail would appear to be in Black's favour and a reason for selecting *10...♗d6* over *10...♗b6*.

12...♘f5 (D)

Black can also play:

a) 12...♗c7 13 ♖e1 ♕d6 14 ♗e3 ♖e8 15 ♘bd4 a6 16 ♘xc6 ♕xc6 (or 16...bxc6 17 b4 a5 18 ♗c5 ♕f6 19 b5 and White is much better, Smagin-Shaboian, Barnaul 1984) 17 ♗d4 ♗e6 18 ♕c2 ♕d7 19 ♗e5 ± Emms-Rossiter, British League (4NCL) 1998/9.

b) 12...♗f5 brings Black close to equality but White still has a slight pull; for example, 13 ♖e1 ♗xd3 14 ♕xd3 ♕c7 15 ♗e3 ♖ad8 16 ♖e2 ♘g6 17 ♖ae1 ± Pavasović-Rezan, Pula 2001.

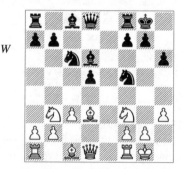

13 ♖e1

The normal move here, but White can try to do without this move; for example, 13 ♗c2 ♖e8 14 ♕d3 g6 15 ♕d1 ♔h7 16 ♘bd4 ♕f6 17 ♘xf5 ♗xf5 18

♗xf5 ♕xf5 19 ♗e3 ♖ad8 20 ♖e1 ♗f8
21 ♕b3 ♕d7 22 ♖ad1 ♗g7 23 ♕c2 ±
Illescas-Smirin, Elista OL 1998.

13...♕f6

The alternative plan is 13...♗c7 14
♗c2 ♕d6 15 ♕d3 g6, when the latest
attempt by White is 16 ♕d1!? h5 17
♗g5 ♗d7 18 ♕d2 ♖ae8 19 ♖ad1 ±
Motylev-Roghani, Erevan 2001.

14 ♗c2 ♖d8 15 ♕d3 g6 16 ♕d2!?
(D)

Instead:

a) 16 ♗d2 a5 17 a4 b6 = Psakhis-
Lputian, Rostov 1993.

b) 16 ♕d1!? ♗f8 17 ♗xf5 ♗xf5
18 ♘bd4 ♗e4 19 ♗e3 ± Tolnai-Uhl-
mann, Debrecen 1988.

B

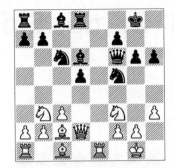

16...♗f8 17 ♕e2 ♗d7 18 ♗xf5
♗xf5 19 ♗e3 ♖e8 20 ♕d2

White has a slight advantage due to
Black's isolated queen's pawn, but the
position is quite playable for Black,
Smagin-Blauert, Vienna 1991.

3 2...d5: Sidelines

1 e4 c5 2 c3 d5 *(D)*

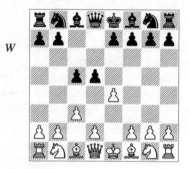

W

3 exd5

Now:

A: 3...♘f6?!   44
B: 3...♕xd5   45

A)

3...♘f6?!

With this rarely-played pawn sacrifice, Black seeks an advantage in development. White can hold on to the extra pawn, and although Black gains some counterplay, it should not be sufficient.

4 ♗b5+

Or:

a) The natural 4 c4 allows Black good play after 4...e6 5 dxe6 ♗xe6 6 ♗e2 ♘c6 7 ♘f3 ♕d7 8 0-0 ♗e7 (8...0-0-0 is also interesting) 9 d3 0-0 10 ♗e3 ♖ad8 11 ♘bd2 b6 12 ♘b3 ♗g4, Rozentalis-Diaz, Trnava 1988.

White has an extra pawn on d3, but it is weak and requires protection. It's extremely difficult to get rid of the weakness by playing d4, as Black controls the centre, so the position is about equal.

b) 4 ♕a4+ ♘bd7 (4...♗d7 is not good in view of 5 ♕b3 ±) 5 c4 g6! (this is better than 5...e6 6 dxe6 fxe6, which opens the e-file: 7 ♘c3 ♗d6 8 ♘f3 0-0 9 d3 ♘e5 10 ♗e2 ♗d7 11 ♕c2 ♗c6 12 ♘e4 and White managed to defend his position and keep an extra pawn in Masek-Orsag, Prague 1992) 6 ♘f3 ♗g7 7 ♗e2 0-0 8 d3 ♘b6 9 ♕c2 e6 (after 9...♕c7 10 0-0 ♘h5 11 ♘c3 ♘f4 12 ♘b5 ♘xe2+ 13 ♕xe2 ♕d7 14 ♘c3 Black has gained the bishop-pair, which should be enough to hold the position, although he lost in Van de Oudeweetering-Schwartz, Dieren 1988) 10 dxe6 ♗xe6 11 0-0 ♗f5. Once again we have a position where White is a pawn up, while Black has active pieces and good possibilities of play on the central e- and d-files.

4...♘bd7 *(D)*

4...♗d7 5 ♗xd7+ ♕xd7 (5...♘bxd7? is too passive: 6 c4 g6 7 ♘f3 ♗g7 8 0-0 0-0 9 ♘c3 ♘b6 10 d3 is excellent for White) 6 c4 e6 7 ♕e2 (7 dxe6 is worse, as it allows the knight to be developed to c6; after 7...♕xe6+ 8 ♕e2 ♘c6 9 ♕xe6+ fxe6 10 ♘f3 e5 Black has good counterplay in the endgame) 7...♗d6 8 dxe6 fxe6 9 ♘f3 ♘c6 10 d3 0-0 11 ♘c3 and White is doing well.

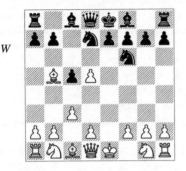

W

5 d4
Or 5 c4:

a) 5...g6 6 ♘f3 ♗g7 7 0-0 0-0 and then:

a1) White shouldn't play the passive 8 d3 ♘b6 9 ♘c3 e6 10 ♗e3 a6 11 ♗a4 ♕c7 12 dxe6 ♗xe6 13 ♗c2 ♖ad8, when we have an unclear position typical of this line: White is a pawn up, but Black has well-placed pieces and more space in the centre, Rozentalis-Domont, Chiasso 1991.

a2) With 8 d4! cxd4 9 ♗xd7 ♗xd7 10 ♘xd4 ♕b6 11 ♘c3 ♕c5 12 b3 White protects his extra pawn. After 12...♘g4 13 ♘de2 b5 14 h3 ♘e5 15 ♗e3 ♕c7 16 f4 White won a piece in Egin-Losev, Moscow 1997.

b) 5...a6 6 ♗xd7+ ♗xd7 7 d4 ♖c8 (not 7...cxd4 8 ♕xd4 b5 9 ♘f3 bxc4 10 ♗g5 e6 11 ♘c3 – analysis by Ravinsky) 8 ♘f3 (8 dxc5 ♕a5+) 8...b5 9 ♘e5 cxd4 10 ♕xd4 e6 11 ♗g5 h6 12 ♕h4 ♗d6 13 ♘g4 ♖xc4 14 ♗xf6 gxf6 with a sharp and unclear position, Zifroni-Manor, Tel-Aviv 1997.

5...cxd4
Or:

a) 5...♘xd5 6 dxc5 e6 7 c6 ±.

b) 5...♕b6 doesn't yield sufficient compensation for the pawn: 6 c4 cxd4 7 ♘e2 e5 8 dxe6 fxe6 9 ♘xd4 ♗c5 10 ♗e3 0-0 11 0-0 ♘e5 12 ♘c3 ♘eg4 13 h3 ♘xe3 14 fxe3 e5 15 ♘a4 ♕c7 16 ♘xc5 ♕xc5 17 ♘c2 ♗e6 18 b4 ♕b6 19 a4 a5 20 bxa5 +− Blatny-Plachetka, Trnava 1988.

6 ♕xd4 g6 7 d6!
White gets rid of his weak pawn and makes things very inconvenient for Black.

7...a6
After 7...exd6 8 ♘f3 Black suddenly finds himself in a difficult situation:

a) 8...♗g7 is bad owing to 9 ♕xd6.

b) 8...♗e7 is poor due to 9 ♗h6.

c) 8...♕e7+ loses the queen after 9 ♔d1! a6 10 ♖e1 +− Ekström-Nemet, Swiss Ch (Potresina) 2000.

8 dxe7 ♕xe7+ 9 ♗e2 ♗g7 10 ♘f3 0-0 11 ♗e3
11 ♕e3 is less good: 11...♖e8 12 0-0 ♕xe3 13 fxe3 (Sermek-Nemet, Lucerne 1994) 13...♘g4 14 ♘g5 ♘xe3 15 ♗xe3 ♖xe3 16 ♗c4 ♘e5 =.

11...♖e8 12 ♘bd2
White has managed to hold on to his extra pawn, and we don't see how Black can make any profit from his better development. 12...♗h6 is simply met by 13 ♘c4 b5 14 ♘d6 ±.

B)

3...♕xd5 4 d4 *(D)*
A reasonable alternative for White is 4 ♘f3, which might temporarily

bemuse Black. There doesn't appear to be any particular advantage to this move-order (as 4 d4 cxd4 is not at all fearsome), but then neither is there any harm; e.g.:

a) 4...e5 5 d4! – *4 d4 e5 5 ♘f3*.

b) 4...♗g4 5 ♕a4+ ♗d7 (at least one person has left the bishop *en prise*) 6 ♕b3 ♘f6 7 d4 – *4 d4 ♘f6 5 ♘f3 ♗g4 6 ♕a4+ ♗d7 7 ♕b3*.

c) 4...g6 5 ♘a3 ♗g7 6 ♗c4 ♕e4+ 7 ♗e2 ♘f6 8 0-0 0-0 9 ♖e1 ♘c6 10 ♗c4 ♕f5 11 ♘c2 b6 12 d4 ♗b7 13 ♘e3 ♕d7 14 ♘e5 ♕c7 15 ♘xc6 ½-½ Sveshnikov-Cebalo, Milan 2000.

d) 4...♘f6 5 ♗e2 ♗g4 (5...e6 is also good, especially as White has committed his bishop to e2) 6 0-0 e6 7 h3 ♗h5 8 d4 (8 c4 ♕d6 9 b4 cxb4 10 a3 ♕b6 11 d4 is very speculative, Ponomariov-Astengo, Biel 2000) transposes to *4 d4 ♘f6 5 ♘f3 ♗g4 6 ♗e2 e6 7 h3 ♗h5 8 0-0*.

B

Now 4...♘c6 and 4...♘f6 are analysed in the following chapters. Here we consider:

If instead 4...cxd4 5 cxd4 e5 (5...g6 – *2...g6 3 d4 cxd4 4 cxd4 d5 5 exd5 ♕xd5; 5...♘c6 6 ♘f3 – 4...♘c6 5 ♘f3 cxd4 6 cxd4*), then:

a) 6 dxe5?! ♕xd1+ (there is no need for Black to play 6...♗b4+ or 6...♕xe5+, though after both moves he probably equalizes) 7 ♔xd1 ♘c6 8 f4 ♗f5 and White will have a lot of problems with his king.

b) 6 ♘f3 and here:

b1) 6...e4? allows 7 ♘e5 followed by 8 ♗c4.

b2) 6...exd4?! 7 ♕xd4 ♘f6 8 ♘c3 ♕xd4 9 ♘xd4 a6 (after 9...♗c5 10 ♘db5 ♘a6 11 ♗g5 0-0 12 ♗xf6 gxf6 13 ♗e2, Black will have some problems holding the position, because his pawns are weak) 10 ♗g5 (10 ♗e2 ♗c5) 10...♘bd7 11 0-0-0 and White is better developed and has an advantage.

b3) 6...♘c6 is best, transposing to *4...♘c6 5 ♘f3 cxd4 6 cxd4 e5*.

B1)
4...e5 5 dxe5

A perfectly reasonable alternative for White is 5 ♘f3 cxd4 (5...e4 6 ♘e5 followed by 7 ♗c4 is good for White; 5...♘c6 – *4...♘c6 5 ♘f3 e5*) 6 cxd4, transposing to *4...cxd4 5 cxd4 e5 6 ♘f3*.

5...♕xe5+

After 5...♕xd1+ 6 ♔xd1 ♘c6, the fact that the c-pawns have not been exchanged off works in White's favour:

a) 7 ♘f3 ♗g4 8 ♗e2 0-0-0+ 9 ♔e1 ♗xf3 10 ♗xf3 ♘xe5 =.

b) After 7 f4 ♗f5, Black can't win back the pawn, but he can play against the white king and pawn-centre: 8 ♘f3 (8 ♗b5 0-0-0+ 9 ♔e2 ♗d7! and, making use of the fact that the white king is on e2, Black threatens 10...♘xe5 or 10...♘d4+) 8...0-0-0+ 9 ♔e1 f6 10 ♗b5 ♘ge7 11 ♔f2 a6 12 ♗xc6 ♘xc6 13 exf6 gxf6 14 ♗e3 ♖d3 and Black's bishop-pair and active pieces give him sufficient compensation.

c) 7 ♗f4 ♘ge7 8 ♘f3 ♗g4 9 ♗e2 ♘g6 10 ♗g3 0-0-0+ 11 ♘bd2 ♗e7 12 ♔c1 ♖he8 13 ♖e1 f5 14 exf6 ♗xf6 15 ♘c4 ♗xf3 16 gxf3 ♗g5+ 17 ♔c2 ♘f4 18 ♗f1 ± Seeger-Jukić, 2nd Bundesliga 1991/2.

6 ♗e2

The dark-squared bishop must go to f4, which is why this move is better than 6 ♗e3 ♘f6 7 ♘f3 ♕c7 (worse is 7...♗d5 8 ♘bd2 ♗e7 9 ♗c4 ♕h5 10 0-0 0-0 11 ♗f4, when White's pieces are better placed, so he has an advantage) and now:

a) 8 ♘a3 doesn't give White anything: 8...a6 9 g3 ♗e6 (not 9...b5? 10 ♗g2 ♗b7 11 ♗f4 ♕e7+ 12 ♔f1, when Black's queen will be in trouble after 13 ♕d2 or 13 ♕c2 and 14 ♖e1, Zak-Pismenny, Moscow 1973) 10 ♗g2 ♘c6 and Black is OK.

b) 8 ♗b5+ ♗d7 (8...♘c6? 9 ♕e2 ♗e6 10 ♘g5 ± Sermek-Kgosimore, Parana 1993) 9 ♕a4 ♗e7 10 0-0-0-0 =.

6...♘f6

6...♗g4 7 ♗e3 ♗xe2 (normally it is good for White to exchange light-squared bishops, since several pawns are already situated on dark squares) 8 ♕xe2 ♘d7 9 ♘f3 ♕e6 10 ♘a3, Donchev-Vuyarov, Bulgaria 1977. The knight is coming to b5 or c4, and White

has a slight advantage, because his bishop is better.

7 ♘f3 ♕c7 8 ♘a3 a6 *(D)*

9 ♕a4+!

9 g3 b5 10 0-0 is not dangerous for Black:

a) 10...♗b7 is possible, as long as after 11 ♘xb5 axb5 12 ♗xb5+, Black plays 12...♗c6, with unclear complications. Instead, 12...♘c6? is a mistake: 13 ♖e1+ ♗e7 14 ♗f4 ♕b6? 15 ♖xe7+ +− Karpachev-Ariskin, Moscow 1998.

b) 10...♗e7 is safer. After 11 ♗f4 ♕b6 12 ♖e1 ♘c6 Black is fine.

9...♗d7 10 ♗f4 ♗d6

The ending after 10...♗xa4 11 ♗xc7 ♘d5 12 ♗g3 is worse for Black; the white knight is coming to c4 and d6.

11 ♗xd6 ♕xd6 12 ♘c4 ♕e6 13 ♕b3 0-0 14 ♘b6 ♖a7 15 ♘xd7

This move is better than 15 ♕xe6 ♗xe6 16 ♘g5 ♗f5 17 0-0-0 h6 18 ♘f3 ♘bd7 and White's initiative is neutralized, Schmittdiel-P.Chandler, Frankfurt 1999.

15...♘bxd7

15...♘xd7 is met by 16 ♕b6.

16 ♕xe6 fxe6 17 0-0-0

White has a useful advantage in the endgame.

B2)
4...e6 *(D)*

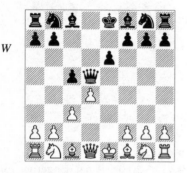

This is a feasible move, which normally transposes to other lines starting with 4...♘f6 or 4...♘c6. Those two moves are more flexible, and though there is no direct refutation of 4...e6, Black has surrendered his possibilities of developing his queen's bishop to g4 or f5. This position can also arise via *2...e6 3 d4 d5 4 exd5 ♕xd5.*

5 ♘a3!? *(D)*

This is the most enterprising attempt to exploit Black's move-order, and has scored very well for White in practice. However, there are two moves that are probably more accurate:

a) The simple 5 ♘f3 ♘f6 transposes to *4...♘f6 5 ♘f3 e6.*

b) 5 ♗e3 and then:

b1) 5...♘f6 6 ♘a3! cxd4 7 ♘b5 ♕d8 8 ♕xd4! ♘c6 9 ♕xd8+ ♔xd8 10 ♘f3 ± Smagin-Jovičić, Yugoslavia 1995.

b2) 5...cxd4 6 cxd4 ♘f6 7 ♘c3 ♕d8 8 ♘f3 ♘c6 – *4...♘f6 5 ♘f3 e6 6 ♗e3 cxd4 7 cxd4 ♘c6 8 ♘c3 ♕d6.*

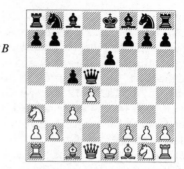

5...♗d7!

This is the best way to neutralize White's threats but is not an obvious move to find. It would be fair to assume that many players choosing 4...e6 rather than 4...♘f6 5 ♘f3 e6 are not familiar with nuances of move-order and are thus less likely to 'know' a move like 5...♗d7!.

Other moves don't prevent the knight jump to b5, after which Black will have some problems.

a) 5...cxd4 6 ♘b5 ♕a6 7 ♕xd4 ♕xd4 8 ♘xd4 ♘c7 (8...♘f6 9 ♘gf3 ♗e7 10 ♗e2 ♘c7 11 ♘e5 ♘d7 12 ♘c4 is a typical 2 c3 Sicilian endgame; although Black is solid, White's queenside majority gives him a small but lasting advantage, Sermek-Bukić, Bled 1993) 9 ♗f4 ♘d5 10 ♗b5+ ♗d7 11 ♗xd7+ ♔xd7 12 ♗g3 ♗d6 13 c4 ♗xg3? (13...♘b6 is correct, with just a slightly inferior position) 14 cxd5 ♗e5 15 dxe6+ fxe6 16 ♘gf3 and White has a serious advantage, due to the weak e6-pawn and the bad location of the black king, Kharlov-Tunik, Kuibyshev 1990.

b) 5...♘f6 6 ♘b5 ♘a6 7 ♗e3 cxd4 8 ♕xd4 ♕xd4 (many players have fallen straight into a trap here: 8...♗c5?? 9 ♕xc5! +–, two examples being Kharlov-Csom, Berne 1992, and Sveshnikov-Osnos, Rostov 1993) 9 ♗xd4 b6 10 ♗e2 ♗b7 11 ♗f3 ♗xf3 12 ♘xf3, Sveshnikov-Novikov, Tallinn 1988. Once again, White has a slight but pleasant endgame advantage.

c) 5...♕d8 6 ♗f4 ♘f6 (6...cxd4 7 ♘b5 ♘a6 8 ♕a4 ♗d7 9 ♕xd4 ♗c6 10 ♘d6+ ♗xd6 11 ♗xd6 and the advantage of the bishop-pair gives White the better chances, Glavina-Pogorelov, Ceuta 1995) 7 ♘b5 (7 dxc5 ♘d5 8 ♗d6 ♗xd6 9 cxd6 ♕xd6 =) 7...♘d5 8 ♗xb8 ♖xb8 9 ♘xa7 ♗d7 10 ♘b5 ♗e7 11 ♘f3 0-0 12 a4. Although White has fallen behind in development, he has won a pawn and we think Black's compensation is insufficient.

We now return to 5...♗d7 *(D)*:

W

6 ♘b5
White has nothing better:
a) 6 ♘f3 cxd4 7 ♘xd4 ♗xa3!? ∓.
b) 6 ♘c2 cxd4 7 ♘xd4 e5 =.
c) 6 ♗e3 cxd4 7 ♗xd4 ♘f6 8 ♗xf6 ♕e4+ 9 ♕e2 ♕xe2+ 10 ♗xe2 gxf6 = Marciano-Sakaev, Paris 1996.
6...♗xb5

This dangerous knight must be exchanged. Worse is 6...♘a6 7 ♗e3 c4 8 a4 ♘f6 (or 8...♗xb5 9 axb5 ♕xb5 10 ♕a4 and the c4-pawn is doomed) 9 ♕e2 ♗xb5 10 axb5 ♕xb5 11 ♕xc4 ♕xc4 12 ♗xc4 ♘c7, when White's bishop-pair and strong centre assure him of the better chances, Westerinen-Åkesson, Gausdal 1996.

7 ♗xb5+ ♘c6 8 ♕f3
White can't get any advantage because the b5-bishop is vulnerable: 8 ♘f3 cxd4 9 ♗xc6+ (9 ♕a4?! ♗c5 10 0-0 ♘e7 11 ♘xd4 ♗xd4! 12 cxd4 a6 ∓) 9...♕xc6 10 ♕xd4 ♘f6 with equality.

8...cxd4 9 ♕xd5 exd5 10 cxd4 ♗b4+ 11 ♗d2 ♗xd2+ 12 ♔xd2 ♘e7
The endgame is absolutely equal.

B3)
4...g6 *(D)*

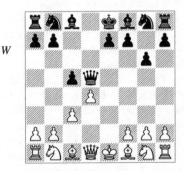

W

This has proved to be a very popular option in recent years, particularly amongst players aiming to win against lower-rated opponents who know the main lines well. Black plans to follow up with ...♗g7, ...♘h6 and ...♘f5 with pressure on d4.

White has two quite distinct main options:

B31: 5 dxc5   50
B32: 5 ♘f3   51

Or:

a) 5 ♗e3 cxd4 6 cxd4 (6 ♕xd4 ♕xd4 7 ♗xd4 f6 = Rozentalis-D.Gurevich, Toronto 1998) 6...♗g7 7 ♘c3 ♕a5 8 ♕b3 ♘h6 9 ♗c4 0-0 10 ♘ge2 ♘f5 and Black is fine, Sziva-Cvitan, Budapest 1991.

b) 5 ♘a3 cxd4 6 ♘b5 ♘a6 7 ♕xd4 ♕xd4 8 ♘xd4 ♘f6 9 ♘gf3 ♘c7 10 ♗f4 ♘cd5 11 ♗e5 a6 12 ♗c4 ♘b6 13 ♗xf6 exf6 14 ♗b3 ♗c5 15 0-0 0-0 = Striković-Popović, Yugoslav Ch (Banja Vrucica) 1991.

B31)
5 dxc5 ♕xc5 6 ♗e3 ♕a5
6...♕c7 is risky for Black, if White is willing to be a little daring:

a) 7 ♘a3 a6 8 ♘f3 ♘f6 9 ♘c4 ♘bd7 10 a4 ♗g7 11 a5 0-0 12 ♗e2 ♖d8 13 ♕d4 ♘h5! 14 ♕d5 ½-½ Sermek-Sakaev, Budapest 1996.

b) 7 ♗xa7!? ♖xa7 (7...♘c6 8 ♗e3 ♘h6 9 ♘a3! ± Krupkova-Bereziuk, Czech League 2000/1; 7...b6 8 ♕d4! ±) 8 ♕d4 ♘c6 9 ♕xh8 ♘f6. White's queen is out of the game and his king is still in the centre. The queen could be trapped after, for example, ...g5, ...♘e5 and ...♘g6. On the other hand, White is an exchange and a pawn up. Serious analysis and practice are still needed to come to a conclusion. Jerić-Veličković, Griže 2001 continued 10 ♘d2 ♖a5 11 ♘gf3 g5 12 ♘c4 ♗c5 13 h3 g4 14 hxg4 ♗xg4 15 ♖d1 ♗xf3 16

gxf3 ♕f4 with continuing compensation, though White did go on to win the game after returning the exchange to free his queen.

7 ♘a3
White does best to play on the queenside immediately, without pausing to play 7 ♘f3. The attempt to attack f7 immediately with 7 ♗c4 ♘c6 8 ♘f3 is not particularly effective:

a) 8...♗g7 9 ♕b3 ♕f5 10 ♘a3 (10 0-0 ♘h6 11 ♘d4 ♘xd4 12 ♗xd4 0-0 ∞) 10...♘h6 11 ♘b5 0-0 12 ♘fd4 ♘xd4 13 ♘xd4 ♕h5 14 ♗e2 ♕a5 15 ♕b5 ♕c7 16 ♕c4 ♕xc4 17 ♗xc4 = Harley-H.Hunt, Cambridge 1999.

b) 8...♘h6 9 ♕b3 e6 10 ♘bd2 ♗g7 11 ♘e4 0-0 12 ♕b5 ♘f5 13 ♗f4 e5 14 ♗g5 ♕xb5 15 ♗xb5 f6 16 ♗d2 ♗e6 ∓ Lane-H.Hunt, British League (4NCL) 1999/00.

7...♘c6
Black has to be careful here. White has some advantage after 7...♗g7 8 ♕b3 ♘c6 (8...♘f6 9 ♕b5+ ♘c6 10 ♕xa5 ♘xa5 11 ♘b5 ♘d5 12 ♖d1; 8...♘h6 9 ♕b5+ ♕xb5 10 ♘xb5) 9 ♗c4 ♘e5 (9...e6 10 ♘b5; 9...♕f5 10 ♘b5 ♔f8 11 ♖d1 ♗d7 12 ♘xa7!? ♘xa7 13 ♕xb7 ♗c3+ 14 bxc3 ♗c6 15 ♕b3 ♗xg2 16 ♗d5 ♗xd5 17 ♕xd5 ♕xd5 18 ♖xd5) 10 ♗b5+ ♘c6 (the alternatives are 10...♗d7 11 0-0-0 ♗xb5 12 ♕xb5+ ♕xb5 13 ♘xb5 ♔f8 and 10...♔f8 11 ♘c4 ♕c7 12 ♘xe5 ♗xe5 13 ♗c4 e6 14 ♘f3) 11 ♘f3 ♗d7 12 0-0 ♘f6 13 ♖ad1 0-0 14 ♖fe1.

8 ♕b3 ♘f6
Now if 8...♘h6 9 ♗c4 ♕f5, then 10 ♘b5! is good for White. Note how by comparison to Harley-H.Hunt above,

White has not 'wasted' a move on ♘f3.

9 ♗c4 e6

9...♘e5 10 ♗b5+ is slightly better for White.

10 ♘f3

Interesting is 10 ♘b5 a6! (10...♗e7 11 0-0-0 0-0 12 ♘f3 ±) 11 ♗b6!? (11 ♘d4 ♘e5 ∞) 11...axb5 12 ♗xa5 bxc4 13 ♕xc4 ♖xa5, when Black has sufficient material for the queen.

10...♗g7 11 ♘b5 0-0 12 0-0 a6 13 ♘bd4 ♘xd4 14 ♗xd4 b5 15 ♗e2 ♗b7

White has a slight space advantage, but Black is very close to equality. Mufić-Godena, Mogliano Veneto 1994 continued 16 c4 ♕c7 17 ♗e5 bxc4 18 ♕c3 (18 ♗xc4 ±) 18...♕e7 (18...♘d5!? ∓) 19 ♗xc4 ♘d5 =.

B32)

5 ♘f3 ♗g7

5...♘f6 *(D)* transposes to a position normally reached via *4...♘f6 5 ♘f3 g6?!* but analysed here to make it easier to compare the two lines. Then:

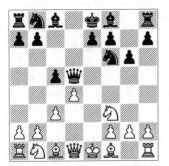

a) 6 ♘a3 doesn't give White an advantage: 6...♗g7 7 ♘b5 (7 ♗c4 ♕e4+ 8 ♗e3 0-0 9 0-0 cxd4 10 ♗xd4 ♘c6

11 ♖e1 ♕f5 = Benjamin-D.Gurevich, USA Ch (Parsippany) 1996) 7...♘a6 8 ♗e2 cxd4 9 ♕xd4 ♕xd4 10 ♘fxd4 0-0 = Shaked-Yermolinsky, USA Ch (Parsippany) 1996.

b) 6 c4!? ♕d8 (6...♕d6 may be better) 7 d5 ♗g7 – *5...♗g7 6 c4!* ♕d8 *7 d5 ♘f6* +=.

c) 6 ♕b3! threatens 7 ♗c4. Black can try:

c1) 6...cxd4 is risky: 7 ♗c4 ♕e4+ 8 ♔f1 e6 9 cxd4 (also possible is 9 ♘bd2 ♕f4 10 ♘xd4 ♕c7 11 ♘2f3 a6 12 ♗g5 ♗e7 13 ♖e1 ♘c6 14 ♘xc6 bxc6 15 ♕a4 0-0 16 ♘e5 ♗d7 17 h4 with active play for White, Barbero-Cebalo, Bratto 1998) 9...a6 10 ♗g5 ♗g7 11 ♘c3 ♕f5 12 ♖e1 ♘c6 13 d5 ♘a5 14 ♕a4+ b5 15 ♕xa5 bxc4, Ekström-Belotti, Mitropa Cup (Charleville) 2000. Here White has a very dangerous initiative, the nastiest continuation now being 16 ♕c5!.

c2) 6...♕xb3 (taking on b3 is also a concession, as White obtains an open file for his rook) 7 axb3 cxd4 (another concession, but 7...♘bd7 8 dxc5 ♘xc5 9 ♗e3 is also bad for Black) 8 ♘xd4 gives White a lot of threats on the queenside, against which Black is unable to defend. For example: 8...♘d5 (or 8...a6 9 ♘b5 ♔d8 10 ♗f4 ♘d5 11 ♗g3) 9 ♗c4 ♘c7 10 ♗f4 ♘ba6 11 ♘b5 ♘xb5 12 ♗xb5+ ♔d8 13 ♖xa6 bxa6 14 ♗c6 ♗f5 15 ♔e2 +− Ekström-Gaprindashvili, Lucerne Wcht 1997.

c3) 6...♗e6!? 7 c4 ♕d7 8 d5 ♗f5 9 ♘c3 ± Emms-Ansell, British League (4NCL) 1998/9.

We now return to 5...♗g7 *(D)*:

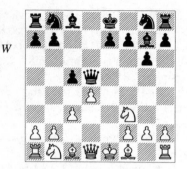

6 c4!

It is odd that this natural move has not been played more often. Instead:

a) 6 ♕b3 ♕xb3 7 axb3 cxd4 8 ♘xd4 ♗xd4 9 cxd4 ♘f6 10 ♘c3 0-0 11 ♗e3 ♗e6 12 ♗c4 ♖d8! 13 ♗xe6 fxe6 ∓ Lorenzo Duran-Kurajica, Malaga 2001.

b) 6 ♗e3 cxd4 7 cxd4 ♕a5+ (not 7...♘h6?? 8 ♕c1 1-0 Vasiukov-Razuvaev, Polanica Zdroj 1972, although some white players have missed this!) 8 ♘c3 ♘h6 9 ♗c4 ♘f5 10 0-0 0-0 11 a3 ♘c6 12 ♕d2 ♘d6 ∞ Mellado-L.Spassov, La Pobla de Lillet 1997.

c) 6 ♗e2 cxd4 7 cxd4 ♘h6 8 ♘c3 ♕a5 9 0-0 0-0 10 ♕b3 ♘f5 11 d5 ♘a6 ∞ Gufeld-Bronstein, USSR Ch (Leningrad) 1960.

d) 6 ♘a3 cxd4 7 ♗c4 and then:

d1) 7...♕d8 8 ♕b3 e6 9 ♘xd4 is slightly better for White, Sveshnikov-Cvitan, Tilburg 1993.

d2) 7...♕a5 8 ♘xd4 ♘f6 9 0-0 0-0 10 ♖e1 e5 11 b4 ♕c7 12 ♘db5 ♕e7 13 ♗e3 b6 14 ♕d6 ± Turner-D'Costa, British Ch (Scarborough) 2001.

d3) 7...♕e4+ 8 ♗e3! (8 ♔f1 ♘h6 9 ♕b3 0-0 10 ♗xh6 ♗xh6 11 ♖e1 ♕f4

12 cxd4 ♘c6 13 ♕e3 ♖d8 is slightly better for Black, Sveshnikov-Sax, Bled 2000) 8...♘h6 (8...dxe3?? loses to 9 ♗xf7+! ♔f8 10 ♕d8+ ♔xf7 11 ♘g5+) 9 cxd4 0-0 10 ♘b5 (10 0-0 ♗g4 11 ♗xh6!? ♗xh6 12 ♖e1, Sveshnikov-Najer, St Petersburg 1998, 12...♕f4! 13 ♖xe7 ♘c6 14 ♖xb7 ♖ab8! gives Black compensation) 10...♘d7 (10...♘c6 11 ♘c3 ♕g4 12 h3! ♕d7 13 d5 ± Stević-Bistrić, Bihac 1999) 11 ♗d3 (11 0-0 ♘b6 12 ♗d3 ♕g4, Harley-H.Hunt, Cambridge 2000, 13 h3 ♕d7 14 ♘e5 ♕d8 15 g4!? ∞) 11...♕g4 12 h3! ♕h5 13 0-0 ♘f5 14 ♗g5! is complex but seems slightly better for White.

6...♕d8

Or:

a) If 6...♕e4+, then 7 ♗e3 is much better for White.

b) 6...♕e6+ 7 ♗e2 cxd4 8 ♘xd4 ♕b6 9 ♘b5 ♗d7 10 ♘1c3 ♗xb5 11 ♘xb5 leaves White slightly better.

c) 6...♕d6 may be best, but we think that after 7 d5 White also has an advantage, due to his strong centre. If Black attacks it by ...e6, White's passed d-pawn can become quite dangerous. Practical tests are required.

7 d5 ♘f6 8 ♘c3 0-0

Now:

a) 9 ♗e3 is best met by 9...♕a5 10 ♕d2 e6 with counterplay for Black. Instead, 9...b6 10 ♗e2 ♘bd7 11 0-0 allowed White a comfortable position in Rizouk-Doghri, Tunez 2000.

b) 9 ♗e2 e6 10 0-0 exd5 11 cxd5 b6 12 a4 with a slight advantage for White, Rozentalis-Piesina, Lithuanian Ch (Vilnius) 2002.

4 2...d5 3 exd5 ♕xd5 4 d4 ♘c6

1 e4 c5 2 c3 d5 3 exd5 ♕xd5 4 d4 ♘c6
(D)

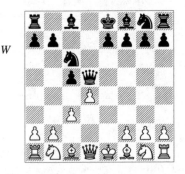

W

Now:
A: 5 dxc5   53
B: 5 ♘f3   55

No other moves offer White anything here:

a) 5 ♘a3 cxd4 6 ♘b5 ♕d8 (another idea is 6...♕e5+!?) 7 ♘f3 a6 8 ♘bxd4 ♘xd4 9 ♕xd4 ♕xd4 10 ♘xd4 e5 = Dončević-Suba, Palma de Mallorca 1992.

b) 5 ♗e3 and Black can choose between a perfectly good closed or a perfectly good open position:

b1) 5...e5 6 c4 (6 dxc5 ♕xd1+ 7 ♔xd1 – *5 dxc5 ♕xd1+ 6 ♔xd1 e5 7 ♗e3*) 6...♕d8 7 d5 ♘d4 ∞ Wahls-Gallagher, Biel 1994.

b2) 5...cxd4 6 cxd4 e5 7 ♘c3 ♗b4 8 ♘f3 exd4 9 ♘xd4 ♘ge7 10 ♘xc6 ♕xd1+ 11 ♖xd1 ♘xc6 12 ♗b5 = Dovzhik-Breder, Paks 2000.

A)

5 dxc5 *(D)*

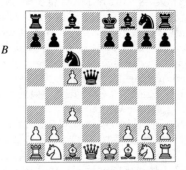

B

A common plan in the modern treatment of the 2 c3 Sicilian. White releases the tension in the centre, trying to gain a queenside pawn-majority and hoping to exploit the position of the black queen, but the idea is premature here and doesn't promise White anything in this particular position.

5...♕xd1+

This is best. White will have to waste a lot of time hiding his king, while his extra pawn is weak and sooner or later will be lost.

5...♕xc5 leads to a more complicated game:

a) 6 ♗e3 is not dangerous for Black; e.g., 6...♕a5 7 ♘f3 ♘f6 8 ♗c4 e6 9 0-0 ♗e7 10 ♘d4 ♗d7 11 ♘d2 ♘xd4 12 ♗xd4 ♗c6 13 ♖e1 0-0, Yudasin-Zsu.Polgar, Pamplona 1990/1. Without queens White is normally slightly better, but if the queens are still on the board, Black has nothing to be afraid of – the position is equal.

b) 6 ♘a3 is White's best chance, starting the typical knight manoeuvre to b5. However, Black has enough resources to neutralize White's initiative:

b1) 6...e5 is not good for Black: 7 ♘b5 ♕e7 8 b3! ♗e6 (8...♕d8 9 ♕xd8+ ♔xd8 10 ♗e3) 9 ♗a3 ♕d8 10 ♕xd8+ ♖xd8 11 ♘c7+ ♔d7 12 ♘xe6 ♔xe6 13 ♗c4+ ♔f6 14 ♗c1 and White obtains an edge due to his bishop-pair, Marković-Zakić, Belgrade 1996.

b2) 6...♘f6 7 ♘b5 ♕e5+ 8 ♕e2 is also good for White.

b3) 6...♕a5 7 ♘f3 ♗g4 8 ♗e2 ♘f6 9 0-0 ♖d8 10 ♕b3 ♖d7 11 ♘c4 ♕c7 12 ♗g5 e6 13 ♖ad1 ♖xd1 14 ♖xd1 ♗e7, F.Röder-Dizdarević, Bad Wörishofen 1988. Black completes his development and equalizes.

6 ♔xd1 e5

The most active move. Instead:

a) 6...♗f5 7 ♗e3 ♘f6 8 ♘f3 – 5 ♘f3 ♘f6 6 dxc5 ♕xd1+ 7 ♔xd1 ♗f5 8 ♗e3.

b) 6...♘f6 7 ♗b5 (7 ♘f3 may be better, transposing to 5 ♘f3 ♘f6 6 dxc5 ♕xd1+ 7 ♔xd1) 7...♗d7 8 ♘f3 e5 9 ♗xc6 ♗xc6 10 ♘xe5 ♗xg2 11 ♖g1 0-0-0+ 12 ♔e2 ♖e8 13 ♖xg2 ♖xe5+ 14 ♗e3 ♗xc5 and a draw was soon

agreed in Schmittdiel-Kaeser, Neuss 1986.

7 b4 a5 8 ♗b5

After 8 b5 ♘d8 followed by ...♘e6, White cannot hold on to his extra pawn.

8...♗d7 9 ♘f3 f6 10 ♗d2 ♘ge7 *(D)*

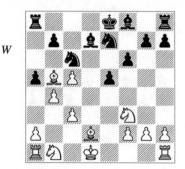

11 ♘a3

Or:

a) After the natural 11 ♖e1 axb4 12 cxb4 ♘d5 13 ♗xc6 ♗xc6 14 ♔c1 ♔f7 15 a3 b6 16 ♖xe5 ♘xb4 17 ♘g5+ ♔g6 18 ♖e6 ♘d3+ 19 ♔c2 ♘e5 20 ♘c3 ♗d7 White has to sacrifice an exchange and fight for a draw, Sveshnikov-Rashkovsky, Moscow Tal mem 1992.

b) 11 ♗c4 also gives Black the initiative: 11...e4 12 ♘e1 ♘e5.

11...axb4 12 ♘c4 bxc3 13 ♘d6+ ♔d8 14 ♘f7+ ♔e8

Black can choose the sharp 14...♔c7 15 ♘xh8 cxd2 or simply go on repeating moves.

15 ♘d6+

White can't take the rook, as after 15 ♘xh8 cxd2 sooner or later Black will win the knight.

15...♔d8 16 ♘f7+ ♔e8

With a draw by repetition – analysis by Sveshnikov and Rashkovsky.

B)

5 ♘f3 *(D)*

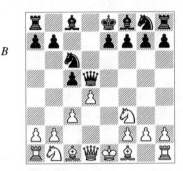

Now:

B1: 5...cxd4   56
B2: 5...♗g4   62
B3: 5...♘f6   68

Alternatively:

a) 5...♗f5 6 ♗e3 and now:

a1) 6...♘f6 and then:

a11) 7 ♕b3 only leads to an equal endgame: 7...♕xb3 8 axb3 cxd4 (not 8...♘d5? as after 9 dxc5 White is just a pawn up, Zifroni-Porper, Tel-Aviv 1992) 9 ♘xd4 ♘xd4 10 ♗xd4 a6 =.

a12) 7 ♕a4 is interesting. White pins the knight and prepares ♗c4. A possible continuation is 7...cxd4 8 ♘xd4 ♗d7 9 ♘b5 ♕e5 10 ♘d2, when the knight goes to c4 or f3 with some initiative.

a2) 6...cxd4 7 ♘xd4 0-0-0 and now 8 ♘d2 gives White comfortable play (8 ♕a4 is not so good, as after 8...♘xd4 9 cxd4 ♗xb1 10 ♖xb1 ♔b8 11 f3 ♖c8 Black is fine).

b) 5...e5 and here:

b1) 6 ♘bd2 is a serious attempt to refute Black's play, but it only leads to an unclear position: 6...exd4 7 ♗c4 ♕f5 (if 7...♕h5 8 0-0 ♘f6 9 cxd4 cxd4 10 ♘b3 White is more active) 8 0-0 ♗e6 9 ♗xe6 fxe6 10 cxd4 cxd4 (after 10...0-0-0 11 dxc5 ♗xc5 12 ♕e1 ♘f6 13 ♘b3 ♗b6 14 ♗e3 ♗xe3 15 fxe3! ♕d5 16 ♖c1 ♔b8 17 ♕g3+ ♔a8 18 ♘c5 White has a strong initiative, Benjamin-Miladinović, Erevan OL 1996) 11 ♘b3 e5 12 ♘xe5!? (recommended by Benjamin; otherwise Black just castles) 12...♘xe5 13 ♘xd4. The position is very sharp. For the piece, White has a strong attack on the open black king, but a lot of analysis and further practical tests are required to come to a conclusion.

b2) 6 ♘xe5 leads to a symmetrical position where White can't expect more than a slight edge. 6...♘xe5 7 dxe5 ♕xe5+ 8 ♗e3 ♗d7 (or 8...♘f6 9 ♗b5+ ♗d7 10 ♗xd7+ ♘xd7 11 ♘d2) 9 ♘a3 and now:

b21) 9...0-0-0 10 ♕b3 ♘f6 11 0-0-0 ♗e7 12 ♗e2 ♗g4 13 ♘c4 ♕c7 14 ♗xg4+ ♘xg4 15 ♕c2 g6 16 ♕e4 gives White an advantage due to the very good knight on c4, Charbonneau-Miladinović, Montreal (3) 2000.

b22) A year later, Miladinović chose instead to castle kingside, which seems wiser: 9...♘f6 10 ♕f3 ♗e7 11 0-0-0 0-0, Khamrakulov-Miladinović, Ano Liosia 2001.

b3) 6 dxe5 is simplest. White obtains a slight edge in the endgame: 6...♕xd1+ 7 ♔xd1 ♗g4 8 ♗f4 ♘ge7 9 ♗e2 ♘g6 10 ♗g3 0-0-0+ 11 ♘bd2

♗xf3 12 ♗xf3 ♘gxe5 13 ♗e2 ♗d6 14 ♔c2 f5 15 ♖he1 ♖he8 16 ♗b5 ±.

c) 5...e6 will eventually transpose to *4...♘f6 5 ♘f3 e6* lines as there is no reason for Black to play his king's knight to any square other than f6. Black has restricted his options by playing this move-order as it is sometimes better to develop the kingside pieces and castle before committing the queen's knight. White then has:

c1) 6 ♗e2 ♘f6 – *4...♘f6 5 ♘f3 e6 6 ♗e2 ♘c6*.

c2) 6 ♘a3 obliges Black to be particularly careful with this move-order:

c21) 6...cxd4?! 7 ♘b5 ♕d8? loses to 8 ♗f4.

c22) 6...a6?! 7 ♘c4!, threatening ♘b6, is good for White.

c23) 6...♘f6 – *4...♘f6 5 ♘f3 e6 6 ♘a3 ♘c6*.

c24) 6...♕d8 7 ♘c2 ♘f6 – *4...♘f6 5 ♘f3 e6 6 ♘a3 ♕d8 7 ♘c2 ♘c6*.

c3) 6 ♗e3 cxd4 (6...♘f6!? – *4...♘f6 5 ♘f3 e6 6 ♗e3 ♘c6!?*) 7 cxd4 ♘f6 – *4...♘f6 5 ♘f3 e6 6 ♗e3 cxd4 7 cxd4 ♘c6*.

c4) 6 ♗d3! is probably the strongest move here, with 6...♘f6 transposing to *4...♘f6 5 ♘f3 e6 6 ♗d3 ♘c6*, while avoiding Black's equalizing option *6...♗e7 7 0-0 0-0*, because delaying the capture on d4 is not as good with the knight already developed to c6.

B1)

5...cxd4 6 cxd4 *(D)*

Now:

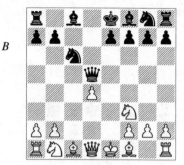

B

B11)
6...♗g4!?

This move is normally given a dubious sign, as it has long been thought that this natural line gives White a big advantage. However, as Chandler first showed in his 1996 book, this line is not as bad as previously suspected. Still, Black is walking a tightrope and few players have yet been attracted to it for Black. However, if Sveshnikov's idea *5...♗g4 6 dxc5!?* becomes more popular, maybe more players will be tempted to try out this route.

7 ♘c3!

White is not forced to enter the complications and can instead play 7 ♗e2, transposing to *5...♗g4 6 ♗e2 cxd4 7 cxd4*.

7...♗xf3

If Black retreats his queen, White simply pushes his central pawn: 7...♕d6 8 d5 ♘e5 9 ♗b5+ ♗d7 10 ♗f4 ♗xb5 11 ♗xe5 ♕a6 12 ♘d4 and the white pieces dominate, I.Zaitsev-Kaufman, Moscow 1968.

8 gxf3 ♕xd4 9 ♕xd4 ♘xd4 10 ♘b5 *(D)*

A strange position. White has sacrificed a pawn, Black can be the first to

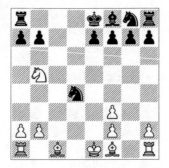

make a fork, but White is most likely to reap the harvest.

10...♘c2+

This materialistic option is probably wisest. Alternatives:

a) 10...♘e6 11 f4! (the direct 11 ♗c4 only leads to a level position: 11...♖c8 12 ♗xe6 fxe6 13 ♘xa7 ♖d8 14 ♗e3 ♘f6 15 ♔e2 g6 and Black is out of danger, Zhachev-Maliutin, Moscow 1990) 11...a6 (11...f5 doesn't stop White's attack either: 12 ♗g2 ♖b8 13 ♗d5 ♔d7 14 ♗e3 a6 15 ♖d1 axb5 16 ♗c4+ ♔e8 17 ♗xe6 +−) 12 f5 axb5 13 ♗xb5+ ♔d8 14 fxe6 fxe6 15 ♗e3 and Black can't resist White's bishops, V.Kirilov-Salata, Riga Ch 1964.

b) 10...0-0-0 11 ♘xd4 ♖xd4 12 ♗e3 chases the black rook:

b1) 12...♖b4 13 ♗c5 and here it is not so easy to find a safe place for the rook. After 13...♖h4 (13...♖xb2? loses at once: 14 ♗h3+ ♔c7 15 ♖c1 +−) 14 ♗xa7 White is much better.

b2) 12...♖d7 13 ♗b5 ♖c7 14 ♗xa7 e6 (or 14...e5 15 ♗b6 ♗b4+ {15...♖c2 16 0-0 should be compared with *14...e6 15 ♗b6 ♖c2 16 0-0*} 16 ♔d1 ♖e7 17 ♖c1+ ♔b8 18 ♗d8 ♖e6 19 ♗c7+ ♔a8 20 ♖c4 +−) 15 ♗b6 ♖c2 16 0-0 ♘e7

17 ♖ac1 ♖xc1 18 ♖xc1+ ♘c6 19 a4 ♔b8 20 a5 ♗e7 21 ♗xc6 ♖c8 22 ♖d1 ♖xc6 23 ♖d7 with good chances to win.

c) 10...e5 (Black is prepared to sacrifice the exchange to develop his pieces) 11 ♘c7+ ♔d7 12 ♘xa8 ♗b4+ (bad is 12...♘f6 13 ♗h3+ ♔c6 14 ♗d2 ♗c5 15 ♖c1 ♖d8 16 ♗g2 1-0 Liss-Gabriel, Singapore U-16 Wch 1990) 13 ♔d1 (13 ♗d2 is also possible, but after 13...♘xf3+ 14 ♔e2 ♘d4+ {or 14...♘xd2 15 ♖d1 ♘e7 16 a3} 15 ♔d3 ♗xd2 16 ♔xd2 ♘e7 17 f4 ♖xa8 18 ♖d1 Black has two pawns for an exchange and we think the position is equal) 13...♘e7 14 ♗e3 ♖xa8 15 f4. White improves his pawn-structure and breaks up Black's centre. Black has only one pawn for the exchange, which is not sufficient; e.g., 15...♘d5 16 fxe5 ♘xe3+ 17 fxe3 ♘f3 18 ♗h3+ ♔e7 19 ♖c1 ♖d8+ 20 ♔e2 ♘g5, Khamrakulov-Elgabry, Cairo 2001, and 15...♗d6 16 ♖c1 ♘ec6 17 fxe5 ♗xe5 18 ♗g2, Rõtšagov-Holmsten, Finnish Cht 1995.

11 ♔d1 ♘xa1

White also has only a slight advantage after 11...♖c8 12 ♘xa7 ♖c5 13 ♗e3 (13 b4 ♘xb4 14 ♗b5+ ♔d8! 15 ♗e3 e6! 16 ♗a4 ♘f6! ∓ Mes-Van der Meiden, corr. 1991) 13...♘xe3+ 14 fxe3, N.Pedersen-Vistisen, Danish Ch (Esbjerg) 1997.

12 ♘c7+ ♔d7

If 12...♔d8, then 13 ♘xa8 e5 14 ♗e3 b6 15 ♗a6 and White's knight is safe.

13 ♘xa8 (D)

13...g6

13...e5? loses since after 14 ♗e3 ♔c6 15 ♗g2 f5 16 ♔e2 b6 17 ♖c1+

♔b7 18 ♘c7 White's knight reaches freedom, while its black counterpart will die.

14 ♗e3

Black's knight is definitely more vulnerable than White's, but it is not clear how to exploit this. Chandler showed that White did not win, as previously thought, after 14 ♗b5+ ♔c8 15 ♗e3 ♔b8 16 ♔e2 because of the reply 16...♗g7! ∞.

14...♗h6

Better than 14...b6 15 ♗b5+ ♔c8 16 ♗f4 ♗h6 17 ♗g3, when Black's king is more exposed, Wuhrmann-Guiot, Paris 1993.

15 ♗b5+ ♔d6 16 ♗xa7 ♘f6 17 ♘b6 ♖d8 18 ♔e2 ♘c2

The knight is almost out!

19 ♖d1+ ♔c7 20 ♖xd8 ♔xd8 21 ♘c4 ♗f4 22 a3 e5

After 22...♗xh2 23 ♗a4, the knight has to return to the corner: 23...♘a1 24 ♗d4 ♘d5 25 b4 b5 26 ♗xb5 ♘b3 27 ♗b2 and White is better – Wolff.

23 h3 ♘d5 24 ♗a4 ♘d4+ 25 ♗xd4 exd4 26 ♔d3

The black knight has finally managed to escape... only to be exchanged immediately, leaving White with a slight endgame advantage, Crouch-Balinas, London 1979.

B12)

6...e5 7 ♘c3 ♗b4 (D)

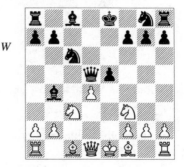

8 ♗d2

Or:

a) 8 ♕d2 has been tried by one of the authors, but the position arising after 8...♗xc3 9 bxc3 exd4 10 cxd4 ♘ge7 11 ♗e2 ♗e6 12 0-0 0-0-0 doesn't promise White anything, as in spite of the bishop-pair and passed d-pawn, Black has good development and can easily blockade the pawn, Rozentalis-Sutovsky, Netanya 1993.

b) 8 ♗e2 and now:

b1) 8...e4 allows an interesting piece sacrifice: 9 0-0! ♗xc3 10 bxc3 exf3 11 ♗xf3 ♕a5 (after 11...♕d7 12 ♖e1+ ♔d8 13 d5 ♘ce7 14 c4 ♘f6 15 ♕b3 ♖e8 16 c5! White's threats are also very dangerous) 12 ♖e1+ ♘ge7 13 d5 0-0 14 c4 ♖d8 15 ♕e2 ♘d4 16 ♕xe7 ♗d7 17 ♗h5 g6 18 ♖d1 (instead of 18 ♗e3 ♘c2 with unclear complications, Rõtšagov-G.Mohr, Moscow OL 1994) 18...♖e8 19 ♗d2 and White stands better in view of his extra pawn.

b2) 8...♘xd4 leads to an equal endgame: 9 ♗d2 ♗xc3 10 ♗xc3 ♘xf3+ 11 ♗xf3 ♕xd1+ 12 ♖xd1 f6 13 ♗a5 ♗e6 (as recommended by Gallagher in *Beating the Anti-Sicilians*; 13...♗d7 is too passive and after 14 ♗xb7 ♖b8 15 ♗d5, White is slightly better, since Black can't take the pawn: 15...♖xb2 16 ♗b3 and the rook is trapped) 14 ♖c1 (14 ♗xb7 ♖b8 15 ♗c6+ ♔f7 16 b3 ♘e7) 14...♘e7 15 ♗xb7 ♖b8 16 ♖c7 ♗d5 17 ♗xd5 ♘xd5 18 ♖xg7 ♖xb2 led to a draw in a few moves in Har-Zvi – Wiersma, Rotterdam U-26 Wch 1998.

Now we return to the position after 8 ♗d2 (D):

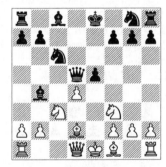

8...♗xc3 9 ♗xc3 e4 (D)

9...exd4 opens the position, which should favour White, who possesses the bishop-pair. After 10 ♘xd4 ♘ge7 11 ♘xc6 ♕xc6, White can choose from:

a) 12 ♕h5 ♗f5! 13 ♗e2 ♕xg2?! 14 ♗f3 ♕g6 15 ♕xg6 hxg6 16 ♗xb7 ± Olesen-B.Stein, Copenhagen 1995.

b) 12 ♕d4 ♗f5! 13 0-0-0 ♕h6+ 14 ♕d2 ± Göhring-Franke, Bundesliga 1980/1.

c) 12 ♗e2 0-0 (12...♕xg2 13 ♗f3 ♕g6 14 ♕e2 is uncomfortable for Black) 13 0-0 ♗e6 14 ♕d4 f6 15 ♖fd1 ± Kavalek-M.Hermann, Bochum 1981.

d) 12 ♗xg7!? ♖g8 13 ♗c3 ♗h3! 14 ♕e2! ♗xg2 15 ♗xg2 ♖xg2 16 0-0-0 ♖g6?! 17 ♕e5! ± Harley-Freeman, Hitchin 1984.

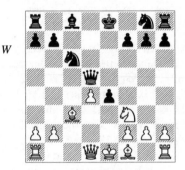

Now White has two options:
B121: 10 ♘e5   59
B122: 10 ♘d2   61
The former was the main line for some time, but Kramnik and Hodgson among others showed that Black's attacking chances could be quite fearsome despite White's bishop-pair. Attention has therefore turned more to the latter option.

B121)
10 ♘e5 ♘xe5 11 dxe5 ♘e7 (D)
12 ♕a4+
Or:
a) 12 ♕e2 0-0 13 ♖d1 and then:
a1) 13...♕xa2?! (it is not good to exchange the central e-pawn for the a-pawn) 14 ♗b4 ♕e6 15 ♕xe4 ♖e8 16 ♗b5 ♘c6 17 0-0 ♕g6 (17...♕xe5? loses immediately: 18 ♕xe5 ♖xe5 19

W

♗xc6) 18 ♕xg6 hxg6 19 ♗c3 and White stands better in the endgame.

a2) 13...♕c6 14 ♖d6 ♕a4 15 b3 (15 ♕c4 is also unclear: 15...♕c2 16 ♖d2 ♕c1+ 17 ♖d1 ♕f4 and now if White plays 18 ♗b4 then Black has the *zwischenzug* 18...♗e6) 15...♕a3 16 ♕d2 ♕c5 17 ♗c4 ♗e6 and then:

a21) If White accepts the pawn sacrifice, Black obtains good counterplay: 18 ♗xe6 fxe6 19 ♖xe6 ♘d5 20 ♗d4 ♕b5 and the white king is stuck in the centre.

a22) Black also sacrifices a pawn after 18 ♖d4 ♘f5 19 ♖xe4 ♖fd8 20 ♕b2 ♕c6 21 f3 ♕c5 22 ♔e2 ♗d5 23 ♗xd5 ♕xd5 24 ♖c1 ♖ac8 and again obtains good play due to his strong knight and the exposed white king, Schmittdiel-Hodgson, Bad Wörishofen 1994.

a23) 18 ♗b4 ♕xe5 19 ♖xe6 fxe6 20 ♗xe7 ♕a1+ 21 ♕d1 ♕c3+ (or 21...♕xd1+ 22 ♔xd1 ♖xf2 23 ♖e1 ∞) 22 ♕d2 ♕a1+ with perpetual check – Hodgson.

b) 12 ♕c2 0-0 13 ♖d1 ♕xa2:

b1) 14 ♕xe4 regains the pawn, but allows Black enough play: 14...♗f5 15 ♕c4 (15 ♕xb7 ♖ad8 16 ♕xe7 ♖xd1+

17 ♔xd1 ♕b1+ is a forced draw) 15...♕xc4 16 ♗xc4 ♖ac8 17 ♗b3 ♗e6 18 ♗xe6 fxe6 19 ♗b4 ♖fe8, J.Polgar-Kramnik, Monaco Amber rpd 1995. After the exchange on e7, the rook ending is equal.

b2) 14 ♗b4 ♗g4 15 ♗xe7 ♗xd1 16 ♕xd1 ♕xb2 17 ♗xf8 ♕c3+! (after 17...♖xf8 18 ♗e2 followed by 0-0, the white bishop is stronger than the three black pawns, Sveshnikov-Tunik, Moscow 1994) 18 ♕d2 (18 ♔e2 is risky, as it leaves White's kingside pieces out of the game) 18...♕a1+ 19 ♔e2 ♕a6+ 20 ♔e3 ♕h6+ with perpetual check.

c) 12 ♗e2 0-0 13 0-0 ♗f5 14 ♕a4 (14 ♕c1 ♕e6 15 ♕g5 h6 16 ♕g3 ♘d5 leads to equality, Hynes-Haydon, British League (4NCL) 1998/9) 14...♕e6 15 ♗c4 ♕g6 16 ♖fe1 a6 17 ♕b3 b5 18 ♗f1 ∞ Mirallès-Gerard, French Cht (Monaco) 2002.

12...♗d7 *(D)*

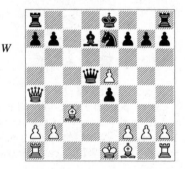

W

13 ♕b4

Or 13 ♕a3 and now:

a) 13...♗g4? is a mistake: 14 h3 ♗h5 15 g4! e3 16 ♖h2 ♗g6 (after 16...exf2+ 17 ♖xf2 ♗g6 18 ♖d1 all White's pieces are extremely active)

17 fxe3 ♕f3 18 ♕a4+ ♘c6 19 ♕f4 and White picks up a pawn, Kramnik-Piket, Monte Carlo Amber rpd 1995.

b) 13...♕e6 (Black protects his knight, prepares to castle kingside and move his queen to f5, where it can take part in the attack on the white king) 14 ♕b4 (14 ♖d1 can lead to unexpected problems for White: 14...0-0 15 ♖d6 ♕f5 16 ♗c4 ♘g6 17 0-0 ♗e6 18 ♗xe6 fxe6 and Black's threats of 19...e3 and 19...♘f4 are very dangerous, Rozentalis-R.Sokolowski, Polish Cht 1999) 14...♗c6 15 ♗b5 ♖c8 (15...♘d5 is premature: 16 ♗xc6+ ♕xc6 17 ♕xe4) 16 0-0 ♘d5 (now this move works) 17 ♗xc6+ ♕xc6 18 ♕xe4 ♘xc3 with a very drawish endgame.

13...♕c6

Black prepares ...♘d5. This is stronger than 13...a5, with the following possibilities:

a) 14 ♕a3 ♕e6 15 ♖d1 0-0 16 ♕d6 ♗c6 and Black is very solid.

b) 14 ♕b6 ♕c6 15 ♗xa5 ♘d5 16 ♕xc6 ♗xc6 17 ♗d2 ± Harley-Gormally, London 1995.

c) 14 ♕d6! ♗c6 (14...♕xd6 15 exd6 ♘f5 16 0-0-0 0-0-0 17 ♗e2 ♖fe8 18 ♖d5 ♗e6 19 ♖hd1! ♖ed8 20 ♖xa5 ♖xa5 21 ♗xa5 ♖xd6 22 ♖xd6 ♘xd6 23 b3 ± Sax-Mohamed, Cairo 1998) 15 ♗e2 ♕xd6 16 exd6 ♘f5 17 0-0-0 0-0 18 ♗g4 ± Karpachev-Stephan, Salzburg 2001.

14 ♖d1

14 ♗c4 stops ...♘d5 but White gets no advantage after 14...a5 15 ♕b3 0-0 16 a4 ♖ac8 17 ♗b5 ♕b6 18 0-0 ♗xb5 19 axb5 ♖c5! 20 ♗xa5 ½-½ Harley-Carlin, London 1995.

14...♘d5

Gallagher thinks that Black has reasonable counter-chances after 14...e3!? 15 ♖d6 exf2+ 16 ♔xf2 ♕c7 17 ♗d3 0-0, but this has never been tested in practice.

15 ♕xe4 ♘xc3 16 ♕xc6 ♗xc6 17 bxc3 0-0 18 f4

White has an extra pawn and therefore a slight advantage. Black has good chances of drawing, but he should not be tempted by the immediate 18...g5? because of 19 ♗c4! gxf4 20 0-0 ♖ae8 21 ♖de1 ± Van Het-Van Egmond, Dutch Cht 1995/6.

B122)

10 ♘d2 ♘f6 (D)

Not 10...♘xd4?? 11 ♕a4+ ♘c6 12 ♗xg7 +–.

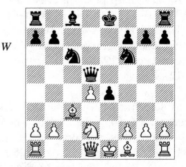

W

11 ♗c4

Or:

a) After 11 ♕b3:

a1) 11...♕g5? allows the blow 12 d5! ♕xd5 (12...♘e5 loses a pawn after 13 ♕a4+ ♗d7 14 ♘xe4!) 13 ♗c4 and White has a very strong initiative.

a2) 11...♕xb3 equalizes: 12 ♘xb3 (12 axb3 is met by 12...0-0 followed by 13...♖d8, attacking the d4-pawn) 12...0-0 13 ♗b5 a6 14 ♗xc6 bxc6 with a very drawish endgame.

b) 11 ♘c4 ♗e6 (the natural move 11...0-0?! allows White to execute his strategic plan of putting his knight on e3 and advancing his d-pawn: 12 ♘e3 ♕g5 13 h4 ♕f4 14 g3 ♕d6 15 d5 ♘e5 16 ♗e2 ♖e8 17 ♗xe5 ♕xe5 18 ♕b3 with a clear positional advantage for White, Blatny-Külaots, Bundesliga 1995/6) 12 ♘e3 ♕d7 13 d5 (otherwise Black plays 13...♘d5 and blockades the pawn) 13...♘xd5 14 ♘xd5 ♕xd5 15 ♕xd5 ♗xd5 16 ♗xg7 ♖g8 17 ♗c3 0-0-0 is fine for Black since it is not so easy for White to finish his development, Antonsen-Molvig, Copenhagen 1995.

11...♕g5 12 d5

A very sharp position arises after 12 ♕b3 0-0 13 0-0-0 a6 14 ♕b6 ♘g4 15 h4 ♕f4 16 ♖hf1 ♘xf2, with interesting unclear complications, Wolf-Marecek, corr. 1982.

12...♘e5

Or:

a) 12...♕xg2 is risky, as the black queen strays from the centre, where the main events are taking place: 13 ♖f1 ♗g4 14 ♕b3 e3 15 fxe3 ♘xd5 16 ♗xg7 +− Blatny (but not 16 ♕xb7? 0-0 17 ♕xc6 ♖ad8, when Black got some attacking chances as compensation for the piece in Blauert-Fuglsang, Lyngby 1990).

b) 12...e3 13 0-0! ♘xd5 (13...exd2 is also hopeless: 14 dxc6 bxc6 15 ♕e2+) 14 ♘e4 ♘xc3 15 ♗xf7+ ♔f8 16 bxc3 e2 (16...♕e5 17 fxe3 and the white rook comes into play) 17 ♕xe2 ♕e7

18 ♗d5 gives White an extra pawn and a strong attack, Ma.Tseitlin-Vydeslaver, Beersheba 1996.

13 ♗b5+ ♗d7 14 ♗xd7+ ♘exd7 15 0-0 0-0 16 d6 ♖fe8 17 ♘c4 ♗e6

17...♘d5 18 h4 ♘xc3 19 hxg5 ♘xd1 20 ♖fxd1 and in the endgame White is still better, Efimov-Zaichik, Prague 1985.

18 ♗xf6 ♖xf6 19 ♕d4 ♖e6

If 19...b5, White wins a pawn: 20 ♕xe4 ♖c8 21 ♕b7 ♖d8 22 ♕c7 +− Emms-Hall, Harplinge 1998.

20 ♖ad1

The far-advanced d-pawn is very dangerous, and White stands better.

B2)
5...♗g4 *(D)*

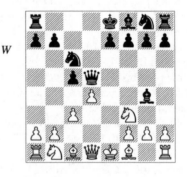

Now:
B21: 6 ♗e2   63
B22: 6 dxc5   67

6 ♘bd2?! is another try, but Black has a strong forcing reply: 6...cxd4 7 ♗c4 ♗xf3 8 ♕b3 ♕e5+ 9 ♔f1 ♗e2+ 10 ♗xe2 ♕c7 11 ♘f3 e6 12 ♗f4 ♗d6 13 ♗xd6 ♕xd6 14 ♘xd4 ♘xd4 15 cxd4 ♘e7 16 ♕xb7 0-0 17 ♕e4 ♖ab8

18 b3 ♖fd8, Vlassov-Tunik, Moscow 1996. After regaining the pawn, Black will have the better position.

B21)
6 ♗e2
This move is usual and well-known. Quite a lot of games have been played, hence clear conclusions can be made. Now:
B211: 6...e6   63
B212: 6...cxd4   65

Or:
a) 6...e5 7 dxe5! ♗xf3 8 ♗xf3 ♕xd1+ 9 ♗xd1 ♘xe5 10 ♗a4+ ♘d7 11 0-0 0-0-0 12 ♗b3! ± Harley-Hodge, Cambridge 2000.
b) 6...0-0-0!? and then:
b1) 7 c4 ♕h5! ∞.
b2) 7 ♗e3 e5!? ∞.
b3) 7 dxc5 ♕xd1+ (7...♕e4!?) 8 ♗xd1 e5 9 b4 e4 10 h3 ± Sveshnikov-Batričević, Tivat open 1995.
b4) 7 h3! is a little-tried recommendation of Gallagher's:
b41) 7...♗xf3 8 ♗xf3 ♕e6+ 9 ♗e3 cxd4 10 cxd4 ♘xd4 11 0-0 with a strong attack for the pawn; for example, 11...♘xf3+ 12 ♕xf3 ♔b8 13 ♘c3 ♕f6 14 ♕g3+ e5 15 ♗g5 ♖d3 16 ♗xf6 1-0 Muzik-Blazkova, Moravia 1998, and 11...♕b6 12 ♘c3 e5 13 ♘d5 ♘xf3+ 14 ♕xf3 ♕e6 15 ♖fd1 ♔b8 16 ♘c7! ♖xd1+ 17 ♕xd1 ♕d6 18 ♕a4 +−.
b42) 7...♗h5 8 c4 (8 0-0 e6 9 ♗e3 ♘f6 ∞; 8 dxc5 ♕e4!?) 8...♕d7 9 d5 ♗xf3 10 ♗xf3 ♘d4 11 ♗e3 e5, and now White should probably not play by analogy with the line *6...e6 7 h3*

♗h5 8 c4 ♕d6 9 d5 ♗xf3 10 ♗xf3 ♘d4 11 0-0 e5 12 ♗e3 0-0-0. This is because White is a tempo down here (Black played ...e7-e5 in one go) and Black's queen is possibly better placed on d7. White does better to open the centre with 12 dxe6 fxe6 13 ♘c3 ±.

B211)
6...e6 *(D)*
Another under-rated move, wrongly considered refuted for quite some time and thus quite a potent weapon in the hands of a well-prepared player.

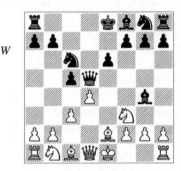

7 h3
The immediate 7 c4 is wrong due to 7...♕f5! 8 d5 exd5 9 cxd5 ♗xf3 10 ♗xf3 ♘d4 11 ♘c3 ♘xf3+ 12 gxf3 0-0-0 and Black is better, Blatny-Z.Almasi, Austrian Cht 2000/1.
7...♗h5 8 c4
White can instead play 8 0-0, with two possible transpositions:
a) 8...cxd4 9 cxd4 ♘f6 10 ♘c3 ♕a5 − 6...cxd4 7 cxd4 e6 8 h3 ♗h5 9 ♘c3 ♕a5 10 0-0 ♘f6.
b) 8...♘f6 − 4...♘f6 5 ♘f3 ♗g4 6 ♗e2 e6 7 h3 ♗h5 8 0-0 ♘c6.
8...♕d6

8...♕d7 is best met by 9 g4! ♗g6 10 d5 exd5 11 cxd5 ♘b4, and then:

a) Not 12 ♘c3?! 0-0-0 13 ♘e5 ♕e8! 14 ♘xg6 (14 ♗f4 ♘xd5 15 ♘xd5 ♗e4 ∓ Polašek-Jakubiec, Czech Cht 1993) 14...hxg6 15 ♗e3 (not 15 a3? ♘xd5 16 ♘xd5, Harley-Stevenson, Cambridge 1987, due to 16...♘f6! ∓) 15...♘f6 16 ♗f3 ∞.

b) 12 ♘e5! ♕xd5 13 ♗b5+ ♔d8 14 0-0 ♔c7 15 ♘c3! ♕xd1 16 ♖xd1 a6 (16...♗d6 17 ♖xd6! +−) 17 ♗f4 ♔b6 18 ♗c4 with a continuing strong attack against the wandering black king, A.Adamski-L.Schneider, Wroclaw 1981.

9 d5

The old 'refutation' 9 g4 ♗g6 10 d5 ♘b4 11 0-0 is itself refuted by 11...exd5 12 cxd5 0-0-0 13 ♘c3 ♘f6! 14 ♕a4?! a6 15 a3 ♗c2 ∓ Short-J.Polgar, Isle of Lewis rpd 1995. Note how the queen is much better placed on d6 rather than d7 after 9 g4 as White does not have the move 11 ♘e5 attacking the queen. However, in the play after 9 d5, Black would probably prefer the queen to be on d7.

9...♗xf3 10 ♗xf3 ♘d4 11 0-0 e5 *(D)*

The well-centralized knight on d4 doesn't compensate for White's strong pawn-centre and lead in development. White prepares an attack on the queenside and has an edge.

12 ♗e3

This seems the most accurate move as it preserves the option of playing the queen's knight to c3 or d2, and also allows for the possibility of playing b4 before ♘c3, when ...cxb4 will not hit the knight. After 12 ♘c3 f5!? 13 ♗e3 ♕d7 14 ♖e1 ♔f7 15 b4 ♘f6 16 bxc5 ♗xc5 17 ♘b5 ♗b4 18 ♗xd4 ♗xe1, a draw was agreed in Egin-Popov, Krasnodar 1997, but White is probably better after 19 ♗xe5 ♗b4 20 ♕d4.

12...♘f6

Or:

a) 12...f5 13 b4! ♕d7 14 ♘d2 ±.

b) 12...0-0-0 13 b4 cxb4 14 ♗xd4 exd4 15 ♘d2 ♔b8 16 ♘b3 ♕b6 17 ♘xd4 ♘f6 18 a3 ± Vadja-Dembo, Budapest 2001.

13 ♘d2

Also perfectly playable is 13 ♘c3 ♗e7 14 ♗xd4 exd4 15 ♘b5 ♕d7 16 d6 ♗xd6 17 ♗xb7 ♖b8, Vlassov-Obodchuk, Moscow 1995, when 18 ♖e1+! ♗e7 19 ♕f3 0-0 20 ♗c6 is good for White – Chandler.

13...♗e7 14 ♗xd4! cxd4

After 14...exd4, Black's centre is quickly undermined by 15 b4! cxb4 16 ♘b3 b6 17 ♘xd4 ± Alvarez.

15 c5! *(D)*

White sacrifices a pawn to clear lines and squares for his pieces.

15...♕xc5 16 ♖e1 ♘d7 17 ♖c1 ♕b4 18 a3 ♕b5 19 d6! ♗xd6 20 ♘c4 ♗c7 21 a4 ♕b4 22 ♕xd4 ♕e7 23 ♕d5 0-0

23...♖b8 24 ♘e3 is strong for White, so Black has to return the material.

24 ♕xb7

White has a clear advantage, Alvarez-Pyrich, e-mail 1997-8.

B212)

6...cxd4 7 cxd4 e6

7...e5?! is best met here by 8 ♘c3:

a) 8...♕a5 9 0-0 (9 ♘xe5 ♗xe2 10 ♘xc6? ♕xc3+! −+) 9...♖d8 (K.Rasmussen-Herzog, Hinnerup jr 1979) 10 ♘xe5! ♗xe2 11 ♘xc6! ±.

b) 8...♗b4 9 0-0 ♗xc3 10 bxc3 e4 (10...exd4 11 ♘xd4! ±; e.g., 11...♗xe2 12 ♕xe2+ ♘ge7 13 ♘xc6 ♕xc6 14 ♗a3 ♕e6 15 ♖fe1 1-0 Röder-Lochte, Pang 1983) 11 ♘g5 (11 ♘d2!? ♗xe2 12 ♕xe2 f5 13 f3! has the point that 13...♘xd4? 14 cxd4 ♕xd4+ 15 ♔h1 ♕xa1 loses to 16 ♕b5+) 11...♗f5 (11...♗xe2 12 ♕xe2 f5 13 f3 ♘f6 14 fxe4 fxe4 15 ♘xe4! ±) 12 ♕a4 (12 f3 is also good) 12...♘h6 13 ♗c4 ♕a5 14 ♕b3 ± Neuschmied-F.Winkler, Austrian Cht 1992.

8 h3

8 ♘c3 is of course also possible, but there is no reason for White not to insert the move 8 h3. In some cases, the tactics work better for White when the bishop is on h5.

8...♗h5 9 ♘c3 *(D)*

9...♕a5

Or:

a) 9...♗b4 10 0-0 ♕a5 (10...♕d6 can be met by 11 ♘b5!? or 11 d5! exd5 12 ♘b5) 11 a3! ♘f6 12 d5! exd5 13 axb4 ♕xa1 14 ♘d2 ♗xe2 15 ♕xe2+ ± is similar to the famous game Alekhine-Podgorny, Prague 1943, though Alekhine still had his h-pawn on h2.

b) 9...♕d8 10 0-0 (10 ♕b3 ♕b6 11 ♕xb6 axb6 12 d5 ± Rausis-Ricter, Cannes 1990) 10...♘f6 11 ♕a4 ♗e7 12 ♖d1 ♘d5 13 ♘xd5 exd5 14 g4 ♗g6 15 ♘e5 and White wins a pawn, M.Vogt-Ac.Müller, Germany 1990/1.

c) 9...♕d7 10 0-0 ♘f6 11 ♘e5 and then:

c1) 11...♘xe5 12 dxe5 ♗xe2 13 ♕xe2 ♘d5 14 ♘xd5 ♕xd5 15 ♖d1 ♕a5 16 ♗g5 with a strong initiative for White, Chandler-Jacoby, Hamburg 1980.

c2) 11...♗xe2 12 ♘xd7 ♗xd1 13 ♘xf6+ gxf6 14 ♖xd1 0-0-0 15 ♗e3, followed by 16 d5, gives White a superior endgame.

c3) 11...♛xd4 12 ♘xc6 ♛xd1 13 ♗xd1 ♗xd1 (13...bxc6 14 ♗a4) 14 ♘xa7 ♖xa7 15 ♖xd1 gives White a slightly better ending.

d) 9...♛d6 10 d5! (10 ♘b5!? ♛d7 11 ♗f4 ♖c8 12 0-0 a6 13 ♘c3 = Hawellek-Helm, Hamburg 1997) 10...exd5 11 0-0 ♘f6 12 ♘b5 ♛d7 (12...♛b8 13 ♛a4 with compensation – Palkovi; 12...♛d8 13 ♗f4 ♖c8 14 ♘e5!? ♗xe2 15 ♛xe2 ♗e7 16 ♘xc6 ♖xc6 17 ♖ae1 a6 18 ♘d4 ♖c4 19 ♗d6! ± Palkovi-Danner, Budapest 1996) 13 ♗f4 ♖c8 14 ♘e5 ♘xe5 (14...♗xe2 15 ♘xd7 ♗xd1 16 ♘xf6+ gxf6 17 ♖axd1 ±) 15 ♗xe5 ♗xe2 16 ♛xe2 ♗e7 17 ♗xf6 gxf6. It is interesting that Kalod has chosen to reach this position twice as Black, but after 18 ♘xa7, taking back a pawn, Black is left with a lot of weaknesses and problems.

10 0-0

The sacrifice 10 d5!?, giving up a pawn to open the e-file, seeks to exploit the fact that Black has chosen to develop his queenside pieces before his kingside pieces. This proved successful for White for a time, but Black has now discovered enough resources to defend the position:

a) 10...0-0-0 11 ♘d2 ♗xe2 12 ♛xe2 exd5 13 0-0 ♘f6 14 ♘b3 ♛c7 15 ♗g5 ♗e7 is possible but unclear.

b) 10...exd5 11 ♘d4 and then:

b1) 11...♘xd4 12 ♗xh5 ♘e6 13 0-0 ♘f6 14 ♖e1 g6 15 ♗g4 ♘xg4 16 ♛xg4 ♗e7 (16...♛b4 17 ♗f4) 17 ♗h6 d4 18 ♘e2 ♛f5 19 ♛xf5 gxf5 20 ♘g3 ♖d8 21 ♘xf5 ♖d5 22 g4 is slightly better for White, Hraček-V.Georgiev, Krynica Z 1998.

b2) 11...♗xe2 12 ♛xe2+ ♗e7 13 ♘xc6 bxc6 14 0-0 ♖d8! (14...♔f8 15 a3 ♖e8 16 ♛d3 ♗f6 17 ♗d2 with good play against Black's weak queenside pawns, Finkel-Rotman, Jerusalem 1996) 15 ♗d2 d4 16 b4 ♛f5 17 ♘e4 ♘f6 18 ♘xf6+ ♛xf6 19 ♖fe1 ♖d7 and Black is now ready to castle, Pisk-Motylev, Ubeda 2000. White needs to find an improvement here to resurrect 10 d5!?.

10...♘f6 (D)

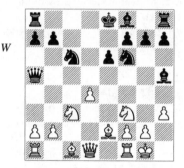

11 ♗e3

Or:

a) 11 a3 and now:

a1) The natural 11...♗e7 is too passive: 12 ♛b3 ♛c7 13 d5 ♘xd5 14 ♘xd5 exd5 15 ♛xd5 ♗g6 16 ♗e3 0-0 17 ♖ac1 ♖ad8 18 ♛b3 gives White a slight edge, Salov-Gelfand, Wijk aan Zee 1992.

a2) 11...♗d6! 12 ♘b5 (not 12 ♛b3? ♗xf3 13 ♗xf3 ♘xd4, Leite-del Rey, Lisbon 1999, since 14 ♛xb7 loses to 14...♖b8) 12...♗b8 13 b4 ♛b6 14 ♘c3 0-0 15 ♗e3 ♛d8 16 ♛d2 ♘e7 17 ♗g5 ♘ed5 with an equal position, Therkildsen-Hamdouchi, Issy les Moulinea 2000.

b) 11 ♕b3 ♕b4 12 ♖d1 ♕xb3
(12...♖d8!?) 13 axb3 ♘d5 (13...0-0-0!?)
14 ♘xd5 exd5 15 g4 ♗g6 16 ♘e5! ∞
Segovia-Georges, Tunja jr Wch 1989.
11...♗d6! *(D)*
11...♗e7 is again too passive: 12
♕b3 ♕b4 (12...♕c7 13 d5 ♘xd5 14
♘xd5 exd5 15 ♕xd5 ♗g6 16 ♖ac1 ±)
13 g4 ♗g6 14 ♘e5 0-0 15 g5! ♕xb3
(15...♘h5? is the wrong move, as after
16 ♘xc6 bxc6 17 ♕d1 ♕xb2 18 ♖c1
♗b4 19 ♘b1, White wins a piece, Ser-
mek-Vl.Georgiev, Cannes 1996) 16
axb3 ♘d5 17 ♘xd5 exd5 18 ♖fc1 and
White is better in this ending, Sma-
gin-Armas, Bundesliga 1990/1.

W

12 a3
After 12 ♕b3 ♕b4 13 g4 ♗g6
White can't play 14 ♘e5 because of
14...♘xd4, while after 14 ♕xb4 ♘xb4
15 ♘b5 ♔e7 Black is fine.
12...0-0 13 ♕b3
Or 13 b4 ♕d8, and then:
a) 14 ♘a4 ♘d5 15 ♕d2 ♕e8!? 16
♘c5 b6 17 ♘e4 ♗b8 18 ♖ac1 ♘ce7
19 ♘e5 f5 20 ♗xh5 ♕xh5 21 ♘g3
♕e8 22 ♘e2 ♗xe5 23 dxe5 (Tzermia-
dianos-Atalik, Athens 1996) 23...h6
with interesting complications.

b) 14 ♕d2 ♖c8 15 ♘a4 ♗b8 16
♖fd1 ♘d5 17 ♖ac1 b6 18 ♘c3 ♘ce7
leaves Black comfortable, Turov-Moty-
lev, Sochi 1998.
c) 14 ♕b3 ♖e8 15 ♖ad1 ♘d5 is
equal, but White has to watch out for
his queenside being undermined: 16
♘e4 a5 17 ♘c5? axb4 18 axb4 ♕b6
winning a pawn, Finkel-Sermek, Olomouc 1996.
13...♖ab8 14 ♖fd1
14 ♕b5 ♕d8 15 ♖ac1 a6 16 ♕g5
♘e7 17 ♗f4 ♗xf4 18 ♕xf4 ♘ed5
gives Black a slight advantage, Mar-
ciano-Istratescu, Batumi Echt 1999.
**14...♖fd8 15 ♖ac1 ♘d5 16 ♘xd5
exd5 17 ♔f1 ♖d7 18 g4 ♗g6 19 ♘e5
♗xe5 20 dxe5**
Now:
a) Skytte-Krejci, Olomouc 2001
continued 20...♖e8? when 21 ♖c5 ♕c7
22 ♖cxd5 ♖xd5 23 ♕xd5 won a pawn,
as 23...♖xe5 would have been met by
24 ♕d7 ♖e7 25 ♕xc7 ♖xc7 26 ♗xa7
exploiting the back rank.
b) 20...♕d8 leaves the chances
evenly balanced after 21 f4 ♗e4 or 21
♗f4 ♖c8 22 ♗f3 d4.

B22)
6 dxc5!?
This is Sveshnikov's latest recommendation. It has been very little tested
in practice, so it leaves a lot of room to
play and invent. Moreover, we think it
gives White an advantage.
6...♕xd1+
After 6...♕xc5 7 ♗e3 (7 ♘a3 ♕a5)
7...♕a5 8 ♕b3 ♕c7 (after 8...0-0-0
White can simply take the pawn: 9
♕xf7 ♘e5 10 ♕f4 g5 11 ♕g3 and

there is no compensation for the pawn) 9 ♘a3 ♗xf3 10 gxf3 it seems that White has a very dangerous initiative.

7 ♔xd1 e5

7...♖d8+ 8 ♘bd2 e5 9 b4 e4 10 h3 ♗h5 11 g4 ♗xg4 12 hxg4 exf3 13 ♔c2 ♘f6 14 g5 ♘g4 15 ♘xf3 (Sveshnikov-Breder, Bled 2001) and now 15...♘xf2 is risky because of 16 ♖h4, so White has a big advantage.

8 b4

Not 8 ♗e3? f5!, with the threat of 9...f4.

8...a5 9 ♗b5 ♘e7 (D)

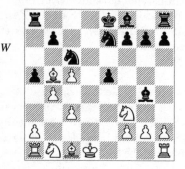

10 a3

Not:

a) 10 ♖e1? axb4 11 cxb4 0-0-0+ 12 ♗d2 ♘xb4 13 ♖xe5 ♘g6 and White is in danger.

b) 10 ♔c2? ♗xf3 11 gxf3 axb4 12 ♖d1 and then:

b1) 12...♖a5? 13 a4 bxa3 14 ♖xa3 ♖xa3 15 ♘xa3 and the white pieces are very active.

b2) 12...♘f5? 13 ♗xc6+ bxc6 14 cxb4 ♘d4+ 15 ♔c3 ♗e7 16 ♘d2 0-0 17 ♗b2 ♗h4 18 ♔c4 ♗xf2 19 ♘e4 gives White a useful advantage, Sveshnikov-Priehoda, Bled 1997.

b3) 12...bxc3! (best, since it immediately removes White's queenside pawn-majority) 13 ♘xc3 ♘f5 leaves Black better, because 14 ♘d5 loses a pawn: 14...♘fd4+ 15 ♖xd4 exd4 16 ♘c7+ ♔d7 17 ♖xa8 ♗xc5.

10...0-0-0+ 11 ♘d2 e4 12 h3 ♗h5

Or 12...exf3 13 hxg4 fxg2 14 ♖g1 ±.

13 g4

White is a pawn up in the endgame.

B3)

5...♘f6 (D)

This is a very important position for the 2 c3 Sicilian, more often arising via the move-order 4...♘f6 5 ♘f3 ♘c6. Black doesn't immediately commit to a plan with ...e6, ...♗g4 or ...e5, but rather waits to see what White does next, and thereby rules out some significant options for White.

Now:

B31: 6 ♗e3   69
B32: 6 dxc5   71

Or:

a) White has tried 6 ♘a3:

a1) 6...a6? is wrong: 7 ♘c4 ♗g4 8 ♘e3 ♕e4 (8...♕d6) 9 ♕b3 ♗e6 10 d5

♗xd5 11 c4 ♗e6 12 ♗d3 ♕f4 13 ♘d5 +– Luther-Vogt, E.German Ch (Glauchau) 1987.

a2) However, Black is comfortable after 6...♗g4 7 ♗e2 cxd4 8 ♘b5 0-0-0 (another solid line is 8...♖c8 9 ♘bxd4 ♘xd4 10 ♕xd4 ♕xd4 11 ♘xd4 ♗xe2 12 ♔xe2 e6 = Spassky-Ribli, Belfort 1988) 9 ♘bxd4 e5 10 ♘xc6 ♕xc6 11 ♕c2 (11 ♕b3 ♗e6 12 c4 ♗c5 13 0-0 ♕c7 14 ♗e3 a6 with equality, Kranzl-Petchar, Austrian Cht 1989) 11...♗c5 12 0-0 ♖he8 13 ♘g5 ♗xe2 14 ♕xe2 ♖d7 15 ♗e3 h6 16 ♘f3 ♘d5 = Haba-Stoica, Eforie-Nord 1988.

b) 6 ♗e2 e6 transposes to *4...♘f6 5 ♘f3 e6 6 ♗e2 ♘c6* with White committed to lines with ♗e2 rather than the more popular ♗d3.

B31)
6 ♗e3 e5!?
An interesting and relatively rare continuation. Alternatives:

a) 6...e6 – *4...♘f6 5 ♘f3 e6 6 ♗e3 ♘c6!?*.

b) 6...♘g4 7 ♘bd2 and then:

b1) 7...♘xe3 8 fxe3 e6 9 ♗c4 ♕d8 (Finkel-Sermek, Groningen open 1993) 10 ♘e4! cxd4 11 exd4 leaves White with good play down the e- and f-files.

b2) 7...cxd4 8 cxd4 (8 ♗c4! is a little better for White) 8...e6 9 ♗d3 ♗d6 10 0-0 ♕h5 with an unclear position, Zude-Bönsch, Bad Wörishofen 1995.

b3) 7...e6 8 ♗c4 ♕d8 9 ♗g5 ♘f6 10 ♘b3 ± Finkel-A.Shneider, Groningen open 1993.

c) 6...♗g4!? and then:

c1) 7 ♘bd2 cxd4 8 cxd4 e6 9 ♗c4 ♕d6 10 0-0 and White's knight is

rather misplaced on d2 for the isolated queen's pawn position.

c2) 7 ♗e2 cxd4 8 cxd4 e6 9 h3 ♗h5 10 ♘c3 and now:

c21) 10...♕a5 11 0-0 – *5...♗g4 6 ♗e2 cxd4 7 cxd4 e6 8 h3 ♗h5 9 ♘c3 ♕a5 10 0-0 ♘f6 11 ♗e3*.

c22) 10...♕d6 11 0-0 ♗e7 – *4...♘f6 5 ♘f3 ♗g4 6 ♗e2 e6 7 h3 ♗h5 8 0-0 ♘c6 9 ♗e3 cxd4 10 cxd4 ♗e7 11 ♘c3 ♕d6*.

c3) 7 dxc5 ♕xd1+ 8 ♔xd1 e5 – *4...♘f6 5 ♘f3 ♗g4 6 dxc5 ♕xd1+ 7 ♔xd1 e5 8 ♗e3 ♘c6 ±*.

c4) 7 c4 ♕h5 8 d5 ♗xf3 9 gxf3 ♘e5 10 ♗e2 ♘ed7 11 ♘c3 ♕e5 12 ♕d2 a6 13 0-0-0 ± I.Werner-Fichtner, Bundesliga wom 1996/7.

d) 6...cxd4 7 cxd4 *(D)* and then:

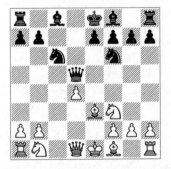

d1) 7...e6 transposes to *4...♘f6 5 ♘f3 e6 6 ♗e3 cxd4 7 cxd4 ♘c6*, and this is how most games continue after 6 ♗e3.

d2) 7...e5?! is well met by 8 ♘c3 ♗b4 9 dxe5:

d21) 9...♘xe5 10 ♕xd5 ♘xd5 11 ♘xe5 ♘xc3 12 a3 ♗d6 13 ♘c4 ♘b5 (13...♘e4 14 f3 b5 15 ♘b6!?) 14 0-0-0 ♗e7 (14...♗c7 15 a4) 15 ♘b6! axb6

16 ♗xb5+ ♔f8 17 ♗xb6 and White wins – Blatny.

d22) 9...♕xd1+ 10 ♖xd1 ♘e4 (or 10...♘g4 11 ♗f4 0-0 12 ♗b5 f6, Blauert-Gabriel, Drumbach 1991, 13 ♗c4+ ♔h8 14 exf6 ♖e8+ 15 ♔f1 ♘xf6 16 ♘g5 ±) 11 ♖c1 ♗e6 12 ♗d3 ♘xc3 13 bxc3 ♗a5 14 0-0 0-0-0 (14...♗xa2 15 c4!) 15 ♗b5 ± Vifleemskaya-Chasovnikova, Russian wom Ch (Elista) 1996.

d3) 7...♗g4!? is a little-tested transpositional option for Black: 8 ♘c3 ♕a5 (8...♗xf3 9 ♘xd5! ♗xd1 10 ♘xf6+ gxf6 11 ♖xd1 ±) 9 h3 ♗h5 and then:

d31) 10 d5 is met by 10...0-0-0! 11 ♗c4 e6, winning a pawn, and White, who is not even castled yet, does not seem in a good position to exploit Black's slightly precarious king position.

d32) 10 ♕b3 ♗xf3 11 gxf3 ♕b4 is level.

d33) 10 g4 ♗g6 11 ♘e5 (11 ♗g2 e6 12 0-0 ♗d6 ∞; 11 ♕b3 ♗e4 12 ♗g2 ♗d5 ∞) 11...e6 (11...♗e4 12 ♘c4 ♕c7 13 ♘xe4 ♘xe4 14 d5 ±) 12 ♗g2 is unconvincing in view of 12...♘xe5 13 dxe5 ♗e4! 14 f3 ♘d5 15 ♗d2 ♗d3 16 f4 ♗e7 17 h4 ♘b4 18 ♖c1 ∞. Instead, Vancini-Caoili, Bratto 2001 continued 12...♖c8?! 13 0-0 ♗b4 14 g5 ♘d5 15 ♘xd5 exd5 16 ♕g4 (16 ♕b3! gives White a clear advantage) 16...0-0 17 h4? ♘xe5 18 dxe5 ♖c4 ∓.

d34) 10 ♗e2 e6 11 0-0 0-0 transposes to 5...♗g4 6 ♗e2 cxd4 7 cxd4 e6 8 h3 ♗h5 9 ♘c3 ♕a5 10 0-0 ♘f6 11 ♗e3. As Black appears to be doing fine there after 11...♗d6!, the little-tested move 7...♗g4!? may actually be Black's most

accurate theoretical option against 6 ♗e3.

We now return to 6...e5 *(D)*:

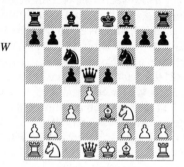

7 dxe5

Or:

a) 7 c4 ♕d6 8 d5 ♘d4 9 ♘c3 a6 10 ♘g5 ♗e7 ∞ Hadzimanolis-Duncan, British League (4NCL) 2000/1.

b) 7 dxc5 ♕xd1+ 8 ♔xd1 – *6 dxc5 ♕xd1+ 7 ♔xd1 e5 8 ♗e3* ∞.

c) 7 ♘xe5 ♘xe5 8 dxe5 ♕xd1+ 9 ♔xd1 ♘g4 10 ♘a3 ♘xe3+ 11 fxe3 ♗g4+ 12 ♗e2 0-0-0+ 13 ♔e1 ± A.Sokolov-Duncan, Gausdal 1996.

7...♕xd1+ 8 ♔xd1 ♘g4 9 ♘a3

This seems best. White has achieved no advantage with other moves:

a) 9 ♗b5 ♘xe3+ 10 fxe3 ♗d7 11 ♗xc6 ♗xc6 12 c4 g6 13 ♘c3 ♗g7 = Saint Amand-Donaldson, Bermuda 1995.

b) 9 ♘bd2 ♘xe3+ 10 fxe3 ♗e7 11 ♗c4 ♗g4 12 h3 ♗h5 13 g4 ♗g6 14 e4 0-0-0 15 ♗d5 ♔c7 16 ♔e2 ♖he8 17 e6 fxe6 18 ♗xc6 (Chandler suggests 18 ♗xe6!? but 18...♗f6 19 ♗f5 ♗f7! 20 g5 g6 21 ♗xg6 ♗xg6 22 gxf6 ♗xe4 is good for Black) 18...♔xc6 19 ♘e5+ ♔c7 20 ♘xg6 hxg6 21 ♖af1 ♖f8 22

♖xf8 ♖xf8 23 ♘f3 g5 24 ♖d1 ♖f4 25
♘d2 ½-½ Motwani-Ward, British Ch
(Norwich) 1994.

**9...♘xe3+ 10 fxe3 ♗g4 11 ♘c4
0-0-0+ 12 ♔e1**

White has a slight advantage. Roz-
entalis-Emms, Bundesliga 1995/6 continued 12...♗e7 13 ♗e2 ♗e6 14 a4
♖d5 15 ♖f1 g5 16 ♖d1 ♖xd1+ 17
♔xd1 ♖d8+ 18 ♔e1 ♔c7 19 ♘fd2 b6
20 h3 a6 21 ♗g4 b5 22 ♗xe6 fxe6 23
axb5 axb5 24 ♘d6 ♗xd6 25 exd6+
♔xd6 26 ♔e2 and White went on to
win the endgame.

B32)

6 dxc5

This is the critical test for this
move-order. Now:

B321)

6...♕xd1+ 7 ♔xd1 (D)

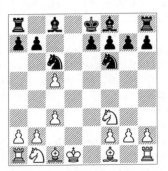

This complex position provides a
great deal of scope for further investigation.

7...e5
Or:

a) 7...♗g4 doesn't make sense as it
neither attacks the c-pawn nor stops
the king's escape to the queenside.
White should play 8 b4 primarily to
create an escape square for his king on
b2, only secondly to defend the c5-
pawn for later. After 7...♗g4, play has
transposed to *4...♘f6 5 ♘f3 ♗g4 6
dxc5 ♕xd1+ 7 ♔xd1 ♘c6*, and there is
further analysis there.

b) 7...♗f5 is much more logical:

b1) 8 ♗b5 0-0-0+ 9 ♔e2 e5 10
♗e3 ♘d5 11 ♗xc6 bxc6 12 ♘xe5
♘xe3 13 fxe3 ♗xc5 14 ♘xc6 ♗g4+
(14...♖d3 15 ♘d4 ♗xd4 16 cxd4 ♖e8
17 ♔f2! followed by 18 ♘c3 with an
extra pawn – Palkovi) 15 ♔f2 ♖d6 16
♘d4 ♖f6+ 17 ♔g1?! (better is 17 ♔e1
♖e8 18 h3 ♗d7 19 ♔e2 ♗xd4 20 cxd4
♗b5+ 21 ♔d1 ♖xe3) 17...♖e8 18 ♘d2
♖xe3 19 ♘2b3 ♗b6 20 h3 ♗e6 21 ♔h2
♗c7+ 22 ♔g1 ♗d5 23 ♘d2 ♖g3 0-1
Werner-Gross, Balatonbereny 1996.

b2) 8 ♗e3 0-0-0+ and then:

b21) 9 ♘bd2 e6 10 ♗b5 ♘d5 11
♗xc6 bxc6 12 ♘e5 ♘xe3+ 13 fxe3
♗xc5 gives Black a strong initiative,
Sveshnikov-Martynov, Val Maubuée
1990, though it should be noted that
Sveshnikov assesses this as slightly
better for White.

b22) 9 ♔c1!? is untested but it is
consistent with ideas tried against the
7...e5 move-order. It seems best for the
king to head to the queenside if at all
possible.

8 b4

This seems more accurate than 8
♗e3 ♘g4!? (8...♘d5 is similar and
also possible; it has the added benefit
of attacking b4 and c3 in some lines

but it doesn't defend e5) 9 b4 a5 10 ♗b5 (10 b5 ♘d8 and the g4-knight defends e5) 10...♗d7 11 ♘bd2 axb4 12 ♗xc6 ♗xc6 13 cxb4 b6 ∞ Bowden-Duncan, British League (4NCL) 1996/7.

8...♗f5 *(D)*

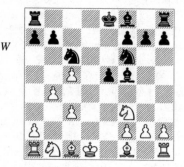

9 ♗e3!

White frees the c1-square for his king. Black gets dangerous compensation after 9 ♗b5 0-0-0+ 10 ♔e2 ♗e7!? (more solid is 10...♘d5 11 ♗xc6 bxc6 12 ♗d2 f6 ∞ Blatny-Gross, Czechoslovak Ch (Trinec) 1988) 11 ♗e3 ♘d5:

a) 12 ♗c4 e4 13 ♗xd5?! exf3+! 14 ♗xf3 ♗d3+ 15 ♔e1 ♘xb4! 16 ♘a3 ♗f6 17 ♔d2 ♗f5+ 18 ♗d4 ♖he8 19 ♘b5?? ♗g5+ 0-1 Ramirez Gonzalez-Martinez Martin, Spanish Cht (Barcelona) 2000.

b) 12 ♗xc6 bxc6 13 ♘xe5 ♖he8 14 ♘xf7? (14 ♘xc6 ♗g4+ 15 f3 ♖d7 16 ♗d2!? may withstand the attack) 14...♘xe3 15 ♘xd8 ♘c4 16 ♘xc6 ♗f6+ 17 ♔d1 ♘b2+ 18 ♔c1 ♘d3+ 19 ♔c2 ♘xb4+ 20 ♔b3 ♘xc6 21 ♘a3 ♖e7 22 ♘b5 ♖b7 23 a4 a6 24 c4 ♘d4+ 0-1 Sermek-Wirthensohn, Bad Wörishofen 1993.

c) Blatny suggests 12 ♖c1!? followed by ♘a3 and ♘c4.

9...0-0-0+

9...♘d5 10 ♔c1 a5!? is an interesting and critical alternative:

a) 11 ♗b5 ♗xb1! 12 ♘xe5 ♘xc3 13 ♗xc6+ bxc6 14 ♗d2 axb4 15 ♗xc3 ½-½ Sveshnikov-Loginov, Russian Ch (Samara) 2000. Black probably has a slight advantage here.

b) 11 b5 ♘d8 and then:

b1) 12 ♘xe5 ♘xe3 13 fxe3 ♗xc5 14 ♗c4! (returning the pawn because otherwise White is passive and worse) 14...♗xe3+ 15 ♔b2 0-0 16 ♖f1 ♗e6 17 ♘a3 ♗c5 18 ♖ad1 (White's more active pieces and Black's weak queenside pawns compensate for Black's bishop-pair) 18...♖c8 19 ♗xe6 ♗xa3+ 20 ♔xa3 ♘xe6 21 c4 was played in Rausis-Wirthensohn, 2nd Bundesliga 1990/1 (which White won). In *Informator 82*, Nadyrkhanov suggested the improvement 21...♘c5. He assessed the position as ∓ but actually after 22 ♘d7 ♖fe8! 23 ♘xc5 ♖xc5 24 ♖d7 ♖xc4, the double-rook endgame is equal and likely to end in a draw by perpetual check within a few moves.

b2) 12 c6!? represents a possible improvement: 12...bxc6 13 ♘xe5 ♗xb1 14 ♔xb1 ♘xc3+ 15 ♔b2 ♘xb5 16 ♘xc6 ♗a3+ 17 ♔c2 ♘xc6 18 ♗xb5 is slightly better for White.

10 ♔c1 ♘d5 11 ♔b2

Defending the c3-pawn. 11 ♗b5 f6 (11...♗xb1 12 ♗xc6 bxc6 13 ♖xb1 ♘xc3 14 ♘xe5! +−) 12 ♔b2 g5 13 ♖d1 ♗e7 14 ♘bd2 also held on to the pawn in Rausis-Maus, Gausdal 1989.

11...f6 12 ♗c4 ♗e7 13 ♘bd2

White is still a pawn up, Skytte-Jiretorn, Stockholm 2001.

B322)
6...♕xc5 7 ♘a3 (D)

This is more accurate than 7 ♗e3 as Black's queen is awkwardly placed and doesn't need to be chased away yet. If the queen moves anyway, White might well prefer to place the bishop elsewhere, such as f4. The a3-knight meanwhile threatens to go to either c4 or b5 depending on events; both moves cut off the black queen's escape to a5. Note how by comparison to play after *4...♘f6 5 ♘f3 ♗g4 6 dxc5 ♕xc5*, the c6-knight here obstructs the black queen, which would ideally like to retreat to c7 at an opportune moment.

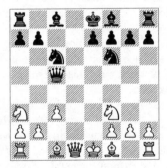

7...e5
Or:

a) 7...♗g4 8 ♗e3 ♕a5 9 ♕b3 0-0-0 10 ♘g5 and White wins a pawn, Schmittdiel-J.Polgar, Dortmund 1990.

b) 7...♕a5 8 ♗f4 ♕f5 9 ♗g3 a6 10 ♗d3 ♕e6+ 11 ♗e2 g6 12 0-0 ♗h6 13 ♖e1 ♕d5 14 ♘c4, Blatny-Basin, Trnava 1989. The knight is going to b6 and White is better.

c) 7...♘g4 8 ♕e2 and then:

c1) 8...♗f5 9 h3 ♗d3!? 10 ♕xd3 ♕xf2+ 11 ♔d1 ♖d8 12 ♕xd8+ ♔xd8 13 hxg4 ± Blatny-Wang Zili, Thessaloniki OL 1988.

c2) 8...a6 9 h3 ♘ge5 10 ♗e3 ♘xf3+ 11 ♕xf3 ♕f5 12 ♕g3 e5 13 ♘c4 ♗e6 14 0-0-0!? ♕g6 15 ♕xg6 hxg6 16 ♘b6 ♖d8 17 ♗c4 ♗xc4 18 ♘xc4 ♗e7 19 a4! ± Shaked-Atalik, Hawaii 1997.

8 ♗e3
Or:

a) 8 ♘b5 is not dangerous for Black: 8...♕e7 9 b3 (after 9 ♗e3 a6 10 ♗c5 ♕xc5 11 ♘c7+ ♔e7 12 ♘xa8 b5 White has won an exchange, but his knight is in danger, Borodkin-Tunik, USSR 1991; 9 ♗g5 a6 10 ♗xf6 gxf6 11 ♘a3 ♗e6 is fine for Black) 9...♗g4 10 ♗a3 ♕d8 11 ♗xf8 ♕xd1+ 12 ♖xd1 ♔xf8 13 ♗e2 ♔e7 is equal, S.Lalić-P.Thipsay, Kuala Lumpur 1992.

b) However, 8 ♘c4 is also interesting: 8...♗g4 9 ♗e3 ♕e7 10 ♕a4 ♗xf3 11 gxf3 (Vi.Ivanov-Barsky, Moscow 1992) 11...♕c7 12 ♖g1 with an initiative.

8...♕a5

After 8...♕e7 9 ♗b5! ♘g4 10 ♘c4 ♘xe3 11 ♘xe3 (11 fxe3 leads to an unclear position: 11...f6 12 ♕a4 ♕c7 13 0-0-0, Sveshnikov-Shneider, Podolsk 1993) 11...♕c5 12 ♕d5 ♕xd5 13 ♘xd5 ♗d6 14 0-0-0, White has a clear advantage.

9 ♘c4 ♕c7 10 ♕a4 ♗d7 11 ♘b6 ♖d8 12 ♘xd7 ♘xd7 13 ♖d1 a6 14 ♗e2

The bishop-pair in a semi-open position gives White the better prospects, Sermek-Riegler, Maribor 1993.

5 2...d5 3 exd5 ♕xd5 4 d4 ♘f6: 5 ♘f3 e6 and Other Lines

1 e4 c5 2 c3 d5 3 exd5 ♕xd5 4 d4 ♘f6 *(D)*

5 ♘f3

Some players have tried alternative move-orders here, either to avoid *5 ♘f3 ♗g4* or to gain some nuance in the systems after 5...e6. White has tried:

a) 5 ♘a3 cxd4 (5...a6!? 6 ♘f3 ♗g4 ∞ Claesen-Chuchelov, Charleroi 2001) 6 ♘b5 ♘a6 7 ♕xd4 ♕xd4 8 ♘xd4 e5 = Vorotnikov-Kharlov, St Petersburg 1998.

b) If White tries to avoid *5 ♘f3 ♗g4* and transpose to *5 ♘f3 e6 6 ♗e3* by playing 5 ♗e3, Black can prevent it by 5...♗g4 6 f3 cxd4 7 cxd4, and now:

b1) 7...♕e6 is an interesting possibility, which leads to a very sharp

position: 8 ♔f2 ♘d5 (8...♘e4+? is bad, because White can play 9 ♔e2! ♗h5 10 g4, winning a piece) 9 ♗c1 ♗f5 10 ♗c4 ♕d7 11 ♘c3 ♘xc3 12 bxc3 ♘c6 13 ♘e2 e5 14 ♘g3 ♗g6 15 ♖e1 0-0-0 with a lot of complications, Rozentalis-Åkesson, Gausdal 2001.

b2) 7...♗d7 8 ♘c3 ♕a5 9 ♗c4 e6 10 ♘ge2 ♗d6 11 ♖c1 0-0 12 0-0 ♗c6 13 ♕d2 ♘bd7, Godena-Gallagher, Swiss Cht 1996/7. The best White can achieve in this position is to make the d5 advance, after which some pieces will be exchanged, leading to an equal endgame.

c) 5 dxc5 ♕xc5 (5...♕xd1+ is less logical here than after *4...♘c6 5 dxc5* as ...♘f6 helps far less in the recovery of the pawn; 5...e6 6 b4!? a5 7 ♕xd5 ♘xd5 ∞ is more plausible, Striković-Cifuentes, Seville 2001) 6 ♘a3 a6 7 ♘c4 ♘bd7 8 a4 b6 9 ♗e3 ♕c7 10 a5 b5 11 ♘b6!? ♘xb6 12 axb6 ♕c6 ∞ Marković-Crisan, Tekija 2001. Marković lost this game but was happy to repeat the line against Arsović (at Jahorina 2001). More tests are needed.

5...e6 *(D)*

Black has three moves of roughly equal value here. 5...♘c6 transposes to 4...♘c6 5 ♘f3 ♘f6, and 5...♗g4 is analysed in the next chapter. 5...g6?! is inferior. It would be nice for Black to put his bishop on g7, but this move slows down his development, a fact that White can exploit by 6 ♕b3! ±. This and other possibilities are analysed under 4...g6 5 ♘f3 ♘f6.

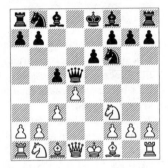

W

Now White has a wealth of options:

A: 6 ♗d3	75
B: 6 ♗e2	81
C: 6 ♘a3	87
D: 6 ♗e3	92

6 ♘bd2 prepares 7 ♗c4, but this construction is too artificial:

a) 6...♘c6 is not the best, but possible. After 7 ♗c4 ♕d8 (7...♕h5 8 ♗e2 cxd4 9 ♘xd4 ♕d5 10 ♘xc6 ♕xc6 11 ♗f3 ± Ochoa-Van der Sterren, Thessaloniki OL 1984) 8 ♘b3 cxd4 9 ♘bxd4 ♘xd4 10 ♘xd4 ♗e7 11 0-0 0-0 12 ♕f3, White's pieces in the centre look promising, but Black has no weaknesses and can activate his own pieces: 12...♕c7 13 ♗b3 ♗d7 14 ♖e1 ♗d6 15 h3 e5 16 ♘c2 ♗c6 17 ♕g3 ♔h8 18 ♕h4 ♘d5 ½-½ Tiviakov-M.Makarov, Podolsk 1992.

b) 6...cxd4! (best) 7 ♗c4 ♕h5 8 cxd4 (or 8 ♘xd4 ♕xd1+ 9 ♔xd1 a6, with equality) 8...♗e7 9 0-0 0-0 10 b3 ♘c6 11 ♗b2 ♖d8 12 ♖c1 ♗d7 13 ♖e1 ♘b4 14 a3 ♘bd5 and Black blockades the isolated pawn with a good position, Schmittdiel-Womacka, Seefeld 1999.

A)

6 ♗d3

This is the most natural move, preparing to castle and developing the bishop to an active square pointing at Black's kingside. For a long time it was the main line. In fact, for some time Black employed the move-order 5...♘c6 to rule out the possibility of 6 ♗d3 because of 6...♗g4. If Black exchanges pawns on d4, White's bishop is well-placed for the resultant isolated queen's pawn position and White's queen's knight is free to develop to c3 with gain of time on Black's queen. The problem with 6 ♗d3 is that it does nothing to force Black to exchange on d4, and Adorjan led the way in showing that Black is OK if he develops his kingside quickly and plays ...♗e7, ...0-0 and ...♖d8, pressurizing the d-pawn. In these lines, the bishop can even prove a liability on d3 as it can be *en prise* if White then wishes to capture on c5 with his d-pawn.

We will look at two lines: the old main line 6...♘c6, which is still theoretically relevant due to the move-order 4...♘c6 5 ♘f3 e6 6 ♗d3! ♘f6 and still suitable for those who as Black wish to play for a win against an isolated queen's pawn, and the equalizing move 6...♗e7.

A1: **6...♘c6**   76
A2: **6...♗e7**   79

A1)
  6...♘c6 *(D)*

W

7 0-0 cxd4

It is less effective for Black to defer exchanging after developing the queen's knight because ...0-0 would have been a more effective tempo than ...♘c6, and because after dxc5 by White, Black would ideally like to recapture on c5 with his queen's knight (via d7 or a6). Thus after 7...♗e7, White can effectively respond 8 c4 ♕d8 9 dxc5. After this:

a) 9...♗xc5 10 ♘c3 0-0 11 ♕e2 ♗d7 12 ♗g5 h6 13 ♗h4 ♗e7 14 ♖ad1 leaves White's pieces more active, Fossan-Efimov, Gausdal 1991.

b) 9...♘d7 10 a3 ♘xc5 11 ♗c2 ♕xd1 12 ♖xd1 a5 13 ♘c3 0-0 14 ♗e3 b6 15 ♘a4 ♖a6 16 ♘xc5 bxc5 17 ♗a4 ♖b6 18 ♗b5 ♗a6 19 a4, Kantsler-Magerramov, Moscow 1981. White has managed to settle on b5, and thus has an advantage.

  8 cxd4 ♗e7 9 ♘c3 *(D)*
  9...♕d8

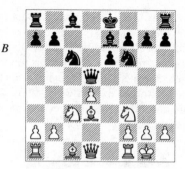

B

This is a fairly common reply but is not the best move. Black naturally retreats his queen out of harm's way, but 9...♕d6 is better as it leaves the queen more actively placed:

a) 10 ♕e2 0-0 11 ♖d1 (if 11 ♗g5 Black can accept the pawn sacrifice: 11...♘xd4 12 ♘xd4 ♕xd4 13 ♖fd1 ♕c5 14 ♘e4 ♘xe4 15 ♕xe4 g6 16 ♗e3 ♕b4 17 ♕xb4 ♗xb4 18 ♗h6 ♖d8 19 ♗e4 ♖xd1+ 20 ♖xd1 ♗a5 and White has enough compensation to achieve a draw, but no more than that, Züger-Pelletier, Biel 1998) 11...♘b4 12 ♗b1 b6 13 ♘e4 ♗a6 14 ♕xa6 ♘xa6 15 ♘xd6 ♗xd6 with an equal endgame – Chandler.

b) 10 ♗g5 0-0 11 ♖c1 and then:

b1) 11...b6? loses to 12 ♗xf6 ♗xf6 13 ♘e4 +−.

b2) 11...♘b4 12 ♗b1 ♘bd5 13 ♘e5 ♗d7 14 ♕d3 g6 15 ♕f3 with an initiative, C.Mann-T.Heinemann, W.German jr Ch 1988.

b3) 11...♖d8! 12 ♘b5 ♕d7 13 ♘e5 ♘xe5 14 ♖c7 ♕d5 15 dxe5 ♕xe5 16 ♖xe7 ♕xg5 17 ♗xh7+ ♔xh7 18 ♕xd8 ♗d7 (18...♕xb5 19 ♖xf7 is dangerous for Black) 19 ♕xa8 ♗xb5 20 g3 ♗xf1 21 ♔xf1 ♕c1+ 22 ♔g2 ♕c6+ with perpetual check, Malaniuk-Gorelov, Saratov 1981.

c) 10 ♗e3 0-0 11 a3 – *6 ♗e3 cxd4 7 cxd4 ♘c6 8 ♘c3 ♕d6 9 a3 ♗e7 10 ♗d3 0-0 11 0-0*.

d) 10 ♘b5 ♕d8 11 ♗f4 ♘d5 12 ♗g3 and then:

d1) 12...0-0 and now rather than 13 ♖c1 ♗d7 14 ♗e4 ♘cb4 = Grefe-Dzindzichashvili, Lone Pine 1980, White should play 13 ♗c4!, transposing to *6 ♗e2 ♘c6 7 0-0 cxd4 8 cxd4 ♗e7 9 ♘c3 ♕d6 10 ♘b5 ♕d8 11 ♗f4 ♘d5 12 ♗g3 0-0 13 ♗c4 ±*.

d2) 12...a6 13 ♘c3 0-0 (13...♘cb4 14 ♗b1 ♘f6 15 ♘e5 ± Henley-Kuligowski, New York 1981) 14 ♖c1 and play is similar to the 6 ♗e2 lines though White's bishop is undoubtedly better placed here on d3 rather than e2:

d21) 14...♘xc3 15 bxc3 b5 16 a4!? (16 ♘e5 ♗b7 17 f4 g6 and we think Black is out of danger) with the point 16...b4?! 17 ♗e4! ♗b7 18 cxb4.

d22) 14...♘f6 15 a3 b6 16 ♗b1 ♗b7 17 ♕d3 ♖c8 18 ♖fe1 g6 19 ♗a2 ± Guido-Caposciutti, Genoa 2000.

10 a3

10 ♖e1 0-0 11 a3 transposes to *10 a3 0-0 11 ♖e1*. The other plan is to play as in the Queen's Gambit Accepted (*1 d4 d5 2 c4 dxc4 3 ♘f3 ♘f6 4 e3 e6 5 ♗xc4 c5 6 0-0 ♘c6 7 ♕e2 cxd4 8 exd4 ♗e7 9 ♘c3 ±*) with 10 ♕e2, but here the bishop is on d3 rather than c4. This difference makes the position OK for Black: 10...0-0 11 ♖d1 ♘b4 12 ♗b1 (12 ♗c4 b6 13 ♘e5 ♗b7 14 a3 ♘bd5 and the position is still complicated, but Black has managed to develop his pieces comfortably and

occupy the main square – d5) 12...b6 13 ♘e5 ♗b7 14 a3 ♘bd5 15 ♘e4 ♘xe4 16 ♕xe4 f5 17 ♕f3 ♗f6 18 ♗a2 ♖c8 and Black is very solid, Van Wely-Kobaliya, Batumi Echt 1999.

10...0-0 (D)

This position can also be reached from the Caro-Kann Defence, Panov-Botvinnik Attack (*1 e4 c6 2 d4 d5 3 exd5 cxd5 4 c4 ♘f6 5 ♘c3 e6 6 ♘f3 ♗e7 7 cxd5 ♘xd5 8 ♗d3 ♘c6 9 0-0 0-0 10 a3 ♘f6*) or the Queen's Gambit Declined, Semi-Tarrasch Variation (*1 d4 d5 2 c4 e6 3 ♘c3 ♘f6 4 ♘f3 c5 5 cxd5 ♘xd5 6 e3 ♘c6 7 ♗d3 cxd4 8 exd4 ♗e7 9 0-0 0-0 10 a3 ♘f6*) though 10...♗f6 is a better equalizing try in both systems. Some of the game references below came from one of those opening systems.

White's most common plan here is a crude mating attack, involving the following steps:

1) ♗c2 and ♕d3 lining up against h7.

2) ♗g5 attacking Black's defending knight on f6 and inducing ...g6.

3) h4 with the idea of h5 softening up Black's kingside further.

4) ♖fe1 and ♖ad1 controlling the centre files, and if possible d5 opening the centre at an appropriate moment, possibly supported by moving the bishop from c2 to b3.

Black, meanwhile, aims to keep a firm grip on the d5-square while gradually seeking exchanges. His principal aim is to reach an endgame where he can round up White's isolated queen's pawn.

11 ♖e1

An important developing move. The rook on the half-open file adds bite to any potential d5 break and, if White ever does break through down the h-file or by a sacrifice on g6, the rook is one step nearer to joining the fray via e3 or e4. To try to avoid the sequence *11 ♖e1 b6 12 ♗c2 ♗a6!?*, White has also tried the move-order 11 ♗c2 b6 12 ♕d3, when 12...♗b7 13 ♖e1 transposes to *11 ♖e1 b6 12 ♗c2 ♗b7 13 ♕d3*, but this does allow Black the interesting option 12...a5!? (threatening ...♗a6 winning the exchange) 13 ♘e4 g6 14 ♖d1 ♗a6 15 ♕e3 ♖e8 16 ♘e5 ♘d5 17 ♕h6 ♕c7 ∓ Jacobs-Adams, London NatWest 1987.

11...b6 12 ♗c2

Another move-order, which avoids the complications of *12 ♗c2 ♗a6!?*, is 12 ♗g5 ♗b7 13 ♗c2. After 13...♖c8 14 ♕d3 g6 15 ♖ad1 ♘d5 16 ♗h6 ♖e8, Black has gained a tempo over *12 ♗c2 ♗b7 13 ♕d3 g6 14 ♗h6 ♖e8 15 ♖ad1 ♖c8* though it is a moot point whether ...♘d5 helps Black. Beliavsky-Karpov, Trud-CSKA ECC 1986 continued 17 ♗a4 a6 18 ♘xd5 ♕xd5 19 ♕e3 ♗f6 20 ♗b3 ♕d7 21 d5 exd5 22 ♕xb6 ±.

12...♗b7

12...♗a6!? is complex:

a) 13 b4 ♖c8 14 ♖e3!? ♗c4 15 b5 ♘a5 16 ♘e5 with an attack, Kaidanov-Anand, Moscow 1987 (by transposition).

b) 13 ♗g5 ♖c8 14 ♕d2 ♘a5 15 ♕f4 ♗b7 16 ♖ad1 ♗d5 (16...♘c4? 17 ♕h4 g6 {17...h6 18 ♗xh6!} 18 d5! ♘xb2 19 d6 +–) 17 ♕h4 g6 18 ♘e5 ♖c7 19 ♖e3 ♘c4 20 ♘xc4 ♗xc4 21 d5!? ♗xd5 22 ♗b3 ♖d7 23 ♗a4 with an initiative, Sermek-Golubović, Pula 1999.

13 ♕d3 *(D)*

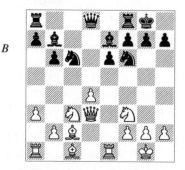

This position contains a very subtle trap that even Karpov has fallen into.

13...g6

This move is forced and it is all thanks to the e1-rook. After 13...♖e8? 14 d5! exd5 15 ♗g5 ♘e4 (15...g6 16 ♖xe7! ♕xe7 17 ♘xd5) 16 ♘xe4 dxe4 17 ♕xe4 g6 18 ♕h4 White has a strong attack – this has occurred in a number of games. White can also play 14 d5! after 13...♖c8? though both a former and a future world champion managed to miss this in Smyslov-Karpov, USSR Ch (Leningrad) 1971.

14 ♗h6 ♖e8 15 ♖ad1 ♖c8 16 ♗b3

16 h4!? ♘d5 17 ♘xd5 ♕xd5 18 ♕d2 ♕d6 19 ♗e4 ± Ribli-Gheorghiu, Warsaw Z 1979, has never been repeated by White, but still seems a good alternative.

16...♘a5

After 16...♘d5, White has a number of options, but one is 17 ♗a4!? – *12 ♗g5 ♗b7 13 ♗c2 ♖c8 14 ♕d3 g6 15 ♖ad1 ♘d5 16 ♗h6 ♖e8 17 ♗a4 ±.*

17 ♗a2 ♘d5 18 ♘e4 ♘f6 19 ♘c3

19 ♘eg5 ♗d5 is fine for Black.

19...♘d5 20 ♘e5

20 ♘e4 ♘f6 ½-½ G.Lee-Gheorghiu, Biel 1990 is a safe option when facing a grandmaster!

20...♗f6 *(D)*

20...♘xc3? loses to 21 ♘xf7 ♔xf7 22 ♗xe6+ ♔f6 23 d5.

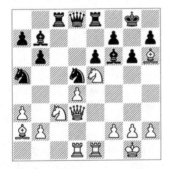

21 ♘e4 ♗g7

White has good chances on the kingside. Rainfray-Solozhenkin, Bordeaux 2001 continued 22 ♕h3 f6 (22...♖c7 is more solid) 23 ♗xg7 ♔xg7 24 ♘f7! ♔xf7 25 ♕xh7+ ♔f8 26 b4 ♕e7 27 ♕h8+ ♔f7 28 ♕h7+ ♔f8 29 ♕h6+ ♔f7 (29...♕g7 30 ♕xg7+ ♔xg7 31 bxa5 ♖c2 32 ♘d6 ±) 30 ♕h7+ (30

♗xd5 ♗xd5 31 bxa5 ♖h8 32 ♕f4 ♔g7 33 axb6 axb6 ±) 30...♔f8 ½-½.

A2)

6...♗e7 7 0-0 0-0 *(D)*

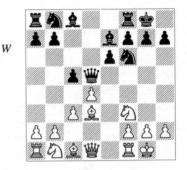

8 c4

White has no satisfactory waiting move:

a) 8 ♕e2 ♘c6 9 ♖d1 cxd4 10 cxd4 and then:

a1) 10...b6 11 ♘c3 ♕h5 12 d5! and Black can't accept the pawn, as 12...exd5? loses a piece to 13 ♗b5.

a2) 10...♖d8 11 ♘c3 ♕h5 12 ♗f4 b6 13 d5 and once again if Black takes the pawn, he loses an exchange: 13...♘xd5? 14 ♘xd5 ♖xd5 15 ♗e4.

a3) 10...♘b4 (Black should take control over the d5-square as otherwise White can advance his central pawn at any moment) 11 ♘c3 ♕d6 (or 11...♕d8) transposes to *6...♘c6 7 0-0 cxd4 8 cxd4 ♗e7 9 ♘c3 ♕d6 (or 9...♕d8) 10 ♕e2 0-0 11 ♖d1 ♘b4.*

b) 8 ♗e3 ♘c6 (or 8...♖d8 9 ♘e5 ♘c6 = Nemec-Vokač, Karvina 1989) 9 c4 (9 dxc5 ♖d8! 10 ♗e2 ♕f5 11 ♕a4 ♗xc5 12 ♗xc5 ♕xc5 = Sveshnikov-Gufeld, USSR 1982) 9...♕h5 10 h3

cxd4 11 ♘xd4 ♘xd4 12 ♗xd4 ♖d8 13
♗e3 ♕e5 14 ♘c3 b6 15 ♕f3 ♗a6 16
♖ad1 ♖ac8 17 ♖fe1 ♗d6 18 g3 ♗c5
with a slight advantage for Black, Am-
brož-Adorjan, Riga 1981.

8...♕h5

Other possibilities:

a) 8...♕d8 9 dxc5 (this is better than
9 ♘c3 cxd4 10 ♘xd4 ♘bd7 11 ♗e3
♘e5 12 ♗e2 a6 13 ♘f3 ♘ed7 14 h3
♕c7 15 ♗d3 b6 16 ♕e2 ♗b7, when
both sides have finished their development and the position is rather complicated, Kaeser-Hort, W.German open
Ch 1986) 9...♘bd7 (9...♘a6 leads to
the same position) 10 ♕e2 (if 10 c6
bxc6 11 ♘c3 c5 12 ♕e2 ♗b7, Black is
fine) 10...♘xc5 11 ♗c2 b6 12 ♘c3
♗b7 (White also has an advantage
after 12...♗a6 13 ♘e5 ♕c8 14 ♗g5
♘cd7 15 ♘xd7 ♕xd7 16 ♖ad1 ♕c7
17 b3 ♗b7 18 ♕d3 ♖fd8 19 ♕h3 h6
20 ♗c1) 13 ♗g5 ♕c7 14 ♘e5 ♖ad8
15 ♘b5 ♕b8 16 ♖fd1 a6 17 ♘d4 ±
(Sax and Hazai).

b) 8...♕d7!? 9 dxc5 (Black also
equalizes after 9 ♘c3 cxd4 10 ♘xd4
♖d8 11 ♗e3 ♘c6) 9...♖d8 (9...♘c6 10
a3! – Sveshnikov) 10 ♘e5 ♕d4 11
♕e2 ♘bd7 12 ♘xd7 ♗xd7 13 ♗e3
♕e5:

b1) The natural 14 ♘d2 is answered
by the strong move 14...♗c6! (after
14...♗xc5 15 ♘f3 ♕h5 16 ♗xc5 ♕xc5
17 ♘e5 ♗c6 18 ♖fd1 White has a
slight edge, Rozentalis-Lukin, Moscow 1983), which leaves White in
trouble, as 15 ♘b3? loses to 15...♖xd3
16 ♕xd3 ♘g4, when White is unable
to protect his king, Kharlov-M.Mak-
arov, Rybinsk 1991.

b2) 14 ♘c3 is very likely to lead to
a draw: 14...♗xc5 15 ♗xc5 ♕xc5 16
♘e4 ♘xe4 17 ♗xe4 ♗c6 ½-½ Mak-
arychev-Anikaev, Frunze 1979.

We now return to the position after
8...♕h5 (D):

9 dxc5

Or:

a) 9 ♘c3 ♖d8 10 ♘e2 cxd4 11
♗g5 ♗d6 12 ♗xf6 gxf6 13 ♘exd4
♘c6 14 ♘xc6 bxc6 15 ♖e1 c5 and
after 16...♗b7 the two bishops will
become quite dangerous, Vi.Ivanov-
A.Donchenko, Moscow 1991.

b) 9 ♗e2 ♖d8 10 ♗e3 (after 10
♘g5 ♕h4 11 ♘f3, Black should accept the draw by 11...♕h5 rather than
risk 11...♕e4 12 ♘c3 ♕c6 ±) 10...cxd4
11 ♘xd4 ♕e5 12 ♘c3 ♗d7 13 ♗f3
♘c6 = Dvoretsky-Polugaevsky, USSR
Ch (Leningrad) 1974.

9...♖d8

Or 9...♗xc5 10 ♘c3 ♘c6 11 ♕e2
♖d8 12 ♘e4 ♘xe4 13 ♗xe4 ♗d7 with
an equal position, Rehorek-Chloupek,
Karvina 1989.

**10 ♗f4 ♕xc5 11 ♕e2 ♘c6 12 ♘c3
♘d4 13 ♘xd4 ♕xd4 14 ♗e4 ♘xe4 15
♘xe4 b5 16 c5**

White can't take the pawn – 16 cxb5 – because of 16...♗b7 17 ♖fe1 ♗b4.

16...♗b7 17 ♗d6 ♕xe4 18 ♕xe4 ♗xe4 19 ♗xe7 ♖d2 20 f3 ♗d5 21 ♖f2 ♖xf2 22 ♔xf2

½-½ Rozentalis-Novikov, Kharkov 1985.

B)

6 ♗e2 *(D)*

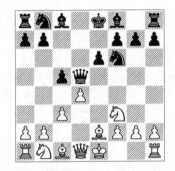

6...♘c6

Instead:

a) An unusual but interesting line is 6...cxd4 7 cxd4 ♗d7 8 ♘c3 ♕a5 9 0-0 ♗c6 10 ♘e5 ♗d6 11 ♗f4 ♗xe5 12 dxe5 ♘d5 = McDonald-Rowson, British League (4NCL) 1997/8.

b) 6...♗e7 7 0-0 0-0 is a strong alternative. White is better placed than in the equivalent position after 6 ♗d3, but still has difficulty in proving more than a very slight advantage:

b1) 8 ♗e3 ♘g4 (8...cxd4 9 cxd4 ♘c6 10 ♘c3 ♕d6 – 6...♘c6 7 0-0 cxd4 8 cxd4 ♗e7 9 ♘c3 ♕d6 10 ♗e3 0-0 =) 9 ♗f4 ♘c6 10 c4 ♕f5 11 ♗c7, Sveshnikov-Adorjan, Sarajevo 1983, and now 11...♘f6 12 ♘c3 cxd4 13 ♘xd4 ♘xd4 14 ♕xd4 ♗d7 is the most

accurate method of reaching equality – Adorjan.

b2) 8 ♘e5 (with the idea of ♗f3) and then:

b21) 8...cxd4 (this exchange is premature) 9 cxd4 ♖d8 10 ♘c3 ♕a5 (after 10...♕xd4 11 ♕xd4 ♖xd4 12 ♘b5 ♖e4 13 ♗f3 ♖xe5 14 ♘c7, White wins an exchange; Black will have some compensation after 14...♘c6 15 ♘xa8 ♘d4, but it's difficult to say if it will be sufficient) 11 ♗f3 ♘bd7 12 ♕e2 ♘xe5 13 dxe5 ♘d5 14 ♘xd5 exd5 15 ♖d1 d4 16 ♕e4 ♕b6 17 b3 and the d-pawn becomes vulnerable, Kharlov-Franco, Saragossa 1994.

b22) 8...♖d8 9 ♗f3 ♕d6 10 ♗f4 ♕b6 11 ♘d2 (alternatively, 11 ♘c4 ♕a6) 11...♕xb2 12 ♘dc4 ♕b5 13 ♖b1 ♕e8 14 ♗xb7 ♗xb7 15 ♖xb7 ♘d5 16 ♕g4 ♘xf4 17 ♕xf4 cxd4 18 cxd4 f6 and Black is fine, Sveshnikov-Novikov, Tashkent 1984.

b3) 8 c4 ♕d8 9 ♘c3 cxd4 and here:

b31) 10 ♘xd4 ♗d7 (10...e5 weakens the d5-square: 11 ♘db5 ♘c6 12 ♗e3 ♗f5 13 ♘d5 ♘xd5 14 cxd5 ♘b4 15 d6 and the white passed pawn becomes very dangerous, J.Polgar-Lautier, Monaco Amber rpd 1995) 11 ♗f3 ♕c8 12 ♕e2 ♘c6 13 ♘xc6 ♗xc6 14 b3 ♖d8 15 ♗g5 h6 16 ♗h4 ♕c7 and Black is OK, though we prefer White, Bjelajac-Adorjan, Vršac 1983.

b32) 10 ♕xd4 ♗d7 11 ♘e5 ♘c6 12 ♘xc6 ♗xc6 13 ♕xd8 ♖fxd8 14 ♗e3 ♔f8 15 ♖fd1 ♖dc8 16 ♖ac1 h6 17 ♔f1 a6 gives White only a symbolic advantage, Anand-Ivanchuk, Shenyang FIDE WCup 2000.

7 0-0 *(D)*

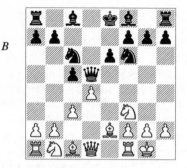

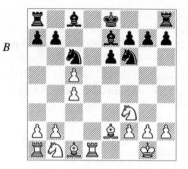

Now:

B1: 7...♗e7 82
B2: 7...cxd4 83

B1)

7...♗e7 8 c4

8 ♗e3 cxd4 (8...♘g4!?) 9 cxd4 (9 ♘xd4 ♘xd4 10 ♗xd4 e5 =) 9...0-0 10 ♘c3 ♕d6 – 7...cxd4 8 cxd4 ♗e7 9 ♘c3 ♕d6 10 ♗e3 0-0 =.

8...♕d8

Or:

a) After 8...♕f5 9 ♘c3 cxd4 (not 9...0-0?? losing the queen to 10 ♘h4) 10 ♘xd4 ♘xd4 11 ♕xd4 e5 12 ♕d3 0-0 13 ♕xf5 ♗xf5 14 ♗e3 White has a slight edge, Sveshnikov-Sunye, Moscow 1989.

b) 8...♕d7!? 9 dxc5 (9 ♘e5 ♕xd4 10 ♘xc6 bxc6 11 ♘c3 0-0 12 ♗e3 ♕e5 ∓ Matthias-Romanishin, Lippstadt 1999) 9...♗xc5 10 ♘c3 b6 11 a3 ♗b7 12 b4 ♗e7 13 ♗f4 0-0 14 ♕xd7! ♘xd7 15 ♖fd1 ♘f6 (the move-order used in Magem-Ionescu, Berga 1995) transposes to 8...♕d8 9 dxc5 ♕xd1 10 ♖xd1 ♗xc5 11 ♘c3 0-0 12 a3 b6 13 ♗f4 ♗e7.

9 dxc5 ♕xd1 10 ♖xd1 (D)
10...♗xc5

This move looks more natural than 10...♘e4, which is also often played. 11 ♗e3 ♗xc5 (11...♘b4 is worse, as after 12 ♘bd2 ♘xc5 13 ♘d4 a5 14 a3 ♘ba6 15 b4 ♘a4 16 ♖dc1 0-0 17 c5 e5 18 ♘4b3 f5 19 g3, the black knights are very bad on the a-file, Ivanchuk-Petursson, Lucerne Wcht 1993) 12 ♘d4 ♗d7 13 ♗f3 ♘xd4 14 ♗xd4, and then:

a) 14...0-0-0 is clever, but wrong:

a1) 15 ♗xg7 only leads to a draw after 15...♘xf2 16 ♖xd7 ♔xd7 17 ♗xh8 ♘g4+ 18 ♔h1 (not 18 ♔f1? ♘xh2+ 19 ♔e2 ♘xf3 20 ♗f6 ♘d4+ 21 ♔d3 ♖g8 −+) 18...♘f2+ with perpetual check, Sveshnikov-M.Makarov, Moscow 1991.

a2) 15 ♗xe4 ♗c6 (15...♖a4? loses to 16 ♘c3!) 16 ♗d5 ♗xd4 17 ♖xd4 exd5 18 c5 ± Malaniuk-Al Modiahki, Calcutta 1995.

b) 14...♗xd4 15 ♖xd4 ♘f6 16 ♘c3 0-0-0 17 ♖ad1 ♗c6 18 ♖xd8+ ♖xd8 19 ♖xd8+ ♔xd8 20 ♗xc6 bxc6 21 f3 leads to an endgame that should be drawn but where Black has some problems to solve. In Sveshnikov-A.Sokolov, Moscow 1991, White managed to win by advancing his queenside pawns.

11 ♘c3 0-0 12 a3 b6

Or 12...a5 13 ♗f4 ♗d7 14 ♘a4 ♗a7 15 ♗d6 ♖fd8 16 ♘c3 ♗e8 17 c5 ♘d7 18 ♘a4 ± Espinosa-Pazos, San Salvador Z 1995.

13 b4 ♗e7 14 ♗f4 ♗b7 15 ♘b5 ♖ad8 *(D)*

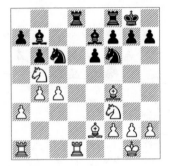

16 ♗c7

16 ♘e5 is an alternative:

a) 16...a6 17 ♘xc6 ♗xc6 18 ♘c3 ♖xd1+ 19 ♖xd1 ♖c8 (19...♖d8? 20 ♗c7 ♖xd1+ 21 ♗xd1 ♘d7 22 ♗a4 ± Magem-Ionescu, Berga 1995) 20 ♗e3 ♖b8 and Black is slightly worse.

b) 16...a5!? 17 ♘xc6 ♗xc6 18 bxa5 bxa5 19 ♗c7 ♖xd1+ 20 ♖xd1 ♖a8 ± Sveshnikov-Serper, Minsk 1986; in the ensuing complex ending, Sveshnikov overpressed and lost.

16...♖xd1+ 17 ♖xd1 ♖c8 18 ♗d6

After 18 ♗f4 ♗a8!, Black is well-prepared to defend his queenside. White is not gaining anything after 19 ♘e5 ♘xe5 20 ♘xa7 ♖c7 21 ♘b5 ♖xc4 22 ♗xe5 ♖c2 23 ♗d3 ♖c8 and a draw is inevitable, Benjamin-Serper, New York 1996.

18...♔f8 19 ♗xe7+ ♔xe7 20 ♘d6 ♖b8

20...♖c7? 21 ♘g5 ♘d8 22 ♘b5 costs Black a pawn.

21 b5! ♘d8 22 ♘e5 ♗d5! 23 ♘f5+ exf5 24 cxd5 ♔d6

White has a slight endgame advantage, Kharlov-Istratescu, Metz 1993. Kharlov suggests 25 f4! as the best way to continue.

B2)
7...cxd4 8 cxd4

With the bishop on e2, it is tempting to play 8 ♘xd4 freeing the f3-square for the bishop: 8...♘xd4 9 cxd4 ♗e7 10 ♘c3 ♕d6 11 ♕b3!? (11 ♗f3 0-0 12 ♗e3 ♘d5 13 ♘xd5 exd5 14 ♕b3 ♗e6 = Sveshnikov-Lerner, Podolsk 1993) 11...♕xd4 (11...0-0 12 ♖d1 ♘d5 13 ♗f3 ♖d8 14 g3! ± Smagin-J.Horvath, Sochi 1987) 12 ♘b5 ♕b6 13 ♗e3 ♕a5 ∞ Sveshnikov.

8...♗e7 9 ♘c3 *(D)*

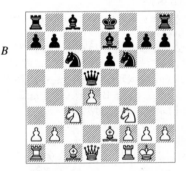

9...♕d6 *(D)*

9...♕d8 is more passive and most importantly doesn't stop ♘e5. 10 ♗e3 0-0 (10...♘d5 11 ♘xd5 ♕xd5 12 a3 followed by ♖c1 ± Sveshnikov) 11 ♘e5 and now:

a) 11...♗d6 12 f4! ± Sveshnikov.

b) 11...♘d5 12 ♘xd5 exd5 13 ♕b3 ♘a5 14 ♕a4 f6 (Sveshnikov-A.Sokolov, Moscow 1983) 15 ♘d3 ±.

c) 11...♘b4 12 ♗f3 ♘bd5 13 ♕b3 ♘xe3 (or 13...a5 14 ♖ac1 ♘xc3 15 bxc3 a4 16 ♕c2 ♘d5 17 c4 ♘b4 18 ♕b1 a3 19 ♖fd1 ± Sveshnikov-J.Polgar, Biel IZ 1993) 14 fxe3 ♘d7 15 ♘c4 (Sveshnikov) gives White a strong pawn-centre and active pieces.

W

10 ♘b5

White's most testing move. Alternatives:

a) 10 ♕b3 0-0 11 ♖d1 b6 12 ♘b5 ♕b8 (12...♕d8 13 ♘e5 ♗b7 14 ♕h3 ∞ Balshan-Speelman, Hastings 1978/9) 13 ♘e5 ♘xd4 = Bowden-Quinn, British League (4NCL) 1998/9.

b) 10 ♗g5 0-0 and then:

b1) 11 ♖c1 ♘d5! (11...b6? 12 ♗xf6 ♗xf6 13 ♘e4) 12 ♗xe7 ♘cxe7 13 ♘e5 b6 14 ♗d3 ♗b7 15 ♘e4 ♕d8 16 ♘g5 ♘f5 17 ♕d2 h6 18 ♘gf3 ♘d6 ∓ Afek-P.Schlosser, Herzliya 1998.

b2) After 11 ♕d2 b6 12 ♖ad1 ♗b7 Black is ready to blockade the isolated pawn by 13...♘d5 (or 13...♘b4 first), so White has nothing better than to advance his d-pawn: 13 ♗f4 ♕d8 14 d5

exd5 15 ♘xd5 ♘xd5 16 ♕xd5 ♕xd5 17 ♖xd5 ♖ad8 with a drawish endgame.

c) After 10 ♗e3, both white bishops are passive but White hopes to activate them by playing ♕d2, ♗f4, ♘e5 and ♗f3. Following 10...0-0 11 ♖c1 *(D)*, Black has:

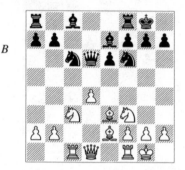

B

c1) 11...♘b4 12 ♘b5 (12 ♕b3 ±) 12...♕d8 13 ♘c7 ♖b8 14 d5!? ♘xa2 15 ♗xa7 ♘xc1 16 ♕xc1 exd5! 17 ♗xb8 ♗d6 ½-½ Harley-J.Sharp, London jr 1987.

c2) 11...a6 12 ♕d2 ♘b4 13 ♘e5 ♘bd5 14 ♗f3 b5 15 ♘c6! ♘xe3 16 ♕xe3 ♗b7 17 ♘xe7+ (17 d5!? ♗xc6 18 dxc6 ±) 17...♕xe7 18 d5 b4 19 d6 ♕d7 20 ♗xb7 ♕xb7 21 ♘a4, Harley-McDonald, British Ch (Norwich) 1994, and now 21...♖fd8 is unclear.

c3) 11...♘g4!? 12 ♕d2 (12 ♗d3 ♘xe3 13 fxe3 g6 is unclear – Khenkin) 12...♘xe3 13 ♕xe3!? ♗d7 (Harley-Summerscale, London 1994) 14 ♖fd1 ♘b4 15 a3 ♘d5 16 ♘xd5 ♕xd5 17 ♗c4 ±.

c4) 11...♖d8 12 ♕d2 and then:

c41) 12...b6? 13 ♗f4 ♕d7 14 ♗b5 ♗d6 (14...♗b7 15 ♘e5 ♕e8 16 ♘e2

♖ac8 17 ♕c2 ♘xd4 18 ♗xe8 ♖xc2 19
♗xf7+ +−) 15 d5! exd5 16 ♗g5 +−
Harley-Hennigan, British Ch (Norwich) 1994.

c42) 12...♘d5 13 ♘e4 ♕b4 14 ♕c2
h6 (14...♘xe3? 15 fxe3 ♕a5 16 a3 h6
17 ♘fd2! ± Benjamin-Yermolinsky,
USA Ch (Parsippany) 1996) 15 a3 ♕a5
(with the idea of ...♗d7-e8) 16 ♘c5
♗xc5 17 dxc5 e5 18 ♗d2 ♕c7 19 b4
♗g4 ∞ Yermolinsky.

c5) 11...b6 and then:

c51) 12 ♘b5?! ♕d7 13 ♘e5 ♘xe5
14 ♖c7 ♕d8 15 dxe5 ♘d5 ∓ Přibyl-
Tal, Erevan 1982.

c52) 12 ♘e5?! ♘xe5 13 dxe5 ♕xe5
14 ♗f3 ♗a6 15 ♖e1 ♖ad8 16 ♕a4
♕a5 17 ♕xa5 bxa5 18 ♗xa7 ♖d2 with
a slight advantage for Black, Biro-
P.Horvath, Budapest 2001.

c53) 12 a3 ♗b7 13 b4 ♖fd8 14
♕b3 ♖ac8 15 ♖fd1 h6 16 h3 ∞ transposes to I.Rogers-Tarjan, Buenos Aires OL 1978.

c54) 12 ♕d2 ♗b7 13 ♗f4 ♕d8 14
♖fd1 ♘b4 15 ♘e5 ♖c8 16 a3 ♘bd5 17
♗f3 ♗a8 18 ♘xd5 ♗xd5 19 ♘c6 ♕d7
20 ♘xe7+ ♕xe7 21 ♗e2 = Sveshnikov-Tukmakov, USSR Ch (Riga) 1985.
Black firmly blockades the pawn,
while White has the bishop-pair.

We now return to the position after
10 ♘b5 *(D)*:

10...♕d8

After the awkward 10...♕b8 White
plays 11 g3 ♘d5 12 ♗c4 a6 13 ♗xd5
axb5 14 ♗e4 0-0 (after 14...♗d7 15 d5
exd5 16 ♕xd5 Black is unable to castle and can't finish his development,
Tisdall-Fossan, Norwegian Ch (Alta)
1996) 15 ♕e2 ±.

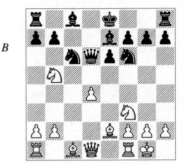

11 ♗f4

After 11 ♘e5 0-0 12 ♘xc6 (12 ♗f3
♕b6 = L.Bronstein-Ricardi, Argentinean Ch (Salta) 1987) 12...bxc6 13 ♘c3,
White would have a slight edge in the
endgame if Black failed to respond
immediately with 13...c5! 14 ♗e3 cxd4
15 ♕xd4 = (Smyslov).

11...♘d5

Or 11...0-0:

a) The slow 12 ♖c1 allows Black to
develop his pieces: 12...a6 13 ♘c3 (13
♘c7 is not dangerous: after 13...♖a7
14 ♕b3 ♗d6 15 ♗xd6 ♕xd6 16 ♕b6
♘d7 17 ♖xc6 ♕xc6 18 ♕xa7 ♕xc7
Black is fine, as White can't win a
pawn by 19 ♗xa6? due to 19...♕a5)
13...♘b4 14 ♕b3 b6 15 a3 ♘bd5 16
♗e5 ♗b7 = Rozentalis-Kaidanov, Vilnius 1984.

b) White should attack the queen:
12 ♗c7! ♕d7 (12...♕d5 13 ♘e5) 13
♘e5 ♘xe5 14 dxe5 (14 ♗xe5 is also
possible) 14...♘d5 15 ♗d6 a6 16 ♗xe7
♕xe7 17 ♘d6 ♗d7 18 ♕d4 ♗c6 19 f4
and White's strong knight assures him
a small but stable edge, Yagupov-
S.Kiseliov, Orel 1994.

12 ♗g3 *(D)*

12...a6

B

Or 12...0-0 13 ♗c4! a6 14 ♗xd5:

a) 14...exd5 15 ♘c7 and now:

a1) 15...♖b8 16 ♖c1 (16 ♘e5? is bad, as Black wins two pieces for a rook and pawn: 16...♗d6 17 ♘xa6 ♗xe5 18 ♘xb8 ♗xb8) 16...♗d6 17 ♘xa6 bxa6 18 ♖xc6 ♗xg3 19 hxg3 ♖xb2, Golod-Röder, Groningen 1995, and now White could play 20 a3 followed by 21 ♕c1, obtaining some advantage because the black bishop is very passive.

a2) 15...♖a7 16 ♕b3 ♗d6 (16...♗g4 doesn't solve all the problems, as after 17 ♖fd1 ♗d6 18 ♘xd5 ♗xg3 19 hxg3 ♗e6 20 ♘f6+ ♕xf6 21 d5 ♗g4 22 dxc6 ♕xc6 23 ♖ac1, Black has an uneasy task trying to neutralize White's activity) 17 ♗xd6 ♕xd6 18 ♕b6 f6 19 ♖ac1 ♖f7 (after 19...♗g4 20 ♖c5 ♗xf3 21 gxf3 White wins a pawn, because 21...♕f4 loses a piece to 22 ♖xc6) 20 ♘e8 ♕d7 (20...♕f4 21 ♖xc6 bxc6 22 ♕d8 ♖f8 23 ♕xc8 ♖e7 24 ♕xa6 ♖fxe8 25 ♕xc6 and the two pawns are better than the exchange – Lautier) 21 ♖fe1 a5 22 ♘c7 h6 23 ♘e6 a4 24 h3 ♖a6 25 ♕c5 and White has a positional advantage, Lautier-J.Polgar, Linares 1994.

b) 14...axb5 15 ♗e4 and then:

b1) After 15...♘b4, as played in S.Lalić-Pogorelov, Saragossa 1995, 16 ♕e2! f5 17 ♗b1 is best, when 17...f4 is bad because of 18 ♕e4.

b2) White also has an advantage in the case of 15...b4 16 ♗c2 followed by 17 ♕d3 and 18 ♗b3.

b3) 15...♖a6 16 ♕e2 f5 17 ♗xc6 (17 ♗d3 ♘b4 18 ♗xb5 f4) 17...bxc6 18 ♗f4 leaves White slightly better due to the bad black bishop on c8 – Sveshnikov.

13 ♘c3 0-0 14 ♖c1

14 ♕b3 is less accurate:

a) 14...♘xc3 15 bxc3 b5 16 ♖fd1 ♗b7 17 a4 b4 18 d5 (18 c4 ♘a5 is good for Black; 18 cxb4 ♘xb4) 18...exd5 19 cxb4 ♘xb4 20 a5 gives White enough compensation for the pawn, but no more than that, Cherniaev-Khenkin, Biel 1994.

b) 14...♘f6! 15 ♖fd1 b5 gives Black a slight advantage, Daniliuk-Galkin, Briansk 1995.

14...♘f6

Or 14...♘xc3 15 bxc3, and then:

a) 15...♗f6 16 a4 ♗d7 17 c4 ♖c8 18 d5 (instead of 18 c5 ♘b4 19 ♗d6 ♗e7 = Smirnov-Kobaliya, Russian Ch (Samara) 2000) and the passed d-pawn becomes very dangerous.

b) 15...b5 16 a4 b4 17 c4 ♗f6 18 d5 exd5 19 cxd5 ♘e7 20 ♕b3 a5 ½-½ Schandorff-Cu.Hansen, Danish Ch (Odense) 1994, but White is better after 21 ♖fd1.

15 a3 *(D)*

Or:

a) 15 h3 is unnecessary because White does not fear the exchange of his dark-squared bishop at the moment, and anyway here allows the immediate 15...b5 16 ♘xb5 axb5 17 ♖xc6 ♖xa2 18 ♕b3 ♕d5 =.

b) Interesting is 15 ♗d3!? b5 16 ♗b1 ♗b7 17 ♖e1 ♖c8 18 a4 b4 19 ♘e2 ♕b6 20 ♕d3 ♖fd8 21 ♗h4 ∞ Acs-Szelag, Rimavska Sobota U-16 Ech 1996. It is worth comparing the similar positions after 6 ♗d3 earlier in this chapter, though obviously here White is one tempo down.

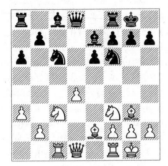

B

15...b6

Not 15...b5? 16 ♘xb5 axb5 17 ♖xc6 winning a pawn.

After 15...♘h5?! 16 ♕d3 ♘xg3 17 hxg3, White is better since he can gain control of the d5-square, and Sveshnikov has won a fair few games from this position.

16 ♗c4

Otherwise:

a) 16 h3 maintains the tension, but allows Black to gain play on the queenside: 16...♗b7 17 ♗d3 ♖c8 18 ♗b1 b5 19 ♕d3 ♘a5 20 ♘e5 ♘c4, J.Polgar-Tiviakov, Madrid 1994.

b) 16 d5 liquidates the centre immediately, and leads to an equal endgame: 16...exd5 17 ♘xd5 ♕xd5 18

♕xd5 ♘xd5 19 ♖xc6 ♗b7, Dončević-Bischoff, Bundesliga 1992/3.

16...♗b7

The position is very complex and tactical opportunities abound for both sides.

16...b5 17 ♗a2 ♕b6 is an alternative:

a) 18 d5 and rather than 18...exd5? 19 ♘xd5 ♘xd5 (S.Kasparov-Yagupov, Pavlograd 2000) 20 ♖xc6! +−, Black should play 18...♖d8!.

b) White can instead play 18 ♕d3 ♗b7 19 b4 ♖ac8, transposing to the line *16...♗b7 17 ♗a2 ♖c8 18 ♕d3 b5 19 b4 ♕b6*.

17 ♗a2 ♖c8 18 ♕d3 b5 19 b4

19 ♖fd1 ♕b6 20 ♘g5 ♖fd8 21 d5 and now 21...h6? 22 ♘xf7! ♔xf7 23 d6 ♗f8 24 ♕f5 ± worked out well for White in Karpachev-Groetz, Salzburg 2001, but 21...b4! is strong.

19...♕b6 20 ♖fd1 ♖fd8

The position is complex, and the chances probably evenly balanced. Here are two examples of how quickly fortune can turn in this position:

a) 21 ♗b1 g6 22 ♕e3? a5! 23 bxa5 ♘xa5 24 ♘e5 ♘b3 0-1 J.Littlewood-Turner, British League (4NCL) 1997/8.

b) 21 ♗h4 ♖d7 22 d5 ♕d8? 23 ♗b1 g6 24 dxc6! ± Cherniaev-A.Petrosian, Erevan open 1996.

C)

6 ♘a3 (D)

This is the move White should play if he feels uncomfortable with an isolated queen's pawn. The idea is to recapture on d4 with the queen's knight after either ♘b5 or ♘c2. This is a lot

B

of moves to make with one piece in the opening, but in compensation Black typically has to retreat his queen to d8 to counter the threat of ♘b5 and ♘c7+, and has thus spent two moves moving his queen nowhere at all!

Black's best responses are:

C1: 6...♘c6   88
C2: 6...♕d8   90

Less good are:

a) 6...cxd4 7 ♘b5 and then:

a1) 7...♕d8 8 ♕xd4 a6 9 ♕xd8+ ♔xd8 and now White can try 10 ♘e5!? axb5 11 ♘xf7+ ♔e8 12 ♘xh8 ♗d7 (12...♗c5? 13 ♗xb5+) 13 ♗d3, when it will cost Black a lot of time and at least one more pawn to win the knight.

a2) 7...♘a6 places the knight awkwardly, and this allows White to get a nice ending by 8 ♕xd4 ♗c5 9 ♕xd5 ♘xd5 10 ♗c4 ♘b6 11 ♗e2 0-0 12 0-0 ♖d8 13 ♗f4 ♘d5 14 ♖fd1 ♗d7 15 ♗g3 ♗e8, Hort-Arakhamia, London (Women-Veterans) 1996. After 16 a3, White is ready to advance his queenside pawns, which gives him the better chances.

b) 6...a6 7 ♘c4 (turning his attention to the b6-square) 7...♘bd7 8 ♗e2

♗e7 9 0-0 0-0 10 ♘fe5 cxd4 11 ♗f3 with a big advantage for White.

c) 6...♗e7 7 ♘b5 ♘a6 and now:

c1) 8 ♗e2 0-0 9 0-0 cxd4 10 ♕xd4 ♕xd4 11 ♘bxd4 ♘c5 12 ♖d1 ♖d8 and White can't exploit Black's undeveloped bishop on c8 as 13 ♘e5?! is well met by 13...♘d5 14 c4 ♘b4 15 ♗e3 f6 16 ♘ef3 e5 17 ♘b5 ♗f5 ∓ Gurieli-Polak, Biel 1998.

c2) The immediate 8 c4 is interesting: 8...♕e4+ (or 8...♕d8 9 ♗e2 0-0 10 0-0 cxd4 11 ♗f4 ♗d7 12 ♘bxd4 ♕b6 13 ♖b1 ♕a5 14 a3 ♖fc8 15 b4 ♕d8 16 ♘e5 with a big advantage, Am.Rodriguez-Adorjan, Thessaloniki OL 1984) 9 ♗e2 cxd4 10 0-0 0-0 11 ♗d3 ♕g4 12 ♖e1 ♘d7 13 ♗e2 (Sveshnikov gives 13 a3 ♘ac5 14 ♗xh7+! as even stronger) 13...♕g6 14 ♘fxd4 ♖d8 15 ♗h5 ♕f6 16 ♗g5! ♕xg5 17 ♗xf7+ ♔xf7 18 ♘xe6 and White has won a rook and two pawns for two pieces, Sveshnikov-A.Sokolov, Sochi 1983.

C1)

6...♘c6 7 ♘b5

The logical continuation, but White also has:

a) 7 ♗e2 ♕d8! – 6...♕d8 7 ♗e2 ♘c6.

b) 7 ♗e3 and then:

b1) 7...♘g4 is bad, because after 8 ♘b5 ♘xe3 9 fxe3 ♕d8 10 d5! exd5 11 ♕xd5 ♕e7 (or 11...♕xd5 12 ♘c7+ ♔d8 13 ♘xd5 followed by 14 ♖d1 or 14 0-0-0) 12 ♘g5 ♗g4? (12...♗e6 is necessary: 13 ♘xe6 fxe6 14 ♕e4 ♖d8 15 ♗c4 with just a slight advantage for White) 13 ♘d6+ ♕xd6 14 ♕xf7+ ♔d8 15 ♕xb7 White obtains a decisive attack, Okhotnik-Magerramov, Uzh-gorod 1988.

b2) 7...cxd4 gives Black an equal game: 8 ♘b5 ♕d7 9 ♘bxd4 ♘d5 10 ♗d3 ½-½ Filipović-Vukić, Bizovac 2002.

7...♕d8

7...♕d7 is risky in view of 8 ♘e5 ♘xe5 9 dxe5 ♘d5 10 c4 ♘b4 11 ♗e3 ♗e7 12 ♕xd7+ ♔xd7 13 0-0-0+ ♔c6 14 a3 ♘a6 15 ♗e2, when White has a very large advantage.

8 dxc5 ♗xc5 9 ♕xd8+ ♔xd8 10 ♗f4 *(D)*

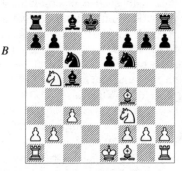

White has the initiative but practice has shown that Black can hold this endgame with precise play.

10...♘d5

10...a6 is perhaps more accurate:

a) 11 ♘d6 ♔e7 12 ♘xc8+ ♖axc8 is fine for Black as all his pieces are already well placed.

b) 11 ♘bd4 ♘xd4 12 ♘xd4 ♔e7 13 ♘b3 ♗d6 14 ♗xd6+ ♔xd6 15 ♗e2 ♔c7 16 0-0-0 ♗d7 17 ♗f3 ♗c6 and Pavasović-Aronian, Bled 1999 was soon agreed drawn.

c) 11 0-0-0+ ♗d7 (11...♔e7?! 12 ♘c7! ♖a7 13 b4 ♗b6 14 ♗d6+ ♔d7

15 b5 gives White a strong attack – Chandler) 12 ♘bd4 ♘xd4 13 ♘xd4 ♔e7 14 ♗e2 and after 14...♖ad8?! 15 ♗f3 ♗xd4 16 ♖xd4 ♗c6 17 ♖xd8 ♖xd8 18 ♗xc6 bxc6 ± White managed to win the ending in Striković-Kolev, Saragossa 1995, but Black should play 14...♗a4!, when he is fine after both 15 ♖d3 ♖hd8 and 15 b3 ♘d5! 16 ♗g5+ f6.

11 0-0-0 ♔e7 12 ♗g3 a6 13 ♘bd4 ♘xd4 14 ♘xd4 ♖d8 15 ♗e2 ♗d6

Black must be careful, because his king is still in the centre. Although it is already an endgame, a lot of pieces are still on the board and the king can become a target: 15...♗d7?! 16 ♗f3 ♗a4 17 ♖d2 ♖d7 18 ♖e1 ♖ad8 19 ♗h4+ ♘f6 20 ♗xb7! ♖xb7 21 ♘f5+ ♔e8 22 ♘xg7+ ♔f8 23 ♘xe6+, winning a rook and three pawns in return for two pieces, Sermek-Andersson, Tilburg 1994.

16 ♗xd6+

Black's rook will be slightly more uncomfortable on d6 than d8, so White exchanges bishops himself. After 16 ♗f3 ♗xg3 17 hxg3 ♘f6 18 ♖d2 ♖b8 19 ♖hd1 ♗d7 20 ♘b3 ♖dc8 Black has equalized, Sermek-Novikov, Croatian Cht (Medulin) 1997.

16...♖xd6 17 ♗f3 ♘f6 18 ♘b3 ♖xd1+

18...♖b8 19 ♘a5 ± Striković-Fran-co, San Sebastian 1994, though Black managed to win that game.

19 ♖xd1 a5 20 ♘d2 ♖b8 21 ♘c4

White has a slight advantage but Black should be able to hold the endgame with precise play, Striković-Pogorelov, Lorca 2001.

C2)
6...♕d8 *(D)*

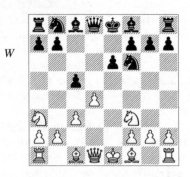

7 ♘c2

The queen has already retreated, so there is no point in the knight heading to b5, where it would just be vulnerable to ...a6. White has a number of alternative possibilities, the most promising of which is to change plans and head for e5 with the knight via c4, playing an isolated queen's pawn position after all.

a) 7 ♗e2 ♘c6 8 ♘c2 – *7 ♘c2 ♘c6 8 ♗e2*.

b) 7 ♗f4 and then:

b1) 7...cxd4 8 ♘xd4 ♘d5 (8...♗xa3 9 ♕a4+!) 9 ♗g3 ♘c6 10 ♘c4 ♗c5 11 ♘xc6 bxc6 12 ♘e5 0-0 ½-½ Pavasović-Dorfman, Cannes 1996.

b2) 7...♘c6 8 dxc5 ♘d5 9 ♗d6 ♗xd6 10 cxd6 ♕xd6 11 ♘b5 ♕e7 12 ♗c4 0-0 13 0-0 ♖d8 14 ♕c2 a6 15 ♘bd4 ♘xd4 16 ♘xd4 ♕c5 17 ♗d3 h6 with an equal position of a type that more normally arises from the French Defence, Dückstein-Vukić, Austrian Cht 1989.

c) 7 ♘c4 (White plans to put his knight on e5 and then to attack the black king on the a4-e8 diagonal, but Black has enough resources to resist) 7...♘c6 (7...♗e7 leads to a typical IQP position: 8 ♘ce5 0-0 9 ♗c4 ♘c6 10 0-0 cxd4 11 cxd4 ♗d7 12 ♕e2 ♖c8 13 ♗g5 h6 14 ♗d2 ♘b4 15 a3 ♘bd5 16 ♖fe1 ♗a4 17 b3 and White has the initiative, Rozentalis-Mikhalchishin, Lvov 1987) 8 ♘ce5 cxd4 (8...♘xe5 9 ♘xe5 a6 10 ♗e3 cxd4 11 ♗xd4 ♗e7 12 ♗d3 gives White more active pieces) 9 ♗b5 ♕d5 10 ♕a4 ♗d7! (10...a6 11 ♗xc6+ bxc6 12 0-0 dxc3 13 bxc3 ♕b5 14 ♕c2 ♘d7 15 c4 ♕b7 16 ♖b1 ♕c7 17 ♕e2 with good compensation for the pawn, Rozentalis-Yudasin, Sverdlovsk 1984) 11 ♘xd7 ♘xd7 12 ♗xc6 bxc6 13 ♕xd4 ♗c5 14 ♕xd5? (14 ♕d2! =) 14...cxd5 leaves Black better in the endgame due to his strong centre, Rozentalis-Yudasin, Lvov 1987.

d) 7 ♗g5 ♘bd7 (Gallagher suggests 7...cxd4 as an improvement) 8 ♘c4 is an interesting new plan for White: 8...♕c7 9 ♗h4 ♗e7 10 ♗g3 ♕c6 11 dxc5 ♗xc5 12 b4 ♗e7 13 ♘d4 ♕e4+ 14 ♘e3 ♘d5?! (14...♘e5 15 ♕c2 ♕xc2 16 ♘dxc2 ♘c6 is better – we think Black has no problems in this endgame) 15 ♗d3 ♘xe3 16 ♗xe4 ♘xd1 17 ♖xd1 0-0 18 ♘b3 ♘f6 19 ♗f3 and the white pieces are very active while the black bishop is still on c8, Baklan-P.Schlosser, Groningen 1998.

7...♘c6

Or:

a) 7...a6 is just a waste of time: 8 ♗d3 cxd4 9 ♘cxd4 ♗d6 10 ♗g5 ♘bd7 11 ♕e2 ♕e7 12 ♖d1 0-0 13 0-0 ♖e8 14 ♗c2 h6 15 ♗h4 ♕f8 16 ♖fe1, Godena-D.Johansen, Istanbul OL 2000. All the white pieces are active, so Black is in trouble.

b) 7...♗e7 8 ♗d3 0-0 9 0-0 ♘bd7 (this is not the best place for the knight, because from here it doesn't exert any pressure on the centre and White can place his pieces comfortably; 9...♘c6 is better, and transposes to 7...♘c6 8 ♗d3 ♗e7 9 0-0 0-0) 10 ♗f4 b6 11 ♕e2 ♗b7 12 ♖ad1 ♕c8 13 ♘e3 ♘h5 14 ♗g5 ♗xf3 15 ♕xf3 ♗xg5 16 ♕xh5 h6 17 f4 cxd4 18 cxd4 ♗f6 19 ♗e4 ♖b8 20 ♘g4 gives White a decisive attack, Vysochin-Volokitin, Ukrainian Ch (Sevastopol) 2000.

c) 7...♘bd7 (again, the knight is going to the wrong place) 8 g3 b6 9 ♗g2 ♗b7 10 0-0 ♗e7 11 ♕e2 0-0 12 ♖d1 ♕c8 13 c4 ♖e8 14 b3 a6 15 ♗b2 b5 16 ♘e3 and the white pieces are better prepared for the tension in the centre. After 16...cxd4 17 ♗xd4 b4 18 ♘e5 ♘xe5 19 ♗xe5 ♘d7 20 ♗b2 White has an advantage due to his strong passed pawn, Finkel-Chuchelov, Dieren 1997.

8 ♗d3 (D)

After 8 ♗e2 ♗e7 9 0-0 0-0 10 ♗g5 cxd4 11 ♘cxd4 ♗d7 12 ♕b3 ♘xd4 13 ♘xd4 ♕c7, Black has solved his development problems and threatens 14...♘g4, Hulak-Suba, Vinkovci 1977.

8...♗e7

This is possibly a little too passive. Alternatives:

a) 8...b6 9 0-0 ♗b7 10 ♗g5 ♗e7 11 ♕e2 (11 dxc5 bxc5 12 ♘e3 0-0 13 ♕c2 h6 14 ♗h4 ♘d5 15 ♗xe7 ♕xe7 16 ♖fe1 ♕c7 = Vuvpetić-Podlesnik, Bled 1992) 11...0-0 – 8...♗e7 9 0-0 0-0 10 ♕e2 b6 11 ♗g5 ♗b7.

B

b) 8...cxd4!? 9 ♘cxd4 ♘xd4 10 ♘xd4 ♗c5 and then:

b1) 11 ♘b3 ♗b6 12 ♕e2 ♗d7 13 ♗e3 ♘d5 = Godena-Mariotti, Italian Cht 1996.

b2) 11 ♗e3 ♗b6 12 0-0 0-0 13 ♖e1 (Beliavsky-Ehlvest, Erevan OL 1996) 13...♘d5 14 ♗d2 ♗xd4 15 cxd4 ♗d7 = Beliavsky.

b3) 11 ♘f3 0-0 12 0-0 b6 13 ♕e2 ♗b7 14 ♗g5 ♕c7!? is fine for Black.

b4) 11 0-0 (now we have reached a position from the currently fashionable Rubinstein French: *1 e4 e6 2 d4 d5 3 ♘c3 dxe4 4 ♘xe4 ♘d7 5 ♘f3 ♘gf6 6 ♘xf6+ ♘xf6 7 ♗d3 c5 8 0-0 cxd4 9 ♘xd4 ♗c5 10 c3*) 11...0-0 12 ♗g5 h6 13 ♗h4 ♗xd4! 14 cxd4 ♗d7 15 ♖e1 ♗c6 = Arencibia-Nogueiras, Cienfuegos 1997.

9 0-0 0-0 10 ♕e2 (D)

Or 10 ♗f4 cxd4 11 ♘cxd4 ♘xd4 12 ♘xd4 ♘d5 13 ♗g3 ♗d6 14 ♖e1 ♗xg3 15 hxg3 ♗d7 16 ♗e4 ♗c6 17 ♕c2 h6 18 ♖ad1 ♕c7 19 c4 ♘f6 20 ♗xc6 bxc6, Sveshnikov-Nevednichy, Ljubljana 1999. White can try to use his queenside pawn-majority, but it is not easy to do so since when the c-pawn moves, Black regains the d5-square for the knight; and Black also has some chances on the kingside.

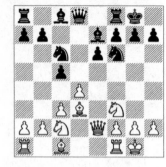

10...b6
Or:

a) 10...♗d7 11 dxc5 ♗xc5 12 ♗g5 ♗e7 13 ♖ad1 ♘d5 14 ♗c1 ♕c7 15 ♕e4 g6 16 ♖fe1 ♗f6 17 ♗h6 ♖fd8 18 ♘e3 ♘xe3 19 ♕xe3 ♗e8 is slightly better for White, Lobzhanidze-Salmensuu, Gausdal 2000.

b) 10...cxd4 11 ♘cxd4 ♘xd4 12 ♘xd4 ± is another Rubinstein French, this time with Black's bishop more passively placed on e7. If Black wishes to exchange on d4, he should do this on move 8 before developing the bishop.

11 ♗g5 ♗b7 12 dxc5 bxc5

12...♗xc5 13 ♖ad1 ♕c7 14 ♗xf6 gxf6 15 ♕e4 f5 16 ♕h4 ± Braun-Postler, W.German Ch (Frankfurt) 1977, and other games since.

13 ♖ad1 ♕c7 14 ♘a3!

The knight heads for c4 but not via the centre, as 14 ♘e3?! is answered by 14...♘d5! = Okhotnik.

14...♖fd8 15 ♘c4 g6 16 ♖fe1 ♘d5 17 g3!

White has a slight advantage, Okhotnik-Inkiov, Paris 1997.

D)
6 ♗e3 (D)

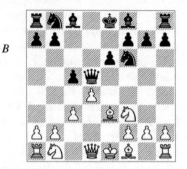

6...cxd4
Or:

a) With 6...♘g4 Black exchanges his knight for White's bishop, but it takes two tempi and also strengthens White's pawn-centre. 7 ♘bd2 ♘xe3 8 fxe3 ♘d7 9 ♗c4 (9 ♗d3 is also possible) 9...♕c6 10 0-0 ♗e7 11 ♗d3 0-0 12 ♘c4 f5 13 ♕b3 and White has a nice position, Rozentalis-Womacka, Bundesliga 1997/8.

b) 6...♘c6!? and then:

b1) 7 ♘a3 – *6 ♘a3 ♘c6 7 ♗e3 =*.

b2) 7 a3 cxd4 8 cxd4 ♗e7 9 ♘c3 ♕d6 – *6...cxd4 7 cxd4 ♘c6 8 ♘c3 ♕d6 9 a3 ♗e7*.

b3) 7 dxc5 ♕xd1+ 8 ♔xd1 ♘g4 9 b4 ♘xe3+ 10 fxe3 a5 11 ♗b5 ♗d7 12 ♘bd2 (12 a3 axb4 13 ♗xc6 ♗xc6 14 cxb4 b6 15 ♘c3 bxc5 16 b5 ± Varavin-Serper, Novosibirsk 1989) 12...axb4 13 ♗xc6 ♗xc6 14 cxb4 and White keeps his extra pawn but Black has the bishop-pair, Poluliakhov-Beshukov, Bydgoszcz 2000. White won that game, but more games are needed to come to a conclusion.

c) 6...♘bd7!? is an interesting attempt to prove that 6 ♗e3 doesn't force the exchange on d4 after all. More tests are needed, but to date this has looked like a promising equalizing option for Black. We suggest White tries 7 c4 (7 ♗d3 ♗e7 8 0-0 0-0 9 c4 ♕d6 10 ♘c3 cxd4 11 ♘xd4 a6 12 ♕e2 = Erenburg-Ortega Hermida, Oropesa del Mar 2001) 7...♕d6 8 ♘c3 cxd4 9 ♗xd4!? (9 ♘xd4 a6 10 ♗e2 ♗e7 11 0-0 0-0 12 a3 ♕c7 ½-½ Vajda-C.Horvath, Budapest 2002) and then:

c1) 9...♗e7 10 ♗d3 0-0 11 0-0 e5 12 ♗e3 with control of the d5- and e4-squares.

c2) 9...a6 10 ♗d3 ♕c7 11 0-0 ♗c5 12 ♖c1 with some advantage.

7 cxd4 *(D)*

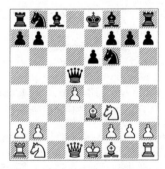

7...♘c6

This is the best square for the queen's knight. Alternatively:

a) 7...♗e7 8 ♘c3 ♕d8 (we would prefer 8...♕d6) 9 ♗d3 0-0 10 0-0 ♗d7 11 ♕c2 ♗c6 12 ♘e5 ♘bd7 13 ♖ad1 ♕a5 14 f4 g6 15 ♘xc6 bxc6 16 f5 exf5 17 ♗h6 ♖fe8 18 ♗xf5 with an initiative, Rozentalis-Lukin, Daugavpils 1989.

b) 7...♗b4+ 8 ♘c3 0-0 9 ♗d3 b6 10 0-0 ♗xc3 11 bxc3 ♗a6 has scored very well for Black, but White should have a comfortable game as he can establish a pawn-centre that is not vulnerable and gives him a lot of space; for example, 12 ♗xa6 ♘xa6 13 ♕e2 (13 ♕a4 ♘c7 14 c4 ± may be better) 13...♕b7 (13...b5!? 14 a4 ♕c4 ∞ Byway) 14 a4 ♘c7 15 c4 ♖ac8 16 ♖fd1 ± (instead of 16 ♖fb1 ♘e4 17 ♗d2?! ♘xd2 = D.Pedersen-Miezis, Andorra 2001).

8 ♘c3 ♕d6

8...♕d8 (with the idea of later putting his queen on a5) and then:

a) 9 ♗c4 ♗e7 10 0-0 0-0 11 ♘e5 ♗d7! (11...♘b4 12 ♕f3; 11...♘a5 12 ♗e2) 12 ♖c1 ♖c8 13 ♗e2 ♘b4 14 ♕b3 ♗c6 15 a3 ♘bd5 16 ♘xc6 bxc6 = Polak-I.Rogers, Biel 1992.

b) 9 a3 ♗e7 10 ♗d3 0-0 11 ♕c2 ♗d7 12 0-0 ♖c8 13 ♖ad1 ♕a5 14 ♖fe1 ♖fd8 15 ♕e2 ♗e8 16 ♗c4 h6, Rozentalis-Gheorghiu, Liechtenstein 1991. Now after 17 h3 Black is solid, but White is more active.

9 a3

The natural 9 ♗c4 doesn't bring White anything: 9...♗e7 10 0-0 0-0 11 ♕e2 a6 12 ♖ad1 b5 13 ♗b3 ♘b4 14 ♗g5 ♗b7 and Black is fine, Rozentalis-Serper, Vilnius 1988.

9...♗e7 10 ♗d3 *(D)*

10 ♕c2!? is an interesting idea to stop 10...b6 (because of 11 ♘b5 ♕d7 12 ♘e5) and thus try to force play into the line *10 ♗d3 0-0 11 ♕c2* after 10...0-0 11 ♗d3. Black can try to take advantage of White's unusual move-order by delaying castling: 10...♗d7

11 &d3 (11 ♖d1 ♖c8 12 &d3 ♘d5 =
Ekström-Kurajica, Dresden Z 1998)
11...♖c8 12 0-0 h6 (Vlassov-*Deep Junior*, KasparovChess 2000), but this is
not especially convincing for Black.

Black has two options here:
D1: 10...0-0   94
D2: 10...b6   95

It is difficult to say which plan is
better for Black: to put his bishop on
b7, where it has good potential to be
activated, but on the other hand is a
long way from the kingside; or to play
...&d7 followed by ...&e8, where it
protects his king but is passive.

D1)

10...0-0 11 ♕c2

This move prevents the immediate
11...b6, because then Black loses a
pawn after 12 ♘e4. White also attacks
the h7-pawn, and while it is protected
for the moment, sooner or later Black
will have to play ...g6 or ...h6, weakening his king's defences.

11 0-0 is the alternative:
a) After 11...♘d5 12 ♕c2 g6 13
♘xd5 exd5 14 ♖ae1 &f6 15 b4 White
gains a small but permanent strategic

advantage: 15...&d7?! 16 ♕d2 &e6
17 &f4 ♕d8 18 &h6 &g7 19 ♕f4 ±
Rozentalis-Epishin, Daugavpils 1989.
b) 11...b6 – *10...b6 11 0-0 0-0.*
11...&d7
The bishop goes to e8 to protect the
black king. Black can also determine
his kingside structure immediately:
a) 11...h6 12 0-0 and then:
a1) 12...b6 13 ♖ad1 &b7 14 ♖fe1
♖ac8? (14...♖fd8 followed by 15...&f8
is needed) 15 ♕c1! ♘d5 16 &xh6 +−
Benjamin-Zimmer, Parsippany 1998.
a2) 12...♖d8 13 ♖ad1 &f8 14 ♖fe1
&d7 15 ♕e2 ♘e7 16 ♘e5 &c6 17 &f4
♘ed5 18 &g3 ♘xc3 19 bxc3 ♕d5 20
f4 gives White a very strong centre,
Rozentalis-Åkesson, Malmö 1997. His
next idea is to play 21 &h4 followed
by 22 f5.
b) 11...g6 12 0-0 b6 13 ♖ad1 &b7
14 ♖fe1 and here:
b1) 14...♖ac8 15 ♕e2 ♖fe8 16 &c4
♘d5 and now 17 ♘e4 gives White
good play on the kingside (instead of
17 &xd5 exd5 18 &h6 f6 with equality, Rozentalis-Hellers, Stockholm Rilton Cup 1990/1).
b2) With 14...♘g4, Black attacks
the bishop, but reduces his control over
the key d5-square. 15 &e4 ♖ac8 16
♕e2 ♘xe3 17 ♕xe3 &f6 18 d5 ♘a5 19
dxe6 ♕xe6 and now 20 &xb7 (instead
of 20 ♘d4 ♕e7 = Rozentalis-Tiviakov, Groningen FIDE 1997) 20...♕xe3
21 ♖xe3 ♘xb7 22 ♖d7 gives White
the better endgame.
12 0-0 ♖ac8
The alternative line 12...h6 13 ♖ad1
♖fd8 14 ♕c1 (Rozentalis-P.Schlosser,
Bundesliga 1999/00) gives White two

dangerous threats with the same piece: 15 ♗f4 and 15 ♗xh6.

13 ♖ad1 ♖fd8 14 ♖fe1 ♗e8 *(D)*

15 ♗c1

White has some other interesting possibilities:

a) 15 ♗g5 h6 16 ♗h4 with some pressure.

b) 15 ♕e2 and now:

b1) 15...♕c7 16 ♗b1 b6 17 ♗g5 h6 18 ♗h4 ♔f8 19 ♗a2 ♘d5 20 ♘xd5 exd5 21 ♕d3, Rozentalis-Kamber, Suhr 1990. White threatens to penetrate to h7, which is difficult to prevent.

b2) 15...g6 16 ♗c4 ♕c7 17 ♗a2 ♕a5 18 ♗g5 ♖d7 19 h3 ♘d5 20 ♗xd5 (a typical exchange – the c3-knight will be stronger than the e8-bishop) 20...exd5 21 ♗xe7 ♖xe7 22 ♕d2 is slightly better for White, Rozentalis-Blatny, Debrecen Echt 1992.

b3) 15...♕b8 16 ♗b1 a6 17 ♗a2 b5 18 ♗g5 h6 19 ♗h4 b4 20 axb4 ♘xb4 21 ♗b1 ♘bd5 22 ♘xd5 ♘xd5 23 ♕e4 gives White a very dangerous attack, Rozentalis-Novikov, USSR Ch (Leningrad) 1990.

b4) 15...♘d5 16 ♘e4 ♕c7 17 ♗b1 ♕b6 (Yanovsky-Dolmatov, Dortmund

1992) 18 ♗c1 ♘a5 19 ♘c5! gives White some advantage, though more tests are needed.

15...h6

Or 15...♔h8 16 ♗e4 ♘xe4 17 ♕xe4 ♗f6 18 ♗g5 ♕e7 19 ♗xf6 ♕xf6 20 d5 exd5 21 ♘xd5 ♕g6 22 ♕e3, when White is better because his pieces are more active, Rozentalis-Staniszewski, Polish Cht (Krynica) 1997.

16 ♕e2 ♗f8 17 ♗b1 g6 18 ♗a2 ♗g7 19 h3

The position is rather complicated, but we prefer White, Rozentalis-Andersson, Tilburg 1993.

D2)

10...b6 *(D)*

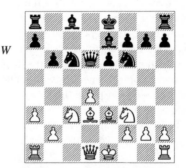

11 0-0

White can try to stop Black castling by 11 ♖c1:

a) If 11...♗b7, White obtains an advantage by 12 ♘b5 ♕d8 (12...♕d7 13 ♘e5) 13 ♘e5 ♖c8 14 ♘xc6 ♖xc6 15 ♘xa7 ♖xc1 16 ♕xc1 with an extra pawn – Nisipeanu and Stoica.

b) However, Black can still castle, as after 11...0-0 12 ♘e4 ♘xe4 13 ♗xe4 ♗b7 14 ♕c2 ♖ac8 15 ♗xh7+ ♔h8 16

♕d3 g6 17 ♗xg6 fxg6 18 ♕xg6 ♗f6 19 ♘g5 ♕d7 White has nothing more than perpetual check.

11...0-0 12 ♕e2 ♗b7 13 ♖ad1 *(D)*

13...♖ad8

It might seem natural to put a rook on the c-file, given that it is the only open file. However, in this specific position, there is no point in doing so, since all the pieces are still on the board, and all the squares on the c-file are under control. Therefore, it is better for both sides to place their rooks on the d- and e-files.

These moves are less accurate:

a) 13...♘g4 14 ♗xh7+! ♔xh7 15 ♘e4 with a strong attack – Gallagher.

b) 13...♖ac8 14 ♖fe1 ♘d5? (Black should play 14...♖fd8) 15 ♘xd5 exd5 (15...♕xd5 16 ♗c4 ♕h5 17 d5 ♘a5 18 ♗a2 ♗xd5 19 ♗xd5 exd5 20 ♗xb6, Manca-Emms, Cappelle la Grande 1993, 20...axb6 21 ♕xe7 ±) 16 ♘e5 ♘xe5 17 ♗f4 ♕d7 18 dxe5 with an advantage for White, Rozentalis-Mikhalchishin, Trnava 1988.

c) 13...h6 14 ♗b1 ♖fd8?! (14...♖ad8 is better) 15 ♕c2 ♖ac8 16 d5 ♘e5 17 ♘xe5 ♕xe5 18 ♗d4 ♕g5 19 ♗xf6

♗xf6 20 ♕h7+ ♔f8 21 ♘e4 ♕f4 22 ♘xf6 (but not 22 d6 g5 with unclear chances, Adams-Poluliakhov, New York 1996) 22...♕xf6 23 dxe6 with a slight edge for White – Adams.

d) 13...♖fd8 14 ♖fe1 ♖ac8 (14...h6 15 ♗c1 ♗f8 16 ♗b1 ♘e7 17 ♘e5 ♘f5, Rozentalis-Andersson, Tilburg blitz 1993, 18 ♘g4 gives White the initiative) 15 ♗c1 h6 16 ♗b1 ♗f8 17 ♘e4 ♘xe4 18 ♕xe4 with an attack on the kingside, Rozentalis-Andersson, Tilburg rpd 1993.

14 ♗b1 ♖fe8

Or 14...♘d5 15 ♘e4 ♕d7 (after 15...♕c7 16 ♗c1 ♘f4 17 ♕e3 ♘g6 18 ♘c3 White takes control over the key d5-square; for example: 18...♘a5 19 ♗a2) 16 ♗c1 f5 17 ♘c3, stressing the weaknesses in the centre (but not 17 ♘eg5 ♗xg5 18 ♘xg5 ♘c7, when Black wins the d-pawn, for which White will have merely sufficient compensation, Rozentalis-Goldin, Vilnius 1988).

15 ♖fe1

Blatny suggests 15 ♕c2 here, but Black is liable to play ...g6 soon anyway without White needing to force it so explicitly.

15...♕b8 *(D)*

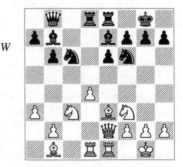

16 ♗g5

This is the most common move here. White attacks the knight that defends both h7 and d5. Some other tries in this position are:

a) 16 ♘g5!? ♗d6 17 ♘ce4 ♘xe4 18 ♗xe4 h6 19 ♘xf7!? ♔xf7 20 ♕h5+ (20 ♕f3+ ♔g8 21 ♗xc6 ♖f8 22 ♕e4 ♗xc6 23 ♕xc6 ♗xh2+ 24 ♔h1 ♗d6 = Blatny) 20...♔g8 21 ♗xh6!, Motwani-J.Bellin, Walsall 1992, and now after 21...♗xh2+ 22 ♔h1 gxh6! (22...♗f4 23 ♗xf4 ♕xf4 24 ♗g6 ♕h6 25 ♗xe8 ♖xe8 26 ♕xh6 gxh6 27 d5 ♘d8 28 dxe6 leads to a better position for White) 23 ♕g6+ ♔f8 24 ♕xh6+ ♔e7 25 ♗xc6 ♗xc6 26 ♕xe6+ ♔f8 27 ♕f6+ ♔g8 28 ♕xc6 ♗d6, White probably has nothing more than perpetual check.

b) 16 ♗a2 g6 17 h3 (stopping ...♘g4 ideas) 17...♕a8 ∞ Pavasović-Kobaliya, Batumi Echt 1999.

c) 16 b4!? g6 17 ♗a2 ♘d5?! (better is 17...♘g4) 18 ♘xd5 exd5 19 ♕d2 ± Vajda-P.Horvath, Budapest 2002.

16...g6

Or:

a) 16...♘a5 17 ♘e5 gives White an advantage.

b) 16...♘d5 17 ♕e4 g6 18 ♕h4 ♘xc3 19 bxc3 ± V.Ivanov-Yakovich, Russian Ch (Elista) 1994.

17 ♗a2 *(D)*

17 h4 ♘g4! 18 ♗xe7 ♖xe7 19 ♘e5 = Jonkman-Tiviakov, Valle d'Aosta 2002.

17...♘h5

Interesting is 17...♘g4!? 18 g3 (18 ♗xe6? ♘xd4 19 ♖xd4 ♖xd4 20 ♗xg4 ♖xg4 21 ♗xe7, as given by Gallagher,

B

is well met by 21...♕f4! −+) 18...♘f6 19 ♕e3 ♘g4 20 ♕e2 ♘f6 21 ♕e3 ♘g4 22 ♕c1 ♘f6 23 d5!? ♘xd5 (23...exd5 24 ♖xe7!) 24 ♗xd5 exd5 25 ♘xd5 ♗xg5 26 ♕xg5 ♖xe1+ 27 ♖xe1 ♕d6 28 ♘f6+, and now:

a) 28...♔g7 29 ♘e8+ ♖xe8 30 ♖xe8 ♕d1+ 31 ♘e1 ♘d4 32 ♕e5+ ♔h6 is given by Gallagher as perpetual check, but White is probably winning after 33 ♕e3+ ♔g7 34 f4! ♘f3+ 35 ♔f2 ♘xh2 36 ♕e5+ ♔h6 37 ♕g5+ ♔g7 38 ♕d8! ♘g4+ 39 ♔g1, though you'd have to be a computer to play this over the board without preparation.

b) 28...♔h8 29 ♕h4 ♔g7 (29...h5 30 ♕g5 ♕f8 ± Gallagher) ½-½ Berelovich-Korneev, Minsk 1998, but Gallagher points out that the continuation 30 ♕xh7+ ♔xf6 31 g4! ♘e5 32 g5+ ♔e7 33 ♘xe5 ♕d5 34 f3 should be winning for White.

18 d5

18 ♗h6 ♗f6 19 ♕e3 ♗g7 20 ♗xg7 ♔xg7 21 ♘e5 ♘f6 22 h3 ♘e7 (Adams-Hulak, Wijk aan Zee 1995) 23 ♕f4 (Chandler) is equal.

18...exd5 19 ♖xd5

White has managed to play the advance d5 and get rid of his potential endgame weakness while maintaining a slight advantage. The game Palkovi-Kovacs, Hungarian Cht 1997/8 finished 19...♗f8 20 ♕d2 ♖xe1+ 21 ♘xe1 ♖xd5 22 ♘xd5 ♗d6 23 h3 ♘e5?! 24 g4! ♘g7 25 ♘f6+ ♔h8 26 ♗h4 ♘d7 27 ♘xd7 ♗h2+ 28 ♔f1 ♕c7 29 ♘f6 g5 30 ♕d3 1-0.

It is interesting to compare the isolated queen's pawn positions which are analysed after 6 ♗d3 (Line A1), 6 ♗e2 (Line B2) and 6 ♗e3 (Line D) in this chapter. The positions in Line A1 are ideal for White but Black did not play the most accurate moves, first exchanging on d4 too early, then retreating the queen to d8 instead of d6. The positions in Line D offer White a wider variety of attacking options than those in Line B2 and are thus slightly to be preferred. White's bishop might look superficially active on g3 where it controls the h2-b8 diagonal, but its options are limited. By contrast, the seemingly passive bishop on e3 can advance to g5 (or h6) or retreat to c1 as the position demands.

6 2...d5 3 exd5 ♕xd5 4 d4 ♞f6 5 ♞f3 ♝g4

1 e4 c5 2 c3 d5 3 exd5 ♕xd5 4 d4 ♞f6 5 ♞f3 ♝g4 *(D)*

W

Black develops his queen's bishop before playing ...e6. With the help of Kasparov, this has replaced 5...e6 as the main line after 2...d5. White has been struggling for some time to find more than equality, and a number of players have given up the 2 c3 Sicilian altogether in despair. However, we don't believe the situation to be so desperate and think there is still much to be discovered, especially after 6 dxc5.

White has tried many different moves in his quest for an advantage:

A: 6 ♕a4+   99
B: 6 ♞bd2   100
C: 6 ♝e2   102
D: 6 dxc5   110

A)
    6 ♕a4+ *(D)*

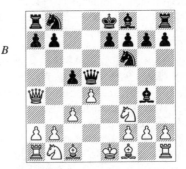

B

6...♝d7
The simplest solution for Black, and a very effective one.

a) 6...♞c6 is not good: 7 ♝c4 ♕e4+ (7...♕d7 8 dxc5 ♝xf3 9 gxf3 e6 10 ♝e3 ♞d5 11 ♝xd5 ♕xd5 12 ♕e4 ± Sveshnikov-Neverov, Moscow 1989) 8 ♝e3 ♝xf3 9 ♞d2 ♝d1!? (9...♕g4 10 ♞xf3 ♕xg2 11 ♔e2 ± Van de Oudeweetering-Van Wely, Rotterdam 1990) 10 ♖xd1 ♕xg2 11 ♔e2 cxd4 12 cxd4 e6 13 ♞f3 ♕g4 14 ♝b5 and White is much better, Stević-Kurajica, Vinkovci 1995.

b) 6...♞bd7 leads to very sharp positions:

b1) 7 ♞e5 0-0-0! 8 ♞xd7 (8 ♞xg4 ♞xg4 9 dxc5 h5 10 c6 ♞c5 11 cxb7+

♔b8 ∓ Cherniaev-Motylev, St Petersburg 1999) 8...♛xd7 9 ♕xa7 cxd4 10 f3 e5 leaves White's king stranded in the centre of the board but might just be playable for him. White actually went on to win in Slapikas-Rõtšagov, Mezezers Z 2000.

b2) 7 ♗c4 ♕e4+ 8 ♗e3 ♗xf3 and then:

b21) 9 ♘d2 ♕c6 10 ♗b5 ♗xg2 11 ♖g1! (11 ♗xc6 ♗xc6 gives Black too much material for the queen) 11...♕c8! 12 ♖xg2 cxd4 13 ♕xd4 a6 14 ♗a4 g6 ∓ Vysochin-Vorobiov, Kiev 2000.

b22) 9 gxf3 ♕xf3 10 ♖g1 cxd4 11 cxd4 ♕c6 12 ♕b3 e6 13 ♘c3 ♖c8 14 ♗b5 ♕d6 15 d5 a6 16 ♗xd7+ ♕xd7 17 ♖d1 with unclear complications, Vogt-Hraček, Altensteig 1995.

7 ♕b3 cxd4 8 ♘xd4

White can't achieve anything if he plays the immediate 8 ♗c4 and loses the possibility to castle after 8...♕e4+ 9 ♔f1 e6 10 cxd4 (after 10 ♘bd2 ♕c6 11 ♘xd4 ♕c7 12 ♘2f3 ♘c6 White has nothing particular on the queenside while he still has a problem with his king, Vysochin-Lerner, Bydgoszcz 2000) 10...♘c6 11 ♘c3 ♕f5 12 ♕xb7 ♖b8 13 ♕c7 ♗e7 14 b3 ♗b4 15 ♗d2 0-0. The white king is still in the centre, so Black has nice compensation for the pawn, according to analysis by Shipov.

8...♘c6! 9 ♗e3 ♘a5!

This is essentially a refutation of the line starting with 6 ♕a4+. Instead, 9...e6?! leads to complicated play: 10 ♘b5 ♕e5 11 ♘d2 a6 12 ♘f3 ♕b8 13 ♘bd4 ♘d5 14 0-0-0 ♘xe3 15 fxe3 ♕c7 16 ♗d3 ♗e7 17 h4 with interesting

chances for both sides, Rozentalis-Degraeve, Belfort 1998.

10 ♕xd5

If White avoids the endgame, Black can simply play 10...e5.

10...♘xd5 11 ♗c1 e5 12 ♘b3 ♘c6

Black has a comfortable endgame due to his better development, Sermek-Avrukh, Pula Z 2000.

B)

6 ♘bd2 (D)

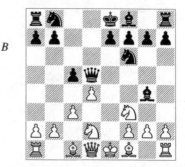

White prepares ♗c4, attacking the queen. However, this plan of development is artificial, so Black can react naturally, developing his pieces.

6...♘c6

Best. This move has proved successful enough for Black to rule out a thorough investigation of other lines, though there are also still possibilities elsewhere for Black:

a) 6...e6 7 ♕a4+ ♘c6 8 ♗c4 ♕d6 9 ♗b5! ♗xf3 (the bishop is potentially loose on g4) 10 ♘xf3 with a slight advantage for White, Palkovi-C.Horvath, Paks 1996.

b) 6...cxd4 7 ♗c4 ♕d7 8 ♕b3 e6 9 ♘e5!? (9 ♘xd4 ♗c5 with equality,

V.Ivanov-Tikhanov, Moscow 1996) 9...♕c7 10 ♗b5+ ♘c6 and then:

b1) 11 ♘dc4!? ♗c5 (11...dxc3 is the critical test, untried to date) 12 ♗f4 (a natural continuation, but the simple idea 12 ♘d3 followed by ♗f4, as suggested by Romero, should give White an advantage) 12...0-0 13 ♗xc6 bxc6 (Shabalov-Dzindzichashvili, USA Ch (Parsippany) 1996) and now Romero gives 14 ♘d3 ♕e7 15 ♘xc5 ♕xc5 16 f3! (16 ♗d6 ♕d5), continuing 16...♕d5 17 0-0-0 ♗f5 18 ♖xd4 ±, but Black can improve with 16...♗xf3! 17 gxf3 ♕f5 =.

b2) 11 cxd4 ♗d6 12 ♘dc4 0-0 13 ♗xc6 bxc6 14 ♗f4?! (14 ♗d2 c5 = Saltaev-Shtyrenkov, Volgograd 1997) 14...♖ab8 15 ♕g3 ♗f5 16 ♘xd6 ♕xd6 17 ♘d3 (17 ♘xc6? ♕xc6 18 ♗xb8 ♘h5! 19 ♕c7 ♕xg2 20 0-0-0 ♕a8! −+) 17...♕xd4 18 ♗xb8 ♕e4+ 19 ♕e3 ♖xb8 20 ♕xe4 ♗xe4 21 0-0-0 ♗xg2 and Black has more than enough for the exchange, Vlassov-Gaisin, Tomsk 2001.

7 ♗c4

7 ♕a4 is a rarer attempt:

a) 7...♗xf3 8 ♘xf3 cxd4 9 cxd4 e5 10 ♗b5 with good play for White, Morgan-Alfred, Cambridge 2000; for example, 10...exd4 11 0-0 ♗c5 12 ♖e1+ with compensation − Morgan.

b) 7...cxd4 8 ♗c4 ♕d7 9 cxd4 e6 10 ♗b5 ♗xf3 11 ♘xf3 ♗b4+ 12 ♔f1 ♗d6 13 ♘e5 ♗xe5 14 dxe5 ♘d5 15 ♗d2 0-0 16 ♗xc6 ½-½ Motylev-Mitin, Moscow 1998.

c) 7...♗d7 8 ♕b3 ♕xb3 9 ♘xb3 cxd4 10 ♘bxd4 ♘xd4 11 ♘xd4 = Vajda-Vučković, Erevan jr Wch 1999.

7...♗xf3 (D)

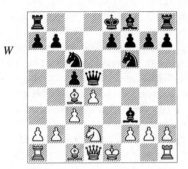

8 ♕b3
Or:

a) 8 ♕a4 ♗d1! (an excellent move found by *Fritz*; 8...♕g5?! is risky, as after 9 ♘xf3 ♕xg2 10 ♔e2 ♕xh1 11 d5 the black king is very unsafe; for example, 11...♖c8? 12 dxc6 bxc6 13 ♕a6 ♖c7 14 ♗f4 ♕xa1 15 ♗xc7 ♕xb2+ 16 ♔f1 ♔d7 17 ♕xa7 ♘d5 18 ♗g3+ ♔e6 19 ♕c7 1-0 Tseshkovsky-Istratescu, Yugoslav Cht (Nikšić) 1997) 9 ♕xd1 ♕xg2 10 ♖f1 cxd4 11 cxd4 ♘xd4 12 ♕a4+ ♘c6 13 ♕b3 e6 14 ♕xb7 ♖b8 ∓ Wahls.

b) 8 gxf3 ♕f5 9 ♕b3 0-0-0 and now:

b1) If White wins a pawn by 10 ♗xf7 he has to swap his bishop and finds himself a long way behind in development: 10...♘d5 11 ♗xd5 ♖xd5 12 ♖g1 (12 ♘e4 e6 13 ♘g3 ♕xf3 14 ♗e3 cxd4 15 ♗xd4 ♗d6 16 ♕d1 ♕g2 is hopeless for White, Votava-Lutz, Erevan OL 1996) 12...e6 13 ♖g3 cxd4 14 ♘e4 ♗e7 15 ♗d2 ♖hd8 16 c4 ♖5d7 17 0-0-0 g6 18 ♗g5 ♗xg5+ 19 ♖xg5 ♕f4+ 20 ♔b1 d3 and Black's central passed pawn gives him a big advantage, Shaked-de Firmian, USA Ch (Parsippany) 1996.

b2) 10 ♗b5 cxd4 11 ♗xc6 bxc6 12 0-0 e6 13 ♘c4 ♕xf3 14 ♘e5 is analysis by Hübner, which he assessed as unclear. However, we don't believe that White has sufficient compensation for the two pawns. For instance, after 14...♕e4 15 cxd4 ♖xd4 Black is close to victory.

c) 8 ♗xd5 ♗xd1 9 ♗xc6+ bxc6 10 ♔xd1 cxd4 11 cxd4 0-0-0 and Black is better.

d) 8 ♕xf3 ♕xf3 9 ♘xf3 cxd4 10 ♘xd4 ♘xd4 11 cxd4 a6 = followed by 12...e6, blockading the isolated pawn.

We return to 8 ♕b3 (D):

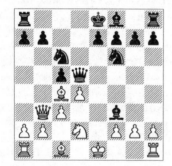

8...♘a5!

Easing the tension in the centre and leading to exchanges. This is better than 8...♗xg2 (Black seeks to give up his queen for sufficient material equivalent) 9 ♗xd5 ♗xd5 10 ♕xb7 ♘xd4 11 ♕a6 ♘c2+, as after 12 ♔e2! ♘xa1 (12...♗xh1 13 ♕a4+ ♘d7 14 ♕xc2 ±) 13 ♖d1 ♖d8 14 ♕a4+ ♘d7 15 ♘f3 White has a strong attack on Black's king which is stuck in the centre, Nisipeanu-S.Kiseliov, Budapest 1997.

9 ♗xd5 ♘xb3 10 ♘xf3 ♘xd5 11 axb3 cxd4 12 ♘xd4 e5 13 ♘f5 a6 14 ♔e2 0-0-0

The endgame is level, Shirov-J.Polgar, Dos Hermanas 1997.

C)

6 ♗e2 e6 (D)

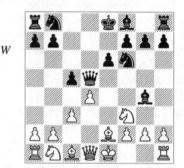

7 h3

This is a useful move for White to throw in. It gives his king an escape-square, potentially saving a tempo later on, and in some lines the threat of g4 immediately breaking the pin works to White's advantage. If White wishes to play ♘a3 however, it is better to leave Black's bishop on g4, so that the possible follow-up ♘c2-e3 attacks the bishop. After 7 ♘a3, Black can react in two ways, both of which are good:

a) 7...♘c6 8 h3 ♗h5 9 ♗e3 cxd4 10 ♘b5 and now:

a1) 10...♖c8 11 ♘bxd4 ♘xd4 (not 11...♗c5? losing to 12 ♘xe6 ♕xe6 13 ♗xc5, Sermek-Mohr, Slovenian Ch (Maribor) 1998) 12 ♗xd4 a6 13 ♕a4+ ♕d7 14 ♕b3 ♗d6 15 ♖d1 ♕c7 16 ♕a4+ ♔e7 17 0-0 and although the black king is not vulnerable, its location in the centre brings Black some trouble, Gdanski-Lautier, Belgrade ECC 1999.

a2) 10...0-0-0! 11 ♘bxd4 ♗c5 12 0-0 e5 13 ♘f5 ♕e4! and White has nothing better than 14 ♕b1, which means that Black is fine – Stohl.

b) 7...a6 and here:

b1) 8 h3 ♗h5 9 c4 ♕d8 10 ♕b3 ♘c6 11 dxc5 (11 ♕xb7? ♘a5 wins for Black) 11...♗xc5 12 0-0 0-0 leaves Black quite comfortable, as the white knight on a3 is out of the game, Zifroni-Avrukh, Tel-Aviv 1997.

b2) 8 ♘c2 cxd4 9 ♘cxd4 e5 10 ♘c2 ♕xd1+ 11 ♗xd1 ♘c6 12 ♘e3 ♗h5 13 ♗b3 ♗c5 14 ♘f5 0-0 15 0-0 ♖fe8 16 h3 ♗xf3 17 gxf3 (Adams-Romero, Leon 1995) and after 17...♘e7 Black has nothing to be afraid of.

7...♗h5 *(D)*

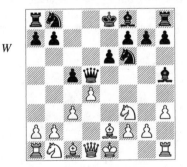

Now:
C1: 8 0-0   103
C2: 8 c4   109

C1)

8 0-0 ♘c6 *(D)*

After 8...♗e7, White can choose between:

a) 9 ♗e3 cxd4 10 cxd4 ♘c6 – 8...♘c6 9 ♗e3 cxd4 10 cxd4 ♗e7.

b) 9 c4 ♕d8 (9...♕d6 10 ♘c3 0-0 11 dxc5 ♕xc5 12 ♗e3 ♕c8 13 ♘d4 ♗xe2 14 ♕xe2 ♘c6 15 ♖ac1 and White is the first to start his queenside play, Rozentalis-Gavrikov, Klaipeda 1988) 10 ♘c3 cxd4 11 ♘xd4 ♗xe2 12 ♕a4+ ♘bd7 13 ♘dxe2 – *8 c4 ♕d8 9 ♘c3 cxd4 10 ♘xd4 ♗xe2 11 ♕a4+ ♘bd7 12 ♘dxe2 ♗e7 13 0-0.*

9 ♗e3

Short's 9 a3!? is an interesting idea which attempts to bypass the *9 ♗e3 cxd4 10 cxd4 ♗b4* idea below, preserves the option of c4, and allows for White to develop the bishop to a more useful square than e3.

a) After 9...♗e7 10 c4 ♕d8 11 dxc5 ♕xd1 12 ♖xd1, the pawn being on a3 is undoubtedly useful. 12...a5 13 ♗e3 ♘e4 and now:

a1) 14 ♘c3!? ♘xc3 15 bxc3 ♗g6 16 ♘d4 0-0-0 = Short-Topalov, Novgorod 1995.

a2) 14 ♘bd2 ♘xc5 15 b4 ♘a4 16 b5 ♘d8 17 ♘e4 is slightly better for White, Sariego-Cruz Lima, Cuban Ch (Las Tunas) 1996.

b) 9...cxd4 10 cxd4 ♗e7 11 ♘c3 ♕d6 and now:

b1) 12 ♘b5 achieves little: 12...♕b8 13 ♘e5 ♗xe2 14 ♕xe2 a6 15 ♘xc6 bxc6 16 ♘c3 0-0 17 ♗g5 ½-½ Conquest-Aronian, Hastings 2000.

b2) Maybe White has nothing better than 12 ♗e3, transposing to *9 ♗e3 cxd4 10 cxd4 ♗e7 11 ♘c3 ♕d6 12 a3*, but he has at least succeeded in avoiding *10...♗b4*.

9...cxd4

Yermolinsky's 9...♖d8!? might be best met by the simple 10 a3 as normally Black plays his king's rook, and not his queen's rook, to d8, but 10 dxc5 ♕xd1 (10...♗xc5 11 ♕xd5 ♖xd5 12 c4! ± Saunders-Fantin, York 2000) 11 ♖xd1 ♖xd1+ 12 ♗xd1 ♘d5 13 b4 should also give White a little something, Cuartas-Dlaykan, Leticia 1985.

10 cxd4

10 ♘xd4 ♗e2 11 ♕xe2 ♘xd4 12 ♗xd4 ♗e7 (12...♗c5 13 ♖d1 0-0-0 14 ♘a3 ♗xd4 15 ♖xd4 ♕a5 16 ♖ad1 ♖xd4 17 ♖xd4 ♖d8 18 ♕c4+ ♔b8 19 ♖xd8+ ♕xd8 20 ♘b5 ± Ftačnik) 13 ♖d1 ♕c6 14 ♘d2 0-0 15 ♘f3 ♖fd8 16 c4 ♕e4 17 ♔f1 b6 18 b3 ♖ac8 19 ♖d3 ♕xe2+ 20 ♔xe2 ♘e4 21 ♖ad1 gives White no more than a symbolic advantage in the endgame, Tiviakov-Lautier, Linares 1995.

10...♗e7

Kasparov's move 10...♗b4 is just as good:

a) 11 ♘c3 and now:

a1) 11...♕a5 12 ♕b3 0-0 13 a3 (13 ♖ac1!? Gallagher) 13...♗xc3 14 bxc3 ♘d5 15 ♖ac1 ♕c7 16 c4 ♘xe3 17 ♕xe3 ♖fd8 with an equal position,

Kramnik-Kasparov, Paris rpd 1994 (by transposition; we don't know where Kasparov would have put his queen after 11 ♘c3).

a2) 11...♕d6 12 ♕b3 0-0 13 a3 ♗xc3 14 bxc3 b6 15 c4 ∞ Petronić-Perunović, Serbian Ch (Kragujevac) 2000.

b) 11 a3 ♗a5 and now:

b1) 12 ♘c3 ♕d6 13 ♘b5 ♕d5! = Seirawan (13...♕e7 is risky: 14 ♘e5 ♗xe2 15 ♕xe2 0-0 16 ♖ac1 ♖ac8 17 ♗g5 and White has an initiative, *Deep Blue*-Kasparov, Philadelphia (1) 1996).

b2) 12 b4 ♗b6 13 ♘c3 ♕d6 14 ♕b3 0-0 15 ♖fd1 ♘d5 =.

11 ♘c3 ♕d6 (D)

It is best to keep the queen in the centre, where it controls the e5-square, defends the c6-knight (useful if White ever plays ♕xb7), and keeps d4 under attack. Instead, 11...♕a5 transposes to *4...♘c6 5 ♘f3 ♗g4 6 ♗e2 cxd4 7 cxd4 e6 8 h3 ♗h5 9 ♘c3 ♕a5 10 0-0 ♘f6 11 ♗e3 ♗e7 ± (11...♗d6! is better).*

12 ♕b3

Instead:

a) 12 ♘b5 ♕b8 13 ♘e5 is not good, since after 13...♗xe2 14 ♕xe2 0-0 15

♘xc6 bxc6 16 ♘c3 ♘d5 17 ♘xd5 cxd5 Black is slightly better, Ljubojević-Kasparov, Moscow OL 1994.

b) 12 a3 0-0 13 ♕b3 ♖fd8 14 ♖fd1 transposes to *12 ♕b3 0-0 13 ♖fd1 ♖fd8 14 a3*, avoiding the lines *12 ♕b3 ♕b4* and *12 ♕b3 0-0 13 ♖fd1 ♕b4*, though as neither option is particularly good for Black, 12 ♕b3 gives Black more chances to go wrong.

c) The main alternative plan for White is 12 ♕d2 0-0 13 ♗f4 (13 ♖fd1 ♖fd8 14 ♖ac1 ♖ac8 15 ♗f4 ♕b4 16 a3 ♕b3 ∓ Nunn-Ward, Kilkenny 1996) 13...♕d8 14 a3 ♗xf3! 15 ♗xf3 ♘xd4 16 ♗xb7 ♖b8 17 ♗a6 e5 18 ♖fd1! (Marković-Atalik, Iraklion 1993), when Atalik gives 18...exf4 19 ♕xd4 ♕xd4 20 ♖xd4 ♖xb2 =.

12...0-0

12...♕b4 transposes to *4...♘c6 5 ♘f3 ♗g4 6 ♗e2 cxd4 7 cxd4 e6 8 h3 ♗h5 9 ♘c3 ♕a5 10 0-0 ♘f6 11 ♗e3 ♗e7 12 ♕b3 ♕b4*, when 13 g4 ♗g6 14 ♘e5 0-0 15 g5! is good for White.

Here, with the queen on d6, Black can ignore the threat of 13 ♕xb7 as this can be met by 13...♖ab8 14 ♕a6 ♖xb2.

13 ♖fd1 ♖fd8

Now 13...♕b4 is well met by 14 d5! ♕xb3 15 axb3 exd5 16 ♘xd5 ♘xd5 17 ♖xd5 ♗xf3 18 ♗xf3 ♗f6 19 ♖d7 ± Okhotnik-Lengyel, Hajduboszormeny 1995.

14 a3 *(D)*

Now Black really was threatening to play 14...♕b4 equalizing easily; e.g., 14 ♖ac1 ♕b4 15 ♕xb4 ♘xb4 16 g4 ♗g6 17 ♘e5 ♘fd5 18 ♘xg6 hxg6 19 ♗f3 ♖ac8 = A.Sokolov-Babula,

Bundesliga 1998/9. Besides stopping ...♕b4, 14 a3 also serves to give the queen a retreat-square on a2 (still controlling the key d5-square) if Black chooses to play ...♘a5.

B

14...a6?!

Black prepares to expand on the queenside with ...b5. This is the most aggressive plan for Black and is quite popular in practice, but our analysis indicates that it may not be sound.

However, the key difficulty with this whole variation for White is that it is very difficult to prove any advantage at all if Black chooses to play ...♘d5 either on this move or the next:

a) 14...♘d5 and then:

a1) 15 ♘xd5 ♕xd5 16 ♕xd5 ♖xd5 17 ♖ac1 (17 g4?! ♗g6 18 ♗c4 ♖dd8 19 ♘e5 ♗e4 ∓ Bashkov-P.Schlosser, Munich ECC 1992) 17...♖ad8 18 b4 leads to equality, Afek-Goormachtigh, Gent 1999.

a2) 15 ♖ac1 ♘xc3!? (15...♖ac8 – *14...♖ac8 15 ♖ac1 ♘d5*; 15...♖ab8 – *14...♖ab8 15 ♖ac1 ♘d5*) 16 ♖xc3 ♖ab8 17 ♖c5 ♗xf3 18 ♗xf3 ♗f6 19 d5 ♘d4! ∞ Acs-C.Horvath, Paks 1996.

b) 14...♖ac8 15 ♖ac1 and then:

b1) 15...♕b8?! 16 d5! ♘xd5 17 ♘xd5 exd5 18 ♖xd5 ♗g6 19 ♖b5! b6 (19...♖d7 20 ♗c4!? ♗d6 21 ♗d5 ± Nunn) 20 ♖d5 ± Nunn-Lutz, Bundesliga 1994/5.

b2) 15...♘d5 16 ♘xd5 ♕xd5 17 ♕xd5 (17 ♕xb7 ♘xd4! 18 ♕xe7 ♖xc1 19 ♘xd4 ♖xd1+ 20 ♗xd1 ♗xd1 21 ♘c6, Senador-Chan, Aden 2002, and now 21...♖c8! 22 ♘xa7 ♖a8 offers Black a slight advantage) 17...exd5 (17...♖xd5 18 g4 ♗g6 19 ♘e5 is a little better for White thanks to the pin on the c-file; for example, 19...♗e4 20 f3 ♗g6 21 ♘xc6 ♖xc6 22 ♖xc6 bxc6 23 ♖c1 ♖d6 24 ♖c4 ± Kunte-Greet, British Ch (Scarborough) 1999) 18 g4 ♗g6 19 ♘e5 ♗d6 20 ♘xc6 bxc6 21 ♖c3 f5!? 22 gxf5 ♗xf5 23 ♖dc1 c5 24 dxc5 ♗e5 ∞ Potkin-Popov, St Petersburg 1998.

c) 14...♖ab8 15 ♖ac1 ♘d5 and then:

c1) 16 ♘e4 ♕c7 17 ♘g3 ♗g6! 18 ♘e5 ♗d6 ∓ Balinov-Löffler, Schwarzach 1998.

c2) 16 ♘b5 ♘a5! 17 ♕c2 ♗g6! 18 ♘xd6 ♗xc2 19 ♖xc2 ♗xd6 with an equal position, Kindermann-Babula, Moscow OL 1994.

c3) 16 ♘xd5 exd5 17 ♕c3 f6 18 b4 ♗f8 19 ♕d2 ♖bc8 20 ♖c3 ♘e7 21 ♖dc1 ♖xc3 22 ♖xc3 ♖c8 23 ♖c5 = Ekström-Lutz, Dresden Z 1998. Perhaps White has the very slightest of advantages here, but Lutz has happily played this line (with 16...exd5) a number of times with no problems and even some success.

15 ♖ac1 *(D)*

15 ♖d2 b5 16 ♖ad1 ♖ac8 17 d5 exd5 (instead of 17...♘a5 with unclear

complications, Speelman-Pigusov, Beijing 1997) 18 ♘xd5 ♘xd5 19 ♖xd5 ♕e6 should lead to a draw.

15...b5 16 d5!

White has got all his pieces on good squares while Black has just spent time playing two pawn moves, so White feels justified in bursting the position open at this point. This move, first introduced by one of the authors, has resulted in a still unresolved theoretical debate over the past few years. Our latest conclusion is that White can come out of the complications on top.

If White wants to keep the position blocked, an alternative plan is 16 ♕a2 ♖ac8 (16...b4 17 ♘a4 bxa3 18 bxa3 ♘d5 19 ♘c5 ♖dc8 ∞ has the point 20 ♗xa6?! ♘cb4 21 axb4 ♘xb4 – Har-Zvi) 17 b4, and then:

a) 17...♗f8 18 g3 ♘e7 19 ♗g5!? ♖xc3!? (19...♕b6) 20 ♖xc3 ♘e4 21 ♖cd3 ♘xg3 22 d5 ♘xe2+ 23 ♕xe2 e5 ∞ is an interesting and sound exchange sacrifice, Braga-Spangenberg, Villa Gesell 1997.

b) 17...♗g6 18 ♘h4 ♘d5 (another idea is 18...♗h5!?) 19 ♘xg6 ♘xc3 20 ♖xc3 hxg6 21 ♖dc1 ♗f6 22 ♗f3 with a slight advantage for White, Sivokho-Ayupov, St Petersburg 2001.

c) 17...h6 is logical and the most common continuation. Black frees a potential retreat-square for the bishop, protects against later back-rank-mate tactics, and prevents White from playing ♗g5. A good example of both sides making progress (rather than just agreeing a draw) was the game Novopashin-Belov, Alushta 1999: 18 ♕b3 ♗g6 19 ♘e1 ♗f8 20 ♗f3 ♘e7 21 ♘d3 ♘ed5 22 ♘xd5 ♘xd5 23 ♘c5 ♕b6 24 ♗d2 ♖b8 25 ♖a1 ♗e7 26 a4 ♗f6 ∞.

16...♘a5

The knight is vulnerable on the c-file so it makes sense to move it with gain of tempo. Alternatively, Black can play:

a) 16...♘xd5 17 ♘xd5 exd5 18 ♖xc6! ♕xc6 19 ♘d4 ♕g6 20 g4 ♗c5 21 ♗d3 ♕f6 22 gxh5 ±. White's minor pieces give him better chances of play on the kingside than Black.

b) 16...exd5 17 g4 (17 ♘xd5 ♘xd5 18 ♖c5 ♕e6 19 ♖cxd5 ♖xd5 20 ♕xd5 ♕xd5 21 ♖xd5 ♗g6 22 ♘d4 ♘xd4 ½-½ Cherniaev-Rausis, Gausdal 1995) 17...♘a5! (17...♗g6? 18 g5 ♘e4 19 ♘xd5 ♘a5 20 ♕b4! ♕xd5 21 ♕xe7 ♘c6 22 ♖xc6 1-0 Kunte-Rodriguez Lopez, Linares open 1999) 18 ♕a2 (18 ♕b4!? ♕xb4 19 axb4 ♘b3 20 gxh5 ♘xc1 21 ♖xc1 ♗xb4 ∞ T.Wall-Summerscale, Oxford 1998) transposes to *16...♘a5 17 ♕a2 exd5 18 g4*.

17 ♕a2 exd5

After 17...♘xd5 18 ♘xd5 exd5 19 ♗c5 ♕f6! (19...♕c7 20 ♗b4 ♘c4 21 b3 ±; 19...♕e6 20 ♘d4 ♕e5 21 ♗xh5 ♗xc5 22 ♗xf7+ ♔xf7 23 ♖xc5 ±) 20 ♖xd5 ♗xc5 21 ♖dxc5 ♗g6 22 a4 ♘b7 23 ♖c7 ♗e4 24 b4, White has regained the pawn and has an advantage thanks to his better placed pieces, Sveshnikov-Sax, Ljubljana 1998.

18 g4 ♗g6 19 g5 ♘e4

After 19...♘e8 20 ♖xd5 (20 ♘xd5 ♕e6 21 ♗b6! ♕xe2 22 ♖d2 ♕e4 is unclear) 20...♕b8 21 ♘e5 ♗d6 22 ♘xg6 hxg6 23 ♘e4, White's pieces are much better placed – Har-Zvi.

20 ♘xd5

White has loosened his kingside, but now threatens both ♘f6+ and ♗b6 winning material. Black cannot meet both threats.

20...♕e6 *(D)*

The immediate counterattack by 20...♘g3? fails because White has too many pieces near the kingside to defend and can even bring his queen back too after 21 b4!, adding two more threats: bxa5 and ♗c5.

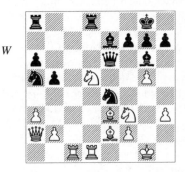

21 ♗b6?!

White wins an exchange but takes a piece away from the kingside. 21 ♘h4! is an interesting and critical alternative:

a) 21...♗xg5 22 ♗g4 ♕e8 23 ♗xg5 ♘xg5 24 ♘c7 ± Har-Zvi.

b) 21...♘c4 22 ♗g4 ♕xd5 (alternatively, 22...♕d6 23 ♗f4 ♕c5 24 ♘xg6 hxg6 25 b4 +–) 23 ♖xd5 ♖xd5 24 ♘xg6 hxg6 25 ♗f3 ♖e5 26 ♖xc4! bxc4 27 ♕xc4 +– Har-Zvi.

c) 21...♘xg5 and then:

c1) 22 ♗g4?! ♘xh3+! (22...♕e5? 23 f4 ♕e4 24 ♖d4 +– Har-Zvi) 23 ♗xh3 ♕xh3 24 ♘xe7+ (or 24 ♘xg6 ♗d6 25 ♘de7+ ♗xe7 26 ♘xe7+ ♔f8 27 ♘d5 ♕g4+ drawing) 24...♔h8 25 ♘exg6+ fxg6 26 ♘g2 ♘c4 27 ♗f4 g5! 28 ♗xg5 (28 ♗g3 ♘d2; 28 ♖xd8+ ♖xd8 29 ♗xg5? ♘e5) 28...♖xd1+ 29 ♖xd1 ♕h5 30 ♖d5 ♖e8 = Chorfi-Cardelli, ICCF e-mail 2000.

c2) 22 ♘xg6! ♘xh3+ (22...hxg6 23 ♗g4! ±) 23 ♔g2 ♕xg6+ 24 ♔xh3 and White should be able to survive the attack and win with the aid of his extra piece.

21...♗d6!

Black doesn't care how much material he loses on the board as a whole, and just tries to ensure he has more pieces on the kingside. This is an important improvement over the first game played in this line (with 16 d5!): 21...♗xg5 22 ♗xd8 ♗xd8! 23 ♗f1 ♕f5 (23...♗h5 24 ♗g2 ♗xf3 25 ♗xf3 ♘g5 ±) 24 ♗g2 ♗h5? (24...♘c4 25 b3 ♗h5! 26 ♖d3 ±) 25 ♘e3 ♕f4 26 ♕d5 1-0 Harley-P.Roberts, British Ch (Dundee) 1993.

22 ♗xa5 (D)

White has nothing better:

a) 22 ♗f1 ♗h5 23 ♘d4 ♕g6 24 ♗xa5 ♕xg5+ 25 ♗g2 ♗xd1 26 ♖xd1 ♖e8 ∞ Har-Zvi.

b) 22 ♔g2 ♗f5 23 ♘f6+ gxf6 24 ♕xe6 fxe6 25 ♗xa5 ♖dc8 = Har-Zvi.

c) 22 ♘f6+ gxf6 23 ♕xe6 fxe6 24 ♗xa5 ♖f8 ∓ Ghaem Maghami-Gadjily, Dubai 2001.

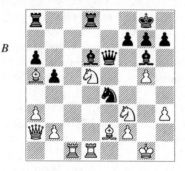

22...♕xh3 23 ♗xd8 ♕g4+ 24 ♔f1 ♕h3+ 25 ♔g1

White is temporarily a rook and knight up, but it is too risky to avoid the draw. 25 ♔e1 ♕h1+ 26 ♗f1 ♕xf3 and now:

a) 27 b4? ♘xf2? (27...♖xd8 ∓) 28 ♕e2! ♕xe2+ 29 ♗xe2 ♘xd1 30 ♗e7? (30 ♗c7! wins a piece) 30...♘e3 and Black is two pawns up, Toomanian-Mohamed, Abu Dhabi 2001.

b) 27 ♗b6 ♖e8 28 ♗e3 ♘xf2 29 ♗e2 ♕h1+ 30 ♔xf2 ♕h4+ 31 ♔f1 ♕h1+ 32 ♗g1? (32 ♔f2 ♕h4+ 33 ♔f1 ♕h1+ draws) 32...♕h3+ 33 ♔e1 ♗g3+ 34 ♗f2 ♕xf2+ 35 ♔d2 ♗e3+ and Black wins – Har-Zvi.

25...♕g4+ 26 ♔f1 ♕h3+

½-½ Potkin-Chekhov, Moscow 1999.

In conclusion, White should try to improve with 21 ♘h4!, but Black can play safe and avoid the complications with 14...♘d5, which should equalize.

C2)
8 c4 *(D)*

8...♕d8
Or:

a) 8...♕d6 allows the manoeuvre of the white knight from b1 to b5: 9 ♘c3 cxd4 10 ♘b5 ♕d8 11 ♗f4!? (11 0-0 didn't bring White an advantage in Schmittdiel-Zsu.Polgar, Polanica Zdroj 1991: 11...♘c6 12 ♗f4 ♖c8 13 ♕a4 ♘d7 14 ♘bxd4 ♗xf3! 15 ♘xf3 ♕f6 16 ♗d2 ♕xb2 17 ♖ab1 ♕a3 18 ♕c2 ♗e7 19 ♖xb7 ♘c5 20 ♖b5 0-0 =) 11...♗b4+ 12 ♔f1 ♘a6 13 ♘c7+ ♘xc7 14 ♕a4+ b5 15 ♕xb4 bxc4 16 ♕xc4 ♘cd5 17 ♕c6+ ♔f8 (or 17...♘d7 with unclear play – Sveshnikov) 18 ♗d6+ ♔g8 19 ♗a6 with a strong initiative for White, Rozentalis-Szekely, Odessa 1989.

b) 8...♕d7 (on d7, the queen is a good target for another knight, because in this case White can play ♘e5 at an appropriate moment) 9 d5 exd5 10 g4 ♗g6 11 ♘e5:

b1) 11...♕e6 12 ♘xg6 hxg6 13 g5 ♘e4 14 cxd5 ♕f5 15 ♗e3 ♘d6 16 ♘c3 ♖xh3 17 ♕a4+ ♔d8 18 ♖xh3 ♕xh3 19 0-0-0 gives White a great

deal of compensation for the pawn, Rozentalis-Loginov, Manila OL 1992.

b2) 11...♕d8 12 ♕a4+ ♘fd7 13 cxd5 ♗e7 14 ♘xg6 hxg6 15 ♘c3 and White is clearly better (but not 15 d6 ♗g5 16 ♕e4+ ♔f8 17 ♗xg5 ♕xg5 18 ♕xb7 ♕c1+ 19 ♗d1 ♘b6 20 ♘c3 ♕xa1 21 ♕e7+ with perpetual check, Godena-Shipov, Cappelle la Grande 1994).

b3) After 11...♕c7 12 ♘xg6 hxg6 13 g5 ♘h5 14 cxd5 the position is far from clear, but we would prefer to be White.

9 ♘c3
9 ♕b3? wastes too much time in order to win a pawn: 9...cxd4 10 ♕xb7 ♘bd7 11 ♘xd4 ♖b8 12 ♕a6 ♗b4+ 13 ♘c3 0-0. Now 14...♘c5 is a threat, so White has to go in for an inferior endgame: 14 ♘c6 ♖b6 15 ♘xd8 ♖xa6 16 g4 ♖xd8 17 gxh5 ♘e4 18 ♗d2 ♗xc3 19 ♗xc3 ♘xc3 20 bxc3 ♘c5, Kveinys-Shipov, Aalborg 1997.

9...cxd4 10 ♘xd4 ♗xe2 11 ♕a4+
(D)

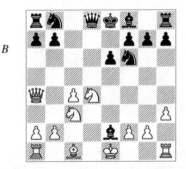

11...♘bd7
After 11...♕d7 12 ♕xd7+ ♘bxd7 13 ♔xe2 the endgame is equal, though

maybe a little bit more pleasant for White in practice.

12 ♘dxe2 ♗e7 13 0-0 0-0 14 ♕c2

Note that the natural 14 ♖d1? is a mistake: after 14...♕c8 15 ♗e3 ♘b6 16 ♗xb6 axb6 17 ♕b3 ♕c7 White has some problems with his c4-pawn, Rozentalis-Kramnik, Bundesliga 1995/6.

14...♖c8 15 b3

White has slightly better chances, with the opportunity both of exploiting his queenside pawn-majority and of piece-play on the kingside. In Rozentalis-Popov, Bydgoszcz 2001, the position after 15...h6 16 ♖d1 a6 was reached by transposition (Black had played the inferior ...h6 earlier) and White developed a nice advantage after 17 ♕d3 ♕a5 18 ♗d2 ♕h5 19 ♘g3 ♕c5 20 ♘ce4 ♕c7 21 ♕f3.

D)

6 dxc5 (D)

In our opinion this move represents White's most promising continuation. The reader would benefit from close comparison of these lines with our other recommendations *4...♘c6 5 ♘f3 ♗g4 6 dxc5* and *4...♘c6 5 ♘f3 ♘f6 6*

dxc5. Black now has two quite distinct ways to continue:

D1: 6...♕xd1+ 110
D2: 6...♕xc5 112

D1)

6...♕xd1+ 7 ♔xd1 e5

7...♘c6 is met by 8 b4!, freeing the b2-square for the king. Then:

a) 8...0-0-0+ 9 ♔c2 e5 10 ♗b5 ♗f5+ 11 ♔b2 ♘g4 12 ♗e3 ♗e7 13 ♘bd2 ♗f6 14 ♗xc6 bxc6 15 ♘c4 ♗e6 16 ♘d6+ ± Jakubiec-Pisk, Prerov 1995.

b) 8...e5 9 ♔c2 ♘d5 10 ♗b5 f6 11 ♔b2! (defending the a1-rook to prepare a3) 11...♗e7 12 ♗e3 ♗xf3 13 gxf3 a5 14 a3 0-0-0 15 ♖g1 g6 16 ♔c2 f5 17 ♗xc6 bxc6 (Khmelnitsky-Christiansen, USA Ch (Parsippany) 1996) 18 c4! ± Christiansen.

8 b4

Safer is 8 ♗e3 ♘c6, and then:

a) 9 ♘bd2?! ♘d5! regains the pawn as 10 b4 is met by 10...♘xc3+.

b) 9 ♔c1!? ♘d5 10 b4 ♗xf3 (removing the attacker of the e5-pawn) 11 gxf3 a5 12 b5 ♘d8 =.

c) 9 ♔c2 ♗f5+ 10 ♔c1 ♘d5 11 b4 transposes to *4...♘c6 5 ♘f3 ♘f6 6 dxc5 ♕xd1+ 7 ♔xd1 e5 8 b4 ♗f5 9 ♗e3 ♘d5 10 ♔c1*. After 11...a5, 12 b5 is a better try for advantage than 12 ♗b5 ♗xb1! ∓ Sveshnikov-Loginov, Russian Ch (Samara) 2000.

8...e4

Now Black can regain a pawn, and even win one more. However, practice has shown that White's 4 vs 2 queenside majority is more potent than Black's kingside pawns, primarily due to the fact that White's pawns are further advanced.

Instead, 8...♘c6 transposes to the line 7...♘c6 8 b4 e5.

9 h3 ♗h5 10 g4 ♘xg4 11 hxg4 ♗xg4 12 ♘bd2 exf3 *(D)*

Relange's suggestion 12...♘c6 prepares to castle quickly and stops White developing his bishop to d3. However, White has a strong reply: 13 ♖h4! ♗xf3+ (Black can't avoid exchanging his bishop: 13...h5 14 ♖xg4 hxg4 15 ♘g5 ±) 14 ♘xf3 exf3 15 ♖e4+ ♗e7 16 ♔c2 a6 17 ♗f4 leaves White much better, since his queenside pawns are more dangerous than Black's on the kingside, and due to his active pieces and bishop-pair. Following 17...h5 18 ♖ae1 ♔f8 19 a4, White went on to win in Rozentalis-Babula, Bundesliga 2001/2.

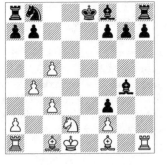

An interesting and complex position has arisen. Black already has a passed pawn and is a pawn ahead, which implies that at some point White will have to waste time capturing the advanced pawn on f3. However, White's pawns are much further advanced. White also has good squares for his pieces: his dark-squared bishop will go to f4, where it can control the h2-b8 diagonal unopposed because the c5-pawn stops Black playing ...♗d6. From f4, the bishop can retreat to h2 to stop the advance of Black's h-pawn while at the same time supporting White's own queenside pawn advance. White's light-squared bishop will try to head for e4, where it can occupy the h1-a8 diagonal and support the queenside pawn advance and at an opportune moment assist in the capture of the f3-pawn. White's knight will go to c4, from where a number of attractive squares beckon, most notably the outpost on d6. White's king can shelter on the queenside, and his rooks can occupy the central open files and launch a potentially devastating attack even without advancing the queenside pawns. All in all, it might seem pretty bleak for Black in this position, but things are not so simple. Recent practice indicates that Black gets reasonable counterchances by sheltering his king on the kingside, starting with ...♔f8, and then charging his pawns forward as quickly as possible by ...h5 and ...g5. Both sides need to be prepared to sacrifice material to delay the opposing pawn advances.

13 ♗d3

The most popular move to date. Alternatives:

a) 13 ♗b5+ enables White to develop more quickly but blocks the b5 pawn advance and doesn't help White capture the f3-pawn: 13...♘c6 14 ♖e1+ ♗e7 15 ♔c2 ♔f8 16 ♘c4 h5 17 ♗f4 h4 18 ♘d6 ♘d8 19 ♖e3 g5 20 ♗h2 is unclear, Miljanić-Genov, Herceg Novi 2002.

b) 13 ♘c4 ♘c6 14 ♕c2 h5 (14...a5 15 b5 ♘d8 ∞ Alekseev-Torbin, Serpukhov 1999) 15 ♗f4 ♗e6 16 a4 ♗e7 17 a5 a6 18 ♖e1 ♔f8 19 ♘b6 ♖d8 20 ♗h3 ♗xh3 21 ♖xh3 g5 22 ♗c7 g4 23 ♗xd8 ½-½ Alekseev-Loginov, St Petersburg 2000.

13...♘c6 14 ♖e1+ ♗e7 *(D)*

Less testing is 14...♗e6 15 ♘xf3 0-0-0 16 ♕c2 ♗e7 (16...h6 17 ♗e3 ± Bosch) 17 ♗g5 h6 18 ♗xe7 ♘xe7 19 ♘d4 ♘d5 20 a3 ♘f4 21 ♗e4 ± Emms-A.David, Escaldes Z 1998.

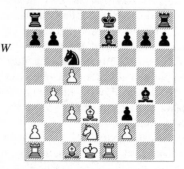

15 ♔c2

White is going to have to play this move eventually, though 15 ♗e4 seems just as good. Here are two good examples of a successful strategy for White after 15...♖d8?! (this just seems to chase the king where it is going anyway; 15...♔f8!?) 16 ♔c2:

a) 16...f5?! 17 ♗xc6+ bxc6 18 ♘c4 ♔f8 19 ♗f4 ♗f6 20 ♖e6 ♔f7 (20...♖c8 21 ♖ae1 ♗h5 22 ♘d6 ♖d8 23 ♖xf6+ gxf6 24 ♗h6+ ♔g8 25 ♖e7 wins for White; 20...♗h4 21 ♖xc6 ♗xf2 22 ♖c7 ±) 21 ♖xc6 ♖d7 22 b5 ♖hd8 23

b6 g5 24 ♗c7 f4 25 ♗xd8 ♖xd8 26 b7 ♗f5+ 27 ♔c1 1-0 Zhigalko-Janocha, Polanica Zdroj 2001.

b) 16...♘e5 17 ♘b3 (not 17 ♗xb7? ♘d3 18 ♖f1 ♘xc1 19 ♗c6+ ♔f8 20 ♖axc1 ♗f5+ 21 ♘e4 h5 ∓) 17...0-0 18 ♗f4 ♘c4 19 ♘d4 ♗h4 20 ♖h1 g5 21 ♖xh4! gxh4 22 ♗xb7 ♖fe8 23 ♖g1 h5 24 ♗xf3 +– Godena-Genocchio, Saint Vincent 1998.

15...♔f8

Instead:

a) 15...0-0-0? 16 b5 ♖xd3 17 ♔xd3 ♗f5+ 18 ♔c4 ♘a5+ 19 ♔b4 ♗f6 20 ♗b2 b6 21 ♘xf3 is winning for White – Nunn.

b) 15...a6 16 ♗e4 ♖c8 17 a4 h5 18 ♘c4! (18 ♗a3?! ♖h6! 19 ♘xf3? ♖f6 ∓ Relange-Nunn, Hastings 1997/8) 18...♔f8 19 b5 axb5 20 axb5 ♘d8 21 ♘d6 ♗xd6 22 cxd6 ± Relange.

16 ♘c4 h5 17 ♗f4 g5 18 ♖xe7!?

18 ♗h2 and 18 ♗d6 are also possible but Black's pawns are already starting to look scary.

18...♘xe7 19 ♗xg5 h4 20 ♘d6 ♖h5 21 ♗f4 b6 22 ♗e4 ♘d5 23 ♗h2 bxc5 24 ♖d1 ♘xc3 25 ♔xc3 cxb4+ 26 ♔xb4

After sacrifice and counter-sacrifice, White retains the advantage but Black has good chances of a draw, Potkin-Najer, Moscow 2002.

D2)

6...♕xc5

By comparison with *4...♘c6 5 ♘f3 ♘f6 6 dxc5 ♕xc5*, Black can feel happier taking on c5 as his knight is still on b8, which means that the queen can retreat to c7 or c8 in one move.

7 ♘a3 *(D)*

7 h3 gives Black the opportunity to relocate his bishop to a more useful square: 7...♗d7! 8 ♘a3 e6 9 ♗e3 ♕a5 10 ♘c4 ♕c7 11 ♘ce5 ♗d6 12 ♘xd7 ♘bxd7 and the bishop-pair gives White no advantage here since Black's pieces are well placed, Shaked-J.Polgar, Tilburg 1997.

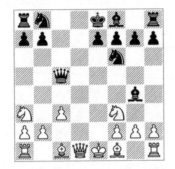

B

7...a6

This is the most common move, but it may not actually be necessary for Black to play this move now. Black should probably seek improvements here.

a) 7...♘c6?! 8 ♘b5 ♖c8 9 ♗e3 ♕h5 10 ♘xa7 ♖d8 11 ♕a4 g6 (Potkin-Frois, Linares 2002) and now 12 ♘xc6 +− is the simplest way to continue.

b) 7...♕c8 8 h3 (many other moves are possible here) 8...♗f5 9 ♗f4 a6 10 ♘c4 ♘bd7 (Pavasović-Bönsch, Portorož 1998) 11 ♗d3 ♗xd3 12 ♕xd3 ♘c5 13 ♕e2 ± Bosch.

c) 7...♘bd7 8 ♗e3 and then:

c1) 8...♕c7 9 h3 (9 ♕a4 followed by 10 0-0-0 should be compared with the main line, though perhaps Black can manage without ...a6) 9...♗h5 10 ♘b5 ♕b8 11 g4 ♗g6 12 g5 ♘e4 13

♘h4! (improving over 13 ♕a4 a6 14 0-0-0 ♗f5 15 ♗d3!? axb5 16 ♕xb5 ♘d6 17 ♗xf5 e6 18 ♕d3 with compensation, Jonkman-Sarbok, Reykjavik 2000) 13...a6 (after 13...e6 14 ♗g2 ♘d6 15 ♘xg6 hxg6 16 ♘xd6+ ♗xd6 17 ♕b3 White wins a pawn) 14 ♘xg6 hxg6 15 ♕d5 ♖h4 16 0-0-0 ♕c8 17 ♖d4 ± Vlassov-Avrukh, Moscow 2002.

c2) 8...♕c8 9 ♕a4 (9 h3 ♗h5 10 ♘c4!, Magomedov-Alia, Cappelle la Grande 1997, 10...♗xf3 11 ♕xf3 g6 ± Magomedov) 9...♗xf3 10 gxf3 a6 11 0-0-0 was the move-order of Rozentalis-Moreno, Linares 2002, analysed below under 7...a6 8 ♗e3 ♕c8 9 ♕a4+ ♘bd7 10 0-0-0 ♗xf3 11 gxf3.

8 ♗e3 ♕c7 (D)

8...♕c8 is also possible, but doesn't seem as good:

a) 9 h3 ♗e6 10 ♗e2 (10 ♘d4 ± Bosch) 10...♗d5 11 0-0 e6 12 c4 ♗c6 13 ♘b1 ♗e7 14 ♘c3 0-0 15 ♖c1 ♖d8 16 ♕b3 ± Shaked-Lerner, Berlin 1997.

b) 9 ♕a4+ ♘bd7 10 0-0-0 ♗xf3 11 gxf3 e6 12 ♖g1 b5 13 ♕b3 g6 14 ♔b1 ♗g7 15 f4 (threatening 16 ♗g2 ♖b8 17 ♗a7) 15...♖b8 16 ♗g2 ♕c7, Rozentalis-Moreno, Linares 2002. Black has wasted too much time and left himself behind in development. Now 17 ♘c2 (instead of 17 f5) leaves Black again unable to castle because of 18 ♘b4.

9 ♕a4+!

An important improvement over 9 h3 ♗h5 10 ♕a4+ ♘bd7, though this is also possible:

a) 11 0-0-0 e6 (11...♗xf3 12 gxf3 ♖d8 13 ♘c4 e6 14 ♗b6 ♕f4+ 15 ♔b1 ♖c8 16 ♖d4 ♕b8 ± Degraeve-Relange, French Ch (Narbonne) 1997) 12 g4

W

♗g6 13 ♗f4 (13 ♗g2 ♗e4 14 ♘b5 ♕b8 15 ♘a7, Rozentalis-Lerner, Groningen FIDE 1997, and now 15...b5 16 ♕xa6 b4 17 c4 ♗c5 gives Black good counterplay – Lerner) 13...♕c8 14 ♘e5 b5 15 ♕a5 ♗e4 16 f3 ♗b7 = Cherniaev-Shipov, St Petersburg 1997.

b) 11 ♗f4 ♕c8 and then:

b1) 12 ♘e5 and here:

b11) 12...b5? 13 ♕d4 e6 is recommended by Bosch, but can be met by 14 ♘xb5! axb5 15 ♗xb5 ♖a5 16 ♕b6 ♕a8 17 f3! ±.

b12) 12...e6 13 g4 (the move-order used in Pavasović-E.Bukić) is well met by 13...b5! (13...♗g6 – *12 g4 ♗g6 13 ♘e5 e6*). Then 14 ♕d4 ♗c5! 15 ♕d2 ♘xe5 16 ♗xe5 ♘e4! gives Black very good play, so White has to resort to 14 ♕a5 ♕b7 15 ♘xd7 ♘xd7 16 ♖g1 =.

b2) 12 g4 ♗g6 13 ♘e5 and now:

b21) 13...b5 14 ♕d4 ♗e4! (and not 14...e6?, Morgan-Nunn, Reading 2000, 15 ♘xb5! axb5 16 ♗xb5 ♖a5 17 ♕b6! ±) 15 ♖g1 e6? (15...♗b7! = with the idea that 16 ♘xb5? fails to 16...♘xe5 17 ♗xe5 axb5 18 ♗xb5+ ♗c6 ∓) 16 ♘xb5! axb5 17 ♗xb5 ♗d5 18 g5 ♕b7 (Morgan-Wise, British Ch (Millfield) 2000) 19 c4 ± (analysis by Morgan).

b22) 13...e6 14 ♗g2 ♗xa3! (better than 14...♘d5 15 ♗xd5 exd5 16 ♘xg6 b5 17 ♕b3 hxg6 18 0-0-0 ± Pavasović-E.Bukić, Slovenian Ch (Bled) 1998) 15 ♕xa3 ♗e4 16 ♗xe4 ♘xe4 17 ♘xd7 ♕xd7 18 0-0 ♕c6 19 ♖ad1 ♘f6 20 ♕d6 (20 ♖fe1 ♘d5 21 ♗g5 h6 22 ♗h4 g5 23 ♗g3 0-0-0 ∞ Morgan) 20...♕xd6 21 ♗xd6 0-0-0 (Morgan-Tan, St Albans 2001), and now after 22 ♖d4 ♘d5 23 ♗g3 ♘e7!, Black should have a draw.

We return to 9 ♕a4+! *(D)*:

B

9...♘c6

Or:

a) If 9...♗d7?! 10 ♘b5! ♗xb5? (10...♕c8 11 ♘e5 ±), then 11 ♗xb5+ ♘bd7 12 0-0-0 ♖d8 13 ♗xd7+ ♘xd7 14 ♖d2 e6 15 ♖hd1 +– Rozentalis-Watanabe, Linares 2002.

b) 9...♘bd7 10 0-0-0 and now:

b1) 10...e6? is bad due to 11 ♖xd7 (this shows the point of not including *9 h3 ♗h5*) 11...♘xd7 (11...♕xd7 12 ♗b5) 12 ♕xg4 ♗xa3 13 ♕xg7. Therefore Black has some problems developing his pieces.

b2) 10...e5 is possible, but the pawn can become vulnerable and Black doesn't take control over the d5-square as is the case after ...e6. White should probably try 11 h3:

b21) 11...♗h5 12 g4 ♗g6 13 ♗g2, and after 13...♗e4 14 g5 b5 15 ♕b3, Black can't play ...♘d5.

b22) 11...♗e6 12 ♗e2 ♗e7 13 ♘g5 ♗d5 14 ♗f3 ♗xf3 15 gxf3! (after 15 ♘xf3? 0-0 followed by 16...b5 Black is first to start his attack) 15...0-0 16 ♘c2 is rather complicated, but we think White has good prospects on the kingside.

b23) 11...♗f5 12 ♗e2 ♗e7 13 g4 ♗e6 14 ♘g5 ♗d5 15 ♗f3 and then:

b231) 15...♕c6 16 ♕xc6 bxc6 17 c4! ♗xf3 18 ♘xf3 ♗xa3 19 bxa3 ♔e7? 20 ♖he1 ± (e5 is vulnerable).

b232) 15...♗xf3 16 ♘xf3 b5 (after 16...0-0 17 g5 b5 18 ♕b3 White has the initiative) 17 ♘xb5 ♕b7 18 ♘d6+ ♗xd6 19 ♖xd6 ♕xf3 20 ♖hd1 0-0 21 g5 ♕xh3 22 gxf6 ♘xf6 23 ♖xa6 and White's queenside pawns must be the more dangerous, thanks to his strong bishop.

10 0-0-0 e6 11 ♘b5 ♕b8

11...♕c8 is met by 12 ♘a7.

12 ♘bd4 ♕c8 13 ♘xc6 ♕xc6 14 ♕xc6+ bxc6 *(D)*

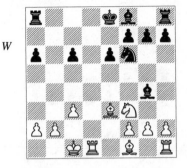

15 ♖d4!

White has an advantage in the endgame as he can attack the weak pawns on the queenside.

15...♗c5 16 ♖a4 ♗xe3+ 17 fxe3 ♗xf3 18 gxf3 a5 19 e4 ♘d7 20 ♖g1 g6 21 ♖g5 e5 22 ♖c4 f6 23 ♖g1 ♖a6 24 ♗h3

White is clearly better, Rozentalis-Lutz, Bundesliga 2001/2.

7 2...♘f6: Sidelines

1 e4 c5 2 c3 ♘f6 3 e5 ♘d5 *(D)*

Now:

A: 4 g3   116
B: 4 d4   120

4 ♘f3 is analysed in Chapter 10.

A)

4 g3

White plans to develop his bishop to g2, attacking the black knight. However, practice shows that the plan is too slow, as White has already made another non-essential pawn move by playing 2 c3.

4...d6

This is the most natural move. The main alternative is to play ...♘c6 and ...♕c7. This provokes White to play f4, an example reason being the line 4...♕c7 5 ♕e2 ♘c6 6 ♘f3 (6 ♗g2 is best, transposing to *4...♘c6 5 ♗g2*

♕c7 6 ♕e2), which is bad in view of 6...g5! 7 h3 ♗g7 8 ♗g2 ♘b6 9 0-0 ♘xe5 10 ♘xg5 c4 11 b3 d5 12 bxc4 ♕xc4 13 ♕h5 h6 14 ♘f3 ♘d3, when Black is much better, Finkel-Timoshenko, Nova Gorica 1997. However, we think that in most cases the inclusion of f4 works in White's favour.

After 4...♘c6:

a) 5 ♕e2 allows Black to play 5...g6 and develop his bishop on g7: 6 ♗g2 ♘c7 7 ♘f3 ♗g7 8 0-0 0-0 9 d4 cxd4 10 cxd4 d6 (only now, once he has castled, does Black attack the centre) 11 h3 ♗e6 12 ♘c3 ♕d7 13 ♔h2 ♖ad8 14 exd6 ♕xd6 15 ♗f4 ♕d7 16 ♘e5 ♘xe5 17 dxe5 ♘d5 18 ♘xd5 ♗xd5 19 ♖fd1 ♕e6 led to a quick draw in Finkel-Dvoirys, Beersheba 1997.

b) 5 ♗g2 and now:

b1) 5...e6 6 ♕e2 ♗e7 7 f4 (7 ♘f3 is too passive: 7...d6 8 exd6 ♕xd6 9 0-0 0-0 10 ♘a3 b6 11 ♘c4 ♕c7 12 a4 ♗b7 13 d3 h6 14 ♗d2 ♖ad8 15 ♖ad1 ♖fe8 16 ♖fe1 ♗f8 17 ♗c1 e5 gives Black comfortable play, Rozentalis-Ljubojević, Moscow OL 1994) 7...0-0 8 ♘f3 d6 9 0-0 dxe5 (9...♖b8 10 d3 b5 11 ♘bd2 ♘b6?! 12 exd6 ♗xd6 13 ♘e4 ♕c7 14 ♗e3 c4 15 ♗xb6 ♖xb6 16 d4 and White's play in the centre and kingside is more dangerous than Black's on the queenside, Rozentalis-Damljanović, Batumi Echt 1999) 10

♘xe5 ♘xe5 11 fxe5 ♖b8 12 d3 b6 13 ♘d2 leaves Black very solid, but White has more space, Rozentalis-Panzalović, Biel 1990.

b2) 5...♕c7 and now:

b21) 6 ♕e2 should be met by 6...e6 (and not 6...♕xe5? 7 ♕xe5 ♘xe5 8 ♗xd5 ♘d3+ 9 ♔e2! {9 ♔d1 ♘xf2+} 9...♘xc1+ 10 ♔e3, when sooner or later White will win the knight) 7 f4, transposing to *6 f4 e6 7 ♕e2*.

b22) 6 f4 e6 7 ♕e2 (7 ♘a3 ♗e7 8 ♘e2 0-0 9 0-0 a6 10 d3 and now 10...b5 gives Black a good position, but not 10...b6?! 11 c4 ♘db4 12 ♘b1 a5 13 ♘bc3, when White has an advantage, Azmaiparashvili-Krasenkow, Groningen FIDE 1997) and then:

b221) 7...a6 8 d3 b5 9 ♘f3 d6 10 c4! (10 0-0 dxe5 11 fxe5 ♗e7 12 a4 ♗b7 13 axb5 axb5 14 ♖xa8+ ♗xa8 is fine for Black, Rozentalis-Shirov, Manila OL 1992) 10...bxc4 11 dxc4 ♘b6 12 exd6 ♗xd6 13 0-0 is slightly better for White – Shirov.

b222) 7...♗e7 8 ♘f3 0-0 (8...a6 9 0-0 b5 10 a4 bxa4 11 ♖xa4 ♘b6 12 ♖a1 c4 13 d3 cxd3 14 ♕xd3 a5 15 ♖d1 ♗a6 16 ♕e4 0-0 17 ♘a3 ♖ab8 with chances for both sides, Rozentalis-Kotronias, Manila OL 1992) 9 0-0 d6 10 exd6 ♗xd6 11 d3 b6 (11...b5 is probably better) 12 ♘a3 a6 13 ♘c4 ♗e7 14 ♗d2 ♗b7 15 ♖ae1 ♖ad8 16 ♗c1, Sivokho-Svidler, St Petersburg 1996. In comparison with the positions arising after 4...d6, White is more active due to the pawn on f4.

5 exd6 *(D)*

5...e6

Black has other options:

a) 5...e5 6 ♗g2 ♕xd6 7 ♘e2 ♘c6 8 0-0 ♗g4 9 h3 ♗h5 10 g4 ♗g6 11 d4 0-0-0 12 ♘a3 ♕f6 13 ♕b3 e4 14 ♘g3 with a very sharp position, Rozentalis-Balinas, Philadelphia 1994.

b) 5...♕xd6 6 ♗g2 ♘c6 7 ♘e2 (after 7 ♘a3 ♘c7 8 ♘c4 ♕d3 9 ♕e2 ♕xe2+ 10 ♘xe2 ♗d7 11 d3 b5! {Cvetković} 12 ♘e3 e5 Black is not worse):

b1) 7...e6 8 0-0 ♗e7 9 ♘a3 0-0 10 d4 cxd4 11 ♘b5 ♕c5 12 ♘bxd4 ♗f6 13 ♘b3 ♕c4 14 ♘f4 ♘xf4 15 ♗xf4 ± Klinger-S.Gross, Balatonbereny 1993.

b2) 7...♗f5 8 d4 cxd4 (8...e6 is met by 9 0-0 threatening 10 c4) 9 ♘xd4 ♘xd4 10 ♕xd4 ♕e6+ 11 ♗e3 ♘xe3 12 fxe3 ♕a6 13 ♕d5 ♗d7!? (13...e6?! 14 ♕xb7 ♕xb7 15 ♗xb7 ♖b8 16 ♗c6+ leaves White a pawn up, Rozentalis-Gelfand, Tilburg rpd 1992) 14 ♕xb7 (14 ♖f1 e6 15 ♕h5 0-0-0! is unclear) 14...♕xb7 15 ♗xb7 ♖b8 16 ♗d5 ♖xb2 17 ♗b3 followed by ♘d2, and Black will have difficulty digging his rook out.

b3) 7...♗g4 8 h3 ♗h5 9 0-0 e6 10 g4 ♗g6 11 d4 ♖d8 12 ♘a3 ♕d7 (the inaccurate 12...♗e7 allows an immediate advance: 13 c4 ♘db4 14 d5 0-0 15 ♗f4 ♘e5 16 ♗g3 and the pinned knight becomes a great problem for Black, Rozentalis-Savchenko, Antwerp 1993) 13 ♘c4 ±.

b4) 7...g6! 8 d4 cxd4 9 ♘xd4 ♗g7 (9...♘xd4 10 ♕xd4 ♕e6+ 11 ♕e4 ♗g7 12 0-0 ♕xe4 13 ♗xe4 ♘c7 14 ♘a3 gives White a slight edge in the endgame, McDonald-Enders, Budapest 1995) 10 ♘xc6 ♕e6+ 11 ♘e5 ♕xe5+ 12 ♕e2 ♕xe2+ 13 ♔xe2 ♗g4+ is fine for Black, Mufić-Palac, Pula 1994.

6 ♗g2 ♗xd6 7 ♘f3

7 ♘e2 (from e2 the knight doesn't control the e5-square, and Black might exploit this fact later) 7...0-0 8 d4 ♘c6 9 0-0 ♘de7 (9...cxd4 10 ♘xd4 – 7 ♘f3 0-0 8 0-0 ♘c6 9 d4 cxd4 10 ♘xd4) 10 ♘a3 cxd4 11 ♘b5 ♗b8 12 ♘bxd4 e5 13 ♘xc6 ♘xc6 14 ♗e3 ♗g4 (the white knight on e2 is restricted by the e5-pawn) 15 ♖e1 ♕xd1 16 ♖axd1 ♗c7 with an equal endgame, Rozentalis-Rogers, Biel 1990.

7...0-0 8 0-0 ♘c6 (D)

W

9 d4

This is the only chance to fight for an advantage. Other moves:

a) 9 d3 gives White a form of reversed King's Indian in which he can expect no more than equality: 9...b6 (after 9...♘e5 10 ♘a3 ♗d7 11 ♘g5 ♗c6 12 ♘c4 ♘f6 13 ♘xe5 ♗xe5 14 ♗xc6 bxc6 15 ♕e2 ♗d6 16 ♘e4 ♗e7 17 ♗e3 White has an advantage, Rozentalis-Gelfand, Tilburg blitz 1992) 10 ♘bd2 ♗b7 11 ♕e2 ♗c7 12 ♘c4 ♖e8 13 a4 h6 14 ♗d2 ♕d7 15 ♖ad1 ♖ad8 16 ♗c1 e5 and Black has managed to seize the centre and the initiative, Short-Kasparov, London rpd (4) 1993.

b) 9 ♘a3 and now:

b1) 9...♘e5 10 d3! – 9 d3 ♘e5 10 ♘a3.

b2) 9...♗d7 10 ♘c4 ♗c7 11 d3 ♖c8 12 a4 b6 13 ♕e2 ♕e7 and now 14 ♗d2 leads to complicated play and is a better try than 14 ♘h4 ♘f4 15 ♗xf4 ♗xf4 = Rozentalis-Gelfand, Tilburg 1992.

b3) 9...b6 10 ♘c4 ♗c7 11 a4 ♗b7 12 d3 ♖b8 13 ♕b3 ♔h8 14 ♖e1 a6 15 ♗d2 ♗a8 16 ♖ad1 b5 17 axb5 axb5 18 ♘e3 ♘ce7 = Wahls-Tischbierek, Biel open 1993.

b4) 9...♗e7 10 d3 b6 11 ♘c4 ♗b7 12 a4 ♕c7 13 ♕e2 ♖ad8 14 ♗d2 ♖fe8 15 ♖ae1 ♗f8 16 ♗g5 f6 17 ♗c1 e5 gives Black a good position, Rozentalis-Rogers, Malmö 1993.

9...cxd4

Or:

a) 9...♗d7?! 10 c4 (this is better than 10 dxc5 ♗xc5 11 ♘bd2 ♗e7 12 ♕e2 ♕c7 13 ♘e4 ♖fe8 14 c4 ♘f6 15 ♘c3 a6 16 b3 e5 with equal chances, Rozentalis-Khalifman, Rakvere 1993) 10...♕b6 11 dxc5 ♗xc5 12 ♕e2 leaves Black's pieces poorly placed.

b) 9...♘de7 10 dxc5 ♗xc5 11 ♕e2 ♘g6 12 h4 ♕c7 13 h5 ♘ge5 14 ♘bd2

♘xf3+ 15 ♕xf3 gives White genuine threats on the kingside, M.Makarov-Filippov, Russian Cht (Moscow) 1994.

c) 9...b6 10 c4 ♘de7 11 ♘c3 ♗b7 12 d5 exd5 13 cxd5 ♘b4 14 ♘g5 h6 15 ♘ge4 ♘bxd5 16 ♗xh6 gxh6 (after 16...♗e5 17 ♗d2, the openness of the black king gives White the better prospects, Magem-Tiviakov, Madrid 1994) 17 ♘xd5 ♘xd5 18 ♕g4+ ♔h7 19 ♕f5+ ♔g7 20 ♖fd1 ♗e7 21 ♘c3 ♕c8 with an equal endgame – Magem.

10 ♘xd4 ♘xd4

Or:

a) 10...♘ce7 is too passive. After 11 c4 ♘f6 12 ♘c3 a6 13 b3 ♖b8 14 ♗b2 b6 15 ♕e2 White controls the centre and therefore stands better, Finkel-Tunik, Beersheba 1996.

b) 10...♗c5 11 ♘xc6 bxc6 and then:

b1) Not 12 ♕a4? ♕b6 13 ♕e4 ♗a6 14 c4 ♖ac8 15 ♘d2 ♘f6 16 ♕c2 ♗d4, when Black has seized an advantage, Finkel-Alterman, Israel 1994.

b2) 12 ♕e2 followed by 13 c4 gives White a slight edge due to his better pawn-structure.

c) 10...♗d7 (simply developing one more piece) 11 ♘f3 (11 c4 ♘de7 12 ♘b5 ♗e5 13 ♘1c3 a6 14 ♘d6 ♕c7 15 c5 ♖ad8 16 ♖e1 ♗c8 17 ♕h5 ♗xd6 18 cxd6 ♕xd6 19 ♘e4 is interesting, when White has the bishop-pair and some activity for the pawn, but it is still difficult to say if this compensation is sufficient, Rozentalis-Shirov, Tilburg 1993) 11...♘e5 12 ♘xe5 ♗xe5 13 ♘d2 ♕c7 14 ♕e2 ½-½ Rozentalis-Shirov, North Bay 1994.

11 ♕xd4 ♕c7! *(D)*

12 ♘d2

White can't win a pawn by 12 ♗xd5 exd5 13 ♕xd5, as the bishop-pair and the light-square holes on White's kingside give Black an enormous initiative.

12 ♖d1 is another try by White, but this is well met by 12...♗d7 (Black is also fine after 12...♗c5; for example, 13 ♕d3 ♗d7 or 13 ♕e4 ♘f6 14 ♕e2 e5) 13 c4 (13 ♗xd5 exd5 14 ♕xd5 ♗c6 15 ♕xd6? ♖fd8 16 ♕xc7 ♖xd1#) 13...♗c5 14 ♕d3 ♘f6 15 ♘c3 ♗c6 ∓ Christiansen-Hodgson, San Francisco 1998.

12...♗d7 13 ♘e4

Or 13 ♕c4 ♗c6 14 ♘f3 ♖ad8 15 ♖e1 e5 ∓ Stolz-Gustafsson, Bundesliga 2000/1.

13...♗b5

13...♗e5 is also sufficient. 14 ♕d3 and then:

a) 14...a6 15 ♖e1 ♗b5 16 ♕f3 ♗c6 17 ♕e2 ♘f6 (Black should choose 17...h6 =) 18 ♗g5 ♗xe4 19 ♗xe4 h6 20 ♗g2 with complications that are good for White, Rozentalis-Tkachev, Hastings 1997/8.

b) 14...♖ad8 15 ♖e1 ♗c6 16 ♕e2 h6 17 ♗d2 ♘f6 18 ♖ad1 ♘xe4 19 ♗xe4 ♗xe4 20 ♕xe4 ♗f6 with a very drawish position, Rozentalis-Akopian, Philadelphia 1994.

14 ♖e1 ♗e7 15 ♘g5 ♖ad8

Only not 15...h6? due to 16 ♘xe6! (16 ♘f3? = Rozentalis-Wojtkiewicz, Bad Godesberg 1994) 16...fxe6 17 ♖xe6 ♘f6 18 ♕e5, regaining the piece with a lot of interest.

16 ♕e4 ♗xg5 17 ♗xg5 ♖d7 18 ♖ad1 h6 19 ♗c1 ♖fd8 20 h3 ♗c6

The exchange of the light-squared bishops is inevitable, and a draw is then the most probable result, Rozentalis-Ftačnik, Lubniewice 1994.

B)

4 d4 *(D)*

4...cxd4

Or:

a) 4...♘c6 allows White to advance his pawns: 5 c4!? ♘c7 6 d5! ♘xe5 7 f4 ♘g6 8 h4 e6 (the knight is also in danger after 8...h5 9 ♗d3) 9 d6 ♘a6 10 g3 ♕f6 11 ♘c3 h5 12 ♘f3 b6 13 ♘e4 ♕f5 14 ♘fg5 ♗b7 15 ♗h3 and the queen is trapped, Adler-Zaid, USSR 1978.

b) 4...e6 5 ♘f3 ♘c6 6 c4 ♘db4 (after 6...♘b6, 7 d5 is very strong) 7

dxc5 (more tricky is 7 d5 exd5 8 cxd5 ♘d4 9 ♘xd4 cxd4 10 a3?! {10 ♗e2 is probably better} 10...♕a5! 11 ♗d2 d3 12 axb4 ♕xa1 13 ♗xd3 ♕xb2 14 0-0 ♕d4! 15 ♕f3 ♗xb4 16 ♕g3 ♗xd2 17 ♘xd2 0-0 ∞ Blauert-Sehner, W.German Ch (Bad Neuenahr) 1989) 7...♘a6 8 a3 ♘xc5 9 b4 ♘e4 10 ♗d3 d5 11 ♕c2 f5 12 exf6 ♕xf6 13 ♗b2 ♕g6 14 0-0 ± Totsky-Losev, Moscow 1996.

c) 4...d6 5 ♘f3 ♘c6 6 ♗c4 e6 7 0-0 cxd4 (7...dxe5 leads to an inferior endgame: 8 dxe5 ♘b6 9 ♗d3 c4 10 ♗e4 ♕xd1 11 ♖xd1 ♗d7 12 b3) 8 cxd4 transposes to *4...cxd4 5 ♘f3 e6 6 cxd4 d6 7 ♗c4 ♘c6 8 0-0*.

Now (after 4...cxd4), 5 ♘f3 is analysed in the next two chapters. Here we analyse:

B1: 5 ♕xd4 120
B2: 5 cxd4 124

Or 5 ♗c4 ♕c7! 6 ♕e2 ♘b6 7 ♗d3 (7 ♗b3 d3) 7...♘c6 8 ♘f3 d5 9 exd6 ♕xd6 10 ♘xd4 ♘xd4 11 cxd4 g6, and Black is fine – Sveshnikov.

B1)

5 ♕xd4

White captures the pawn with his queen, attacking the knight. However, as usual, putting the queen in the centre is not a good thing to do in the opening. Moreover, White has already spent one tempo preparing to recapture on d4 with the c3-pawn. Therefore this line doesn't bring any trouble to Black.

5...e6 *(D)*

6 ♘f3

Or:

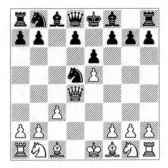

W

a) 6 ♗d3 ♘c6 7 ♕e4 d6 8 exd6 ♗xd6 9 ♘f3 f5 10 ♕e2 0-0 11 0-0 ♕f6 gives Black a strong centre and a good position – Sveshnikov.

b) With 6 ♗c4, White attacks the knight, but in many cases c4 will be a poor square for the bishop. 6...♘c6 7 ♕e4 and now:

b1) 7...f5 is active, but probably not the best move in this case: 8 ♕e2 (8 exf6 is a strategic mistake, as Black will have a good pawn-centre: 8...♘xf6 9 ♕e2 d5 10 ♗b5 ♗d6 11 ♘f3 0-0 12 0-0 ♕c7 13 ♖e1 e5 ∓ Slapikas-Kveinys, Mezezers Z 2000) 8...♘de7 9 ♘f3 ♘g6 10 0-0 ♕c7 11 ♖e1 ♗e7 (Black can also remove White's e-pawn with 11...♘cxe5, leading to an unclear position after 12 ♘xe5 ♘xe5 13 ♕xe5 ♕xc4 14 ♕xf5 ♗e7 15 ♕h5+ g6 16 ♕e5 0-0 17 ♘d2, Tobor-Kaplan, Balatonbereny 1993) 12 a4 0-0 13 ♘a3 a6 14 b4 b6 15 ♗b3 ♗b7 16 ♘c4 gives White more space, Slapikas-Sturua, Istanbul OL 2000.

b2) 7...♘de7 (Black withdraws his knight immediately, stressing the poor location of the white bishop) 8 ♘f3 ♘g6 9 0-0 ♕c7 10 ♖e1 b6 11 ♗b3 ♗b7 12 ♕e2 f6 13 exf6 gxf6 14 ♘a3

♗xa3 15 bxa3 0-0-0 16 ♘d4 ♘f4 17 ♗xf4 ♕xf4 leads to an advantage for Black, Timoshchenko-Zaichik, USSR 1977.

6...♘c6

6...d6 also gives Black equality: 7 ♘bd2 (or 7 exd6 ♕xd6 8 ♗b5+ ♗d7 9 ♗xd7+ ♕xd7 10 0-0 ♘c6 11 ♕e4 0-0-0 12 ♘bd2 f6 13 ♘d4 e5 14 ♘xc6 ♕xc6 is also level, Azmaiparashvili-Gelfand, Madrid 1996) 7...♘c6 8 ♗b5 ♗d7 9 ♗xc6 ♗xc6 10 ♘c4 dxe5 11 ♘cxe5 ♕b6 12 ♕xb6 axb6 13 ♘d4 ♖c8, Motwani-C.Werner, Cappelle la Grande 1996. Sooner or later White will have to take on c6, improving Black's pawn-structure.

7 ♕e4 (D)

B

7...d6

Or:

a) 7...♕c7 and then:

a1) 8 ♗c4 (again, this is not the best place for the bishop) 8...♘de7 9 ♗f4 ♘g6 10 ♗g3 a6 11 ♘bd2 b5 12 ♗d3 d6 13 exd6 ♗xd6 14 ♕e3 ♘f4 and White has to exchange one of his bishops for the black knight, Gdanski-Krasenkow, Polish Ch (Brzeg Dolny) 1996.

a2) 8 ♘bd2 b6 9 g3 ♗b7 10 ♗g2 ♘de7 11 0-0 ♘g6 12 ♕e2 ♗e7 13 ♖e1 0-0 with complicated play, Vorotnikov-I.Ivanov, Beltsy 1979.

a3) 8 g3 ♘de7 9 ♘a3 (making use of the fact that Black can't take the knight with his bishop) 9...♘g6 10 ♘b5 ♕b8 11 ♗f4 a6 12 ♘d6+ ♗xd6 13 exd6 b5 14 ♗g2 ♗b7 15 0-0-0 0-0 16 ♕e2 b4 17 c4 ♘a5 18 b3 ♘xf4 19 gxf4 ♕d8 20 ♖hg1 with a strong attack on the king, Rozentalis-Lanc, Trnava 1988.

b) 7...f5 *(D)* is better here than after 6 ♗c4 ♘c6 7 ♕e4, because now the queen's retreat to e2 will disturb the development of the light-squared bishop:

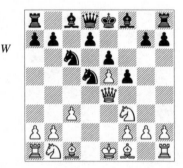

b1) 8 exf6 is not good, as it gives Black a strong centre: 8...♘xf6 9 ♕h4 d5 10 ♗d3 ♗d6 11 ♗g5 (or 11 ♗g6+ ♔e7 12 ♗c2 h6 13 ♗g6 ♗d7 14 ♗f4 e5 15 ♗g3 ♗e8 16 ♗xe8 ♖xe8, when Black is better, Novopashin-Sveshnikov, Volgodonsk 1981) 11...♔f7 12 ♘d4 h6 13 ♗e3 ♘e5 14 ♗c2 g5 15 ♕h3 ♘g6 16 g3 e5 17 ♘f5 ♘e7 18 f3 d4 with a dangerous initiative, Vorotnikov-Sveshnikov, Lvov 1983.

b2) 8 ♕e2 and now:

b21) 8...b6 9 g3 a5 10 c4 ♗a6 11 ♗g2 ♗b4+ (after 11...♗c5 12 0-0 0-0 13 b3 f4 14 ♗b2 a4 15 ♕d1 ♘de7 16 ♘c3 White has finished his development and has an advantage, Rogers-Shirov, Brno 1991) 12 ♗d2 0-0 13 0-0 and then:

b211) 13...♕b8 14 b3 ♘de7 15 a4 ♕e8 16 ♘c3 ♘g6 17 ♖ad1 gives White more space and a better position, Vorotnikov-Najer, Moscow 1998.

b212) 13...♕c7 14 b3 ♗xd2 15 ♕xd2 ♘xe5!? 16 cxd5 ♗xf1 17 ♔xf1 f4! 18 ♕d1 ♕c5! 19 ♘bd2 ♘g4 gives Black enough compensation for the material, Magem-B.Lalić, Manresa 1995.

b22) 8...d6 9 g3 ♕c7 (9...dxe5 10 ♘xe5 ♗d6 11 ♘xc6 bxc6 12 c4 ♘f6 13 ♗g2 ♕c7 14 0-0 0-0 15 b3 ♗e5 16 ♗b2 ♗xb2 17 ♕xb2 e5 18 ♘c3 e4 19 f3 gives White a small strategic advantage, Schmittdiel-Bönsch, Bundesliga 1998/9) 10 exd6 ♗xd6 11 ♗g2 0-0 12 0-0 ♘f6 13 c4 (13 ♘d4 is not dangerous for Black: 13...♘xd4 14 cxd4 ♗d7 15 ♘c3 a6 16 ♕d1 ♖ad8 17 ♕b3 b5 = Finkel-De Vreugt, Dieren 1997) 13...e5 14 c5 ♗e7 15 ♘c3 a6 16 ♕c4+ ♔h8 17 b4, Vorotnikov-Gorbatov, Moscow 1992. It seems that White has achieved more on the queenside than Black has in the centre.

b23) 8...♕c7 (Black chooses a plan where he doesn't exchange off the e5-pawn, but rather tries to attack it) 9 g3 ♘de7 10 ♘a3 (after 10 ♗f4 ♘g6 11 ♘bd2 ♘xf4 12 gxf4 ♘e7 13 0-0-0 ♘d5 14 ♘c4 b5 Black wins the e-pawn and gains an advantage: 15 ♘d6+ ♗xd6

16 exd6 ♕xd6 17 ♘e5 0-0, Mellado-Tukmakov, Barcelona 1993) 10...♘g6 11 ♘b5 ♕b8 12 ♗f4 a6 13 ♘bd4 ♘xd4 14 ♘xd4 b5 15 ♗g2 ♗b7 16 0-0 ♗e7 17 ♖fd1 0-0 18 ♖d3, Rozentalis-Yakovich, Tallinn 1986. White has more space and can try to attack the d7-pawn, but Black is solid and also attacks the e5-pawn.

8 ♘bd2 *(D)*

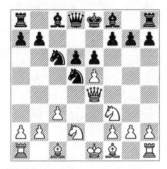

8...dxe5

The simplest way. Other options:

a) 8...♗e7 is probably too passive: 9 ♘c4 f5 (9...dxe5 10 ♘cxe5 ♘xe5 11 ♘xe5 0-0 12 ♗d3 ♘f6 13 ♕e2 ♗d6 14 ♘c4 gives White a slight edge due to his more active pieces, Malaniuk-Basin, Kostroma 1985) 10 ♕e2 dxe5 11 ♘cxe5 ♘xe5 12 ♘xe5 0-0 13 g3 ♕c7 14 ♗d2 ♗f6 15 f4 ♗xe5 16 ♕xe5 ♕xe5+ 17 fxe5 ♗d7 18 c4 ♘e7 19 ♗e2 and White is better in the endgame due to his two strong bishops, Finkel-Greenfeld, Beersheba 1996.

b) 8...♕c7 9 ♘c4 dxe5 10 ♘cxe5 ♘f6 11 ♕a4 ♗d6 12 ♘xc6 ♗d7 13 ♗g5 ♕xc6 14 ♕xc6 ♗xc6 15 ♘d4 ♗d7 with an equal endgame, Sveshnikov-Pigusov, Sochi 1987.

c) 8...♗d7 9 ♘c4 ♘xc3 10 bxc3 d5 11 ♕f4 dxc4 12 ♗xc4 ♗e7 13 0-0 0-0 14 ♗d3 with an unclear position, Sveshnikov-Beliavsky, USSR Ch (Tbilisi) 1978.

9 ♘xe5 ♘xe5

Or 9...♘f6 10 ♕a4 (after 10 ♘xc6 ♕xd2+! 11 ♗xd2 ♘xe4 Black is fine), and now:

a) 10...♕d5 11 ♘df3 ♗d6 12 ♗f4 ♕e4+ 13 ♕xe4 ♘xe4 14 ♗b5 0-0 15 ♖d1.

b) 10...♗d7 11 ♘xd7 ♕xd7 12 ♗b5 ♖c8 13 ♘e4 ♗e7 14 ♘xf6+ ♗xf6 15 ♗f4 a6 16 ♗e2 ♘e5 17 ♕xd7+ ♔xd7 18 0-0-0+ ♔e7 19 ♖he1 and White has the advantage of the bishop-pair, Sveshnikov-Browne, Wijk aan Zee 1981.

c) 10...♕c7 is probably best. After 11 ♘xc6 ♗d7 12 ♗b5 bxc6 13 ♗e2 ♗e7 14 ♘c4 ♘d5 15 0-0 0-0 16 ♖e1 ♖ad8 17 ♗d2 c5 18 ♕a5 ♕b8, White's pawn-structure is better, but Black's pieces are well placed, Hort-Polugaevsky, Biel 1990.

10 ♕xe5 *(D)*

10...♕c7

Or:

a) After 10...♞f6 11 ♞c4 ♗e7 12 ♕g3 White has some initiative, Sveshnikov-Shtyrenkov, USSR 1981.

b) 10...♕d6 11 ♕e4 (11 ♗b5+ ♗d7 12 ♗xd7+ ♕xd7 – *10...♕c7 11 ♗b5+ ♗d7 12 ♗xd7+ ♕xd7*) 11...♗e7 12 ♞c4 ♕c7 13 ♗d3 ♗f6 14 0-0 ♗d7 15 f4 ♗c6 16 ♕e2 0-0 17 ♞e5 g6 with unclear chances, Sveshnikov-Estevez, Cienfuegos 1979.

11 ♗b5+

11 ♞f3 ♕xe5+ 12 ♞xe5 ♗d6 13 ♞c4 ♗c7 14 ♞e3 ♞e7 15 ♗d2 ♗d7 = Campora-Spraggett, Spanish Cht (Cala Galdana) 1994.

11...♗d7 12 ♗xd7+ ♕xd7 13 0-0

After 13 ♞e4 ♕c7 14 ♕d4 ♞b6 15 0-0 ♖d8 16 ♕e3 ♗e7 Black successfully finishes his development, Rozentalis-Martin del Campo, Mendoza tt 1985.

13...♕c7! 14 ♕e2

14 ♕e4 ♗d6 15 ♞f3 0-0 = Campora-Yudasin, Spanish Cht (Cala Galdana) 1994.

14...♗d6 15 ♞f3 ♖c8 16 g3 0-0 17 ♞d4 ♕c5

The position is equal, Rogers-Yudasin, Moscow OL 1994.

B2)

5 cxd4 d6 *(D)*

5...e6 6 ♞f3 is analysed under *5 ♞f3 e6 6 cxd4*.

There are some independent options after 5...♞c6:

a) 6 ♗c4 ♞b6 (6...e6 7 ♗xd5 exd5 8 ♞c3 d6 =) 7 ♗b3 g6!? (7...d5 8 ♞e2!? ♗f5 9 0-0 e6 10 a3 ♖c8 11 ♞bc3 ♗e7 12 ♔h1 a6 13 ♗a2 ♞c4 14 ♞g3 ♗g6 15 f4 ∞ Antonio-Liu Dede,

Vung Tau Z 2000) 8 h4 h5 9 ♞f3 d5 ∞ Okhotnik-Manik, Kosice 1997.

b) 6 ♞f3 g6?! (6...d6 – *5...d6 6 ♞f3 ♞c6*; 6...e6 – *5 ♞f3 e6 6 cxd4 ♞c6*) 7 ♕b3! e6 (7...♞b6 8 d5 ♞a5 9 ♕b5 wins for White) 8 ♞c3 ♞xc3 9 bxc3 ± J.Littlewood-Ca.Hansen, British League (4NCL) 1998/9.

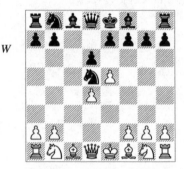

6 ♞f3

One of the authors tried to deviate from the main lines with 6 ♗c4 for a time, but Black found adequate responses after 6...♞b6:

a) 7 ♗b5+ and then:

a1) 7...♗d7 is a natural move but leads straight into complications after the spectacular 8 e6!:

a11) 8...fxe6 9 ♗d3 ♗c6 (9...g6 10 h4) 10 ♕g4 ♕d7 11 ♞h3 ♞a6 12 a3 g6 13 ♞g5 e5 14 ♞e6 e4 15 ♗xe4 ♗xe4 16 ♕xe4 ♕c6 17 ♕xc6+ bxc6 with equal chances, Rozentalis-Vitolinš, Daugavpils 1989.

a12) 8...♗xb5 9 ♕h5 ♕c8 10 ♕xb5+ ♕c6 (after 10...♔d8 11 ♗e3 ♕xe6 12 d5 ♕d7 13 ♗xb6+ axb6 14 ♕xb6+ ♕c7 15 ♕e3 ♕c5 16 ♕d2 Black has lost his right to castle, so White is probably slightly better, Rozentalis-Aseev,

Klaipeda 1988) 11 exf7+ ♔d8 12 ♘c3 ♕xb5 13 ♘xb5 ♔d7 14 ♘f3 ♘c6 15 ♗e3 e6 16 0-0 ♗e7 17 ♖fe1 ♖hf8 18 ♖e2 ♖xf7 with an equal endgame, Rozentalis-Arbakov, Uzhgorod 1987.

a2) 7...♘c6 is a more solid move:

a21) White can't play 8 ♘c3? since 8...dxe5 9 d5 a6 10 ♗a4 ♘xa4 11 ♕xa4 b5 12 ♘xb5 ♗d7 13 ♘c3 ♘d4 14 ♕d1 ♗f5 leaves him in trouble, Rozentalis-Sadler, Hastings 1997/8.

a22) 8 d5!? a6 9 ♗xc6+ bxc6 10 dxc6 dxe5 11 ♕h5 ♕c7 12 ♘f3 e4 (12...♕xc6?! 13 ♕xf7+! ∞ Cohen-Harley, Cambridge 2001) 13 ♘g5 (13 ♘d4 e5; 13 ♘e5 g6) 13...g6 14 ♕h4 ♕xc6 15 0-0 ♗b7 16 ♘c3 ♗g7 ∓.

a23) 8 exd6 ♕xd6 9 ♘c3 ♗d7 10 ♘ge2! (Esaulkov-Cherniaev, Moscow 1999) 10...e5!? 11 ♗e3 exd4 12 ♘xd4 ♘xd4 13 ♗xd7+ ♕xd7 14 ♕xd4 ♕xd4 15 ♗xd4 ♗b4 = Har-Zvi.

a24) 8 ♘f3 – *6 ♘f3 ♘c6 7 ♗c4 ♘b6 8 ♗b5*.

b) 7 ♗b3 dxe5 8 ♕h5 (the endgame after 8 dxe5 ♕xd1+ doesn't promise anything, so White tries to remove his queen) 8...e6 9 dxe5 ♘c6 10 ♘c3 (or 10 ♘f3 ♕d3 11 ♘c3 ♗b4 12 ♗d2 ♘a5 13 ♗d1 ♘ac4 14 ♗e2 ♕g6 15 ♕xg6 hxg6 16 ♘b5 ♘xd2 17 ♘xd2 ♔e7 with some advantage for Black) 10...g6 11 ♕g5 ♕xg5 12 ♗xg5 ♗g7 13 ♗f6 0-0 and Black is not worse in the endgame.

6...♘c6 *(D)*

7 ♗c4

Or:

a) 7 exd6 (White gives up his centre, so this move can't be good) 7...♕xd6 8 ♘c3 g6 9 ♗c4 ♘b6 10 ♗b3 ♗g7 11

0-0 0-0 12 d5 ♘a5 13 ♗g5 ♘xb3 14 ♕xb3 ♗g4 15 ♘d2 ♖ac8 leaves Black better, Sznapik-Kuligowski, Polish Ch playoff (3) (Warsaw) 1978.

b) 7 ♗d2!? (Devereaux) is one of the as yet almost untested avenues of the 2 c3 Sicilian. The idea is 7...♗g4 8 ♘c3 (though 8 ♗c4 e6 is also possible), when after 8...♘xc3?! 9 ♗xc3 White has avoided getting a weak pawn on c3. Black can instead play 8...dxe5 9 dxe5 ♘db4 10 ♗f4 ♗f5 11 ♖c1 ∞ or vary a move earlier with 7...dxe5 8 dxe5 g6 9 ♕b3! ♗g7 10 ♗c4 e6 11 ♘c3 ±.

c) 7 ♘c3 allows Black a comfortable endgame: 7...dxe5 (7...♘xc3 8 bxc3 dxe5 is dubious in view of 9 d5) 8 dxe5, and now:

c1) 8...♘db4 moves the knight from the centre to the edge, and allows White an advantage: 9 a3 ♕xd1+ 10 ♔xd1 ♘a6 11 b4 ♗g4 (11...♘c7 12 ♘b5 ♘xb5 13 ♗xb5 ♗d7 14 ♖e1 0-0-0 15 ♗d2 ± OII) 12 b5 0-0-0+ 13 ♗d2 ♘xe5 14 bxa6 ♘xf3 15 gxf3 ♗xf3+ 16 ♔c2 ♗xh1 17 ♗h3+ e6 18 ♖xh1 bxa6 (Kiik-Rõtšagov, Tallinn 1990) 19 ♘e4 gives Black a rook and three pawns for bishop and knight, but the white pieces are very active and the black king will have a lot of problems – Oll.

c2) With 8...♗e6, Black develops his queenside first and though he disturbs his kingside development, White can't profit from this:

c21) 9 ♘b5 ♕b6 10 ♘bd4 ♗g4 and Black is fine.

c22) 9 ♘d4 ♘xc3 10 bxc3 ♕a5 costs White a pawn.

c23) 9 ♕a4 ♘xc3 (not 9...♘db4?! 10 ♗b5 a6? 11 ♕xb4 axb5 12 ♕xb5 ♕a5 13 ♕xb7 ♘xe5 14 0-0 ♘xf3+ 15 ♕xf3 +– Voitsekhovsky-Filippov, Russian Ch (St Petersburg) 1998) 10 bxc3 ♗d5 11 ♗e2 ♕a5 and Black has nothing to fear in the endgame.

c3) 8...♘xc3 is a good move, and the most natural. Following 9 ♕xd8+, the endgame is OK for Black after either recapture:

c31) 9...♘xd8 10 bxc3 ♗d7 11 ♗e3 (or 11 ♘d4 ♘c6 12 ♖b1 0-0-0 13 e6 fxe6 14 ♗f4 e5 15 ♘xc6 ♗xc6 16 ♗xe5 ♖d5 ½-½ Lputian-Sveshnikov, Sochi 1985) 11...e6 12 a4 a6 13 ♗d3 ♖c8 14 ♔d2 ♗c5 15 ♗d4 h6 16 ♖hb1 ♖c7 17 ♔e3 ♗xd4+ 18 cxd4 ♘c6 19 ♘d2 ♘e7 = Al.Karpov-Brodsky, Russian Cht (Smolensk) 2000.

c32) 9...♔xd8 10 bxc3 ♗g4 11 ♖b1 (White also achieves nothing after 11 e6 ♗xe6 12 ♘g5 g6 13 ♘xe6+ fxe6 14 ♗c4 ♗g7 = Torre-Xu Jun, Shenzhen 1992) 11...♗xf3 12 gxf3 ♔c7 13 e6 fxe6 14 ♗c4 e5 15 ♗e3 g6 16 ♔e2 ♗g7 17 ♗d5 b6 18 ♗e4 e6 gives White compensation for the pawn, but nothing more, Rizouk-Bacrot, Linares open 2001.

7...♘b6

The black knight retreats, while also attacking the bishop. White rarely plays 5 cxd4 these days, as the rich volume of practice shows that Black equalizes easily here.

Other moves:

a) 7...e6 – 5 ♘f3 e6 6 cxd4 d6 7 ♗c4 ♘c6.

b) 7...dxe5 is risky: 8 ♗xd5 ♕xd5 9 ♘c3 ♕d6 (9...♕c4 10 d5 ♘b8 11 ♘xe5 ♕a6 12 ♕f3 ♕f6 13 ♕e2 g6 14 ♘c4 ♔d8 15 ♘e4 ♕f5 16 ♗g5 with a very strong initiative, Kaidanov-Kalinichev, Leningrad 1975) 10 d5 ♘d4 11 ♘xd4 exd4 12 ♕xd4 e5 13 ♕d3 ♗d7 14 0-0 f5 (14...♕g6 15 ♕xg6 hxg6 16 f4! ± Kwiatkowski-Ward, British Ch (Blackpool) 1988) 15 ♖e1 ♔f7 16 a4 a6 17 b3 e4 18 ♕h3 ♖c8 19 ♗a3 ♕c7 20 ♗b2, Regan-Grünfeld, USA 1979. The unsafe black king and the strong passed pawn give White the better chances.

Now we return to the position after 7...♘b6 (D):

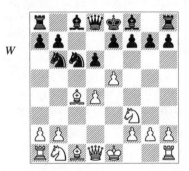

Now White can choose between:

The sacrifice 8 ♗xf7+? is not correct. The simplest reply for Black is to return the extra piece: 8...♔xf7 9 ♘g5+ ♔g8 10 e6 ♕e8 11 d5 ♘d8 12 ♘c3 h6 13 ♘h3 ♘xe6 14 dxe6 ♗xe6 15 ♘f4 ♗f7 and Black is a pawn up with a clear advantage, Berman-Minasian, Las Vegas 1993.

B21)
8 ♗b3!? dxe5

The right move, as the subsequent complications are not dangerous for Black.

8...d5 would be a natural move, were it not for the loss of tempo (...d6-d5) that it involves:

a) 9 ♘c3 ♗g4 10 ♗e3 e6 11 h3 ♗h5 12 ♕e2 ♗e7 13 0-0 0-0 leaves Black well developed, Zhachev-Kiseliov, Moscow 1988.

b) 9 h3 ♗f5 10 ♘c3 e6 11 0-0 ♗e7 12 ♗c2 ♗g6 13 ♗xg6 fxg6 14 ♘e2 0-0 15 b3 ♖f7 16 ♘e1 ♘d7 17 ♘d3 g5 18 ♗e3 ♘f8 19 ♕d2 ♘g6 = Arencibia-Vera, Cuban Ch (Matanzas) 1995.

c) 9 ♘h4! (to prevent the black bishop from being developed to an active location on g4 or f5) 9...e6 10 g3 ♗e7 11 ♕g4 g6 12 ♘f3 f5 13 ♕f4 ♗d7 14 ♘c3 leaves White better due to his space advantage. If Black tries to change matters by 14...g5 15 ♘xg5 ♗xg5 16 ♕xg5 ♕xg5 17 ♗xg5 ♘xd4 18 ♗d1, then White obtains the superior ending thanks to his bishop-pair, Vi.Ivanov-Karasev, Moscow 1986.

9 d5

9 ♘xe5 leads to an equal endgame: 9...♘xe5 10 dxe5 ♕xd1+ 11 ♗xd1 ♘c4 12 f4 e6 13 ♗f3 ♗d7 14 ♗xb7

♖b8 15 ♗e4 ♘xb2 16 ♘d2 ♘a4 and Black is fine, Laub-Ikonnikov, Geneva 1993.

9...♘a5

9...♘b4 is also possible:

a) 10 ♘xe5 ♘4xd5 11 0-0 (11 ♕f3!?) 11...e6 12 ♘c3 ♗d6! ∞.

b) 10 ♘c3 e6 11 ♗g5 ♗e7 (not 11...f6? 12 ♘xe5! +–) 12 ♗xe7 (12 dxe6 ♗xg5! 13 exf7+ ♔f8 14 ♘xg5 ♕xg5 15 0-0 ♘c6 16 f4 ♕e7 17 ♕h5 ♗e6 ∓ Potkin-Shaposhnikov, St Petersburg 1998) 12...♕xe7 (12...♔xe7 13 ♘xe5 ♘6xd5 14 ♘xd5+ ♘xd5 15 0-0 and Black's extra pawn does not compensate for his poor development and weak king position, Rechel-Heidrich, 2nd Bundesliga 1998/9) 13 d6 ♕f6 14 ♘e4 (14 0-0 is probably better) 14...♕g6 15 ♕e2 ♘c6 16 ♖d1 (16 0-0 f5! ∓ Pavasović-Volzhin, Budapest 1995) 16...0-0 17 0-0 ♘d7 with a tense and unclear position.

10 ♘c3 ♘xb3

Or:

a) 10...f6 11 0-0 g6 12 ♗e3 ♗d7 13 ♘d2 ♖c8 14 ♕e2 ♗g7 15 f4 exf4 16 ♗xf4 gives White good compensation for the pawn, Sermek-Filippov, Bled 2001.

b) 10...g6 11 ♘xe5 ♘xb3 (11...♗g7 12 ♗f4 ♘d7?, Rausis-Sadler, Gausdal 1995, 13 ♘xf7! ♔xf7 14 ♗c7! +–) 12 ♕xb3 ♗g7 13 ♗f4 0-0 14 ♖d1 ♗f5 15 0-0 ♘d7 16 ♖fe1 ± Hoffman-Quiroga, Argentinean Ch (Villa Martelli) 1998.

11 ♕xb3 e6

Not 11...e4 12 ♘g5 ♗f5 13 ♗e3 h6 14 ♘e6! ± Novak-Gombac, Opatija 2002.

12 ♘xe5 exd5

Black should avoid 12...♘xd5 13 ♕b5+ ♗d7 14 ♕xb7 ♘xc3 (14...♗b4 15 0-0!? Gallagher) 15 bxc3 ♕c8 16 ♕f3 ± Sveshnikov.

13 ♗e3 ♗d6 14 ♕b5+ (D)

14...♔f8!

This is best. Instead:

a) 14...♘d7 is bad because of 15 ♘xf7 ♔xf7 16 ♕xd5+ ♔e7 17 0-0-0 ♘f6 18 ♕g5, when White's attack is very dangerous.

b) 14...♗d7 15 ♘xd7 ♕xd7 16 0-0-0 ♕xb5 17 ♘xb5 ♔d7 18 ♗xb6 axb6 19 ♖xd5 gives White a slightly better endgame, Vi.Ivanov-R.Gasanov, Moscow 1994.

15 ♘f3

White's original idea in this line was the spectacular 15 0-0-0?!, with the point 15...♗xe5 16 ♘xd5 ♗d6! (16...♘d7? loses to 17 ♕b4+! ♔e8 18 ♖he1 – Gallagher) 17 ♘xb6 axb6 18 ♗xb6 ♗d7 19 ♖xd6 regaining the sacrificed piece – Vi.Ivanov. However, after 15...♗e6, White's king is more exposed to tactical danger on the queenside than it would have been on the kingside, so the prosaic 15 ♘f3 followed by 16 0-0 therefore makes

more sense. After 15 0-0-0?! ♗e6, White has tried:

a) 16 f4 ♗xe5 17 fxe5 h6 18 h4 ♔g8 19 ♔b1 ♕c7 20 ♗xb6 ♕xb6 21 ♕xb6 axb6 22 ♘xd5 ♖a5 and Black is better, Van der Werf-Van Wely, Wijk aan Zee 1995.

b) 16 ♘f3 ♖c8 17 ♔b1 ♘c4 18 ♘xd5 a6 19 ♕b3 ♕a5 20 ♗b6 ♘xb6 21 ♕xb6 ♕xb6 22 ♘xb6 ♖c6 and Black's bishops will be more effective than White's knights, Pavasović-Jelen, Ljubljana 1997.

15...♗e6

After 15...♗g4!? White may do best to revert to the plan of queenside castling by 16 0-0-0 (16 ♗xb6 ♕xb6 17 ♕xb6 axb6 18 ♘xd5 ♗xf3 19 gxf3 ♗e5 ∓; 16 ♘d4!?) 16...♖c8 17 ♔b1 ♗e6, as he gains a tempo in comparison with *15 0-0-0?! ♗e6 16 ♘f3 ♖c8 17 ♔b1*. However, the position is still far from clear; e.g., 18 ♖he1 ♘c4 19 ♘xd5 a6 20 ♕b3 ♗f5+ 21 ♔a1 ♗c2 22 ♕xb7 ♗xd1 23 ♖xd1 ∞ Zak-Kullamaa, USSR 1984.

16 0-0 ♘c4

After 16...♕e8, White can either play 17 ♗xb6 axb6 18 ♕xb6 ♕c6 = or try 17 ♖ad1, transposing to Mukhametov-Makarov, Omsk 1996, which continued 17...♕xb5 18 ♘xb5 ♗e7 19 b3! h6 20 ♖fe1 (20 ♖c1!?) 20...♗b4 21 ♖e2 ♖d8! 22 ♘xa7 =.

17 ♕xb7 ♕c8 18 ♕xc8+ ♖xc8 19 ♗d4 ♗c5

This move is too accommodating. 19...♘xb2 20 ♘b5 ♘c4 21 ♘xd6 ♘xd6 22 ♗xa7 leaves White with the better bishop, but 19...a6 20 b3 ♘a5 21 ♘a4 ♘c6 is fine for Black.

20 ♗xc5+ ♖xc5 21 ♘a4 ♖c8 22 b3 ♘a3 23 ♘d4

White has a marginal advantage here and went on to win the ending in Pavasović-Jelen, Ljubljana 2002, but as the improvements above indicate, Black need not fear this line. White can play this line, hoping that his opponent will not know or find the play up to and including 14...♚f8!, and can at least be reassured that 15 ♘f3 ♗e6 16 0-0 (unlike 15 0-0-0?!) leaves him no worse and with chances to outplay his opponent in the ensuing endgame.

B22)
8 ♗b5 *(D)*

8...dxe5

This is the most popular move. Black can also play:

a) 8...♗d7 and then:

a1) 9 exd6 and here:

a11) 9...exd6 10 ♘c3 ♘b4 11 ♗xd7+ ♕xd7 12 0-0 ♗e7 13 ♕b3 (Cherniaev-Ljubojević, Antwerp 1994) 13...♘c6 14 d5 ±.

a12) 9...e6 10 ♗g5 ♕b8 11 ♘c3 ♗xd6 12 0-0 0-0 13 ♖e1 a6 14 ♗d3

♘b4 with chances for both sides, Godena-Efimov, Genoa 1998.

a2) 9 ♘c3 and now:

a21) 9...e6 is probably too slow. 10 0-0 – 5 ♘f3 e6 6 cxd4 d6 7 ♗c4 ♘c6 8 0-0 ♘b6 9 ♗b5 ♗d7 10 ♘c3 ±.

a22) 9...dxe5, opening the centre, is best. Then:

a221) The pawn sacrifice 10 d5 doesn't promise White sufficient compensation: 10...♘b4 11 ♘xe5 ♗xb5 12 ♘xb5 g6 13 ♕b3 ♘4xd5 14 ♗e3 e6 15 ♗d4 ♗g7 and Black is just a pawn up, Sveshnikov-Zaid, USSR 1976.

a222) After 10 dxe5 g6 11 0-0 ♗g7 12 ♗f4 0-0 13 h3 a6 White has more space, but his central pawn can become a target, so the position is level, Zhuravliov-Al.Khasin, USSR 1976.

b) 8...d5 closes the centre, but again the pawn has spent two moves reaching d5. 9 0-0 (9 ♘h4!? is interesting but has never been tested) 9...♗g4 10 h3 ♗xf3 11 ♕xf3 e6 12 ♗e3 ♖c8 13 ♘d2 a6 14 ♗xc6+ ♖xc6 15 ♖fc1 ♘c4 16 ♕e2 ♘xd2 17 ♖xc6 bxc6 18 ♕xd2 ♕b6 and White cannot exploit the weakness of the black c-pawn, as his bishop is rather bad, Sturua-Minasian, Erevan OL 1996.

9 ♘xe5 ♗d7 *(D)*
10 ♗xc6

Other moves don't give White an advantage either:

a) 10 ♘xd7 ♕xd7 11 ♘c3 (11 0-0 g6 12 ♘c3 ♗g7 13 d5 ♗xc3 14 dxc6 bxc6 15 ♗xc6 ♕xc6 16 bxc3 0-0 is slightly better for Black, Pavasović-Jelen, Slovenian Ch (Maribor) 1998) 11...e6 and here:

W

a1) 12 0-0 ♗e7 13 ♕g4 0-0 14 ♗xc6 (14 ♖d1 ♖fd8 15 ♗h6 g6 16 ♖ac1 ♖ac8 17 h4 a6 18 ♗xc6 ♖xc6 19 ♗g5 ♖c4 and Black seizes the initiative, Emms-Macieja, Batumi Echt 1999) 14...bxc6 15 ♗h6 ♗f6 16 ♖fd1 ♔h8 17 ♘e4 ♕e7 18 ♗g5 ♗xg5 19 ♕xg5 ♕b4 = Godena-Ki.Georgiev, Bastia 1999.

a2) 12 ♕g4 h5 (a typical move: White is forced to remove his queen from the g4-square, where it could control the key squares d4 and g7) 13 ♕f3 a6 14 ♗xc6 ♕xc6 15 ♕xc6+ bxc6 16 ♔e2 ♔d7 17 ♗e3 ♘d5 18 ♖ac1 ♗d6 with a very drawish endgame, Sveshnikov-Sakaev, Russian Ch (St Petersburg) 1998.

b) 10 ♘c3 also leads to equality:

b1) 10...e6 and now:

b11) 11 ♕g4 is not dangerous for Black: 11...♘xe5 12 dxe5 ♗xb5 13 ♘xb5 ♕d7 14 ♘c3 ♕d3 15 ♗d2 ♘c4 16 0-0-0 ♖c8 17 ♗f4 ♕g6 18 ♕xg6 hxg6 19 ♔b1 ♘a3+ 20 ♔a1 ♘c2+ with perpetual check, Sveshnikov-Tal, USSR Ch (Tbilisi) 1978.

b12) 11 0-0 – *5 ♘f3 e6 6 cxd4 d6 7 ♗c4 ♘c6 8 0-0 ♘b6 9 ♗b5 ♗d7 10 ♘c3 dxe5 11 ♘xe5* ±.

b2) With 10...♘xe5 Black goes for exchanges, as he has nothing to fear in the endgame: 11 dxe5 ♗xb5 12 ♘xb5 ♕xd1+ 13 ♔xd1 ♘d5 (13...0-0-0+ leads to a forced draw after 14 ♔e2 ♖d5 15 a4 ♖xe5+ 16 ♗e3 ♘d5 17 ♖ac1+ ♔b8 18 ♖hd1 e6 19 ♔f3 ♖f5+ 20 ♔e2 ♖e5 and the players repeat moves, Novik-Maliutin, Jurmala jr 1989), and now:

b21) 14 ♔e2 a6 15 ♖d1 0-0-0 16 ♘d4 (after 16 ♘a3 e6 17 ♘c4 ♗e7 18 ♗d2 b6 19 g3 ♔b7 20 ♘e3 ♘c7 Black has the superior pawn-structure, Sveshnikov-Kasparov, USSR Ch (Minsk) 1979) 16...e6 17 ♗g5 ♖d7 18 ♖ac1+ ♔b8 19 ♘b3 h6 20 ♗e3 ♗e7 21 g3 b6 and Black's chances are slightly better, Golod-Tsesarsky, Givataim rpd 1998.

b22) 14 ♗d2 e6 15 ♔e2 ♗e7 16 ♖ac1 ♔d7 17 ♖hd1 ♖hc8 18 ♘c3 ♘xc3+ 19 ♗xc3+ ♔e8 and a draw was soon agreed in Sveshnikov-Andersson, Wijk aan Zee 1981.

10...♗xc6 11 ♘xc6 bxc6 12 0-0 *(D)*

B

12...g6

The other good possibility, 12...e6, leads to more complicated play:

a) 13 ♞c3 ♝e7 14 ♝f4 0-0 15 ♖e1 (after 15 ♝e5 ♛d7 16 ♛e2 a5 17 ♖fd1 f6 18 ♝g3 ♖fe8 19 ♖ac1 a4 Black has some initiative, Dolmatov-Vaiser, Novosibirsk 1993) 15...♛d7 16 ♝e5 ♞c4 17 ♛e2 ♞xe5 18 dxe5 ♖fd8 19 ♖ad1 ♛c7, Zarnicki-Alterman, Erevan OL 1996. Both sides have a weak pawn: White on e5 and Black on c6.

b) 13 ♛g4 h5 14 ♛e4 ♖c8 15 ♞c3 ♝e7 16 ♝e3 0-0 17 ♖ac1 ♞d5 18 ♛f3 g6 (Rozentalis-Shirov, Erevan OL 1996) 19 ♞a4 is equal.

13 ♖e1

After 13 ♞c3 ♝g7 14 ♝e3 0-0 15 ♛e2 ♞d5 Black is fine, Maciejewski-Brodsky, Karvina 1992.

13...♝g7 14 ♝g5 *(D)*

14...0-0

14...♞c8 is also a clever move: 15 ♛f3 0-0 16 ♛xc6 ♖b8 17 ♛c2 (the natural move 17 ♖e2? loses a pawn after 17...♛xd4 18 ♞c3 ♖xb2 19 ♖xb2 ♛xc3 20 ♛xc3 ♝xc3, Keitlinghaus-Stohl, Bundesliga 1998/9) 17...♛xd4 18 ♞c3 with equal chances.

15 ♝xe7 ♛xd4 16 ♛xd4 ♝xd4 17 ♞d2 *(D)*

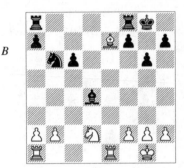

17...♖fb8

This is better than 17...♖fe8 18 ♝a3 c5 19 ♔f1 c4 20 ♖xe8+ ♖xe8 21 ♖c1 ♖c8 22 ♞e4, when White has some chances in the endgame.

18 ♖ac1

Now, Black can meet 18 ♝a3 with 18...♞a4.

18...♝xb2 19 ♖xc6 ♞d5

A draw is inevitable – Alterman.

8 2...♘f6 3 e5 ♘d5 4 d4 cxd4 5 ♘f3: 5...e6 and Other Moves

1 e4 c5 2 c3 ♘f6 3 e5 ♘d5 4 d4 cxd4 5 ♘f3 *(D)*

5...e6

Black opens a pathway for his king's bishop and takes control over the d5-square. However, we don't think this is Black's best plan. It gives White a stable central position with more space, though there is still plenty of complicated and unclear play. Other moves:

a) 5...♘c6 is analysed in the next chapter.

b) 5...b6 6 ♗c4 (6 cxd4 e6 – *5...e6 6 cxd4 b6*) 6...♗b7 7 0-0 e6 8 ♘xd4 (8 cxd4 transposes to *5...e6 6 cxd4 b6 7 ♗c4 ♗b7 8 0-0*, while avoiding Black's alternative 7...♗a6) 8...♕c7 9 ♕e2 a6 10 ♖d1 g6?! 11 b3 ♗g7 12 f4 b5 13

♗xd5 ♗xd5 14 ♗a3 ♘c6 15 ♘xc6 ♗xc6 16 ♘d2 ♕b7 17 ♘f1 is good for White, as he controls the dark squares, Sveshnikov-Al.David, Bled 1996.

c) 5...d6 is an important and fairly common move which often transposes to other lines but has some nuances worth noting. White can choose from:

c1) 6 cxd4 – *5 cxd4 d6 6 ♘f3*.

c2) 6 exd6 ♕xd6 7 ♘xd4 a6 8 ♘d2 g6 ∞ Vogt-Cvitan, Swiss Cht 1999.

c3) 6 ♗c4 ♘b6 (6...e6 7 cxd4 – *5...e6 6 cxd4 d6 7 ♗c4*) 7 ♗b3 and then:

c31) 7...d5 means that Black has played ...d6-d5 in two moves, and this is enough to give White a small but stable advantage after 8 cxd4 ♘c6 9 ♘c3 ♗g4 10 ♗e3 e6 11 h3 – Sveshnikov.

c32) 7...dxe5 8 ♘xe5 e6 9 0-0 ♘c6 10 ♘xc6 (10 ♘f3!?) 10...bxc6 11 cxd4 ♗e7 12 ♘c3 0-0 13 ♗f4 ♗a6 14 ♖e1 c5 (Black exchanges his weak pawn, but this doesn't solve all his problems) 15 dxc5 ♕xd1 16 ♖exd1 ♗xc5 17 ♘e4 ♗e7 18 ♖ac1 ♖fc8 19 ♘d6 ♖xc1 20 ♖xc1 ♖d8 21 ♖c6 ♗xd6 22 ♖xd6 ♖xd6 23 ♗xd6 gives White a queenside majority and the better endgame, Kharlov-Yudasin, Kemerovo 1995.

c33) 7...♘c6 is best, transposing to *5...♘c6 6 ♗c4 ♘b6 7 ♗b3 d6*.

c4) 6 ♕xd4 e6 7 exd6 (after 7 ♘bd2 ♘c6, 8 ♕e4 transposes to *5 ♕xd4 e6 6 ♘f3 ♘c6 7 ♕e4 d6 8 ♘bd2*, while 8 ♗b5 has been tried as an attempt to exploit the move-order, but without much success) 7...♕xd6 8 ♗d3 (8 ♘a3 is also logical) 8...♘c6 9 ♕e4 ♗e7 10 0-0 ± Tzermiadianos-Pountzas, Aegina 1997. This is White's only serious attempt to exploit Black's move-order; the point is that White's queen being on d4 forces Black to recapture on d6 with the queen rather than the bishop; in the line after *5 ♕xd4 e6 6 ♘f3*, Black would first kick the queen with *6...♘c6 7 ♕e4* and only then continue *7...d6*.

6 cxd4 *(D)*

6 ♗c4!? is an important alternative for White to consider, as it aims to rule out Black's option of playing ...b6:

a) 6...dxc3?! 7 ♗xd5 cxb2 8 ♗xb2 ♕a5+ 9 ♘c3 ♗a3 10 ♕b3 ♗xb2 11 ♕xb2 exd5 12 ♖d1 ♘a6 13 0-0 ♘c7 14 ♘d4 ± Antonio-Bellon, Thessaloniki OL 1988.

b) 6...b6?! 7 ♗xd5 exd5 8 ♕xd4 ±.

c) 6...♘c6 7 ♗xd5?! (7 cxd4 – *6 cxd4 ♘c6 7 ♗c4*) 7...exd5 8 cxd4 d6 ∓.

d) 6...♘b6 7 ♗b3 (7 ♗d3 is also possible) 7...dxc3!? (7...d6 8 cxd4 – *6 cxd4 d6 7 ♗c4 ♘b6 8 ♗b3*) 8 ♘xc3 d5 9 exd6 ♕xd6 (9...♗xd6 10 0-0 ♘c6 11 ♕e2 0-0 12 ♖d1 ♘d5 13 ♘xd5 exd5 14 ♗xd5 ♕e7 15 ♕xe7 ♗xe7 16 ♗e3 ♘b4 17 ♗b3 ♗f5 18 ♖ac1 ± Emms-Cummings, British Ch (Hove) 1997) 10 ♕e2 ♘c6 11 0-0 a6 12 ♖d1

♕c7 ∞ Blauert-Rotshtein, Groningen 1992.

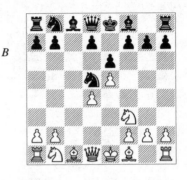

B

Now:

A: **6...♘c6** 133
B: **6...d6** 135
C: **6...b6** 141

6...♕c7 is a subtle alternative. Black prevents 7 ♘c3 and 7 ♗c4, but White can safely play 7 ♗d3 ♘c6 8 0-0 ♘cb4 9 ♗e4 f5 10 exf6 ♘xf6 11 ♘c3 ♘xe4 12 ♘xe4 ♕c2 13 ♘c3 with a slight advantage, as in Godena-Janssen, Cannes 1998.

A)

6...♘c6 7 a3!?

With this ambitious move, White aims to gain a tempo in some lines by playing the king's bishop to d3 in one go rather than to c4 first and then back to d3. An immediate 7 ♗d3 is well met by 7...d6 8 0-0 ♘db4! = so White first makes the useful move a3. This idea is more effective against 6...♘c6 than other move-orders as Black does not have the option of playing ...♗d7 and ...♗c6. Nevertheless, it might still be better for White to play 7 ♗c4 d6, transposing to *6...d6 7 ♗c4 ♘c6*. This has the added practical advantage of leaving White one less line to learn!

7...d6 8 ♗d3 *(D)*

8...dxe5

Instead:

a) 8...♕a5+ 9 ♗d2 ♕b6 10 ♘c3! ♘xc3 11 ♗xc3 is slightly better for White, Chandler-Kasparov, Wattignies U-16 Wch 1976.

b) 8...♗e7 9 0-0 0-0 10 ♖e1 leaves White a clear tempo up on the line *6...d6 7 ♗c4 ♘c6 8 0-0 ♗e7 9 a3 0-0 10 ♖e1* followed by ♗d3. White has very good attacking prospects.

c) The immediate 8...g6 gives White the option of 9 ♗g5 (after 9 0-0 ♗g7 10 ♖e1 0-0, Black will eventually exchange on e5 anyway, transposing to lines we consider via *8...dxe5*) 9...♕c7 10 exd6 ♕xd6 11 ♘bd2 ♗g7 12 ♘c4 ♕c7 13 ♖c1 0-0 14 0-0 with the slightest of advantages for White, Benjamin-V.Milov, New York 1997.

9 dxe5 g6

This is the best move, but not one Black is likely to come up with unless he has prepared to play this line. Black takes two moves to develop his king's

bishop but thereby places it aggressively, targeting White's vulnerable e5-pawn, rather than passively on e7. White's slow development with 7 a3 gives Black time to get away with this. Nor can White exploit the dark-squared weaknesses that ...g6 creates: his bishop cannot get to the a3-f8 diagonal because of the pawn on a3, and his knights cannot get to f6 or h6 while keeping e5 defended. Other plans allow White to justify his opening strategy fully:

a) Grabbing the e5-pawn immediately with 9...♕c7 10 0-0 ♘xe5 11 ♘xe5 ♕xe5 offers White strong compensation following 12 ♗b5+ ♗d7 13 ♗xd7+ ♔xd7 14 ♖e1 ♕d6 15 ♕f3 ♗e7 16 ♘c3, Vogt-Reich, Bundesliga 1993/4.

b) Attacking on the kingside with 9...♗e7 10 0-0 g5!? is a reasonable try, but is well met by 11 ♖e1 g4 12 ♘fd2 ♘f4 13 ♗f1 h5 14 b4 ± Golod-G.Kuzmin, Iraklion 1995.

10 0-0 ♗g7 11 ♖e1 0-0 *(D)*

White has more space, but endings are likely to be better for Black because of the potential weakness of the e5-pawn, especially if only the dark-squared bishops are left. Therefore, White does best to keep pieces on and take his chances in the middlegame by seeking to launch a kingside attack and/or playing a knight to d6.

12 b4

White makes another pawn move, but it does gain more space and prepare a smoother development of the queenside. Alternatives:

a) 12 ♘c3 ♘xc3 13 bxc3 ♕a5 14 ♕e2 ♕xc3 15 ♗d2 ♕c5 16 ♖ec1 ♕e7 17 ♗b5 ♖d8 18 ♗xc6 bxc6 19 ♖xc6 ♗b7 20 ♗g5 ♕e8 ∓ Etchegaray-Gallagher, Lausanne 2000.

b) 12 ♕e2 b6 (12...f6!? is an interesting attempt to exploit Black's lead in development by building up pressure on the f-file) 13 ♗d2 (13 h4!?) 13...♗b7 14 ♘c3 ♘a5! 15 ♖ad1 ♘b3 ∞ Adams-Anand, Paris rpd 1992. Then 16 ♗g5 is met by 16...♘xc3 17 bxc3 ♗xf3 18 ♕e3 ♕c7 ∓.

12...b6 13 ♕b3

After 13 ♗b2 ♗b7, White still can't play 14 ♘bd2? because of 14...♘dxb4! 15 axb4 ♕xd3, and 14 ♘c3?! ♘xc3 15 ♗xc3 ♘e7 16 ♗e4 ♗xe4 17 ♖xe4 ♕xd1+ 18 ♖xd1 ♘d5 ∓, Westerinen-Tisdall, Gausdal 1997, shows precisely the kind of piece exchanges that White should avoid.

13...♗b7 14 ♘bd2 ♖c8 15 ♗b2 ♘f4 16 ♗e4 ♖c7 17 ♘c4

White's knight is going to reach d6, so he has a slight advantage, Brynell-Cramling, Swedish Cht 1998/9.

B)

6...d6 (D)

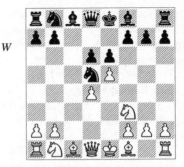

7 ♗c4

This is clearly the best try here, as other moves don't promise much:

a) After 7 ♗d3 Black can react in two ways, obtaining good play in either case:

a1) 7...dxe5 8 ♘xe5 (after 8 dxe5 ♘b4 Black obtains a good endgame) 8...♘d7 9 0-0 ♗d6 10 ♕h5 g6 11 ♕e2 ♕f6 12 ♗b5 a6 13 ♗xd7+ ♗xd7 14 ♘c3 ♘xc3 15 bxc3 ♗a4 16 ♕e4 0-0 17 ♘g4 ♕e7 18 d5 ♗d7 and Black takes over the initiative, Jusić-Rotshtein, Cannes 1995.

a2) 7...♘b4 8 ♗b5+ ♗d7 9 ♗e2 ♗c6 10 0-0 ♘d7 11 exd6 ♗xd6 12 ♘bd2 0-0 13 ♘c4 ♗c7 14 ♗g5 f6 15 ♗h4 ♘d5 with a very solid position, Beikert-Stohl, Bundesliga 1998/9.

b) After 7 ♘c3 Black also has two fine continuations:

b1) 7...♘c6 8 ♗d3 (White also has nothing after 8 ♘xd5 exd5 {this position can also arise from an Alekhine} 9 ♗e2 dxe5 10 ♘xe5 ♗d6, when after 11 ♕a4?!, Pazos-Anand, Dubai OL 1986, 11...♗xe5 12 dxe5 0-0 13 f4 ♕h4+ White is in trouble – Anand) 8...dxe5 9 dxe5 ♗b4 10 0-0 ♘xc3 11 bxc3 ♗xc3 12 ♖b1 ♗xe5 13 ♘xe5

♘xe5 14 ♗b5+ ♘c6 15 ♕a4 ♗d7 16 ♖d1 0-0 and it is White who has to fight for a draw, Kosikov-Gavrikov, Daugavpils 1978.

b2) 7...♘xc3 8 bxc3 ♕c7 (the same method as in the line *6...b6 7 ♘c3 ♘xc3 8 bxc3 ♕c7*; instead, 8...♘c6 is poor: 9 ♗f4 ♗e7 10 ♗d3 dxe5 11 ♘xe5 ♘xe5 12 ♗xe5 ♗f6 13 ♗b5+ ♗d7 14 ♗xf6 gxf6 15 ♗xd7+ ♕xd7 16 ♕f3 gives White a small positional advantage, Levi-Canfell, Melbourne 1991) and then:

b21) 9 ♕c2 ♘d7 10 ♗f4 dxe5 11 ♗xe5 (after 11 ♘xe5 ♗d6 12 ♗b5 0-0 Black is fine) 11...♘xe5 12 ♘xe5 ♗d6 13 ♗b5+ ♔f8 14 f4 b6 15 0-0 g6 16 ♖ae1 ♗b7 17 ♖e3 ♔g7 and Black finishes his development satisfactorily, Lehmann-Kraut, Bundesliga 1989/90.

b22) 9 ♗d2 ♘d7 10 exd6 (the fact that White exchanges on d6 without waiting for Black to play ...♗e7 first is a great achievement for Black, but 10 ♗d3 is not dangerous for Black either: 10...dxe5 11 0-0 g6 12 ♖e1 ♗g7 13 ♖c1 0-0 14 ♘xe5 ♘xe5 15 ♗f4 b6 16 ♗xe5 ♗xe5 17 ♖xe5 ♗b7 and Black has solved all his problems, Romanovich-Sivokho, St Petersburg 1995) 10...♗xd6 11 ♗d3 b6 and now White has nothing better than 12 0-0 ♗b7, transposing to the line *6...b6 7 ♘c3 ♘xc3 8 bxc3 ♕c7 9 ♗d2 ♗b7 10 ♗d3 d6 11 0-0 ♘d7 12 exd6 ♗xd6 ∓*, because an attempt to deviate can be disastrous: 12 ♘g5 ♗b7 13 ♘e4 ♗f4 14 ♕g4? ♗xd2+ (14...♗xe4!?) 15 ♔xd2 0-0-0 16 ♕g3 e5 and the white king is in danger, Sveshnikov-Filippov, Russian Ch (Moscow) 1999.

c) 7 a3 prevents ideas like ...♘b4 and ...♗b4, but loses precious time. Black can use this tempo to obtain good play with 7...♗d7 8 ♗d3 ♗c6 9 0-0 ♘d7 *(D)*:

c1) 10 ♕e2 ♕c7 11 ♗d2 dxe5 12 dxe5 g6 (White has problems protecting his central pawn) 13 ♘c3 ♘xc3 14 ♗xc3 ♗g7 15 ♖ac1 0-0 16 ♗b4 ♖fc8 17 ♗d6 ♗xf3 and Black wins the e5-pawn, Azarov-Bologan, Minsk Z 2000.

c2) 10 b4 a6 11 ♖e1 ♕c7 12 ♘bd2 ♘c3 13 ♕c2 ♗a4 14 ♕b2 ♘d1 15 ♕b1 ♘c3 and Black can draw by attacking the queen, Vogt-Sermek, Lucerne 1994.

c3) 10 ♖e1 and now:

c31) 10...♖c8 (Black can develop his queenside first, as he controls the centre and his kingside is safe enough) 11 ♗d2 (11 ♘g5 dxe5 12 ♘xe6? looks nice, but is incorrect: 12...fxe6 13 ♕h5+ ♔e7 14 ♗g5+ ♘5f6 15 dxe5 ♘xe5 16 ♗f5 g6 −+ Dolzhikova-Volzhin, Hamburg 1999) 11...♗e7 12 ♘c3 dxe5 13 ♘xe5 ♘xe5 14 dxe5 ♘xc3 15 ♗xc3 0-0 = Kuntz-Vaulin, Budapest 1991.

c32) 10...♗e7 11 b4 a6 12 ♘bd2 ♕c7 13 ♗b2 0-0 14 ♖c1 ♖fd8 15 ♗e4

♘7b6 16 ♕c2 h6 17 ♕b3 ♕d7 18 ♗b1 with a complicated position, Acs-Ruck, Hungarian Ch (Budapest) 1996.

c33) 10...dxe5 11 dxe5 ♘c5 12 ♗f1 a5 13 ♘bd2 ♘f4 14 ♕c2 ♘cd3 and Black dominates in the centre, Engel-bert-Reddmann, Hamburg 1991.

We return to 7 ♗c4 *(D)*:

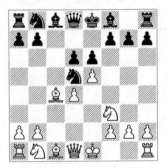

Black now has:

B1: 7...♘b6   137
B2: 7...♘c6   138

Or:

a) After 7...♗e7 8 0-0 0-0 9 ♕e2 (or 9 ♖e1) 9...♗d7 (9...♘c6 – *7...♘c6 8 0-0 ♗e7 9 ♕e2 0-0*) 10 ♘c3 ♘xc3 11 bxc3 ♗c6 12 ♗f4 dxe5 13 ♘xe5 ♗d5 14 ♗d3 ♘d7 15 c4 ♘xe5 16 ♗xe5 ♗c6 17 ♖ad1 ♗f6 18 ♗c2 ♖c8 19 ♗xf6 ♕xf6 20 d5 exd5 21 cxd5 ♗d7 22 ♗b3 White has a strong passed pawn and the better chances, Dolma-tov-Zapata, Tilburg 1993.

b) 7...dxe5 8 dxe5 ♗b4+ 9 ♘bd2 ♘b6 gives White two ways to obtain a promising position:

b1) 10 ♗b3 ♗d7 11 ♕e2 ♘c6 12 0-0 ♕c7 13 ♘e4 (Ponomariov-Taima-nov, Cannes 1998) 13...0-0 (it is risky

to accept the pawn sacrifice: 13...♘xe5 14 ♗f4 ♘xf3+ 15 ♕xf3 ♕c6 16 ♖ac1 ♕b5 17 ♕g3 gives White many threats) 14 ♗f4 and White has finished his de-velopment, protected his central pawn and is ready to attack on the kingside.

b2) 10 0-0 ♘xc4 11 ♕a4+ ♘c6 12 ♘xc4 ♕d3 13 ♘d6+ ♗xd6 14 ♖d1 ♕a6 15 ♕xa6 bxa6 16 exd6 e5 17 ♗e3 ♗d7 18 ♘d2 and White's far-advanced passed d-pawn gives him an advantage in the endgame, Svidler-Taimanov, St Petersburg Ch 1995.

c) 7...♗d7 8 ♗xd5 exd5 9 ♘c3 dxe5 10 dxe5 ♗e6 11 ♘d4 ♘c6 12 0-0 ♗c5 13 ♗e3 ♗xd4 14 ♗xd4 0-0 15 ♕d2 ♖c8 16 ♘b5 f6 17 exf6 ♘xd4 18 ♘xd4 ♕xf6 19 ♖fe1 and White has obtained a strategic advantage in a very simple way, Degraeve-Vescovi, Bastia 1998.

B1)
    7...♘b6 8 ♗d3
8 ♗b3 is also possible: 8...dxe5 (8...♘c6 is analysed under *5...♘c6 6 ♗c4 ♘b6 7 ♗b3 e6 8 cxd4 d6*; then 9 exd6 gives White an advantage) 9 ♘xe5 (the endgame after 9 dxe5 ♕xd1+ 10 ♗xd1 ♘c6 gives Black good play: 11 0-0 ♘c4 12 ♖e1 ♘b4 13 ♗a4+ ♗d7 14 ♗xd7+ ♔xd7 15 ♘c3 ♔e8 16 ♖d1 ♖c8 17 ♖b1 h6 18 h4 ♗c5 ∓ Bojko-vić-J.Polgar, Novi Sad wom OL 1990) 9...♘8d7 10 0-0 ♘xe5 11 dxe5 ♕xd1 (now the rook comes into play) 12 ♖xd1 ♗d7 13 ♘c3 ♗c6 14 ♗e3 ♗e7 15 a4 0-0 16 ♘b5 ♗xb5 17 axb5 ♖fc8 18 g3 ♔f8 19 ♖dc1 and White has the bishop-pair and more space, Maliu-tin-Golod, Minsk 1993.

8...♘c6

Here the plan 8...♗d7 9 0-0 ♗c6 10 ♘c3 ♘8d7 11 ♕e2 ♗e7 12 ♖d1, Godena-Marinelli, Catania 1995, is less effective for Black. The centre is stable, and White can attack on the kingside.

9 0-0 dxe5

9...♘b4 is interesting:

a) 10 ♗g5 ♗e7 11 ♗xe7 ♕xe7 12 ♗e4 d5 13 ♗d3 ♘xd3 14 ♕xd3 ♗d7 15 ♘c3 0-0 is equal, Smagin-Rublevsky, Russian Cht (Kazan) 1995.

b) 10 ♗b5+ ♗d7 11 ♘c3 ♗e7 12 ♕b3 ♗xb5 13 ♘xb5 ♘c6, Daniliuk-Scherbakov, Krasnodar 1997. The exchange of light-squared bishops is in Black's favour.

c) 10 ♗e2 is best. After 10...♗e7 11 a3 ♘4d5 12 ♗d3 ♗d7 13 ♕e2 ♗c6 14 ♘c3 ♘xc3 15 bxc3 0-0 Black is solid, but White has good prospects on the kingside, Smirnov-Vaulin, Russian Cht (Smolensk) 2000.

10 dxe5 ♘b4 11 ♗e4 ♕xd1 12 ♖xd1 (D)

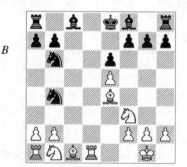

12...♗d7!?

Black launches into a complex variation, but after 12...♘4d5 13 a4 a5 14 ♘c3 ♘xc3 15 bxc3 ♗c5 16 ♘d4, he could find nothing better than 16...♗d7 17 ♗xb7 ♖a7 18 ♗f3 ± in Timman-Handke, Amsterdam 2001.

13 ♗xb7 ♘c2 14 ♗xa8 ♘xa8 15 ♘c3 ♘xa1 16 ♘e1

The knight is trapped, while White is a pawn up.

16...♘b6 17 ♗e3 ♘c4 18 ♗d4 ♘xb2 19 ♖xa1

White has regained a knight and Black has regained a pawn. However, Black's kingside is still not developed and this leaves Black's king in difficulties.

19...♘c4 20 ♖b1 ♗c8 21 ♘d3

White is clearly better, Sveshnikov-Filippov, Bled 2001.

B2)

7...♘c6 8 0-0 (D)

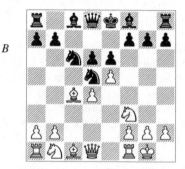

8...♗e7

After 8...♘b6, White could play 9 ♗d3 transposing to *7...♘b6 8 ♗d3 ♘c6 9 0-0*, but can probably get more advantage by means of 9 ♗b5 ♗d7 10 ♘c3:

a) 10...♘b4 is wrong because of 11 ♗g5 ♗e7 12 ♘e4 dxe5 13 ♘d6+ ♔f8

14 ♘xb7 ♕c7 15 ♗xe7+ ♔xe7 16 ♕b3 ♘6d5 17 ♗xd7 ♕xb7 18 ♘xe5, when White is simply a pawn up, Svesh-nikov-Mamoshin, Odessa 1972.

b) 10...♗e7 11 exd6 ♗xd6 12 a3 ♘e7 13 ♗d3 ♘g6 14 g3 ♗c6 15 ♖e1 0-0 16 h4 gives White an initiative on the kingside, Izvozchikov-Donchenko, USSR 1975.

c) 10...dxe5 11 ♘xe5 and then:

c1) 11...♘xe5 12 dxe5 ♗xb5 13 ♘xb5 a6 (13...♕xd1 14 ♖xd1 ♘d5 15 ♗e3 ♘xe3 16 fxe3 ♖c8 17 ♖ac1 ♖xc1 18 ♖xc1 and Black can't defend his queenside) 14 ♘d6+ ♗xd6 15 exd6 ♘d5 16 ♗f4 and the d-pawn is very dangerous.

c2) 11...♗e7 12 ♕g4 ♗f6 (12...0-0 13 ♖d1 gives White unpleasant pres-sure in the centre and kingside) 13 ♘e4 ♘xe5 (after 13...0-0 14 ♘xf6+ ♕xf6 15 ♗xc6 ♗xc6 16 ♗g5 ♕f5 17 ♕xf5 exf5 18 ♘xc6 bxc6 19 ♖ac1 White has a favourable endgame) 14 ♘d6+ ♔f8 15 dxe5 ♗xe5 16 ♘xf7 ♔xf7 17 ♕h5+ ♔g8 18 ♕xe5 ♕f6 19 ♕e2 ♗xb5 20 ♕xb5 and Black has a difficult position because of the weak pawns and undeveloped king's rook, Rozentalis-Cramling, Malaga 2000.

9 a3

Since Black's knight is already de-veloped on c6, Black can't adopt a set-up with the bishop on c6 and knight on d7, attacking the centre. Therefore, White can play this preventative move, which seems to be his best chance to fight for an advantage. Otherwise:

a) Giving up the centre by 9 exd6 doesn't promise anything: 9...♕xd6 10 ♘c3 0-0 11 ♕e2 a6 12 ♖d1 b5 13 ♗xd5 exd5 14 ♘e5 b4 15 ♘xc6 ♕xc6 16 ♘xd5 ♕xd5 17 ♕xe7 ♗b7 18 ♕g5 f5 19 ♗f4 ♖f6 20 f3 ♖g6 21 ♕h5 ♖g4! 22 ♗g3 ♖xd4 and a draw soon re-sulted in Emms-B.Lalić, British League (4NCL) 1998/9.

b) 9 ♕e2 0-0 *(D)* (in this position after 9...♘b6 White can go to b3: 10 ♗b3 d5 11 ♘c3 ♗d7 12 ♗f4 a6 13 ♖ac1 ♖c8 14 ♖fd1 leads to a typical French-type position where the centre is stable and White has the better chances; for example: 14...♘a5 15 ♗c2 g5 16 ♗e3 ♘ac4 17 ♗d3 g4 18 ♘e1 ♘xe3 19 fxe3 ♗g5 20 g3 ± Dolma-tov-V.Milov, Haifa 1995), and now:

b1) 10 ♖d1 ♘a5 (after 10...♘b6 White can again go to b3: 11 ♗b3 d5 12 ♘c3 ♗d7 13 ♗c2 with a compli-cated position that is slightly better for White, Fridh-Wedberg, Swedish Ch (Degerfors) 1978) 11 ♗d3 ♘b4 12 exd6 ♕xd6 13 ♗e4 f5 14 ♗d3 ♘xd3 15 ♕xd3 ♘c6 and Black has managed to exchange off White's light-squared bishop and has nothing to be afraid of.

b2) With 10 ♘c3, White weakens his pawn-structure, but exchanges off the most important black piece – the d5-knight. 10...♘xc3 11 bxc3 dxe5 12 dxe5 *(D)* and then:

b21) 12...♕c7 is a natural but slow move. Black doesn't threaten anything and White can develop his initiative: 13 ♕e4 (13 ♗d3 is also interesting; for example: 13...♖d8 14 ♖e1 ♗d7 15 ♗g5 h6?! 16 ♗xh6! gxh6 17 ♕e4 f5 18 exf6 ♗xf6 19 ♕h7+ ♔f8 20 ♖e4 with a very strong attack, Rausis-Piesina, Riga Z 1995) 13...♗d7 (or 13...b6 14 ♗g5 ♗b7 15 ♗d3 g6 16 ♕h4 ♖fe8 17 ♖ae1 ♗f8 18 ♖e3 ♘e7 19 ♘d4 with serious threats, Sax-Kagan, Hastings 1977/8) 14 ♖e1 ♖ac8 15 ♗d3 with an initiative (not 15 ♗g5 ♘xe5! 16 ♗xe7 ♘xf3+ 17 gxf3 ♕xc4 18 ♗xf8 ♕xe4 19 fxe4 ♔xf8 20 ♖ab1 ♖c7 with a very drawish endgame, Sveshnikov-Cvitan, Tilburg 1993).

b22) 12...b6 13 ♕e4 ♗b7 14 ♗d3 g6 15 ♗h6 ♖e8 16 ♖ad1 ♕c7 17 ♕f4 ♖ad8 18 h4 ♘a5 19 ♘g5, Sveshnikov-Am.Rodriguez, Cienfuegos 1979. The position is very sharp, but it seems to us that White's chances are better.

b23) 12...♕a5 is best. Black immediately attacks the weak pawns, denying White time to create a kingside attack: 13 ♕e4 (practice shows that the sacrifice of the c3-pawn is not dangerous for Black: 13 ♖b1 ♕xc3 14 ♖b3 ♕a5 15 ♕e4 ♖d8 16 ♗g5 h6 17 ♗e3 ♕a4 and White possesses no real threats, Godena-V.Milov, Swiss Cht 1999) 13...♕a4 (Black pins the bishop along the rank; sooner or later White will have to remove his bishop and allow the exchange of queens) 14 ♗g5 h6 15 ♗xe7 ♘xe7 16 ♖ab1 ♗d7 17 ♗d3 ♕xe4 18 ♗xe4 ♗c6 and a draw soon resulted in the game Adams-Tkachev, Cannes rpd 2001.

b3) 10 ♖e1 (White prophylactically protects the e5-pawn, but Black can attack another central pawn) 10...♕b6 (10...♗d7 is worse: 11 ♘c3 ♘xc3 12 bxc3 dxe5 13 dxe5 ♘a5 14 ♗d3 ♗c6 15 ♘d4 ♕d5 16 ♕g4 g6 17 ♗h6 ♖fc8 18 h4 with a dangerous initiative for White, Sveshnikov-Kožul, Ljubljana 1997) 11 ♕e4 dxe5 12 dxe5 ♗c5 (attacking one more weak pawn) 13 ♖e2 ♘d4 14 ♘xd4 ♗xd4 15 ♘d2 ♗xb2 16 ♗xb2 ♕xb2 17 ♘b3 ♕a3 18 ♖d2 ♗d7 19 ♗xd5 exd5 20 ♕xd5 ♗c6 = Sveshnikov-Yakovenko, Russian Ch (Samara) 2000.

b4) 10 ♕e4 (the best chance for White after 9 ♕e2 is to continue the queen manoeuvre without any delay) 10...♕c7! 11 ♗d3 g6 (11...f5! 12 exf6 ♘xf6 13 ♕e2 d5 ∞ gives Black good French-type play, Sermek-Cvitan, Bled 1996) 12 ♗h6 ♖d8 13 ♘bd2 dxe5 14 dxe5 ♗d7 (after 14...♘b6 threatening 15...♘d7, Sermek-Kožul, Maribor 1993, White has to play 15 ♘b3 keeping more active chances) 15 ♖ac1 ♗e8 16 ♖fe1 ♖ac8 17 ♗f1 ♕b8 18 ♘c4 b5

19 ♘d6 ♗xd6 20 exd6, Smagin-Lech-tynsky, Karvina 1987. It's not so easy to assess this position, where White has sacrificed a pawn to exchange Black's dark-squared bishop and exploit the holes on the kingside.

9...0-0 10 ♖e1 ♕c7 11 ♗d3

11 ♕e2 is also possible: 11...♖d8 12 h4!? dxe5 13 dxe5 ♘b6 (Har-Zvi recommends 13...b6 and putting the bishop on a more active location) 14 ♗a2 ♘d4 15 ♘xd4 ♖xd4 16 ♘c3 ♖d8 17 ♕g4 ♗d7 18 ♗h6 ♗f8 19 h5 gives White a comfortable attack on the king, Smagin-Filippov, Russian Ch (St Petersburg) 1998.

11...dxe5 12 exe5 ♖d8 13 ♕e2 *(D)*

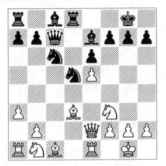

13...g6

With 13...♘a5, Black tries to go to b3 in order to exchange the white bishop, but after 14 ♖a2!, Black can't reply 14...♘b3 as White wins a pawn by 15 ♗xh7+ ♔xh7 16 ♕d3+.

14 ♗d2 b6 15 ♘c3 ♘xc3 16 ♗xc3 ♗b7 17 h4 ♖d7 18 h5 ♖ad8 19 ♗b5 ♕c8 20 ♕e3 a6 21 ♗f1 ♗c5 22 ♕f4

Black has developed all his pieces to nice locations, but he doesn't have any real threats, while White has a

dangerous attack on the kingside, Kharlov-Gallagher, Calcutta 2001.

C)

6...b6 *(D)*

In order to exchange the light-squared bishops after ...♗a6, or simply to develop the bishop to b7.

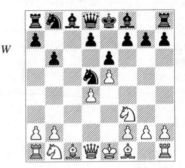

Now:

C1: 7 ♘c3   142
C2: 7 ♗d3   147

There are some other less well tested but perfectly reasonable possibilities:

a) 7 a3 ♗e7 (7...♗a6 may be best) 8 ♘bd2 0-0 9 ♘e4 f5 10 exf6 ♘xf6 11 ♗d3 ♗b7 12 ♘xf6+ ♗xf6 13 0-0 (Z.Almasi-J.Polgar, Groningen FIDE 1997) transposes to a line analysed via *7 ♗d3 ♗b7 8 0-0 ♘b4 9 ♗e2 ♗e7 10 ♘c3 0-0 11 a3 ♘d5 12 ♘e4 f5 13 exf6 ♘xf6 14 ♘xf6+ ♗xf6 15 ♗d3*.

b) 7 ♘bd2 ♗a6 (7...♗b7 8 ♘e4 ♗e7 9 ♗d3 0-0 10 0-0 – 7 ♗d3 ♗b7 8 ♘c3 ♗e7 9 0-0 0-0 10 ♘e4) 8 ♗xa6 ♘xa6 gains White a tempo over *7 ♗d3 ♗a6 8 ♗xa6 ♘xa6* but this may not be enough for an advantage: 9 ♘e4 ♗e7 10 0-0 0-0 11 ♗d2 ♘ac7 12 ♖c1 f5 13 exf6 gxf6 14 ♗h6 ♖f7 15 ♘fd2 ♗f8 with a complicated but probably equal position, Hort-Ftačnik, Bundesliga 1994/5.

c) 7 ♗c4 is a very important alternative requiring more tests:

c1) 7...♗b7 8 0-0 ♘a6 (8...♗e7 is worse, because after 9 ♗xd5 ♗xd5 10 ♘c3 ♗c4 11 ♖e1 0-0 12 d5 exd5 13 ♘xd5 ♘c6 14 ♖e4 ♗xd5 15 ♕xd5 White is better, Smagin-Kupreichik, Eupen 1994) 9 ♗g5 (9 ♘g5 h6 10 ♘e4 ♖c8 11 b3 ♕h4 12 ♕e2 ♘ab4 ∞ Rüfenacht-Elwert, corr. 1998) 9...f6 10 exf6 gxf6 11 ♘e5! fxg5 12 ♕h5+ ♔e7 13 ♗xd5 ♗xd5 14 ♕xg5+ ♔e8 15 ♕h5+ ♔e7 and now 16 ♕g5+ ½-½ was the finish of M.Marić-Skripchenko, Yugoslav wom Cht 1999, but 16 ♘c3! improves; e.g., 16...♘c7 17 ♕f7+ ♔d6 18 ♕f4 ♔e7 19 ♘f7 ±.

c2) 7...♗a6 8 ♗xd5 (8 ♗xa6 – 7 ♗d3 ♗a6 8 ♗xa6) 8...exd5 9 ♘c3 (9 a3 ♗e7 10 ♘c3 0-0 11 ♘e2 d6 = Petschar-Plachetka, Oberwart 1991) 9...♗b4 10 ♕b3!? ♗xc3+ 11 bxc3 ♗c4 12 ♕c2 ♗e7 13 ♘d2 ♗a6 14 ♕a4 ♕e6 15 ♗a3 ♕g4! (15...♗d3?! 16 0-0-0 ± Marković-Kutuzović, Bled 2000) 16 f3!? ♕xg2 17 0-0-0 ♕e2 ∞.

C1)
7 ♘c3 ♘xc3

For 7...♗b7 8 ♗d3, see 7 ♗d3 ♗b7 8 ♘c3.

8 bxc3 (D)

8...♕c7

Or:

a) Now after 8...♗a6 9 ♗xa6 ♘xa6 White can try to exploit his space advantage and strong pawn-centre; for

B

example: 10 h4 ♕c8 11 ♕d3 ♘c7 12 0-0 d5 13 exd6 ♗xd6 14 c4 ♕a6 15 ♖d1 h6 16 ♘d2 0-0-0 17 ♕b3 g5 18 h5 ± Yanovsky-Rausis, Dortmund 1990.

b) 8...♗b7 9 ♗d3 transposes to 7 ♗d3 ♗b7 8 ♘c3 ♘xc3 9 bxc3, when after 9...♕c7 White has the additional option 10 0-0!?.

9 ♗d2

Or:

a) 9 c4? doesn't work: 9...♗a6 10 ♕a4 b5 11 cxb5 ♕c3+ 12 ♔d1 ♗b7 13 ♕c2 ♕xa1 14 ♗d3 ♘c6 15 bxc6 ♗xc6 16 ♔d2 g6 17 ♔e2 ♖c8 –+ Sveshnikov-Pugachov, St Petersburg 1994.

b) 9 ♕c2 ♗b7 10 ♗e2 d6 11 0-0 ♘d7 12 ♗f4 ♖c8 13 ♖fd1 ♗e7 is fine for Black, Bednar-Stohl, Mlada Boleslav 1993.

c) 9 ♗b2 ♗a3 (Black exchanges the dark-squared bishops, gaining time; instead, 9...d6 leads to a complicated position: 10 ♗d3 ♘d7 11 exd6 ♗xd6 12 0-0 ♗b7 13 c4 0-0, Peptan-Kuijf, Groningen 1995) 10 ♕b3 ♗xb2 11 ♕xb2 ♗b7 12 ♗e2 0-0 13 0-0 d6 14 exd6 ♕xd6 15 c4 ♘d7 16 ♖fd1 ♖ac8 with equal chances, Relange-Lesiège, Bermuda 1998.

d) With 9 ♗e2!? White sacrifices a pawn to gain some time. Current practice seems to show that White gets sufficient compensation for the pawn (but no more than that), but our feeling is that White is walking more of a tightrope than Black and we wouldn't be surprised if this assessment changed in the future in Black's favour: 9...♕xc3+ (9...♗b7 10 0-0 d6 11 ♗f4 ♞d7 12 ♖e1 ♗e7 and the fact that the bishop is on e2 rather than d3 enables White to play an immediate 13 d5! ± Pavasović-Sadatnajafi, Dubai 2001; therefore Black should accept the pawn by either 9...♕xc3+ or 9...♗b7 10 0-0 ♕xc3) 10 ♗d2 ♕a3 (10...♕c7 11 ♖c1 ♞c6 12 0-0 ♗b7 13 d5! exd5 14 ♗f4 ∞ Sermek-Medvegy, Cairo 2001) 11 ♖c1 ♞c6 (11...♗a6? 12 ♞g5! ♗b7 13 ♖c7 ♗xg2 14 ♖g1 ♗d5 15 ♖c8+ ♔e7 16 ♕b1 +−) 12 ♖c3 ♕e7 13 ♞g5 (13 0-0 h6, S.Pedersen-Schandorff, Torshavn 1997, 14 ♕a4 ♗b7 15 ♖fc1 ∞ S.Pedersen) 13...f5! 14 exf6 ♕xf6 15 ♞xe6! dxe6 16 ♗b5 ♗d7 17 ♗xc6 ♗xc6 18 ♖xc6 = Van Mil-Krasenkov, Budapest 1989.

We now return to the position after 9 ♗d2 *(D)*:

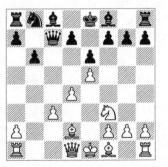

9...♗b7

This is the most natural developing move. However, by attacking the centre immediately with 9...d6 Black can attempt to reach the same positions while ruling out one of White's options (9...♗b7 10 ♗d3 d6 11 0-0 ♞d7 12 ♗f4). White then has the following choice:

a) 10 ♗b5+ ♞d7 (10...♗d7 is a mistake, as the bishop should go to b7: 11 a4 ♞c6 12 exd6 ♗xd6 13 0-0 0-0 14 ♖e1 ♞e7 15 ♕e2 ♖ac8 16 ♗a6 ♖b8 17 h4 with an initiative for White, Smagin-Borriss, Bundesliga 1992/3) 11 0-0 a6 12 exd6 ♗xd6 13 ♗d3 ♗b7 14 h3 0-0 15 ♖e1 ♗f4 and here Black is fine, Dolmatov-Tukmakov, Burgas 1995.

b) 10 ♗d3 ♞d7 and now White can play:

b1) 11 ♞g5 ♗b7 12 ♕h5 g6 13 ♕h3 dxe5 14 0-0 (14 ♗xg6 hxg6 15 ♕xh8 ♕c4 leads to unclear complications; e.g., 16 ♕g8 0-0-0 17 ♕xf7 exd4 18 cxd4 ♗b4) transposes to *9...♗b7 10 ♗d3 d6 11 0-0 ♞d7 12 ♞g5 dxe5 13 ♕h5 g6 14 ♕h3*.

b2) 11 0-0 dxe5 and then:

b21) 12 ♞xe5 ♞xe5 13 ♗f4 ♗d6 14 dxe5 and here:

b211) It's quite risky to take the pawn: 14...♗xe5 15 ♕a4+ ♔e7 16 ♕b4+ ♔f6 (16...♗d6 17 ♗e4 ♖b8? {17...♗a6 is better, giving up the exchange} 18 ♖ad1 ♗d8? 19 ♖xd6 ♖xd6 20 ♖d1 +−) 17 ♗e3 g5? 18 f4 gives White a decisive attack, Werner-Löffler, Badenweil 1995.

b212) 14...♗e7 15 ♕g4 ♔f8 16 ♗e4 ♗b7 17 ♗xb7 ♕xb7 18 ♖ad1 h5

19 ♕e2 g6 and Black is able to finish developing, Dückstein-Arakhamia, Vienna (Women vs Veterans) 1993.

b22) 12 ♖e1 and then:

b221) 12...g6 13 ♕a4 ♗g7 14 ♘xe5 0-0 15 ♗e4 ♘xe5 16 ♗xa8 ♘g4 (Mojzlan-Timoshchenko, Slovakia 1995; or 16...♗d7 17 ♕d1 ♖xa8 18 ♗f4 ±) and now after 17 f4! ♗d7 18 ♕d1 White is an exchange up.

b222) 12...♗d6 13 dxe5 ♗e7 14 ♘g5 ♗xg5 15 ♗xg5 h6 16 ♕h5 ♗b7 17 ♖ad1 ♘c5 18 ♗c2 ♗d5 19 ♖d4 gives Black major problems with his king, Schmittdiel-Borriss, Bundesliga 1999/00.

b223) 12...♗b7 is best, transposing to *9...♗b7 10 ♗d3 d6 11 0-0 ♘d7 12 ♖e1 dxe5.*

10 ♗d3 d6 11 0-0 ♘d7 *(D)*

Or:

a) 11...♘c6 12 exd6 ♗xd6 13 ♖e1 0-0-0 (13...0-0!?) 14 ♕e2 h6 15 ♗a6 ♘a5 16 ♖ac1 ♗xa6 17 ♕xa6+ ♕b7 18 ♕d3 ♔b8 19 c4 and White is much better, Peptan-Cholushkina, Manila wom OL 1992.

b) 11...dxe5 12 ♘xe5 ♘c6 13 f4 ♗d6 14 ♕h5 g6 15 ♕h3 with an initiative for White.

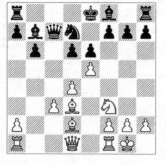

W

12 ♘g5!?

This is the most popular move at present, but is perhaps not the best. White has some safer options:

a) 12 exd6 allows Black to develop his bishop comfortably: 12...♗xd6 13 h3 0-0 14 ♖e1 ♗f4 15 ♗xf4 ♕xf4 16 ♘e5 ♘xe5 17 ♖xe5 ♖ac8 18 ♕c2 g6 19 ♖ae1 ♖fd8 ∓ Røyset-Rausis, Gausdal Peer Gynt 1995.

b) 12 ♖e1 is a natural move that unfortunately doesn't promise White anything:

b1) 12...♗e7 is not best, as Black wastes precious time:

b11) 13 ♗g5 fails to refute Black's play: 13...♗xg5 14 ♘xg5 dxe5 15 ♕h5 ♘f6 16 ♕h3 (16 ♘xe6? ♕c6 17 d5 ♕xe6! −+ Har-Zvi) 16...e4 17 ♘xe4 ♘xe4 18 ♗xe4 ♗xe4 19 ♖xe4 0-0 and Black is at least not worse, Wach-Landenbergue, Ptuj Z 1995.

b12) 13 exd6 (now that Black has spent one tempo moving his bishop, it's time for this exchange) 13...♗xd6 14 c4 0-0 15 h3 ♖ac8 16 ♗c3 and White is ready to play in the centre and on the kingside, Rozentalis-Lesiège, Montreal 1995.

b2) 12...dxe5 13 ♘xe5 (13 dxe5 gives Black good play, as his knight obtains a nice square on c5 and White's e5-pawn can become a target: 13...♗e7 14 ♘d4 ♘c5 15 ♗c2 h5 16 a4 a6 17 ♕e2 ♖d8, Rozentalis-I.Sokolov, Malmö 1997) 13...♘xe5 14 ♖xe5 ♗d6 and then:

b21) 15 ♗b5+ ♗c6 (15...♔f8 16 ♖h5 g6 17 ♖h4 h5 18 ♖c1 e5 19 ♗g5 ♔g7 is also fine for Black, Fiorito-Panno, Trelew 1995) 16 ♕f3 0-0-0

(16...♖c8 leads to unclear complications: 17 ♗xc6+ ♕xc6 18 d5 ♕b7 19 ♖g5 ∞) 17 ♗xc6 ♗xe5 18 a4 ♖d6 and White only has some compensation for the exchange, Sequera-Akopian, Mamaia jr Wch 1991.

b22) 15 ♖h5 g6 (15...0-0-0 is incorrect because after 16 a4 g6 17 ♖h3 f5 18 a5 bxa5 19 ♖b1 White has dangerous threats on the queenside, Spassky-Arakhamia, Roquebrune (Women vs Veterans) 1998) 16 ♖h3 0-0. Black can castle kingside, as White doesn't have enough resources for a successful attack. Then:

b221) 17 ♗h6?! ♖fe8 18 ♕g4 e5 19 ♕h4 and now 19...♗e7? 20 ♗g5 ♗xg5 21 ♕xg5 ♕xc3 22 ♖c1 ♕xd4 (A.Grosar-Striković, Geneva 1991) allows White to break through by 23 ♗xg6! fxg6 24 ♖xh7. However, Black should play 19...♕xc3! 20 ♖c1 ♕xd4 21 ♕f6 ♗f8 22 ♗c4 ♗d5 23 ♖d3 ♖e6! ∓.

b222) 17 ♕g4 f5 18 ♕e2 ♖ae8 19 ♖e1 ♔h8 20 ♗b5 ½-½ Pinal-Bellon, Cienfuegos 1985.

c) 12 ♗f4 ♗e7 (after 12...0-0-0 13 exd6 ♗xd6 14 ♗xd6 ♕xd6 15 ♕e2 ♔b8, Novik-Akopian, Jurmala jr 1987, White can start his attack first by continuing 16 a4) 13 ♖e1 0-0 14 ♖e3 g6 15 ♖c1 ♖fd8 (Black must be careful, because after 15...♖ac8 White can develop his initiative: 16 ♕e2 ♖fd8 17 ♘g5 dxe5 18 dxe5 ♘c5 19 ♗c2 and White has a lot of threats, Van de Oudeweetering-Vrenegoor, Enschede 1991) 16 ♕e2 dxe5 17 ♘xe5 ♘xe5 18 ♗xe5 ♗d6 and after the exchange of bishops, the position will be equal,

Slapikas-Sarakauskas, Lithuanian Ch (Kaunas) 2001. However, this line might represent best play for White after 7 ♘c3, depending on the assessment of the complications below.

We now return to 12 ♘g5 *(D)*:

12...dxe5 13 ♕h5 g6 14 ♕h3 ♗e7
White was threatening 15 ♗xg6, so Black doesn't have many possibilities. 14...♗g7 15 ♖ae1 ♗d5 16 f4 exd4 17 c4 ♗xc4 18 ♗xc4 ♕xc4 19 f5 ♘c5 20 ♘xf7 gives White a very dangerous attack, Brynell-B.Kristensen, Torshavn 1997.

15 ♖fe1
It is difficult to decide which rook to play to e1. 15 ♖ae1, intending to follow up with a quick f4, is more aggressive but also less flexible, as White is almost committed to playing f4 against most of Black's possible plans. Nonetheless, it does have its points:

a) It is particularly effective against 15...♗d5 (a move which is given in many places as best against 15 ♖ae1), as 16 f4 gives White good attacking chances; e.g., 16...exd4 17 cxd4 ♗c4 18 f5 gxf5 19 ♕h5 ♗xg5 20 ♗xg5

♕d6 21 ♖xf5 ♖f8 22 ♗xc4 ♕xd4+ 23 ♔h1 ♕xc4 24 ♗h6 ± Matsuura-Rocha, Brazil 1999.

b) 15...♗xg5 16 ♗xg5 f5 17 ♕h6! ♔f7 18 ♗b5 is good for White – see the analogous line after *15 ♖fe1*; the rook positions make little difference here.

c) 15...♖f8?! 16 ♕xh7! 0-0-0? 17 ♘xf7 ♘f6 18 ♕h3 ♖xf7 19 ♕xe6+ ♕d7 20 ♕xf7 ♗xg2 was drawn by perpetual check after 21 ♔xg2 ♕g4+ in Westerinen-Djurhuus, Torshavn 1997 seemingly because of the rook's position on f1, but White can win by 21 ♖xe5!, as played in G.Szabo-Perunović, Ballatonlelle 2000.

d) 15...h6 16 f4 ♗xg5 17 fxg5 h5 is unclear; it is also unclear here whether White would prefer a rook on a1 or f1.

e) White's rooks are also slightly better placed in the line 15...a6 16 f4 ♗xg5 17 fxg5 0-0 18 ♖e3 exd4 19 cxd4 ♕d6, but Black is fine after 20 ♕h4 (20 ♕g4!? ∞) 20...♕d5 21 ♖f2 f5! = Jamrich-Rajlich, Budapest 2001.

We now return to the position after 15 ♖fe1 *(D)*:

15...a6

A clever waiting move by Black. Alternatives:

a) 15...♖f8? 16 ♕xh7! e4 (16...0-0-0 17 ♘xf7 ♘f6 18 ♕h3 ♖xf7 19 ♕xe6+ and White wins, Stević-Grosar, Mravinci 1995, and many other games since) 17 ♘xe4 0-0-0 18 ♕h3 and White is simply a pawn up, Pavasović-Peptan, Ljubljana 1997.

b) 15...♗xg5?! 16 ♗xg5 f5?! 17 ♕h6 (17 dxe5? 0-0 18 ♖e3 ♖f7 19 ♖d1 ♘c5 20 ♗c2 ♖d7 and Black is out of danger, Pavasović-Epishin, Nova Gorica 1997) 17...♔f7 18 ♗b5 a6 19 ♗xd7 ♕xd7 20 dxe5 ♕c6 21 f3 ♕c5+ 22 ♔h1 ♕f8 23 ♕h4 h6 24 ♗f6 ♖h7 25 ♕d4 +− Potkin-Zakharstov, Russian Ch (Elista) 2001.

c) 15...♗d5 16 f4!? (16 c4 ♗b7 ∞) 16...exf4 17 c4 ♗xg5 18 cxd5 0-0 is unclear, Syrtlanov-Medvegy, Koszalin 1999.

d) 15...h6 and then:

d1) 16 ♗xg6 fxg6 17 ♘xe6 ♕c4 ∓ Har-Zvi.

d2) 16 ♘xe6 fxe6 17 ♕xe6 ♕c6 18 ♗xg6+ ♔d8 19 ♕xc6 ♗xc6 20 dxe5 ♗xg2! ∓ Har-Zvi.

d3) 16 dxe5 ♘c5 17 ♗b5+ ♔f8 18 ♘f3 ♔g7 19 ♖ad1 a6 20 ♗f1 ♖ad8 and Black has finished his development and stands well, Vadja-Marjanović, Bucharest 1999.

d4) 16 ♖ad1 a6! 17 ♘f3 exd4 18 cxd4 ♗d5 ∓ Pap-Rajlich, Budapest 2000.

d5) 16 f4 ♗xg5 17 fxg5 h5 18 a4 (18 ♗xg6?! fxg6 19 ♕xe6+ ♔d8 20 ♕xg6 ♕c6 21 ♕xc6 ♗xc6 22 dxe5 ♘c5 ∓) 18...0-0 19 ♖e3 with compensation – Vi.Ivanov.

d6) 16 a4 ♔f8 17 f4 ♔g7 18 ♘xf7!? ♔xf7 19 fxe5 ♘f8 20 ♖f1+ ♔g7 (perhaps 20...♔e8!? is better) 21 ♕g3 with a strong attack for White, Vadja-Rajlich, Eger 2002. The rook returns to f1 after all!

16 a4 *(D)*

White also waits, trying to improve his position. There is still plenty of scope for investigation here:

a) 16 f4 ♗xg5 17 fxg5 0-0 18 ♖e3 exd4 19 cxd4 ♕d6 20 ♕g4 with compensation – Vi.Ivanov.

b) 16 ♖ad1 h6 – *15...h6 16 ♖ad1 a6*.

c) 16 ♖ac1 ♗xg5 17 ♗xg5 f5 ∞ Susak-Sermek, Pula 1996. Sermek, an expert on the white side of the 2 c3 Sicilian, feels happy to enter this complex position having ruled out White's ♗b5.

d) 16 dxe5 ♘c5 17 ♗c2 0-0-0! (taking advantage of the attack on d2 to bring the king to safety on the queenside; without this resource Black could be in trouble here) 18 ♗f4 ♖df8 19 ♕h6 ∞ Vi.Ivanov.

16...♖c8 17 ♕h6 ♗f8 18 ♕h3 ♗e7 19 ♕h6

White doesn't have to repeat moves. He can also try 19 dxe5 ♘c5 20 ♗c2, especially now that 20...0-0-0 has been ruled out. Black does now have the resource 20...♕d8! since after 21 ♘f3? ♗xf3 22 ♕xf3 White is not hitting a rook on a8, but the uncomfortable-looking 21 ♕e3 h6 22 ♘h3 is perfectly playable for White since Black still has difficulty with his king position. Tests are needed.

19...♗f8 20 ♕h3 ♗g7

Black too can play for a win.

21 f4

Now:

a) 21...exf4? 22 ♘xe6! fxe6 23 ♕xe6+ ♔f8 24 ♗xf4! ♕xf4 25 ♖f1 +− Har-Zvi.

b) 21...e4?! and then:

b1) In the game Zakharov-Neverov, Perm 1997, Black's attempts to play for a win were justified after 22 ♘xe4?! 0-0 ∓. If Black gets his king to safety (on the kingside or queenside) in this whole variation, White is always left with a weakness on c3 to worry about.

b2) After 22 ♗xe4! Har-Zvi analyses 22...♘f6 23 ♗xb7 ♕xb7 24 f5 gxf5 25 ♕xf5 and 22...♗xe4 23 ♖xe4 as better for White.

c) 21...exd4! 22 ♘xe6! fxe6 23 ♕xe6+ ♔f8 24 ♕e7+ draws – Har-Zvi.

C2)

7 ♗d3 *(D)*

This is a natural move and may now offer White more chances than in the over-analysed 'main line' 7 ♘c3, even though it allows Black to exchange the

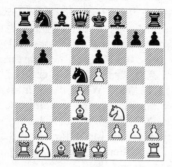

light-squared bishops by ...♗a6. Black has three main replies:

C21: 7...♗b4+ 148
C22: 7...♗a6 151
C23: 7...♗b7 152

Other possibilities such as 7...♗e7 or 7...♕c7 are also playable, but usually quickly transpose to either 7...♗a6 or 7...♗b7 lines depending on Black's next move.

C21)
7...♗b4+
This is a popular choice. Black has a slight space disadvantage and so seeks to exchange pieces. However, he may actually do better to keep the dark-squared bishops on the board.
8 ♗d2 (D)
8...♗xd2+ 9 ♕xd2
Instead:
a) 9 ♘bxd2 ♘f4! (9...♗a6 10 ♘e4 0-0 11 ♖c1 f5 12 ♘d6 ♗xd3 13 ♕xd3 ♘f4 14 ♕f1 ♘c6 15 g3 ♘d5 16 a3 a6 17 ♕e2 leaves White better due to his strong knight on d6, Pinkus-Modr, Dortmund 1989) 10 ♗f1 0-0 11 g3 ♘d5 12 ♗c4 ♗a6 = Heppekausen-J.Adamski, Aachen 1993.

b) 9 ♘fxd2!? is an interesting alternative:
b1) 9...♗a6 10 ♘e4 0-0 11 ♘bc3 ♘xc3 (11...f5 12 ♘xd5 fxe4 13 ♗xa6 ♘xa6 14 ♘c3 ♕g5 15 0-0 e3 16 f3 ♘b4 17 ♕e2 ♖ac8 18 ♖ad1 ± M.Anderton-Sheldon, British League (4NCL) 1997/8; 11...♗xd3 12 ♕xd3 ♘c6!?) 12 bxc3 ♗xd3 13 ♕xd3 ♘c6 (13...d5 14 exd6 f5 15 ♘d2 ♕xd6 16 0-0 ♘d7 is slightly better for White, Saunders-Lund, British League (4NCL) 1996/7) 14 0-0 f6 (14...♘e7 15 f4 f5 16 exf6 gxf6 17 ♕h3 ♔h8 18 ♖f3 ♘f5 19 g4 ± Blatny-Jansa, Namestovo 1987) 15 exf6 gxf6 16 f4 d5 17 ♘g3 ♕d7 18 ♘h5 ♕f7 19 ♕h3 ♔h8 20 ♖ae1 ± Brynell-Schandorff, Torshavn 1997.

b2) 9...0-0 10 ♘c3 ♗b7 11 ♗e4 (11 0-0 ♘f4 12 ♗e4 d5! 13 exd6 ♗xe4 14 ♘dxe4 f5 15 ♘f6+!? ♖xf6 16 ♕f3 ♘h3+ 17 ♕xh3 ♕xd6 =; 11 ♘de4 f5 12 exf6 ♘xf6 ∞) 11...d6!? (11...♘xc3 12 bxc3 ♗xe4 13 ♘xe4 is similar to 9...♗a6 10 ♘e4 0-0 11 ♘bc3 ♘xc3 12 bxc3 ♗xd3 13 ♕xd3 but with the queen on d1 instead of d3) 12 ♕f3 (12 ♗xd5 exd5 13 ♘f3 ♘c6 14 0-0 dxe5 15 dxe5 d4 ∓) 12...♘c6! 13 ♕h3 h6 14 ♘xd5 exd5 15 ♗xd5 dxe5 16 ♗xc6

♗xc6 17 dxe5 ♕d4 and Black has a slight advantage.

9...♗a6 10 ♗e4!

This seems a brave move, leaving the white king in the centre of the board, but 10 ♘c3 ♘xc3 11 bxc3 ♗xd3 12 ♕xd3 d5 doesn't offer White many prospects.

10...♘c6 11 ♗xd5

This aims for a good knight vs bad bishop ending. Another approach is 11 ♘c3 ♘xc3 12 bxc3 ♖c8 13 h4 ♕c7 14 ♖h3 with balanced attacking chances, Luther-Pekarek, Namestovo 1987.

11...exd5 12 ♘c3 ♘b4

After 12...♘e7, White could try attacking with 13 h4!? but also has time to run his king into relative safety on the queenside by 13 0-0-0 d6 14 ♖he1 0-0 15 ♔b1 ♕d7 16 ♔a1. Brynell-Couso, Swedish Ch (Linköping) 2001 continued 16...♖ad8 17 ♕f4 h6 18 exd6 ♘g6 19 ♕g3 ♕xd6 20 ♕xd6 ♖xd6 21 g3 with a better ending for White.

13 a3!?

This was an over-the-board innovation by one of the authors (Harley-Pigott, London 1994). Swapping pieces immediately with the clever 13 ♘b5 doesn't offer White any advantage; for example, 13...♘c2+ 14 ♕xc2 ♗xb5 15 ♕b3 ♗c4 16 ♕a3 ♖c8 17 ♖c1 ♕e7 18 ♕xe7+ ♔xe7 19 a3 ♗d3 20 ♔d2 ½-½ Gallagher-Sandipan, Calcutta 2001. 13 0-0-0?! is clearly unwise due to 13...♖c8 14 a3 (14 ♔b1 ♗d3+ 15 ♔a1 ♘c2+ 16 ♔b1 ♗g6 ∓) 14...♘a2+ 15 ♔b1 ♘xc3+ 16 bxc3 0-0 ∓.

13...♘d3+ 14 ♔d1 *(D)*

14...d6

B

Black indirectly defends the d-pawn and threatens to open the position with ...dxe5 followed by ...d4. This forces White to play 15 ♘e1 immediately and take back with the king's rook after 15...♘xe1 16 ♖xe1 rather than the queen's rook, which makes it less easy for White to get his king to safety on the queenside and also leaves the h2-pawn undefended. However, it is far from clear if White can risk 15 ♘xd5 yet anyway, and Black has an alternative plan of ...f6 aiming to keep the doubled pawns on the d-file but threatening to open the f-file and exploit White's light-square weaknesses with ...♕e8 and ...♕g6. This alternative strategy is illustrated in the variations below:

a) 14...♗c4? 15 ♔c2 ♖c8 16 ♖hd1! 0-0 (16...b5!? 17 b3 b4 18 bxc4 dxc4 19 ♘e4 b3+ 20 ♔b1 is much better for White) 17 ♕e3 and White wins two knights for a rook, Harley-G.Morris, British League (4NCL) 1998/9.

b) 14...♖c8 15 ♘xd5!? 0-0 (after 15...♗c4 16 ♘e3 ♗b3+ 17 ♔e2 ♘f4+ 18 ♔f1 f6 19 g3 ♘g6 20 ♔g2 White's king finds safety on the kingside) 16 ♘f4 (16 ♘e1 ♗c4!?) 16...♘xf4 17

♕xf4 f6 (17...♗c4 18 ♖c1 ±) 18 ♖e1! ♗b7 19 ♖e3 ±.

c) 14...0-0 and then:

c1) 15 ♘xd5?! d6 16 ♘f4 ♘xf4 17 ♕xf4 dxe5 gives White very good attacking chances against the white king stranded in the centre.

c2) 15 ♘e1 ♘xe1 16 ♖xe1 ♖c8!? (16...♕h4?! 17 ♘xd5! ♗b7 18 ♕f4! ♕h5+ 19 g4 ♕h3 20 ♘e7+ ♔h8 21 ♔c2 ♖fe8 22 ♖e3 ♕g2 23 ♘f5 ♖ac8+ 24 ♔d2 g5 25 ♕g3 ♕c6 26 ♘d6 ♕c2+ 27 ♔e1 ♕xb2 28 ♖d1 +−; 16...f6 17 ♔c2!? {or just 17 f4 ±} 17...fxe5 18 ♖xe5 ♕h4 19 f3! ±) 17 ♘xd5 ♗b7 18 ♘f4 is unclear.

c3) 15 ♔c2 ♖c8 16 ♘e1 (16 ♖ad1 f6 17 ♕e3 fxe5 18 dxe5 ♘f4 19 g3 ♘g2! 20 ♕d2 ♖xf3 21 ♕xd5+ ♖f7 22 ♕xg2 ♗e2 23 f4 ♗xd1+ 24 ♖xd1 ∓) 16...♘xe1+ 17 ♖axe1 f6 18 f4 (18 ♔b1?! doesn't move the king to safety − rather the opposite because the king no longer supports the pawn move to b3: 18...♗c4 19 ♖e3 a5 20 f4 b5 21 ♘e2?! b4! 22 axb4? axb4 23 ♕xb4 ♕e8! and Black is much better, Harley-H.Hunt, Cambridge 2001) 18...♕e8 19 b3 fxe5 20 ♖xe5 ♕f7 21 g3 ±.

15 ♘e1 ♘xe1 16 ♖xe1 0-0 *(D)*

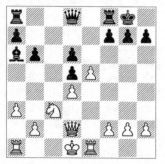

17 f4

White tends to prefer 17 ♔c2, immediately connecting the rooks and intending to follow up with b3 and ♔b2, bringing the king to safety. However, after 17...dxe5 18 ♖xe5 ♕d6! 19 ♖ae1 ♕g6+ 20 ♔c1 ♕xg2 21 ♘xd5 the position is very unclear, though White did go on to win in Olesen-P.Hagesæther, Gausdal Troll 1995.

An alternative idea for White is 17 ♕f4, supporting the centre with the queen rather than the f-pawn. Compare 17 ♔c2 ♖c8 18 ♕f4 ♖c6 19 exd6 ♖xd6 20 ♖e5 ♗c8 21 ♖ae1 ♗e6 ± Harley-Pigott, London 1994. Note that 17 ♕f4 is more accurate, and that White could then consider keeping the king in the centre at d2.

17...♕d7

Black tries to exploit White's light-squared weaknesses.

18 b3

As 18 ♔c2 is now met by 18...♕f5+, White prepares the way for the king to get to b2, even via c1 if necessary.

18...dxe5

Instead:

a) 18...♖fe8 19 ♔c2 transposes to Bricard-Janssen, Wijk aan Zee 1996, which continued 19...♗b5 20 ♔b2 ♗c6 21 ♘d1 a5 22 ♘e3 a4 23 b4 ♗b5 24 g4 ±.

b) 18...♖ac8 19 ♔c2 dxe5 20 ♖xe5 f6 21 ♖e3 has the point that 21...♕f5+ 22 ♔b2 ♕xf4 is answered by 23 ♘xd5 ±.

19 ♖xe5 f6 20 ♖e1 ♖ac8 21 ♔c2 ♖fe8 22 ♔b2 ♕f5 23 ♖e3

White has managed to keep a slight advantage and can look forward to the endgame, N.Pedersen-L.Hansen, Danish Ch (Randers) 1996.

C22)

7...♗a6 *(D)*

Exchanging just the light-squared bishops may be a better option for Black.

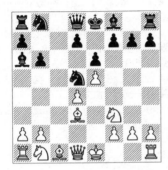

8 0-0

White aims to gain a little time by letting Black swap bishops. Instead:

a) 8 ♗xa6 ♘xa6 (this knight is not as badly placed here as it might appear, since within two moves it can reach the important d5-square) 9 0-0 ♗e7 10 ♘bd2 0-0 11 ♘e4 ♘ac7 12 ♗g5 f6 13 exf6 ♘xf6 14 ♗xf6 (14 ♘c3 ♘fd5 15 ♗d2 ♖c8 16 ♕a4 offers White some advantage, Sermek-Grosar, Ljubljana 1992) 14...gxf6 15 ♖c1 d5 16 ♘g3 is a good example of how to play these kind of positions for White. Now 16...♕d7 17 ♘h4 ♗d6 18 f4! ± was Adams-Benjamin, New York 1996, but Adams points out that 16...♗d6 is more accurate, with an unclear position. Note that that game began with 7 ♗c4 ♗a6, so Adams did not have the option of 8 0-0.

b) 8 ♘c3 aims to obtain control of d5 before Black can play ...♘a6 and ...♘ac7. After 8...♘xc3 9 bxc3, the inferior 9...♕c8?! 10 ♗xa6 ♕xa6 11 ♘g5! ♕b7 12 ♕g4 ± saw White's plan working out well in Marković-Šolak, Serbian Ch (Sabac) 1998, but 9...♗xd3 10 ♕xd3 d5 11 exd6 ♗xd6 seems fine for Black.

8...♗e7

Instead, Black can try to stop White playing ♘c3:

a) 8...♕c7 9 ♗xa6 ♘xa6 10 ♕e2 ♘ab4 (Shaked-Kobaliya, Wijk aan Zee 1998) and now Har-Zvi suggests 11 a3 ♘c6 12 ♗d2.

b) 8...♕c8 9 a3 h6 (9...♗e7 10 ♖e1 ♗xd3 11 ♕xd3 ♘a6 12 ♘c3 ± Blatny) 10 ♖e1 ♗xd3 11 ♕xd3 ♘a6 12 ♘bd2 ♘ac7 13 ♘e4 ♕a6 14 ♕c2! ♖c8 15 ♗d2 ♗e7 16 ♘d6+! ± ♗xd6 17 exd6 ♘a8 18 ♕b3 0-0 19 ♘e5 f6 20 ♘xd7 ♖fd8 21 ♕h3! wins for White, Blatny-Mokry, Czechoslovak Ch (Prague) 1986. This is another good example of how to play these kind of positions for White.

9 ♘c3 ♘xc3 10 bxc3 ♗xd3

10...♕c8 is well met by 11 ♗g5! ♕xc3 12 ♖c1 ♕a3 13 ♗e4 ♗xg5 (or 13...♘c6 14 ♖xc6 ♗xg5 15 ♖c2 ±) 14 ♘xg5 ♘c6 (Harley-Lyell, London 1997) 15 d5!:

a) 15...exd5 16 ♕xd5 0-0! (16...♕e7 17 ♖xc6 0-0 18 ♗xh7+ ♔h8 19 ♗c2 ♕xg5 20 ♕xd7 ♕h5 21 ♖c3 ♗xf1 22 ♖h3 ♗e2 23 f3 +−) 17 ♗xh7+ ♔h8 18 ♕e4! (18 ♗b1 ♗xf1 19 ♕e4 ♗d3! −+; 18 ♖fe1 ♕e7 19 f4 g6 ∞) 18...f6! (18...♗xf1 19 ♕h4 +−) 19 ♗g6 fxg5 20 ♕g4 ♔g8 21 ♕h5 ♖fc8 22 ♗f7+

♔f8 23 ♗b3 ♔e7 24 ♖fd1 and White wins.

b) 15...♗xf1 16 dxc6 0-0 17 ♗xh7+ ♔h8 18 ♔xf1 (18 ♕h5?? ♗e2! −+) 18...dxc6 19 ♖c4 g6 (19...♕a6 20 ♕h5 +−) 20 ♖h4 ♔g7 21 ♗xg6! fxg6 22 ♕d7+ +−.

c) 15...♘xe5 16 dxe6 ♗xf1 17 ♗xa8 0-0 18 exf7+ ♔h8 19 ♕xf1! ♖xa8 20 ♖e1 +−.

11 ♕xd3 0-0 (D)

An easy trap for Black to fall into is 11...d5? 12 exd6 ♕xd6 13 ♗a3! ♕c7 (13...♕xa3 14 ♕e4 costs Black his a8-rook) 14 ♗xe7 ♔xe7 15 ♖ad1 ♘d7 16 d5 ± Fossan-Iskov, Gausdal 1988, and many other games since.

12 d5

Instead:

a) 12 ♗f4 ♘c6 13 d5 exd5 14 ♕xd5 ♕c7 15 ♖ad1 ♖ad8 16 ♕e4 ♕c8 17 ♖d3 ♖fe8 18 ♘g5 g6 19 ♖h3 d5 gives Black sufficient counterplay, Godena-Hraček, Pula Echt 1997.

b) 12 c4 d5 13 exd6 ♕xd6 (alternatively, 13...♗xd6 14 ♘g5) 14 ♕e4 ♘d7 15 ♗f4 ♕b4 16 ♕c6 ♖fd8 17 ♗c7!? worked out well for White after 17...♖ac8 18 ♖fd1 ♗f6 19 ♖ab1 ♕a3

20 d5 ± in J.Shaw-Jansa, Port Erin 1998.

12...exd5 13 ♖d1

A subtle move by White, stopping Black's knight developing to its favoured square – a6. After 13 ♕xd5 ♘a6, the position is unclear.

13...♘c6

Or 13...♕c8 14 ♗g5 ♘c6 15 ♕xd5 ♖d8 16 ♕e4 h6 17 ♗f4 ♕a6?! 18 e6! fxe6 19 ♖xd7 ♖xd7 20 ♕xe6+ ♔h8 21 ♕xd7 ± Ristić-Nikčević, Vrnjačka Banja 1999.

14 ♕f5 ♗c5 15 ♘g5 g6 16 ♕h3 h5 17 ♖xd5 ♕e7 18 ♗f4

White has a clear advantage, Perez-Jansa, Andorra 2000.

C23)
7...♗b7 (D)

8 ♘c3

8 0-0 is an alternative move-order, with both pros and cons:

a) 8...♗e7 and then:

a1) 9 ♘c3 transposes to *8 ♘c3 ♗e7 9 0-0*, with White having avoided the line *8 ♘c3 ♘xc3*.

a2) Some players dislike the idea of the weak pawn on c3 altogether and have tried 9 ♘bd2 with the idea of 9...0-0 10 ♘e4 transposing to *8 ♘c3 ♗e7 9 0-0 0-0 10 ♘e4*. Instead, 9...♘b4 (or 9...♘f4) 10 ♗e4 ♗xe4 11 ♘xe4 0-0 leaves White a few tempi up in comparison with *7...♗a6 8 ♗xa6 ♘xa6 9 0-0 ♗e7 10 ♘bd2 0-0 11 ♘e4*.

b) 8...♘b4!? is the critical test of this move-order: 9 ♗e2 ♗e7 10 ♘c3 0-0 11 a3 ♘d5 12 ♘e4 (12 ♗d3 ♘xc3 13 bxc3 ♘c6 14 ♕c2 g6 ∞ Managadze-Veličković, Athens 1999) 12...f5 13 exf6 ♘xf6 14 ♘xf6+ (14 ♘c3 ♘a6 15 d5 exd5 16 ♘xd5 ♗xd5 17 ♗xa6 ♕c7 and Black has activity of his own, Sermek-Pavasović, Nova Gorica 1998) 14...♗xf6 15 ♗d3 transposes to a position that can also arise via *8 ♘c3 ♗e7 9 0-0-0-0 10 ♘e4 f5 11 exf6 ♘xf6 12 ♘xf6+ ♗xf6 13 a3* and *7 a3 ♗e7 8 ♘bd2 0-0 9 ♘e4 f5 10 exf6 ♘xf6 11 ♗d3 ♗b7 12 ♘xf6+ ♗xf6 13 0-0*. After 15...♗d5 (15...♘c6 16 ♗e4 ±) 16 ♘e5 ♗xe5 17 dxe5 ♕h4 18 f4 ♘c6 19 ♗e3 ♘e7 (19...g5 20 ♕e1 ♕xe1 21 ♖axe1 gxf4 22 ♗xf4 ♘d4 23 ♗h6 ♖xf1+ 24 ♖xf1 ♖c8 25 ♖f4 ♘f5! offers White a slight advantage, Harley-Watts, Cambridge 1988) 20 ♕e1, Black's active pieces provide compensation for the bishop-pair, but White probably has slightly better chances, Z.Almasi-J.Polgar, Groningen FIDE 1997.

We now return to 8 ♘c3 *(D)*:

8...♗e7

After 8...♘xc3 9 bxc3 ♕c7 (9...♗e7 10 0-0 – 8...♗e7 9 0-0 ♘xc3 10 bxc3), White could play 10 ♗d2 transposing to *7 ♘c3 ♘xc3 8 bxc3 ♕c7 9 ♗d2*

♗b7 10 ♗d3, but can also try the more enterprising 10 0-0!?:

a) 10...d6 11 ♗f4 ♘d7 12 ♖e1 ♗e7 leaves White a tempo up in comparison with the major line *7 ♘c3 ♘xc3 8 bxc3 ♕c7 9 ♗d2 ♗b7 10 ♗d3 d6 11 0-0 ♘d7 12 ♗f4 ♗e7 13 ♖e1* because the white bishop has been developed to f4 immediately without going to d2 first. This tempo means that Black hasn't yet castled, and after 13 ♖e3! ♖c8 14 ♖c1, Black can't risk 14...0-0 because of 15 ♘g5! h6 16 ♕h5 with a strong attack. Black can instead try 14...h6 (or 14...g6) 15 d5!? (a thematic idea in this whole variation, but maybe premature here) 15...♗xd5 16 exd6 (16 ♗a6 ♗xf3 17 ♖xf3 dxe5 18 ♗xc8 ♕xc8 19 ♗e3 ∞) 16...♗xd6 17 ♗xd6 ♕xd6 18 ♗a6 ♖c5 19 c4 ♕c7 20 ♗b5, when, rather than 20...♗xf3 21 ♖xf3 ± Van de Oudeweetering-Blees, Dutch Cht 2001, Black can defend better with 20...♗c6! 21 ♘d4 ♘b8!, when White has difficulty proving his compensation for the pawn.

b) 10...♕xc3!? is critical but almost untested. 11 ♗e3 ♘a6 12 ♖c1 ♕a3 13 ♘g5 gave White strong compensation in Mäki-Pirttimäki, Jyväskylä 1996.

9 0-0 0-0 *(D)*

Or 9...♘xc3 10 bxc3 d6 11 ♗f4 (11 ♖e1 ♘d7 12 ♗f4 dxe5 13 ♘xe5 ♘xe5 14 ♗xe5 0-0 15 ♕h5 ± Smagin-Sadler, Vienna 1991) 11...♘c6 12 ♖e1 (after 12 ♕e2 dxe5 13 dxe5 ♕c7 14 ♖ad1 0-0-0 the black king is safe on the queenside, Kharlov-Prokopchuk, Russian Clubs Cup (Maikop) 1998) 12...dxe5 13 ♘xe5 ♘xe5 14 ♗xe5 ♗f6 15 ♕h5 ♗xe5 16 ♗b5+ ♔f8 17 dxe5 ♕d5 18 ♗f1 ♗c6 19 ♖ad1 and Black is in serious danger, Dončević-Tal, Bundesliga 1991/2.

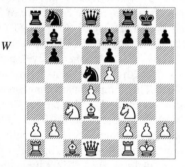

W

10 ♕e2

10 ♘e4 is an important alternative:

a) 10...f5 11 exf6 ♘xf6 (11...gxf6 12 ♗h6 ♖f7 13 ♘c3 ♗f8 14 ♗d2 ♖g7 15 ♗c4 ♘e7 16 d5 exd5 17 ♗b3 ± Sermek-Pilz, Austrian Cht 1998/9) 12 ♘fg5! ♘xe4 13 ♘xe4 ♘c6 (13...♗a6 14 d5! ± Harley-Edwards, Cambridge 1985; 13...d5 14 ♘c3 ♗a6 15 ♘b5! ± Harley-Keehner, Hastings 1990/1) 14 ♕h5 g6 15 ♕g4 ♘b4 (15...♘xd4 16 ♗h6 ♖e8 17 ♘d6! ♗xd6 18 ♗xg6! ±) 16 ♗b1 (Harley-O'Shaughnessy, London 1995) 16...♘d5 17 ♗h6 ♖f5 18 ♘g3 ♘f6 19 ♕e2 ♖a5 ±.

b) 10...♘c6!? has the points 11 ♘fg5 h6 12 ♘f6+? ♗xf6! 13 exf6 hxg5 −+ and 11 ♗g5 ♘xd4!. Ferretti-Fauland, Cappelle la Grande 1993 continued 11 a3 ♖c8 (11...f5 12 exf6 ♘xf6 13 ♘xf6+ ♗xf6 14 ♗e4 ±) 12 ♖e1 ♘a5 13 ♗g5 (13 b4!? ♘c4 14 ♕b3 ±) 13...f6 14 exf6 gxf6 15 ♗h6 ♖f7 16 ♘g3 ♗f8 17 ♗xf8 ♕xf8 with an unclear position. More tests are necessary.

10...♘xc3

Or:

a) 10...f6 11 ♘xd5 ♗xd5 12 ♗e4 ♗xe4 13 ♕xe4 ♘c6 14 exf6 ♗xf6 15 d5 exd5 16 ♕xd5+ ♔h8 17 ♗g5 ± Vi.Ivanov.

b) After 10...f5, the reply 11 ♗d2!? was tried with success in Illescas-J.Polgar, Linares 1994, which continued 11...a6 12 ♗c4! ♘xc3 (12...♘c7 13 d5!) 13 bxc3 b5 14 ♗d3 ♗a3 15 ♖fb1 ±. Black improved in Adamson-Storey, Newcastle 1998 with 11...♔h8 12 ♗c4 ♘c7 (with the point 13 d5 exd5 14 ♗b3 ♗a6) 13 ♖ac1 (13 ♖fd1 seems stronger) 13...g5!? ∞.

11 bxc3 d6 12 exd6 ♕xd6

12...♗xd6? 13 ♘g5 ± Vi.Ivanov.

13 a4 *(D)*

13 ♗g5 ♗xg5 14 ♘xg5 gives White no advantage. White's main chances here rest in playing ♘g5, but the immediate 13 ♘g5 is met by 13...h6 14 ♘h7? (14 ♘e4 =) 14...♖c8! 15 ♕g4 ♔h8! 16 ♕h5 (Vi.Ivanov) 16...♖xc3 17 ♗xh6 ♕d5 −+. Therefore, White improves his position first with the text-move and waits to see how Black develops.

13...♘c6

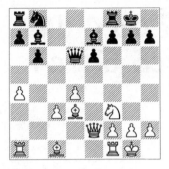

Black wants to stop 14 a5. 13...♕c7 is the main alternative:

a) 14 ♘g5 makes more sense for White than a move earlier but is still not clearly strong:

a1) 14...♗xg5?! 15 ♗xg5 ♕xc3? (15...♘d7 16 ♕e3 ♖fc8 17 ♖ac1 ±) 16 ♖ac1! ♕xd4 17 ♖fd1! ♕xa4 18 ♖c4! ♕a5 19 ♕h5? (19 ♗xh7+! ♔xh7 20 ♕h5+ ♔g8 21 ♖h4 f5 22 ♗f6! ♖xf6 23 ♕e8+ ♖f8 24 ♕xe6+ ♖f7 25 ♖d8#) 19...h6? (19...g6 20 ♕h6 ♕e5 ∞) 20 ♖g4 ♖d8 21 ♗f6! 1-0 Vi.Ivanov-Losev, Moscow Ch 1995 (analysis based on that by Vi.Ivanov in *Informator 65*).

a2) 14...h6! 15 ♘xe6 (15 ♘h7? ♖d8 16 ♕g4, suggested by Vi.Ivanov, is refuted by 16...♕xc3! 17 ♗xh6 ♕xd4 −+) 15...fxe6 16 ♕xe6+ ♖f7 (but not 16...♔h8? 17 ♕g6 ♔g8 18 ♗xh6 ♗f6 19 ♕h7+ ♔f7 20 ♖fe1 +− Vi.Ivanov) and White will end up with two pawns and a rook for a knight and bishop. The position is unclear.

b) White can simply play 14 ♗d2. Now 14...♘c6 can be met by 15 ♘g5 as 15...h6? runs into 16 ♕e4, and after 14...♘d7, White can play 15 a5 with an advantage.

14 ♘g5 ♗xg5

Here 14...h6 is not so good: 15 ♕e4 g6 16 ♘f3 ♔g7 17 ♕e3 ♖h8 18 ♗b2 ± Vi.Ivanov.

15 ♗xg5 e5 16 a5! exd4 17 a6 ♖ae8

17...♗c8 18 ♕e4 f5 19 ♗c4+ ♔h8 20 ♕d5 ♕xd5 21 ♗xd5 ♘d7 22 cxd4 is better for White.

18 ♕c2

Black has the better chances after 18 ♗xh7+ ♔xh7 19 ♕h5+ ♔g8 20 axb7 dxc3; e.g., 21 ♖a4 ♕g6 22 ♕xg6 fxg6 23 ♖c4 ♘a5 24 ♖c7 ♖b8 25 ♗e7 ♖fe8 26 ♗b4 ♖xb7 27 ♖xc3 ♖e4 28 ♗xa5 bxa5 with an unusual double-rook ending with two sets of doubled pawns against three connected pawns.

18...h6?!

Perhaps this move is wrong and Black should play 18...♗a8. White may have an edge after 19 ♗xh7+ ♔h8 20 ♗f5, but the position is complex.

19 ♗c1

19 axb7 hxg5 20 cxd4 ♘xd4 21 ♕d1 a5 seems good for Black, who just needs to round up the b7-pawn.

19...♗a8 20 ♗a3

White has won the exchange, but Black has reasonable compensation. After 20...♕d5 21 c4 ♕g5 22 f4 ♕f6 23 ♗xf8 ♔xf8 24 ♕d2 ♖e3 25 ♖ae1, a draw was agreed in Potkin-Neverov, Pardubice 2000. However, White had good chances for a win in the final position. For instance: 25...♕e7 26 ♖e2 ♕b4 (26...♘b4 27 ♖fe1!) 27 ♕xb4+ ♘xb4 28 ♖xe3 dxe3 29 ♗e2 ♘xa6 30 ♖a1 ♗b7 31 ♔f1 followed by 32 ♗f3 with a probably winning position.

9 2...♘f6 3 e5 ♘d5 4 d4 cxd4 5 ♘f3 ♘c6 6 ♗c4 ♘b6 7 ♗b3

1 e4 c5 2 c3 ♘f6 3 e5 ♘d5 4 d4 cxd4 5 ♘f3 ♘c6 6 ♗c4

White seeks to develop quickly, and is prepared to give up a pawn to maintain hopes of an initiative.

6 cxd4 transposes to *5 cxd4 ♘c6 6 ♘f3*, which offers White fewer chances.

6...♘b6

In our opinion, this is Black's best option. 6...e6 gives White a position with more space. 7 cxd4 transposes to *5...e6 6 cxd4 ♘c6 7 ♗c4*; Black has ruled out White's alternative plan *7 a3* followed by *♗d3*, but this is counteracted by Black's early development of the queen's knight, which hinders Black from developing his queen's bishop to c6.

7 ♗b3 *(D)*

B

Now Black has two good options to choose from:

A: 7...g6   157
B: 7...d6   161

Alternatively:

a) Black very rarely accepts White's pawn sacrifice immediately by 7...dxc3 8 ♘xc3, but while 8...e6 9 ♗g5!? ♗e7 10 ♗xe7 ♕xe7 11 ♕d2 ± and 8...d6 9 exd6, transposing to *7...d6 8 exd6 dxc3 9 ♘xc3*, are clearly good for White, who is ahead in development, 8...g6 deserves more attention. White sacrificed another pawn and gained more than enough compensation in Dolgov-Chepa, corr. 1990 with 9 ♘g5 e6 10 ♘ge4 ♘xe5 11 ♗g5 ♗e7 12 ♘d6+ ♔f8 13 ♗h6+ ♔g8 14 ♘ce4 but this wouldn't be so easy to play over the board.

b) 7...e6 8 cxd4 d6 transposes to a position that can also be reached after *5...e6 6 cxd4 d6 7 ♗c4 ♘b6 8 ♗b3 ♘c6* from the previous chapter but there we recommend *8 ♗d3* instead. White probably does best to play 9 exd6, transposing to *7...d6 8 exd6 e6 9 cxd4* ±, as after both 9 ♕e2 dxe5 10 dxe5 ♘b4 11 0-0 ♕d3! and 9 0-0 dxe5

10 dxe5 ♕xd1 11 ♖xd1, Black is close to equality.

c) After 7...d5, White should exchange pawns by 8 exd6 (because 8 cxd4 ♗g4 9 ♗e3 e6 gives Black an improved type of French Defence) and transpose to the main line *7...d6 8 exd6*.

A)

7...g6 *(D)*

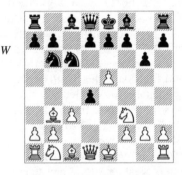

Black also seeks to develop his pieces first, and only then to struggle for the centre. This move was introduced to common practice through a win by Bologan against one of the authors in 1995, quoted below, and has since become a popular option for players seeking a win with Black. In fact, Black has actually achieved a plus score to date, and not just because of surprise value. However, we believe that with accurate play, White can maintain some advantage.

8 ♘g5

This move, by which White attacks Black's kingside immediately, is probably best. The alternative is 8 cxd4 ♗g7 (8...d5!? 9 exd6 ♕xd6 10 ♘g5 e6

– *8 ♘g5 d5 9 exd6 e6 10 cxd4 ♕xd6*), and then:

a) 9 ♘c3 0-0 10 h4? (this attempt to attack the black king allows Black to seize the initiative; the natural 10 0-0 is better but allows Black a comfortable position after 10...d6 11 exd6 ♕xd6) 10...d5 11 h5 ♗g4 12 hxg6 fxg6 13 ♗e3 a5 14 a3 e6 15 ♕e2 a4 16 ♗c2 ♘c4 with a big advantage for Black, Rozentalis-Bologan, Belfort 1995.

b) 9 d5!? is very sharp, but also isn't dangerous: 9...♘xe5 10 ♘xe5 ♗xe5 11 ♗h6 e6 (according to Finkel, it is too risky to win more material by 11...♗xb2, as after 12 ♘d2 ♗xa1 13 ♕xa1 f6 14 d6 White obtains a huge initiative) 12 ♘c3 ♕h4 13 ♕d2 f6 (but not 13...♘c4 14 ♗xc4 ♕xc4 15 ♖c1 b6 16 f4 ♗f6 17 b3 ♕b4 18 a3 with a strong attack for White, Finkel-Mariasin, Israel 1996) 14 dxe6 dxe6 15 0-0-0 ♗d7 16 ♗e3 (16 g3 ♕b4 17 f4 ♗xc3 18 bxc3 ♖c8 and the c-pawn falls) 16...0-0-0 17 f4 ♗c7 18 g3 ♕h5 and White has only some compensation for the pawn, Jenni-Fressinet, Lausanne 2000.

c) 9 ♗f4 (White takes control of d6 and thereby stops Black recapturing on d6 with the queen) 9...d6 10 exd6 0-0 and now:

c1) On 11 h3, Black can even play 11...♘xd4 12 ♘xd4 e5 13 ♗g3 exd4 14 0-0 ♗f5 15 ♘d2 ♘c8 16 ♘c4 b5 17 ♘e5 ♘xd6 18 ♘c6 ♕d7 19 ♘xd4 ♘c4 with some pressure, Ekström-Fressinet, Mitropa Cup (Charleville) 2000.

c2) 11 0-0 exd6 12 h3 ♘a5 and now 13 ♗c2 is equal. White shouldn't allow the bishop to be exchanged as after 13 ♘c3 ♘xb3 14 ♕xb3 ♗f5 15 ♖fe1 ♕d7 Black has an advantage, Smagin-Bologan, Novgorod 1995.

8...d5

Or:

a) 8...♘xe5?! 9 ♕xd4 f6 (9...♗g7? loses to 10 ♗xf7+ ♔f8 11 ♘e6+) 10 ♕xe5 d5 11 ♕e2 fxg5 12 ♗xg5 ± Sveshnikov.

b) 8...e6 can be met by the solid 9 cxd4 d6 (9...♗b4+ 10 ♘c3 d6 11 exd6 ♕xd6 12 ♗e3 ±) 10 ♕f3 ♕c7 11 ♕f6 ♖g8 12 exd6 ♗xd6 13 ♘c3 ± or the ambitious 9 ♘e4 ♘xe5 10 ♕xd4 ♗g7 11 ♗g5 ♕c7 12 ♗f6 ♗xf6 13 ♘xf6+ ♔e7 14 0-0 d6 15 ♕h4, which gave White a good attack for the pawn in Garma-Laylo, Manila Z 2001.

9 exd6 e6 *(D)*

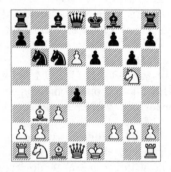

W

10 ♕f3

Other moves seem to offer Black good chances:

a) 10 cxd4 ♕xd6 (10...♗g7 11 d5!; 10...h6 11 ♘e4 transposes to *10 ♘e4 h6 11 cxd4* and is a serious alternative) 11 ♕f3 ♕e7 12 ♗e3 ♗g7 13 ♕e4 (13 ♕f4 0-0 and now 14 0-0 ♘xd4! ∓ or 14 ♘f3 e5 ∓) 13...0-0 14 ♘f3 f5 15 ♕d3 ♔h8 16 0-0 f4 17 ♗d2 ♘xd4 18

♘xd4 ♕d7 19 ♗c3 e5 gave Black good counterplay in Khamrakulov-Sermek, Cairo 2001.

b) 10 ♘e4 and then:

b1) 10...♗xd6!? has rarely been seen but wins a pawn. 11 ♗g5 ♗e7 12 ♗xe7 ♕xe7 13 cxd4 0-0 14 0-0 ♖d8 is good for Black, so White has to try 11 cxd4 ♗b4+ 12 ♘bc3 ♕xd4 13 0-0 0-0 14 ♗e3 ♕xd1 15 ♖axd1 with compensation for the pawn.

b2) 10...h6 11 cxd4 ♗g7 12 0-0 (12 ♗e3 f5!; 12 d5 exd5 13 ♗xd5 ♘xd5 14 ♕xd5 ♗e6 15 ♕d1 f5 16 ♘ec3 0-0 17 0-0 ♕d7 ∓ Mogilarov-Felgaer, Oropesa del Mar U-18 Wch 1998) 12...♘xd4 (this has to be played immediately since after 12...0-0 13 ♘bc3, 13...♘xd4 is met by 14 ♗xh6! and 13...♔h7 by 14 d5 ±) 13 ♗e3 ♘f5 ∞ Kharlov-Dydyshko, Swidnica rpd 1997. It is unclear whether the d6-pawn is weak or strong, but the risks seem greater for White.

10...♘e5

Other moves are rare here, mainly because of the dynamic chances offered by the text-move. However, neither move by Black's f-pawn is easy to counter without preparation:

a) 10...f6!? needs to be met by 11 ♘xe6 (11 ♗xe6 ♗xd6 12 ♘f7 ♕e7 13 ♘xd6+ ♕xd6 ∓) 11...♗xe6 12 ♗xe6 ♗xd6 13 ♕h3 (13 0-0 ♗xh2+! 14 ♔xh2 ♕d6+ 15 ♗f4 ♕xe6 16 cxd4 ♘xd4 17 ♕d1 ♕d7 18 ♖e1+ ♔f7 ∓; 13 ♕e2 ♕e7 14 0-0 d3 ∞) 13...f5 14 0-0 ♕f6 15 ♖e1 ♔d8 16 ♗b3 (16 ♕h6 f4) 16...♔d7! 17 cxd4 (improving on the passive move 17 ♗d2 of Filipović-Čabrilo, Yugoslav Cht (Tivat) 1995)

17...♘xd4 18 ♘c3 ♖ae8 19 ♗e3, as given by Chekhov, which looks good for White.

b) 10...f5 and now:

b1) 11 ♘xe6?! is not good here, as Black can reply 11...♗xe6 12 ♗xe6 ♕xd6 (in the 10...f6 case, White would have been able to play 13 ♕xf6 here) 13 ♕e2 d3!? 14 ♕e3 ♘e5 15 ♗b3 0-0-0 with an advantage.

b2) 11 0-0 ♗xd6 12 ♖e1 preserves the tension:

b21) 12...0-0 (Marković-Mizetić, Niš 1998) 13 ♘xe6 ♗xe6 14 ♖xe6 ♔g7 15 ♕h3 and White starts a strong attack by simple means.

b22) 12...♕c7! seems more logical, when 13 ♘xe6 ♗xe6 14 ♖xe6+ ♔d7 15 h3 ♖ae8 is unclear.

b3) Therefore we recommend 11 ♗xe6:

b31) 11...♗xd6!? 12 0-0 ♘e5 13 ♕d1! dxc3 14 ♘xc3 gives White an advantage; e.g., 14...♗xe6 15 ♘xe6 ♕e7 16 ♘b5! ± or 14...h6 15 ♘b5 ♗b8 16 ♗xc8 ♕xd1 17 ♖xd1 ♘xc8 18 ♘e6 ♔e7? 19 ♘bc7 ♗xc7 20 ♘xc7 ♖b8 21 ♗f4 +–.

b32) 11...♗xe6 12 ♘xe6 ♕xd6 13 ♘xd4 ♘xd4 14 cxd4 ♕d5! definitely gives Black some compensation for the pawn (and the d4-pawn is difficult for White to hold anyway). Black actually went to win in Handoko-Xu Jun, Singapore tt 1995, but White can preserve a slight advantage with 15 ♕e3+! ♗e7 16 0-0.

We now return to 10...♘e5 *(D)*:

11 ♕e4

It is difficult to know where best to place White's queen, both here and

W

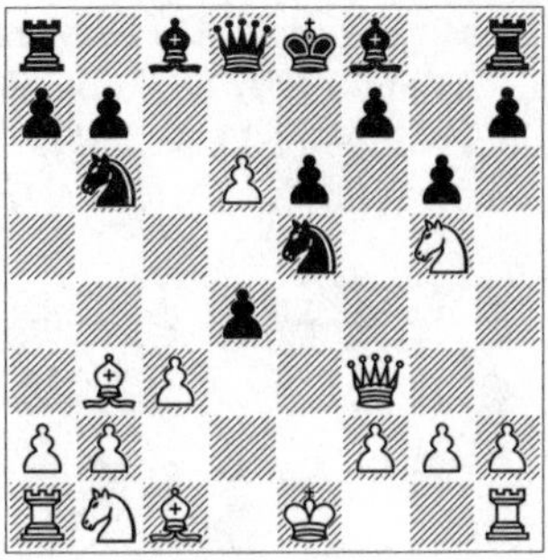

over the following moves. The alternatives are:

a) 11 ♕h3 ♗g7 12 0-0 ♘ec4 13 ♖e1 (13 ♘e4 ♘xd6 14 ♗g5 f6 15 ♘xd6+ ♕xd6 16 ♗d2 e5 ∓; 13 ♖d1!?) 13...h6 14 ♘e4 (14 ♘xf7?! ♔xf7 15 ♘a3 ♘xd6 16 ♗xe6+ didn't give White enough in Blatny-Dao Thien Hai, Amsterdam 1996) 14...♘xd6 15 ♘xd6+ ♕xd6 16 cxd4 is unclear. Black's kingside is weakened, but White's isolated queen's pawn is weak and it is to Black's advantage that a pair of knights has been exchanged.

b) 11 ♕g3 ♗g7 (11...♗xd6 12 0-0 ♘c6 13 ♗f4 ♗xf4 14 ♕xf4 0-0 occurred in Acs-Šolak, Rimavska Sobota U-16 Ech 1996, when White could have ventured 15 ♖d1 e5 16 ♘xf7! ♕c7 17 ♘g5+ ♔g7 18 ♕g3 ♖f4 19 f3!? ♗d7 20 ♘a3 ♖d8 21 ♘b5 ♕b8 22 ♗e6 ±) 12 0-0 0-0 (12...♕xd6 13 ♖d1) 13 cxd4 (13 ♕h3 h6 14 ♘e4 f5 15 cxd4 ♘f7 16 ♘c5 ♕xd6 is unclear, Acs-Stocek, Budapest 1996) 13...♘c6 (13...♘ec4 14 ♘e4 f5 15 ♗g5! ♕d7 16 ♘bd2! ± Peredy-Sziebert, Budapest 1996) 14 ♖d1 h6 15 ♘f3 ♘a5 16 ♗c2 ♗d7 17 ♘e5 ♖c8 18 ♗e4 ♗c6 19 ♘xc6 ♘xc6 20 ♘c3 ♘xd4 21 ♔h1

♘c4 was played in D.Pedersen-Aagaard, Århus 1999, and now White should have found 22 ♗xh6! ±.

We now return to 11 ♕e4 (D):

11...♗g7

This is now considered the best reaction, planning to recapture on d6 with the e5-knight! Instead:

a) 11...♗xd6 12 ♕xd4 0-0 13 0-0 ± Bangiev.

b) 11...♕xd6 and then:

b1) 12 cxd4 ♘c6 13 0-0 allows Black the option of 13...♕xd4!?, when neither 14 ♕f3 ♘e5 15 ♕g3 ♗g7 16 ♘c3, given by Chekhov, nor 14 ♖d1 ♕xe4 15 ♘xe4 ♗e7 16 ♗h6 ♗d7 17 ♗g7 ♖g8 18 ♗f6 ♘a5 19 ♗c2 ♖c8 20 ♘bc3 ♗c6 ∓ is convincing for White.

b2) 12 0-0 and here:

b21) 12...d3?! is well met by 13 ♗f4 ♗g7 14 ♖e1 h6 15 ♘h3 ♘bd7 16 ♗a4 ±.

b22) 12...dxc3!? is untested and unclear; e.g., 13 ♘xc3 ♗g7 14 ♖d1 ♕c6! or 13 ♖d1 ♕b8! 14 ♘xc3 ♗g7 15 ♗f4 h6 16 ♘f3 ♘xf3+ 17 ♕xf3 ♗e5.

b23) 12...♗g7 13 cxd4 (13 ♗f4 ♕c6! gives Black a slight advantage) 13...♘c6 14 ♖d1 0-0 15 ♘c3 (15 ♕h4

h6 16 ♘f3 ♕e7 17 ♕e4 ♗d7 18 ♘c3 leads to a complicated game, Zifroni-Khuzman, Tel-Aviv 1996) 15...♕e7 (Bangiev gives 15...♘e7 16 ♗f4!? ♕b4 17 ♖ac1, with an initiative for White, and 15...♘xd4?! 16 ♘b5 ♘xb5 17 ♖xd6 ♘xd6 18 ♕h4 ±) 16 ♘f3 leaves White's pieces more active. After the inaccurate continuation 16...♘a5 17 d5! ♖d8 18 ♗f4 White gained a big advantage in Emms-Tukmakov, Copenhagen 1996.

12 cxd4 ♘ec4 13 ♘f3

The knight has served its purpose in forcing ...e6 and now retreats to defend d4 and free g5 for the bishop. This does seem somewhat passive, but White can't really take advantage of his knight being on g5. 13 ♕f4?! prevents the white bishop from getting to g5 and doesn't help White get to the h-file. A better try is 13 ♕d3, when after 13...♘xd6 14 0-0 0-0 15 ♖d1, 15...♗d7 16 ♘c3 ♗c6 17 ♕h3 h6 18 ♘f3 ♘f5 19 d5 ♘xd5 20 g4 ♘d6 21 ♘xd5 exd5 22 ♗xh6 allowed White to obtain a good initiative in Kalezić-Perunović, Herceg Novi 2000. However, Rogozenko's suggestion 15...♘f5 16 ♘c3 ♕xd4 17 ♕h3 ♕h4 18 ♕xh4 ♘xh4 is better, when White no longer has any real compensation for the pawn.

13...♘xd6 14 ♕e2

A good alternative for White is 14 ♕d3, keeping control over the key d5-square. Then after 14...0-0 15 ♘c3 ♗d7, White can improve on 16 0-0 ♗c6 17 ♗g5 ♗f6 18 ♗xf6 ♕xf6 19 d5 = Poddubny-Volzhin, Russian Ch (Elista) 2001 by playing 16 h4! h5 (16...♗c6 17 h5) 17 ♗g5 ♗f6 (17...♕c7

18 ♗f4) 18 0-0, when White is more active.

14...♘f5

In *Informator 83*, Volzhin suggests 14...0-0 as an improvement, presumably with the point 15 ♘c3 ♘f5 16 ♗g5 ♘xd4!?, but one idea for White is 15 ♗g5 ♗f6 16 h4!?.

15 ♗g5 ♕d6

Or:

a) 15...♘xd4?! 16 ♗xd8 ♘xe2 17 ♗xb6 axb6 18 ♔xe2 ♗xb2 19 ♘bd2 ♗xa1 20 ♖xa1 ± Matulović.

b) 15...♗f6 16 ♗xf6 ♕xf6 and White can try to take advantage of his queen being on e2 instead of d3 by playing 17 ♕e5! ± (rather than 17 d5 0-0! =).

16 ♘c3 (D)

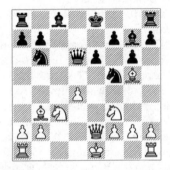

16...0-0

After 16...♘xd4 17 ♘xd4 ♗xd4 (17...♕xd4?? 18 ♖d1 and mate on d8 if the queen moves), White has good compensation following either 18 ♖d1 or 18 0-0-0!? – Rogozenko.

17 ♘e4!

17 ♖d1 ♗d7 18 0-0 ♗c6 19 ♘e4 ♗xe4 20 ♕xe4 ♘d5 ½-½ Certić-Matulović, Belgrade 1996.

17...♕b4+ 18 ♗d2 ♕e7 19 a3 ♖d8 20 ♗g5 f6 21 ♗d2 ♘d5 22 0-0

The position was agreed drawn in Demkovich-Morokhin, Ukraine 1999, but White has a slight advantage and could play on.

B)

7...d6 8 exd6

8 cxd4 – *5 cxd4 d6 6 ♘f3 ♘c6 7 ♗c4 ♘b6 8 ♗b3!?*.

8...♕xd6 (D)

Or:

a) 8...dxc3?! 9 ♘xc3 exd6 (the alternative 9...♕xd6 10 0-0! transposes to *8...♕xd6 9 0-0 dxc3 10 ♘xc3 ±*) 10 ♘g5 d5 (10...♘e5 11 f4!) 11 0-0 (11 ♘xd5 ♘xd5 and now 12 ♗xd5 ♗b4+ 13 ♔f1 0-0 ∓ or 12 ♕xd5 =) 11...♗e7 (11...h6 12 ♘xf7! ♔xf7 13 ♘xd5 ♘xd5 14 ♗xd5+ ♔f6 15 b3! ± Gola-Arkhipov, Moscow 1989) 12 ♕h5 g6 13 ♕h6 ♗e6 (13...♗f8 14 ♖e1+ ♘e7 15 ♘ge4! dxe4 16 ♘xe4 ♕c7 17 ♕h4 +– *NCO*) 14 ♖e1 ♕d7 15 ♗f4 with dangerous compensation for the pawn, but the position is still far from clear.

b) 8...e6 gives White comfortable play as Black has wasted time playing his knight to b6; e.g., 9 cxd4 ♗xd6 10 0-0 ♘e7 11 ♘c3 ♗d7 12 ♘g5 h6 13 ♘ge4 ♗c7 14 ♕g4 ♘f5 15 ♖d1 0-0 16 ♘c5 ♗c8 17 g3 ♘d5 18 ♘xd5 exd5 19 ♕f3 ♘e7 20 ♗f4 and White has a small but lasting strategic advantage, Short-Krasenkow, Groningen FIDE 1997. In ...e6 lines, White rarely chooses to play exd6 when the knight is still on d5, as Black is then well positioned for the resulting isolated queen's pawn position.

Now White has two main options:
B1: 9 ♘a3!?   162
B2: 9 0-0   165

Instead, recapturing the pawn now would be inconsistent:

a) 9 cxd4 ♗e6 gives Black easy play against the isolated queen's pawn: compare *9 0-0 ♗e6 10 cxd4*.

b) 9 ♘xd4 ♘xd4 10 ♕xd4 ♕g6!? 11 0-0 (11 ♕f4! is the best try, but Black is fine after 11...♗d7 12 0-0 ♗c6) 11...♗h3 12 ♗a4+ ♘xa4 13 ♕xa4+ ♗d7 14 ♕f4 ♗c6 and Black has secured the bishop-pair, Balbi-Sorokin, Buenos Aires 1997.

B1)
9 ♘a3!?

The aggressive option, and worth considering for White if you are willing to take the risk that your opponent will not be both brave enough and well prepared enough to play the most accurate response.

9...dxc3!

The alternatives are:

a) 9...♗e6 is not good here, since after 10 ♘b5 ♕d7 11 ♗xe6 ♕xe6+ 12 ♗e3! White wins a precious tempo:

a1) 12...♖c8 13 ♘fxd4 ♘xd4 14 ♕xd4 a6 15 ♘a7 +− Striković-Drei, Forli 1988.

a2) 12...0-0-0 13 ♘fxd4 ♕d5 14 ♕b3 and Black is in trouble, Sermek-Sosa Macho, Paranana 1993.

a3) 12...♕d7 13 ♘bxd4 e6 (after 13...♘c4 14 ♕e2 ♘xe3 15 ♕xe3 e6 16 0-0-0 ♕c7 17 ♕g5 White was slightly better in Smirnov-Lopushnoi, Tomsk 1997) 14 ♘xc6 ♕xc6 15 ♕d4!? ♖d8 16 ♕g4 ± Vlassov-Donchenko, Moscow 1998.

b) 9...a6 is very solid. After 10 0-0, Black has a number of playable options:

b1) 10...dxc3!? 11 ♘g5 (11 ♕e2 e6 − *10...e6 11 ♕e2 dxc3*) 11...e6 12 ♕h5 gives White good play but deserves more tests.

b2) 10...♗e6 11 ♗xe6 ♕xe6 and then:

b21) 12 ♘xd4 ♘xd4 13 ♕xd4 gives us a position from the line *9 0-0 ♗e6 10 ♗xe6 ♕xe6 11 ♘xd4 ♘xd4 12 ♕xd4*, but with the moves ♘a3 and ...a6 included, which should be in White's favour, but Black might be able to exploit the fact that White's knight is away from the kingside: 13...♖d8 14 ♕h4 h5 (14...♕c6 15 ♘c2 e6 16 ♘d4 ♕c7 17 ♗g5 ♗e7 18 ♘f5 and White's threats become very dangerous, Ni Hua-Nakamura, Seattle tt 2001) 15 h3 f6! 16 ♕b4 g5 17 c4 g4 18 h4 ♕c6 19 ♗e3 with an unclear position probably in White's favour, De Wit-Filipek, Belgian Cht 2001/2.

b22) 12 ♖e1!? ♕d5 13 ♘xd4 ♘xd4 14 ♗e3 ♘b5 15 ♗xb6 ♕xd1 16 ♖axd1 ♘xa3 17 bxa3 e6 18 a4 ♗e7 19 ♖d3

0-0 20 ♖d7 favours White, Vajda-Nakamura, Budapest 2002.

b3) 10...♗f5 – *4 ♘f3 ♘c6 5 ♗c4 ♘b6 6 ♗b3 d5 7 exd6 ♕xd6 8 ♘a3 a6 9 0-0 ♗f5 10 d4 cxd4.*

b4) 10...e6 and then:

b41) 11 ♕e2 is not dangerous, because after 11...dxc3 12 bxc3 ♗e7 13 ♖d1 ♕c7 14 c4 0-0 15 ♗b2 ♘d7 16 ♖ac1 ♘c5 17 ♗c2 b6 18 ♗b1 ♗b7 Black is simply a pawn up, Dovzhik-A.Schneider, Hungarian Cht 1992.

b42) 11 ♘xd4 also favours Black: 11...♘xd4 12 cxd4 ♗e7 13 ♕f3 0-0 14 ♖d1 ♕c6 15 ♕g3 ♗d7 16 ♗h6 ♗f6 17 ♖e1 ♕c8 18 ♗c2 (Black is fine after 18 ♘c2 ♗c6) 18...♖e8 19 ♗f4 ♗c6 20 ♗e5 ♕d8 and Black takes control over the central squares with a comfortable game, Sermek-S.Kiseliov, Ljubljana 1992.

b43) 11 cxd4 ♗e7 gives Black a reasonable IQP position because the white knight is poorly placed on a3 rather than on c3 controlling the d5-square. This enables Black to equalize: 12 ♗e3 0-0 13 ♘e5 ♘xe5! (better than 13...♗f6 14 ♖c1 ♗d7 15 ♘ac4 ♘xc4 16 ♘xc4 ♕c7 17 d5 exd5 18 ♘b6 ± Blatny-Stocek, Lazne Bohdanec 1996 or 13...♘b4 14 ♕h5 ♘6d5 15 ♘ac4 ♕d8 16 a3 ♘f6 17 ♕h3 ♘bd5 18 ♗c2 with an initiative on the kingside, Praznik-Zontakh, Bled 1995) 14 dxe5 ♕xd1 15 ♖axd1 (or 15 ♖fxd1 ♘d5 16 ♗xd5 exd5 17 ♖xd5 ♗e6 18 ♖dd1 ♖fd8 with full compensation for the pawn) 15...♘d5 16 ♗xd5 exd5 17 ♘c2 ♗e6 18 ♘d4 g6 19 h3 h5 and a draw is the most probable result, Marković-Ilinčić, Yugoslav Cht 2001.

We now return to 9...dxc3 *(D)*:

10 ♕e2?!

This is the consistent follow-up, but against well-prepared opposition, it may already be time to bale out.

a) 10 ♘b5?! is not the answer. After 10...♕xd1+ 11 ♔xd1 ♖b8! (Black can also play 11...cxb2 12 ♗xb2 ♖b8 13 ♘e5 e6 14 ♘c7+ ♔e7 15 ♘a6 ♖a8 16 ♘c7 ♖b8 ½-½ Shaked-Hodgson, Bermuda 1997) 12 ♗f4 cxb2 13 ♖b1 ♗f5, Black was clearly better in Rabiega-Van Wely, Frankfurt 2000.

b) 10 ♕xd6! leads to a drawish endgame after 10...exd6 11 ♘b5 ♖b8 12 ♘g5 ♘e5 13 0-0 ♗d7 14 ♘xc3 ♗e7 15 ♘ge4 0-0 16 ♗e3 ♗e6 17 ♖fd1 ♖fd8 18 ♗xb6 axb6 19 ♘d5, when White controls the light squares, compensating for Black's extra pawn, Beulen-Van der Vliet, Dutch Cht 1995/6.

10...cxb2

This leads to very sharp and relatively unexplored positions. 10...♗f5 is a safer way to play. 11 ♘b5 ♕d7 12 ♘e5 ♘xe5 13 ♕xe5 ♖c8 (13...f6 is unclear, because after 14 ♘c7+ ♔d8 15 ♘e6+ ♗xe6 16 ♕xe6 ♕xe6+ 17 ♗xe6 ♘a4 18 b4 a5 19 ♗e3 axb4 20

0-0-0+ Black is three pawns up, but White has a strong attack against the black king, Hraček-Stohl, Czech Cht 1995/6) 14 0-0 ♘c4 (14...♗d3 15 ♘xa7) 15 ♗xc4 ♖xc4 16 ♘xc3 (16 ♗f4? is bad: 16...f6 17 ♕b8+ ♖c8 18 ♘c7+ ♔f7 19 ♕xb7 e5 20 ♕b3+ ♔g6 and Black wins a piece, Palkovi-Wells, Budapest 1997) 16...e6 17 ♖e1 ♖c5 18 ♕g3 ♗g6 19 ♗f4 ♗e7 20 ♖ad1 ♕c6 21 ♗e3 ♖c4 22 ♕b8+ ♕c8 23 ♕xc8+ ♖xc8 24 ♗xa7 and White has managed to regain the pawn, but in the endgame he is slightly worse, Vajda-Rogozenko, Romanian Ch (Iasi) 1999.

11 ♗xb2

11 ♕xb2 is an untested alternative.

11...♕b4+ 12 ♔f1 *(D)*

12 ♘d2 has also been suggested but, like 11 ♕xb2, only seems to have the merit of preserving White's right to castle. With two pawns sacrificed, White needs something rather more concrete.

B

White's bishop on b2 makes it difficult for Black to develop his kingside, while the a3-knight is ready to leap into b5 at an appropriate moment. White's most simplistic plan is ♘b5, ♖d1 and

♘c7#, but Black has enough time to extricate himself and get developed.

12...♗f5

This clever move is played with the idea of ...♖d8 and ...♗d3. 12...♗g4 is less clear, because after 13 ♘b5 ♗xf3 (or 13...0-0-0 14 ♖c1 ± Sveshnikov; 13...♕f4 14 ♗e5! ♕f5 15 ♘c7+ ∞; however, Matulović's 13...♖d8!? may be an improvement) 14 gxf3 ♕f4 15 ♗c1! ♕b8 16 ♕e4, White has a dangerous initiative; for example, 16...e5 17 ♕f5 ♘d8 18 ♗b2 or 16...♘d7!? 17 ♗f4 e5 18 ♖d1! (threatening to play 19 ♗xf7+) 18...♕c8 19 ♖g1! (19 ♗xf7+ ♔xf7 20 ♕d5+ ♔f6!) 19...♘c5 20 ♕d5 ♘xb3 21 ♗xe5.

13 ♖d1

After 13 ♖c1 ♖d8 14 ♘c2 ♕xb3 (14...♕f4 is also good) 15 axb3 ♗d3 16 ♘cd4 ♗xe2+ 17 ♔xe2 ♘xd4+ 18 ♘xd4, Black correctly returned one pawn with 18...e6! 19 ♘b5 ♗b4 to gain a clear advantage in the endgame in Rüfenacht-Frostick, corr. 1999.

13 ♘b5? fails to 13...0-0-0! 14 ♘e5 ♖d2! −+.

13...♖d8!

White is hoping for play such as 13...e6? 14 ♘b5 ♖c8 15 ♘fd4 a6? 16 ♘d6+! +− Van Mil-Yakovich, Leeuwarden 1992.

14 ♖xd8+ ♘xd8 15 ♘d4 ♗d7

White doesn't have enough compensation for two pawns, and the best he can hope for is to win one back and hold the endgame.

16 ♘ab5

16 h4 was tried in Salai-Krakops, Pula Echt 1997. Then Har-Zvi suggests 16...♘a4!? 17 ♘ac2 ♕a5 18 ♗a3 ♘c3

19 ♕e3 e6, when we can see no compensation for White.

16...♗xb5 17 ♘xb5 a6 18 ♘d4 e6 19 g3 ♗e7 20 ♘c2 ♕b5 21 ♕xb5+ axb5 22 ♗xg7 ♖g8 23 ♗d4 ♘c4

Black is slightly better, but White managed to hang on to draw in Sermek-Sher, Ljubljana 1994.

B2)
9 0-0 *(D)*

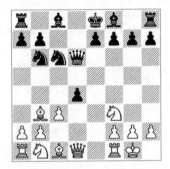

9...♗e6

Black probably has to neutralize White's light-squared bishop, as the other options give White a strong initiative:

a) 9...dxc3?! 10 ♘xc3 ♕xd1 11 ♖xd1 ♗g4 (11...a6 12 ♗e3 ♘d7 13 ♘d5 wins for White) 12 ♘b5 ♖c8 13 ♗e3 a6 (Agnos-Lawson, British Ch (Southampton) 1986) 14 ♘bd4! ±.

b) 9...d3?! 10 ♘a3 ♗f5 11 ♘b5 ♕d7 12 ♗f4 ♖c8 13 ♘xa7 ♘xa7 14 ♘e5 ♕b5 15 ♘xf7 with a dangerous attack for White, Schmittdiel-Gutman, Lugano 1987.

c) 9...♗f5 10 ♘xd4 ♘xd4 11 cxd4 (White plans to put his queen on f3, the knight on c3 and push d5 at the

right moment) 11...e6 (11...♗xb1 gives White the advantage of the bishop-pair: 12 ♖xb1 e6 13 ♕f3 ♕d7 14 ♖e1 ♗b4 15 ♖e4 ♘d5 16 ♖e5 ♘e7 17 ♕g4 ♘g6 18 ♖e2 h5 19 ♕e4 ♗e7 20 d5 ± Rozentalis-Jaracz, Polish Cht (Augustow) 1996) 12 ♘c3 ♗e7 13 ♕f3 0-0 (13...♕xd4 14 ♕xb7 ♗d6 15 ♕c6+ ♔e7 16 ♘b5 ♕e5 17 ♕b7+ and Black's king is stuck in the centre, Lautier-J.Polgar, Hilversum 1993) 14 d5 ♕d7 (14...♖ad8 15 ♖e1 ♕b4 16 dxe6 ♗xe6 17 ♕xb7 ♖d7 18 ♕e4 and White is simply a pawn up, Pavasović-Nguyen Anh Dung, Istanbul OL 2000) 15 dxe6 ♗xe6 16 ♖d1 ♕c8 17 ♗xe6 fxe6 18 ♕e4 leaves White better, Mi.Tseitlin-Velikov, Pernik 1981.

d) 9...g6 10 ♘a3 a6 11 ♘g5 e6 12 ♕f3 ♕e7 13 ♗f4 ± Olesen-Ward, Gausdal 1995.

e) 9...e6 10 cxd4 ♗e7 11 ♘c3 0-0 12 ♖e1 ♘d5 13 a3 b6 14 ♘e4 ♕c7 15 ♕d3 ♗b7 leads to a typical position with an isolated pawn, in which White has the better chances according to Sveshnikov.

We return to 9...♗e6 *(D)*:

Now:

B21: 10 ♗xe6 166
B22: 10 ♘a3!? 169

Instead, 10 cxd4 gives Black the better game: 10...♗xb3 11 ♕xb3 e6 12 ♖d1 ♕b4 13 ♕e3 ♗e7 14 a3 ♕d6 15 b4 0-0 16 ♘bd2 ♖fd8 and White has to fight for a draw, McDonald-Emms, British League (4NCL) 1999/00.

B21)

10 ♗xe6 ♕xe6 11 ♘xd4 (D)

It's finally time to regain the pawn. After 11 a4 ♖d8 12 a5 dxc3 13 ♕c2 ♘b4 14 ♕xc3 ♘6d5 15 ♕b3 ♕a6 16 ♘c3 e6 17 ♘xd5 ♖xd5 18 ♗d2 ♘c6, White had no compensation in Kiik-Külaots, Estonian Ch (Tallinn) 2000.

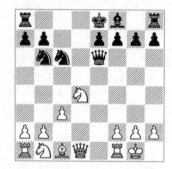

Now:
B211: 11...♘xd4 166
B212: 11...♕d7 168

Less good is 11...♕d5, as after an exchange on d4, the white knight can come to c3 with tempo: 12 ♕e2 e6 (after 12...♘xd4 13 cxd4 e6 14 ♘c3 ♕d7 15 d5! ♘xd5 16 ♘xd5 ♕xd5 17 ♖d1 the white rooks will penetrate into Black's position via the open c-

and d-files, Sveshnikov-Rashkovsky, USSR 1983) 13 ♖d1 ♘xd4 14 cxd4 ♗e7 15 ♘c3 ♕d7 16 d5 0-0 17 dxe6 ♕xe6 18 ♕xe6 fxe6 and the weak black e-pawn defines White's slight edge, Sveshnikov-Rashkovsky, USSR 1985.

B211)

11...♘xd4
This is the most popular move, and often leads to sharp complications.

12 ♕xd4
If 12 cxd4, Black is fine after both 12...♕d7 13 ♘c3 e6 14 ♕g4 ♘d5 and 12...g6 13 ♖e1 ♕f6 14 ♘c3 ♗g7.

12...♖d8 (D)

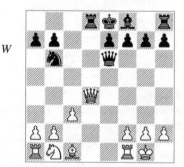

13 ♕h4
This move is the one most often played. White wants to put the bishop on g5 and attack the e7-pawn. Alternatives:

a) 13 ♕e3 leads to an endgame that is not dangerous for Black: 13...♕xe3 14 ♗xe3 ♘c4 15 ♗xa7 ♘xb2 16 ♘a3 e6 17 ♘c2 ♖d2 18 ♘d4 ♗a3 19 ♖fb1 ♘a4 20 ♖xb7 0-0 21 ♘f3 ♖c2 22 ♘d4 ♖d2 ½-½ Mikhalchishin-Ki.Georgiev, Sarajevo 1985.

b) After 13 ♕b4 ♕c6 14 a4 a6 15 ♕b3 e6 16 ♞d2 ♝e7 17 ♞f3 0-0 Black has completed his development and stands well, Blatny-Stohl, Pardubice 1993.

c) 13 ♕f4 g6 (13...♕c6 is worse: 14 ♞d2 g6 15 ♕e5 f6 16 ♕e2 ♝g7 17 a4 0-0 18 ♕xe7 ♖fe8 19 ♕b4 and Black doesn't have enough compensation for the pawn, Smagin-Nijboer, Essen 2001) 14 ♝e3 ♝g7 15 ♕b4 0-0 16 ♝xb6 ♕xb6 17 ♕xb6 axb6 18 a4 ♖a8 19 ♖a3 ♖fd8 20 ♖e1 ♝e5 with a level endgame, Sveshnikov-Vasiukov, Moscow 1987.

13...♕e2 *(D)*

Or:

a) After 13...♕c6 14 ♖e1 e6 15 ♝g5 ♖d5 16 ♞d2 h6 17 ♝e3 ♝c5 18 ♞e4 ♝xe3 19 ♖xe3 0-0 20 ♖g3 White's threats on the kingside are very dangerous, Sveshnikov-Szekely, Leningrad 1984.

b) 13...h5 (with the positional threat of 14...♕g4) 14 h3 (the endgame after 14 ♕f4 ♕g4 15 ♕e5 h4 16 h3 ♕g6 17 ♕b5+ ♕c6 18 ♕xc6+ bxc6 is about equal, Nikolaidis-Miladinović, Korinthos 2001) and now:

b1) 14...♕e2?! reaches a position similar to that after *13...♕e2* but with the difference that the pawns are already on h5 and h3. This is in White's favour: he has a bolt-hole for his king on h2 and, a very important detail in many variations, Black will be not be able to play ...f6 or ...f5 as the g6-square is weakened and the white queen can go there with mate. 15 ♝e3 ♕xb2? (15...e6) 16 ♞d2 ♖xd2 17 ♖ab1 ♕c2 (17...♕xc3 18 ♝xd2 ♕xd2 19

♖fd1 ♕a5? 20 ♕g3 +– Rogozenko; then 20...f6 allows 21 ♕g6#) 18 ♖fc1 ♕d3 19 ♝xd2 ♕xd2 20 ♖d1 ♕e2 21 ♕g3 e5 22 ♖e1 h4 23 ♕h2 and White's attack becomes decisive, Savić-V.Mikhalevski, Neum ECC 2000.

b2) 14...♕c4 15 ♕g3 h4 (15...♕d3 16 ♝e3 ♞c4 17 ♞a3! ♞xe3 18 fxe3 ♖h6 19 ♕f4 ♖f6 20 ♕a4+ ♖d7 21 ♕xa7 doesn't give Black enough compensation – Sveshnikov) 16 ♕f3 ♕d5 17 ♞d2 ♕xf3 18 ♞xf3 e6 19 a4 ♞d5 20 a5 a6 21 ♖a4 gives White a slightly better endgame because of the weak pawn on h4, Van de Oudeweetering-Gustafsson, Dutch Cht 2001.

b3) 14...f6!? 15 ♞d2! g5 16 ♕g3 g4 17 h4 ♕e2 18 ♞b3 ± V.Ivanov-Simantsev, Voronezh 2001.

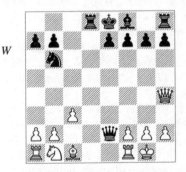

Black is threatening 14...♖d1, so White has to be ready to sacrifice material.

14 ♝d2

The right move; the idea is to prepare 15 ♖e1. White has also tried:

a) 14 ♞d2 and then:

a1) 14...e6 15 ♕g3 ♝d6 16 ♕xg7 ♝e5 17 ♕g5 ♖d3 (Acs-Volzhin, Budapest 1996) and now White can obtain an advantage by means of 18 f4! ♗d6 19 ♖f2 ±.

a2) 14...♖xd2 15 ♗xd2 ♕xd2 – *14 ♗d2 ♖xd2 15 ♘xd2 ♕xd2.*

a3) 14...h5 15 h3 g5 16 ♕g3 g4 17 h4 ♗g7 18 ♘b3 0-0 19 ♘d4 ♗xd4 20 cxd4 ♕e4 21 ♗d2 ♘d5 22 ♖ae1 ♕g6 and Black's strong knight on d5 compensates for his weakened kingside, Acs-A.Schneider, Budapest 1995.

b) With 14 ♗e3 White is ready to sacrifice his whole queenside, but practice shows that Black can accept it and defend successfully: 14...♕xb2 (14...e6 is probably sufficient for a draw: 15 ♗xb6 axb6 16 ♘a3 ♗xa3 17 ♕a4+ ♔e7 18 ♕xa3+ ♖d6 19 ♕b4 ♕h5 20 ♖ad1 ♖hd8 followed by 21...♕c5, as in Marković-Ves.Georgiev, Belgrade 2000) 15 ♘d2 ♖xd2 and now White has two possibilities, but neither is dangerous for Black:

b1) 16 ♖ab1 ♕xc3 17 ♗xd2 ♕xd2 18 ♖fd1 ♕a5 19 ♕e4 g6 20 ♕xb7 f6 21 h3 ♔f7 −+ Murshed-Rahman, Dhaka 1999.

b2) 16 ♗xd2 ♕xd2 17 ♖fd1 ♕h6 18 ♕g3 ♕c6 19 ♖ab1 (after 19 ♖d4 f6 20 ♕b8+ ♘c8 21 ♖ad1 ♔f7 22 ♖d7 g5 23 ♕xb7 ♕xb7 24 ♖xb7 ♗g7 the two pieces will show their strength – analysis by Shirov and Cherniaev) 19...♘c8 20 ♕b8 b6 and everything is protected.

14...h5

Or:

a) 14...♖xd2 15 ♘xd2 ♕xd2 16 ♖fd1 ♕h6 17 ♕g3 ♕c6 18 ♖d4 (18 ♕b8+ leads to a draw: 18...♘c8 19 b4 e6 20 a4 ♗e7 21 b5 ♕c5 22 ♕xb7 0-0 23 a5 ♗f6 24 b6 axb6 25 a6 ♗xc3 26

a7 ♘xa7 = Malaniuk-Azmaiparashvili, Tallinn 1981) 18...e6 19 ♖ad1 ♗e7 20 ♕xg7. White wins two pawns on the kingside and has slightly the better chances.

b) 14...e6 15 ♖e1 ♕d3 16 ♗g5 ♖d5 17 ♘d2 ♕g6 18 ♘f3 h6 19 ♖ad1 with a clear initiative – Ionov and Livshits.

c) After 14...♕c4 15 ♕g3 ♕d3 16 ♗e3 ♘c4 17 ♘a3! (Sveshnikov), all White's pieces are developed, while the black ones are still in their initial locations.

15 h3

15 ♖e1 ♕g4 16 ♕xg4 hxg4 17 ♗e3 ♘c4 is good for Black, Sveshnikov-Dvoirys, Cheliabinsk 1986.

15...♘c4 16 ♖e1 ♕d3 17 ♗c1

White has managed to remove the black queen from e2 and can temporarily return his bishop to c1.

17...a6

17...f6 18 b3 ♘b6 19 ♗e3 e5 20 ♘d2 ± Cheutshenko-Rõtšagov, Estonian Ch (Tallinn) 2000. The h5-pawn is weak, which makes it problematic for Black to castle.

18 b3 ♘d6 19 ♕a4+ ♕b5 20 ♕f4

Not 20 ♕xb5+ ♘xb5 21 a4 ♘c7, when the endgame is equal, Sveshnikov-Salov, Leningrad 1984.

20...e6 21 c4 ♕f5 22 ♘c3

White's queenside pawn-majority gives him slightly better chances.

B212)

11...♕d7 *(D)*

The most solid move.

12 ♗e3

12 ♘xc6 gives Black two viable options:

W

a) 12...♛xc6 13 ♘d2 g6 14 ♘b3 ♖d8 15 ♕e2 ♗g7 16 ♗g5 0-0 17 ♖ad1 (17 ♗xe7? loses a piece to 17...♖de8; 17 ♕xe7 allows Black nice compensation after 17...♘c4 18 ♕e2 ♖fe8 19 ♕c2 f6) 17...h6 18 ♗e3 ♘d5 = Slobodjan-Cyborowski, Ohrid Ech 2001.

b) 12...♛xd1 13 ♖xd1 bxc6 14 a4 e5 15 a5 ♘d5 16 ♘d2 0-0-0 17 ♘c4 f6 18 ♗e3 ♖d7 = Savić-Ilinčić, Yugoslav Ch (Herceg Novi) 2001.

12...e6 13 ♘d2 ♘d5 14 ♘c4

14 ♕g4 leads to an equal endgame: 14...e5 15 ♕xd7+ ♔xd7 16 ♘xc6 ♔xc6 17 ♘c4 f6, Zelić-Rashkovsky, Zadar 2000.

14...♗e7

14...♘xe3 15 fxe3 opens the f-file and strengthens the white centre.

15 ♘xc6 ♛xc6!

15...bxc6 damages Black's pawn-structure and gives White a slight edge.

16 ♕e2

White can't profit from the fact that the black king is still in the centre, since after 16 ♘e5 ♘xe3 17 fxe3 ♕b5 18 ♘xf7? 0-0! the knight is trapped.

16...♘xe3 17 ♘xe3

The position is equal, Rozentalis-Lesiège, Montreal 2001.

B22)

10 ♘a3!? *(D)*

Given that the natural move 10 ♗xe6 doesn't promise White an advantage against the most precise play by Black, White has instead tried to exploit the fact that Black's kingside is not yet developed by starting an attack in the centre and on the queenside. However, this attack comes at the cost of a pawn.

B

10...dxc3!

Again, just as after *9 ♘a3!?*, this is the best move, but is only likely to be played by those who are both brave and well-prepared. White has more chances of gaining an initiative here than after *9 ♘a3!? dxc3!*, but the disadvantage of 10 ♘a3 dxc3 is that these lines tend to be somewhat better known.

White is quite happy if Black declines the pawn: 10...♗xb3 (10...a6 – *9 ♘a3!? a6 10 0-0 ♗e6*) 11 ♕xb3 (after 11 axb3 Black easily gets a good position: 11...a6 12 cxd4 e6 13 ♘c4 ♕c7 14 ♗g5 ♗e7 15 ♖c1 ♕d8 16 ♗xe7 ♘xe7 17 ♕d3 ♘bd5 and White has weak pawns, Yudasin-Rechlis, Israeli Cht 1997) and then:

a) 11...e6 12 ♖d1 (the active 12 ♘b5 only leads to a draw: 12...♕d7 13 ♘bxd4 ♗c5 14 ♗e3 ♗xd4 15 ♖fd1 0-0 16 ♘xd4 ♘d5 17 ♘xe6 fxe6 18 c4 ♘a5 19 ♕d3 ♘xc4 20 ♕xc4 ♘xe3 = Kotronias) and now:

a1) 12...d3 is risky: 13 ♘b5 ♕d7 14 c4 ♖d8 15 ♘xa7 ♘xc4 16 ♕xc4 ♘xa7 17 ♗e3 ♘c6 18 ♗b6 ♕d5 19 ♕a4 ♖d7 20 ♘e1 ♗d6 21 ♖xd3 and the black pieces are in danger, Schmittdiel-Enders, Bundesliga 1990/1.

a2) 12...♕d5 doesn't solve Black's problems either: 13 ♘b5 0-0-0 14 ♘xa7+ ♘xa7 15 ♕xb6 ♗c5 16 ♕a5 ♘c6 17 ♕a8+! (to force black king to c7, where it can be checked from f4) 17...♔c7 18 ♕a4 e5 (after 18...d3 19 ♘e1 ♕f5 20 ♕f4+ ♕xf4 21 ♗xf4+ e5 22 ♗g3 White wins a pawn) 19 cxd4 ♘xd4 20 ♘xd4 ♗xd4 21 ♗e3 and White is better due to Black's exposed king – Blatny.

a3) 12...♗e7 13 ♘b5 ♕b8 14 ♘bxd4 0-0 15 ♘xc6 bxc6 16 c4 ♕c7 17 ♕c2 ♖ad8 18 ♗e3 ♗f6 19 ♖ac1 and White's superior pawn-structure gives him a small but stable advantage, Seger-Loew, Bundesliga 1993/4.

b) 11...♕d5 12 ♘b5 ♖c8 13 ♘fxd4 ♘xd4 14 ♘xd4 e6 15 ♖d1 ♗c5 16 ♕b5+ ♕d7 (16...♔e7?! 17 ♕e2 ♖hd8 18 ♗e3 ♕e5 19 ♕g4 ± Benjamin-Wolff, New York 1996) 17 ♕e2 ♕e7 18 ♘b3 0-0 19 ♘xc5 ♕xc5 20 ♗e3 ♕c7 21 ♗d4 ± Rozentalis-Pigusov, Tallinn 1986. Once White has provoked ...f6 he will try to exchange the minor pieces and exploit Black's weaknesses in the major-piece endgame.

11 ♕e2

White doesn't achieve anything by 11 ♘b5 ♕xd1 12 ♖xd1 ♖c8 13 ♗xe6 fxe6 (not 13...cxb2?? 14 ♗xc8 bxa1♕ 15 ♘c7#) 14 ♘xc3 (or 14 bxc3 ♘c4 15 ♘g5 e5 16 ♘e6 ♔f7 17 ♘g5+ with a draw, Smagin-Gavrikov, USSR Ch (Kiev) 1986) 14...h6 15 ♘e4 g5 16 h4 gxh4 17 ♘xh4 ♗g7 18 ♘f3 ♖d8, when Black has nothing to be afraid of in the endgame, where he has an extra (albeit weak) pawn – Sveshnikov.

11...♗xb3 12 ♘b5

This move-order reduces Black's options. If instead 12 axb3 then one possibility is 12...0-0-0 (M.Anderton-Marley, British League (4NCL) 1996/7) with the point that 13 ♘b5 may be met by 13...♕d3.

12...♕b8

After 12...♕d7 13 axb3 ♖d8 14 ♗f4 ♕f5 15 ♘d6+ ♖xd6 16 ♗xd6 cxb2 17 ♖ab1 ♘d5 18 ♖xb2 ♕d7 19 ♗c5 White has an exchange for two pawns, and slightly better chances, Down-Lysenko, Dublin 1991.

13 axb3 (D)

Black is significantly behind in development, and has to counter three possible attacking plans by White:

a) g3 or ♕e4 (or even ♖a4 if the b6-knight moves away) preparing the devastating ♗f4 and ♘c7+.

b) ♗e3 threatening both ♗xb6 axb6, ♖xa8 ♕xa8, ♘c7+ winning the queen, and ♘xa7 ♘xa7, ♗xb6 winning back a pawn, and adding a queenside majority to a development advantage.

c) Playing a knight to d4 with ideas of ♘xc6 removing a defender, or ♘f5 turning attention to Black's unprotected kingside.

Black has two reliable options here:

B221: 13...e5   171
B222: 13...g6   174

Other moves are less dependable:

a) The attempt to free Black's position immediately with 13...a6 14 ♘bd4 ♘xd4 15 ♘xd4 e6 is met by 16 ♘xe6 – Sveshnikov and Yudasin.

b) 13...e6 14 g3 e5!? (14...♘d5 15 bxc3 ♕c8 16 c4 ♘c7 17 ♗b2 a6 18 ♗xg7 and White regains a pawn while keeping his attack going, Blauert-Kveinys, Groningen 1992) and now:

b1) If White wants to play 15 bxc3 ♗e7 16 ♗g5, then 16...♗xg5 17 ♘xg5 h6 18 ♘e4 0-0 is better for Black than *13...e5 14 bxc3 ♗e7 15 ♗g5 ♗xg5 16 ♘xg5 h6 17 ♘e4 0-0* since White cannot transfer his rook to the kingside along the third rank.

b2) 15 ♘bd4 is a better version for White of *13...e5 14 ♘bd4* as he can later save a tempo protecting against back-rank mates.

c) 13...c2!? 14 ♗e3! a6 15 ♗xb6 axb5 (Marcelin-Tukmakov, Cappelle la Grande 1998) 16 ♘d4! offers White good chances.

B221)
13...e5 *(D)*

14 ♘bd4

Or:

a) 14 bxc3 ♗e7 15 ♗g5 used to be common, but Black found several safe replies:

a1) 15...a6 leads to a draw: 16 ♗xe7 ♘xe7 17 ♘xe5 0-0 18 ♘d4 ♘g6 19 ♘xg6 hxg6 = Onishchuk-Nijboer, Wijk aan Zee 1996.

a2) 15...♘c8 is relatively untested but logical; e.g., 16 ♗xe7 ♘8xe7 17 ♖fd1 0-0 18 ♖d7 ♘g6 19 ♖ad1 ♕c8 20 ♕c4 (Harley-Coleman, British League (4NCL) 1996/7) 20...♘d4! 21 ♕xc8 ♘xf3+ 22 gxf3 ♖fxc8 23 ♖xb7 a6 24 ♘c7 ♖d8! 25 ♖xd8+ (25 ♘d5!? is unclear) 25...♖xd8 26 ♔f1 ♘f4 27 ♔e1 ♘d3+ 28 ♔e2 =.

a3) 15...♗xg5 16 ♘xg5 h6 17 ♘e4 0-0 18 ♖fd1 ♖d8 19 ♘bd6 ♕c7 20 ♕g4 gives White a strong position in the centre and on the kingside, but after 20...♘e7 it is only sufficient for a draw: 21 ♘b5 ♖xd1+ 22 ♖xd1 ♕c6 23 ♘bd6 ♖d8 24 ♘f6+ ♔f8 25 ♘h7+ with perpetual check, Sermek-Sveshnikov, Slovenian Cht (Ljubljana) 1997.

a4) 15...f6 is played if Black wants to fight. 16 ♗e3 and now:

a41) 16...♘d5 and then:

a411) 17 ♘h4 a6 18 ♕h5+ ♔f8 19 ♘g6+ hxg6 20 ♕xh8+ ♔f7 21 ♕xb8 ♖xb8 22 ♘a3 ♘xc3 and, with two pawns for an exchange, Black is probably better, Sivokho-Ionov, St Petersburg 1996.

a412) 17 ♘xa7 ♘xe3 18 ♘xc6 ♖xa1! 19 ♖xa1 bxc6 20 ♕xe3 ♕xb3 21 ♘d2 ♕e6 22 ♖a8+ ♗d8 ∓.

a42) 16...♘c8 17 ♘h4 (17 c4 0-0 18 c5 ♔h8 19 ♕c4 f5! 20 ♗g5 a6 21 ♘c3 e4 22 ♗xe7 ♘8xe7 23 ♘g5 ♘e5 ∓) 17...0-0 18 ♕g4 gives White very active-looking pieces, but practice has shown that Black has enough resources to defend the position. After 18...a6 19 ♘f5 g6 20 ♘xe7+ ♘6xe7 21 ♕c4+ ♔g7 22 ♘c7 ♘d6 23 ♕c5 ♖c8, Black had an advantage in Benjamin-Ilinčić, Erevan OL 1996.

b) After 14 ♘fd4 (D) Black can transpose to the main line, but he also has some other interesting possibilities leading to unclear complications:

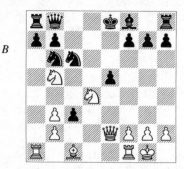

b1) 14...♘xd4 15 ♘xd4 – *14 ♘bd4 ♘xd4 15 ♘xd4*.

b2) 14...g6? 15 ♘xc6 bxc6 16 ♘xa7! ♕c7 17 ♗e3 ♗d6 18 ♘b5! cxb5 19 ♗xb6 ♕c6 20 ♖xa8+ ♕xa8 21 ♕xb5+ ± Yanovsky-Timoshenko, Voskresensk 1992.

b3) 14...♘d7 15 bxc3 g6 16 f4 ♗c5 17 fxe5 0-0 18 e6 ± Jenni-Palac, Biel 1998.

b4) 14...♗c5 15 ♘f5 0-0 (15...g6? 16 ♗e3 ± Swinkels-Hofland, corr. 1994) and now both 16 ♗h6!? g6! and 16 bxc3 are suggested by Sveshnikov.

b5) 14...♗e7 15 ♘f5 0-0 (Ferguson-Sutovsky, Guarapuava U-18 Wch 1995) 16 bxc3 a6 17 ♗h6! (Chandler) 17...gxh6 (17...axb5 18 ♖xa8 ♘xa8 19 ♗xg7 with a dangerous attack) 18 ♕g4+ ♗g5 19 ♘xh6+ ♔h8 20 ♕xg5 ♕d8 (20...f6 21 ♕e3 ♘d5 22 ♕c5 ±) 21 ♕h5 ♕f6 and Black is OK.

b6) 14...c2! 15 ♘xc6 (15 ♘f5!?) 15...bxc6 16 ♘d4 ♕d6 ∓ Rüfenacht-Cu.Hansen, corr. 1998.

There is still scope for new ideas in the above lines, but in the absence of any improvements, 14 ♘bd4 has to be recommended.

We now return to 14 ♘bd4 (D):

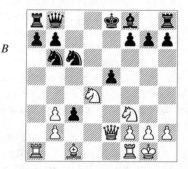

14...♘xd4

Or:

a) 14...♗d6 15 bxc3 (the immediate 15 ♘f5 gives Black a good position after 15...g6 16 ♘xd6+ ♕xd6 17 bxc3 f6 18 ♗a3 ♕e6 19 ♘d4 ♘xd4 20 cxd4 e4 – Salov and Ionov) 15...0-0 16 ♘f5 and White's attack on the kingside can become dangerous – Kochiev and Soloviev.

b) 14...f6 15 bxc3 and now:

b1) Black can't swap knights by 15...♘xd4 because White replies 16 cxd4, attacking the centre.

b2) 15...♕c8 16 ♘xc6 bxc6 17 ♖a5 creates serious pressure on the e5- and a7-pawns (but not 17 ♘h4? g6 18 f4 ♗c5+ 19 ♗e3 ♗xe3+ 20 ♕xe3 0-0 21 fxe5 ♕e6, when Black is simply a pawn up, Rõtšagov-Sadler, Pula Echt 1997).

b3) 15...♔f7 16 ♘xc6 bxc6 17 ♕e4 ♕d6 18 ♖a5! (the rook is located ideally on a5, as it attacks the a-file and all the central squares on the 5th rank) 18...♘d7 19 ♖e1 (increasing the pressure on e5) 19...♗e7 20 ♗a3 c5 21 b4 cxb4 22 ♗xb4 ♕b6 23 ♕f5 ♖ad8 24 ♖axe5 with a decisive attack, Rozentalis-Lesiège, Montreal 2000.

15 ♘xd4 f6

After 15...cxb2 16 ♗xb2 ♗d6 17 ♘f5 0-0 18 ♘xd6 ♕xd6 19 ♗a3, White wins an exchange for two pawns. The position is open, so the white rooks will be active and White will have some advantage.

16 bxc3 ♔f7 *(D)*

After 16...♗d6 17 ♘f5 g6 18 ♘xd6+ ♕xd6 19 f4 ♘d7 20 ♖d1 ♕c7 21 ♗a3 White has a huge initiative and now 21...♔f7? loses a piece to 22 ♕c4+, Palkovi-Grabics, Budapest 1994.

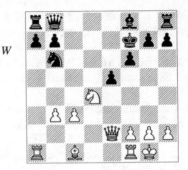

17 ♘b5

White threatens 18 ♗e3, so the next few moves are forced.

17...a6 18 ♗e3 axb5 19 ♗xb6 ♖xa1 20 ♖xa1 ♕e8 21 ♖a5 *(D)*

Or 21 ♕f3 ♕c6 22 ♕xc6 bxc6 23 ♖a8 ♖g8 24 ♖c8 ♗e7 25 ♖xc6 ♖a8 26 h3 ♖a6 with advantage to Black.

Black is undeveloped and his king is rather precariously situated on f7, but White has to spend some time regaining his pawn. The question is whether Black can disentangle himself in time and equalize.

21...b4

This is the most popular choice, but 21...♕c6 seems to be a better equalizing try; e.g.:

a) 22 ♖xb5 ♕xc3 23 h3 (23 ♗e3
♗e7 24 ♖xb7 ♕a1+ 25 ♕f1 ♕xf1+ 26
♔xf1 ♗e6 =) 23...♗e7 24 ♗e3 ♕c6
25 ♖b6 ♕d5 26 ♕c2 ♖d8 27 ♕xh7 e4
½-½ Rozentalis-Dydyshko, Glogow
2001.

b) 22 ♕xb5 ♕xc3 23 ♕d5+ ♔g6
24 g4 ♕c6 25 ♕xc6 bxc6 26 ♖a8 ♔f7
27 ♗c5 h6 28 ♖a7+ ♔g6 29 ♖a8 ♔f7
30 ♖a7+ ½-½ Blauert-Jirovsky, 2nd
Bundesliga 1992/3.

22 c4

22 cxb4 leads to a very drawish
ending: 22...♕e6 23 ♕c4 ♕xc4 24
bxc4 ♗xb4 25 ♖a7 ♖c8 26 ♖xb7+
♔e6, Luther-Sadler, Gausdal 1994.

**22...♕c6 23 ♖b5 ♗d6 24 ♗a5 ♖a8
25 h3 ♗c5**

After 25...♔g8, 26 ♗xb4 gives White
an advantage, and is better than 26
♕e1, which allows the black bishop
into the game: 26...♗c5 27 ♗xb4 ♗d4
28 ♗c3 ♗c5 29 ♗b4 ½-½ Lautier-
Gelfand, Linares 1994.

26 ♗xb4 ♗d4 27 ♖d5

Marciano-Nataf, French Ch (Vichy)
2000. White is slightly better, due to
the relative openness of the black king
and the possibility of making a passed
pawn on the queenside.

B222)
13...g6 (D)

This simple developing move only
appeared in practice a few years ago,
but appears to raise a number of serious questions about the viability of the
whole line with 10 ♘a3!?. White has
to play some very imaginative moves
to avoid simply ending up a pawn
down for nothing.

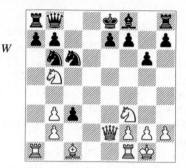

W

14 ♗e3

Originally 13...g6 was rejected because of analysis by Kochiev and Soloviev: 14 ♖d1 ♗g7 15 ♘d6+ ♔f8 16
♘xf7 ♔xf7 17 ♘g5+ ♔e8 18 ♕e6
♘d8 19 ♖xd8+ ♕xd8 20 ♕f7+ ♔d7
21 ♗f4 with, they claimed, a strong attack (quoted in *Informator* and *ECO*
for many years). However, there are a
whole host of improvements for Black
over moves 16 to 19, and it is hard to
see anything promising for White at
an earlier stage in the sequence.

Let's take a closer look. After 14
♖d1 ♗g7 15 ♘d6+ (more positional
play doesn't help White: 15 bxc3 0-0
16 ♕e4 {16 ♗e3 ♖d8 17 ♗xb6 axb6
18 ♖xd8+ ♕xd8 19 ♖d1 ♕c8 20 ♕e3
♖a6 ∓} 16...a6 17 ♘bd4 ♘xd4 18
cxd4 ♕c7 ∓ Rechel-Kotronias, Metz
1998) 15...♔f8 16 ♘xf7 (Rechel gives
16 ♗f4 cxb2 17 ♖ab1 ♔g8 −+ and 16
♘e4 cxb2 17 ♗xb2 h6 ∓) we have:

a) 16...cxb2 17 ♗xb2 (here a draw
was agreed in the game Nadyrkhanov-
Atakisi, Antalya 2002) 17...♗xb2 18
♕xb2 ♔xf7 19 ♘g5+ ♔g8 20 ♘e6
♕e5 −+ Rechel.

b) 16...♔xf7 17 ♘g5+ with a further branch:

b1) 17...♔f8 18 ♗f4! cxb2 19 ♖ab1 (19 ♗xb8 bxa1♕ 20 ♖xa1 ♗xa1 21 ♗c7 ♗f6 wins for Black) 19...♕c8 20 ♘e6+ ♔f7 21 ♘xg7 ♔xg7 22 ♗e5+ (22 ♕xb2+ ♔f7 23 ♖d3 ♕f5 24 ♖f3 ♘d4!) 22...♘xe5 23 ♕xe5+ ♔f7 24 ♖xb2 with some compensation but nowhere near enough for a whole piece!

b2) 17...♖e8 18 ♕e6 and here:

b21) 18...♘d8 19 ♖xd8+ and now Black's last chance to improve over the Kochiev/Soloviev analysis is 19...♔xd8 20 ♗e3! (20 ♘f7+ ♔e8 21 ♗g5 ♕c7 22 ♘xh8 ♕e5! ∓) 20...c2 21 ♗xb6+ axb6 22 ♘f7+ ♔c7 23 ♕xe7+ ♔c6 24 ♕e6+ ♔c7 =.

b22) 18...♘e5 19 ♗e3 (19 f4 c2 20 ♖e1 ♕c8 ∓) 19...c2 20 ♖dc1 ♘bd7 21 f4 ♘f8 22 ♕d5 h6 23 ♘e4 ♘c6 24 ♖xc2 ♕d8 25 ♕b5 ♗d4 26 ♗xd4 ♕xd4+ 27 ♘f2 ♕d7 28 ♖d1 ♕c7 29 ♖cd2 ♔f7 30 ♘e4 ♕b6+ 0-1 Burtasova-Smirnov, St Petersburg 2001.

Now we return to the position after 14 ♗e3 (D):

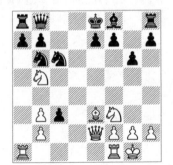

B

14...♘c8

Or:

a) 14...♘d7 15 bxc3 ♗g7 16 ♖fd1 ♘de5 (16...♘f6 17 ♗b6! costs Black

the exchange) 17 ♗b6! ♘xf3+ 18 ♕xf3 ♗e5 19 ♘xa7! is good for White.

b) 14...a6 15 ♗xb6 axb5 16 ♗c7! ♕c8 17 ♖xa8 ♕xa8 18 ♗e5 ♘xe5 19 ♕xe5 f6 20 ♕xb5+ ♔f7 21 bxc3 ± Rechel.

c) 14...♘d5 is a serious but as yet untested alternative. White needs to respond very accurately to stay in the game. Best seems to be 15 ♗xa7! (15 ♘xa7 ♘xe3! 16 ♘xc6 ♖xa1! 17 ♖xa1 bxc6 18 fxe3 ♗g7 19 bxc3 ♗xc3 20 ♖c1 ♗g7 21 ♖xc6 ♕xb3 22 ♖c8+ ♔d7 23 ♖c1 ♖d8! 24 ♘g5 ♔e8 ∓) 15...cxb2 16 ♕xb2 ♘xa7 17 ♖xa7 ♖xa7 18 ♘xa7 (18 ♕xh8 ♖a5 is a more adventurous route for White but is very murky and difficult to evaluate) 18...♘f6 19 ♕d4 with compensation (Rechel). However, by giving back the pawn with 19...♗g7 20 ♕a4+ b5 21 ♘xb5 0-0, Black might be slightly better as White's b-pawn could later become a weakness.

15 ♖a4!

A fantastic (and necessary) move, preparing ♗f4. This is much more effective than 15 ♕c4 ♗g7 16 ♗f4 ♘b6! 17 ♗xb8 ♘xc4 18 ♗f4 cxb2 19 ♖ad1 ♘d6 ∓ Pap-Flumbort, Novi Sad 2002.

15...♗g7 16 ♗f4 e5 17 ♘xe5 ♘xe5 18 ♗xe5 ♗xe5 19 f4 0-0 20 fxe5 cxb2 (D)

White is temporarily two pawns down but will soon pick one up on b2, and the combination of White's active pieces, control of the half-open f-file and Black's weakened dark squares on the kingside give White adequate compensation.

W

21 ♖e4

This feels rather slow, but may be a better practical try than 21 ♖af4:

a) After 21...♘b6? 22 ♕xb2 ♘d5 23 ♖4f3 ♕c8 24 ♘d6, White developed strong pressure on the kingside in Alekseev-Aseev, St Petersburg 2000.

b) 21...f5! 22 ♖h4 (22 exf6 ♕xf4! 23 ♖xf4 b1♕+; 22 ♕xb2 a6 23 ♘a3 ♖e8 24 ♖e1 ♘d6 ∓ Rogozenko) 22...a6 23 ♕c4+ ♚h8 24 ♕c5 ♖g8 25 ♕d4 h5 26 ♕f4 ♖g7 27 ♖xh5+ gxh5 28 ♕h6+ with a draw, Vysochin-Rausis, Cairo 2002.

21...a6 22 ♘d4 ♘e7 23 ♕xb2 ♘c6 24 ♘f3

24 ♘xc6 is enough for equality but no more than that.

24...♕a7+ 25 ♚h1 ♖ae8 26 ♕d2 (D)

B

Now Black has to be accurate but has sufficient defensive resources:

a) 26...b5 27 ♕f4 ♖e7 28 ♘g5 ♖fe8? (after 28...♕c5 the weakness of White's back rank helps Black defend) 29 ♕f6 ♕d7 30 ♘xh7 ♖xe5 31 ♖xe5 ♘xe5 32 ♕h4 offered White strong pressure on the kingside in Alekseev-Bakre, St Petersburg 2000.

b) 26...♕b8 defends based on the points 27 ♕f4 f5 and 27 ♕h6 f6.

10 2...♘f6 3 e5 ♘d5 4 ♘f3

1 e4 c5 2 c3 ♘f6 3 e5 ♘d5 4 ♘f3 *(D)*

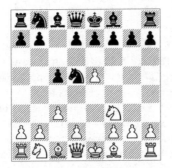

This has now become the most popular move-order and thus the main line. White sometimes simply plays 5 d4 and transposes immediately to the previous chapters, but more often he tries to develop his pieces first, and only pushes the d-pawn later when everything is prepared and Black has committed himself. The primary reason for this has been the success of the lines discussed in the previous chapter for Black, namely after *4 d4 cxd4 5 ♘f3 ♘c6 6 ♗c4 ♘b6 7 ♗b3 d6 8 exd6 ♕xd6, 9 ♘a3!? dxc3!* and *9 0-0 ♗e6 10 ♘a3!? dxc3!*.

4...♘c6

Or:

a) 4...e6 and here:

a1) 5 c4 ♘e7 6 d4 cxd4 7 ♕xd4 ♘bc6 8 ♕e4 ♘g6 9 ♘c3 ♘a5 10 ♗d2 ♘cxe5 11 ♘xe5 ♕xe5 12 ♕xe5 ♘xe5 13 ♘b5 ♔d8 14 ♗c3 f6 15 0-0-0 b6 denies White real compensation for the pawn, Afek-Timoshchenko, Pardubice 1998.

a2) 5 b4 cxb4 6 c4 ♘c7 7 d4 d6 8 exd6 ♗xd6 9 ♗d3 ♘c6 10 0-0 ♗e7 11 ♗e4 ♗f6 12 ♗b2 0-0 gives White a nice centre, but it doesn't look like it compensates for Black's extra pawn, I.Zaitsev-Rõtšagov, Jyväskylä 1997.

a3) 5 d4 cxd4 – *4 d4 cxd4 5 ♘f3 e6*.

a4) 5 ♗c4 and now:

a41) 5...d6 6 0-0 dxe5 7 ♘xe5 ♗d6 (7...♘d7 8 d4) 8 d4 0-0 9 ♘d2 cxd4 10 cxd4 ♘c6 11 ♘df3 ♘ce7 12 ♕e2 ♗d7 13 ♘g5 ♗c6 14 ♕h5 ♘f6 15 ♕h3 gives White a very dangerous attack, Rozentalis-Vaulin, Bydgoszcz 2000.

a42) 5...b6 6 0-0 ♗b7 7 d4 cxd4 – *4 d4 cxd4 5 ♘f3 b6 6 ♗c4 ♗b7 7 0-0 e6*.

a43) 5...♘b6 6 ♗b3 c4 (6...d6 7 exd6 ♘c6 – *4...♘c6 5 ♗c4 ♘b6 6 ♗b3 d5 7 exd6 e6*; this line is good for White) 7 ♗c2 d6 8 exd6 (8 d4 cxd3 9 ♕xd3 ♘c6 10 exd6 ♕xd6 11 ♕e2 ♗e7 12 0-0 0-0 13 ♘bd2 ♘d5 with complicated play, Thorhallsson-Van Wely, New York 1996) 8...♗xd6 9 b3 ♘c6 10 0-0 ♘e5 is a recommendation of Cvetković, but after 11 ♘xe5 ♗xe5 12 ♕h5 ♕c7 13 ♖e1 White obtains a serious initiative.

b) 4...d6 is an important alternative:

b1) 5 ♘a3!? ♘c6 – *4...♘c6 5 ♘a3 d6.*

b2) 5 ♗c4 ♘b6 (5...dxe5 6 ♘xe5 e6 7 0-0 – *4...e6 5 ♗c4 d6 6 0-0 dxe5 7 ♘xe5*) and now:

b21) 6 ♗xf7+? ♔xf7 7 ♘g5+ ♔g8 8 ♕f3 ♕e8 9 e6 g6 ∓ Golod.

b22) 6 e6!? ♘xc4 7 ♕a4+ ♘c6 8 exf7+ ♔xf7 9 ♕xc4+ d5!? 10 ♕xc5 e5 with good compensation, Stević-Palac, Croatian Ch (Pula) 2000.

b23) 6 b3!? ♘c6 7 exd6 ♕xd6 8 d4 cxd4 9 cxd4 ♗f5 10 ♘c3 e6 11 0-0 ♗e7 12 d5 ♘xd5 13 ♘xd5 exd5 14 ♕xd5 ♕xd5 15 ♗xd5 0-0 soon led to a draw in L.B.Hansen-Hellers, Malmö 1993.

b24) 6 ♗b3 c4 7 ♗c2 (7 ♗xc4?! ♘xc4 8 ♕a4+ ♘c6 9 ♕xc4 dxe5 ∓ Golod) 7...dxe5 8 ♘xe5 ♘8d7! 9 ♕h5 (9 ♘xd7 is better, but White still can't expect to achieve any advantage) 9...g6 10 ♕e2 ♘xe5 11 ♕xe5 f6 12 ♕e2 ♕d5 13 0-0 ♗f5 gives Black an advantage, Pavasović-Palac, Pula 2001. More tests are needed but this line could prove critical.

b3) 5 exd6 ♕xd6 6 d4 cxd4 – *4 d4 cxd4 5 ♘f3 d6 6 exd6 ♕xd6.*

b4) 5 d4 cxd4 transposes to *4 d4 cxd4 5 ♘f3 d6.* If this is the best White can do, 4...d6 may seriously hinder White's hopes of independent play after 4 ♘f3. If White really wants to avoid the line *4 d4 cxd4 5 ♘f3 ♘c6 6 ♗c4 ♘b6 7 ♗b3 d6*, we would have to recommend the line 6 ♕xd4 e6 7 exd6 (discussed via *4 d4 cxd4 5 ♘f3 d6*), which attempts to exploit Black's move-order.

We now return to 4...♘c6 *(D)*:

5 ♗c4

Besides 5 d4 cxd4, transposing to *4 d4 cxd4 5 ♘f3 ♘c6*, White has experimented with other ideas here:

a) 5 b4?! cxb4 6 c4 ♘c7 (6...♘b6 7 d4 d6 8 e6! fxe6 9 ♗d3 gives White some compensation, Schmittdiel-Watzke, St Ingbert 1994) 7 d4 d5 8 exd6 exd6 (8...♕xd6 9 ♗b2 ♗g4 10 d5 with strong compensation, Sermek-Cirkvenčić, Ljubljana 1999) 9 d5 ♘e5 10 ♗e2 ♗e7 11 ♘d4 0-0 12 0-0 ♘a6 13 a3 bxa3 14 ♖xa3 does not give White enough compensation, Zagema-Van der Vliet, Dutch Cht 1995/6.

b) 5 ♘a3 has been resurrected recently and may reward further investigation. Black can respond in a number of ways:

b1) 5...e6 is a mistake: 6 ♘c4 b5 (6...d6 7 exd6 ♗xd6 8 ♘xd6+ ♕xd6 nets White the bishop-pair) 7 ♘e3 ♘xe3 8 fxe3 ♕b6 9 d4 d6 10 exd6 ♗xd6 11 ♗d3 and White has a good centre and the better position, Baklan-Anapolsky, Ukrainian Cht 1999.

b2) 5...♘b6 6 ♗e2 d6 7 exd6 e5 8 d4 cxd4 9 cxd4 e4 10 ♘g5 ♗xd6 11 ♘xe4 ½-½ Baklan-Pelletier, Bundesliga 1999/00.

b3) 5...d6 6 exd6 and now:

b31) 6...♛xd6 7 d4 cxd4 8 ♞b5 ♛d8 9 ♝c4!? ± (Fressinet) gives White what he is looking for.

b32) 6...exd6 is the simplest reaction. The knight's position on a3 is too artificial, and Black is fine.

b4) 5...g6 and then:

b41) 6 g3 ♝g7 7 ♝g2 d6 (7...♞c7 8 ♛e2 0-0 9 0-0 d6 ∞ Bisguier-Fischer, Stockholm IZ 1962) 8 exd6 ♛xd6 9 0-0 0-0 10 d4 cxd4 11 ♞b5 ♛c5 = Heidenfeld-Portisch, Madrid Z 1960.

b42) 6 ♛b3 ♞b6 7 d4 cxd4 8 cxd4 ♝g7 9 ♝f4 d5 10 exd6 ♝e6 11 ♛d1 0-0 12 ♝e2 exd6 13 0-0 ∞ Jonkman-Halkias, Linares 2000.

5...♞b6 6 ♝b3

Or:

a) White can't expect anything after 6 ♝e2, because the bishop goes to a rather passive location:

a1) 6...d6 7 exd6 e5 (7...♛xd6 8 d4 cxd4 9 cxd4 ♝f5 10 ♞c3 e6 11 0-0 ♝e7 12 ♞b5 ♛b8 13 g3 ♞d5 14 ♞c3 0-0 15 ♞xd5 exd5 16 ♝f4 ♝d6 17 ♞e5 ♞xe5 18 dxe5 ♝xe5 19 ♛xd5 ♝xf4 20 ♛xf5 ♛e5 led shortly to a drawn in Korneev-Lautier, Spanish Cht 1999) 8 d4 cxd4 9 cxd4 e4! 10 ♞g5 ♝xd6 11 ♞xe4 ♝b4+ 12 ♞bc3 ♛xd4 13 0-0 ½-½ Adams-Khalifman, Wijk aan Zee 1995.

a2) 6...g6 7 d4 cxd4 8 cxd4 ♝g7 9 ♝f4 d6 10 exd6 exd6 11 0-0 ♞d5 12 ♝g3 0-0 13 ♞c3 ♞de7 14 d5 ♞b4 15 ♛b3 ♞a6 with complicated play, Daniliuk-Poluliakhov, Krasnodar 1997.

b) 6 ♝b5 a6 7 ♝e2 has recently been tried by Sveshnikov, the idea being that ...a6 weakens c5. After 7...d6

8 exd6 ♛xd6 9 0-0, Sveshnikov-Van Wely, Tallinn rpd 2002 continued 9...g6 10 d3 ♝g7 11 ♞bd2 ♛c7 12 ♞e4 ♞d7 13 ♝e3 b6 and, having forced ...a6 and ...b6, White entered a favourable IQP position with 14 d4 cxd4 15 cxd4 ♝b7 16 ♜c1 ♛b8 17 ♛d2 ±. However, Black could have played 9...♝f5 instead, pressurizing the d3-square. Then after 10 d4 cxd4 11 ♞xd4 ♞xd4 12 cxd4 e6 the pawn being on a6 would be useful for Black as it exerts control over b5; e.g., 13 ♝f3 ♛c7 14 ♞c3 ♝d6.

We return to the position after 6 ♝b3 *(D)*:

Black can now choose between:

A: 6...d5   180

B: 6...c4   184

6...g6 is a perfectly playable alternative:

a) 7 0-0 ♝g7 8 ♜e1 0-0 9 ♞a3 d6 10 exd6 ♛xd6 11 d4 cxd4 12 ♞b5 ♛d8 13 ♞bxd4 ♞xd4 14 ♞xd4 ∞ Gheng-Jianu, Bucharest 2001.

b) 7 d3 ♝g7 8 a4 ♞a5 9 ♝c2 d5 10 exd6 ♛xd6 11 ♞bd2 ∞ Yudin-Bibko, Novosibirsk 2001.

c) 7 d4 cxd4 – *4 d4 cxd4 5 ♘f3 ♘c6 6 ♗c4 ♘b6 7 ♗b3 g6.*

A)

6...d5 (D)

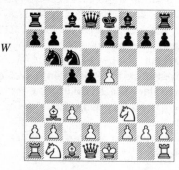

7 exd6

After 7 d4?! cxd4 8 cxd4 ♗g4 9 ♘c3 e6 Black has a sort of French Defence with a good light-squared bishop.

7...♕xd6 (D)

Or:

a) 7...e5? 8 d4! c4 9 ♗a4 ♘xa4 10 ♕xa4 exd4 11 ♘xd4 ♗xd6 12 ♘xc6 ♕d7 13 ♘d2 ♕xc6 14 ♕xc6+ bxc6 15 ♘xc4 and White has won a pawn, Sermek-Soln, Maribor 1998.

b) 7...e6 8 d4 ♗xd6 9 0-0 0-0 10 ♖e1 ♗e7 11 ♗e3 (11 dxc5 ♕xd1 12 ♖xd1 ♗xc5 13 ♗f4 ♖d8 14 ♖xd8+ ♘xd8 15 ♘bd2 ♗d7 = Morozevich-Lautier, Wijk aan Zee 2002) 11...cxd4 12 cxd4 ♘d5 13 ♘c3 ♘xe3 14 ♖xe3 ♗f6 15 ♘e4 ♗d7 16 ♕d2 ♗e7 17 a3 ♕a5 18 ♖c3 ♖ad8 19 ♖d1 ♗c8 20 ♕c1 leaves White much more active, Sveshnikov-Tratar, Nova Gorica 1996.

c) 7...exd6!? 8 d4 ♗g4 9 dxc5 (9 h3 ♗h5 10 ♗e3 ♗e7 11 dxc5 dxc5 12 ♘a3 0-0 13 0-0 ♕c8 14 ♗f4 ♖d8 15

♕e2 ♕f5 with a nice position for Black, Ivanchuk-Kasparov, Dortmund 1992) 9...dxc5 10 0-0 ♗e7 11 ♘a3 0-0 12 ♗f4 ± Ivanchuk.

d) 7...c4 8 ♗c2 – *6...c4 7 ♗c2 d6 8 exd6.*

Now White has two main options:

A1: 8 0-0   180

A2: 8 ♘a3   182

A1)

8 0-0 ♗e6 (D)

Or:

a) 8...♗f5 9 d4 e6!? (*9...cxd4 – 4 d4 cxd4 5 ♘f3 ♘c6 6 ♗c4 ♘b6 7 ♗b3 d5 8 exd6 ♕xd6 9 0-0 ♗f5*; this line favours White) 10 ♘a3 ♕d7 11 ♗f4 a6 12 ♘h4 (12 ♗e3 cxd4 13 ♘xd4 ♘xd4 14 ♗xd4 ♗xa3 15 bxa3 ♕c6 ∞ Sermek-Dominguez, Istanbul OL 2000) 12...♗g6 (12...cxd4 13 ♘xf5 exf5 14 cxd4 gives White a great initiative) 13 dxc5 ♕xd1 14 ♖axd1 ♗xc5 15 ♘xg6 hxg6 16 ♘c4 and White has a slight advantage in the endgame because of his bishop-pair.

b) 8...c4 9 ♗c2 – *6...c4 7 ♗c2 d6 8 exd6 ♕xd6 9 0-0.*

9 ♘a3

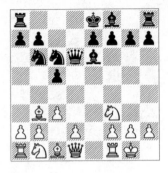

W

Or:

a) 9 d4 cxd4 – *4 d4 cxd4 5 ♘f3 ♘c6 6 ♗c4 ♘b6 7 ♗b3 d5 8 exd6 ♕xd6 9 0-0 ♗e6.*

b) 9 ♕e2 and now:

b1) 9...♗f5!? is an interesting tactical idea: 10 d4 cxd4 11 ♘xd4 ♘xd4 12 cxd4 ♕g6!? 13 ♕b5+ and now 13...♔d8?! followed by ...♗d3 wins the exchange but leaves White with the bishop-pair and Black with a precarious king position. 13...♗d7 is better, although 14 ♕e5 gives White control over the key d5-square, and therefore an advantage.

b2) After 9...♗xb3 10 axb3 e6 11 ♖d1 ♗e7 12 d4 cxd4 13 ♘xd4 ♘xd4 14 ♖xd4 ♕c6 15 ♘d2 0-0 16 ♘f3 a6!, Black is ready to meet the planned 17 ♘e5 with 17...♕b5!, so White has to waste time with 17 b4, but following 17...♗f6 18 ♖d3 the a-pawn is not under attack any more and Black can play 18...♖ad8. Since 19 ♗g5 is then bad due to 19...♗xg5 20 ♘xg5 ♕b5, Rozentalis-Ribli, Bundesliga 2001/2 concluded 19 ♖xd8 ½-½.

9...♗xb3

Black can again try 9...c4 10 ♗c2 g6 and now:

a) 11 b3 ♗g7 – *6...c4 7 ♗c2 d6 8 exd6 ♕xd6 9 0-0 g6 10 ♘a3 ♗g7 11 b3 ♗e6.*

b) 11 d4 cxd3 12 ♘b5 ♕d7 13 ♕xd3 ♕xd3 14 ♗xd3 0-0-0 15 ♗e2 a6 16 ♘bd4 ♘xd4 17 cxd4 f6 with an equal endgame, Benjamin-Gavrikov, Horgen 1994.

10 axb3 *(D)*

10 ♕xb3, hoping for 10...e6 11 d4 cxd4 – *4 d4 cxd4 5 ♘f3 ♘c6 6 ♗c4 ♘b6 7 ♗b3 d6 8 exd6 ♕xd6 9 0-0 ♗e6 10 ♘a3 ♗xb3 11 ♕xb3 e6 ±*, is well met by 10...♕d3! blockading the d-pawn. After 11 ♕b5 0-0-0 12 ♘g5 (12 ♕xc5 e5 13 ♕e3 ♗xa3 14 bxa3 ♘c4 leaves Black clearly better in the endgame) 12...c4 13 ♘xf7 ♖d5 the white queen is trapped, Sermek-Gelfand, Ljubljana 2001.

B

10...a6

This move is played primarily to keep the a-pawn itself safe. Instead:

a) 10...e6 is bad: 11 ♘c4 ♕d8 12 d4 cxd4 13 ♘xd4 ♘xd4 14 ♘xb6 ♕xb6 15 ♗e3 ♖d8 16 ♗xd4 ♗c5 17 ♗xc5 ♕xc5 18 b4! ♕c6 19 ♕g4 winning a pawn, Sveshnikov-Filippov, Russian Ch (Elista) 1995.

b) 10...♕d3 11 ♖e1 ♖d8 12 ♖e3 ♕d7 13 ♘c4 ♘xc4 14 bxc4 e6 (Christiansen-Seirawan, USA Ch (Chandler) 1997) 15 b3!? ♗e7 16 ♗b2 0-0 17 d4 gives White a slight edge.

11 ♘c4 ♕d8 12 ♕e2

A new idea. Instead:

a) After 12 ♘xb6 ♕xb6 13 d4 cxd4 14 ♘xd4 ♘xd4 15 ♗e3 ♕xb3! 16 ♕xd4 ♖d8 (Shovunov-Stillger, Budapest 1996) 17 ♕a7 f6 White's advantage in development is temporary, while Black is a pawn up. This line shows why *10...a6* was a better move than *10...e6*.

b) 12 d3 e6 13 ♘xb6 (13 ♗e3 ♘d5!) 13...♕xb6 14 ♗e3 ♕c7 15 d4 cxd4 16 ♘xd4 ♗e7 gives White the tiniest of advantages – almost nothing.

12...e6 13 ♖d1 ♕c7

13...♘xc4 14 bxc4 followed by 15 d4 gives White a slight advantage.

14 d4 cxd4 15 ♘xd4 ♘xc4

After 15...♘xd4 16 ♖xd4 ♘xc4 (after 16...♗c5, 17 ♗f4! is strong) 17 ♖xc4 ♕b6 18 b4, White is ahead in development.

16 ♕xc4

White has a slight advantage. Practical tests are required.

A2)

8 ♘a3 *(D)*

8...a6

Or:

a) 8...♗f5 9 d4 cxd4 10 ♘b5 ♕d7 11 ♘bxd4 ± Yudasin.

b) 8...♗e6 and then:

b1) 9 0-0 – *8 0-0 ♗e6 9 ♘a3*.

b2) 9 d4 ♗xb3 (9...cxd4 – *4 d4 cxd4 5 ♘f3 ♘c6 6 ♗c4 ♘b6 7 ♗b3 d6*

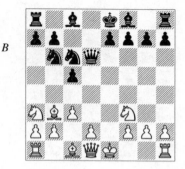

8 exd6 ♕xd6 9 ♘a3 ♗e6 ±) 10 ♕xb3 cxd4 and now:

b21) 11 ♘b5 ♕d7 12 ♘bxd4 ♘xd4 13 ♘xd4 e6 14 0-0 ♗e7 15 ♖d1 0-0 16 ♘b5 ♕c6 17 ♗e3 ♗c5 18 ♗xc5 ½-½ Pavasović-Kharlov, Ljubljana 2002.

b22) 11 0-0 transposes to *4 d4 cxd4 5 ♘f3 ♘c6 6 ♗c4 ♘b6 7 ♗b3 d6 8 exd6 ♕xd6 9 0-0 ♗e6 10 ♘a3 ♗xb3 11 ♕xb3 ±*. White has achieved his objective of a favourable transposition to the previous chapter.

9 0-0 ♗f5

Or:

a) 9...♗e6 10 d4 cxd4 – *4 d4 cxd4 5 ♘f3 ♘c6 6 ♗c4 ♘b6 7 ♗b3 d6 8 exd6 ♕xd6 9 ♘a3 a6 10 0-0 ♗e6*.

b) 9...e6 10 ♕e2 (10 d4 cxd4 – *4 d4 cxd4 5 ♘f3 ♘c6 6 ♗c4 ♘b6 7 ♗b3 d6 8 exd6 ♕xd6 9 ♘a3 a6 10 0-0 e6*) 10...♗e7 11 d4 cxd4 12 ♖d1 ♗f6 13 ♘c2 ± Novak-Priehoda, Slovakian Ch (Topolcianky) 1993.

10 d4 cxd4

This position can also be reached via *4 d4 cxd4 5 ♘f3 ♘c6 6 ♗c4 ♘b6 7 ♗b3 d6 8 exd6 ♕xd6 9 ♘a3 a6 10 0-0 ♗f5*, though in that move-order we recommend *9...dxc3!* for Black. We have chosen to analyse this position here because it is critical for this variation.

11 ♘xd4

This knight exchange makes particular sense here. If the bishop were still on c8, Black could quickly try to manoeuvre the bishop to c6 via d7 to help blockade d5; and with the bishop on f5, White has freed up the f3-square for his queen, from where it will attack the f5-bishop and threaten a d5 pawn-break, undermining the defending e6-pawn.

11...♘xd4 12 cxd4 e6 13 ♕f3 *(D)*

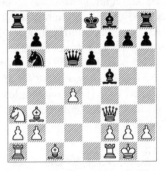

B

13...♕d7

13...♕c6?! is also met by the undermining 14 d5!. After 14...♘xd5, 15 ♖d1 renews the threat. Thus, Black retreats with 15...♘b6, whereupon White plays 16 ♕g3, stopping Black developing by attacking g7, and planning to follow up with ♗e3 or ♗f4 and then ♖ac1 with a crushing attack. If Black returns again with 16...♘d5, White breaks through by 17 ♘c4 ♖d8 18 ♘e3! ♗g6 19 ♘xd5 exd5 20 ♗g5 with a winning position, Sermek-Kiseliov, Ljubljana 1992.

14 d5!

White needs to try this pawn sacrifice since Black can equalize easily against other lines:

a) 14 ♗f4 ♗xa3! 15 bxa3 0-0 and Black is fine, Manor-Yudasin, Rishon-le-Zion 1996.

b) 14 ♘c2 ♗xc2! is equal, Sevillano-D.Gurevich, Philadelphia 1995.

c) 14 ♘c4 ♘xc4 15 ♗xc4 ♖c8 16 ♗b3 ♗c2! and with the light-squared bishops exchanged, Black has nothing to be afraid of.

d) 14 ♖e1 ♗e7 15 ♗g5 ♗xg5 16 ♕xf5 ♗e7 17 ♕e4 ♖d8 18 d5 ♘xd5 19 ♖ad1 0-0 20 ♖xd5 ½-½ Sveshnikov-Novgorodsky, St Petersburg 1997.

14...♘xd5

14...exd5?! 15 ♕g3! (Okhotnik) hinders Black's development and keeps White on top.

15 ♖d1 ♗xa3

An alternative idea is 15...♖d8, when White can keep the pressure on with 16 ♘c4 – Okhotnik.

16 bxa3 0-0 *(D)*

W

17 h4

This is played with the idea of g4 and h5 trapping the bishop, but also clears the back rank as the immediate

17 ♗xd5 exd5 18 ♖xd5 is met by 18...♕e6! 19 ♕xf5?? ♕e1#.

White has also tried first developing his queen's bishop by 17 ♗b2 ♖ad8 and only then 18 h4:

a) 18...f6 19 ♖d4 and now, rather than 19...♗g6 20 h5 ♗f7 21 h6 ± Sermek-Soln, Dresden Z 1998, Har-Zvi notes the improvement 19...♖fe8 20 ♖ad1 ♕c8 21 g4 ♗g6 22 h5 ♗f7 23 h6 gxh6!? 24 ♗xd5 ♖xd5 25 ♕xf6 ♖xd4 26 ♖xd4 e5, when Black is doing well.

b) 18...♕b5! has the point 19 g4 ♗g6 20 h5?! ♗c2 21 ♖xd5?? ♖xd5 22 ♕c3 ♖g5! (Har-Zvi), and gives Black good play.

17...♖ac8

This move is now forced and indirectly defends against White's threats, the ideas being 18 g4 ♗c2 and 18 ♗xd5 exd5 19 ♖xd5 ♕e6 20 ♕xf5 ♕e1+ 21 ♔h2 ♖xc1.

18 ♖d2

This is Okhotnik's recommendation, which he assesses as slightly better for White. White's bishop-pair gives him definite compensation for the pawn, though Black should be able to hold the position with precise play. For example, the position after 18...♖c5 19 ♗b2 occurred in Okhotnik-A.Shneider, USSR 1987. The game continued 19...♕c8 20 a4 a5 21 ♖ad1 h6?! 22 ♗xd5 exd5 23 ♖xd5 b6? 24 ♕g3 f6 25 ♗xf6! ±, which shows what can happen if Black is not careful.

The move-order actually used in that game, 18 ♗b2, allows Black the possibility of 18...♗c2!, when Okhotnik analysed 19 ♗xg7!? (19 ♕g4? f5 ∓)

19...♗xd1 (19...♔xg7? 20 ♕g4+ ♔h8 21 ♖xd5 ±) 20 ♕g3 ♗h5! 21 ♗b2+ (21 ♗xf8+?! ♔xf8 22 ♕e5 ♗g4! ∓) 21...♗g6 22 h5 with unclear compensation for the exchange (*Informator 43*).

B)

6...c4

This double-edged move gains space and hinders White's queenside development and defence of e5, but leaves a slightly vulnerable pawn on c4. After a later b3 cxb3, axb3, White gets an open a-file and a central pawn-mass, but the c3- and b3-pawns are slightly weak. (A similar pawn-structure can also arise after *2...e6*; e.g., *3 d4 d5 4 exd5 exd5 5 ♘f3 ♘c6 6 ♗e3 c4 7 b3 cxb3 8 axb3*, but there Black has a pawn on d5 instead of e7.) This leads to complex positions that are difficult to assess.

7 ♗c2 (D)

Now:

B1: 7...d6   185
B2: 7...♕c7   187

After 7...g6, the most accurate way to continue seems to be to attack the c4-pawn with ♕e2 followed by ♘a3. Other moves are of course possible but will generally simply transpose to lines considered under *7...d6 8 exd6 ♕xd6 9 0-0 g6*. After 8 ♕e2:

a) 8...♗g7 9 ♘a3 0-0 10 0-0 ♘a5 11 b4 cxb3 12 axb3 d6 13 d4 ♘c6 14 h3 (14 exd6 seems better, leaving White two tempi up on other lines) 14...dxe5 15 dxe5 ♗e6 16 ♘b5 ♗d5 ½-½ Nunn-Tkachev, London Lloyds Bank 1994, though Sveshnikov considers that White is better after 17 ♘bd4.

b) 8...d6 9 ♘a3! d5 10 h3 ♗g7 11 0-0 ♘d7 12 e6 fxe6 13 ♘g5 gives White the better chances, Adams-Gelfand, Wijk aan Zee 1994.

c) 8...d5 9 exd6 ♕xd6 10 ♘a3 ♗e6 (10...♕e6!?) 11 b3 cxb3 12 axb3 ♗g7 13 d4 0-0 14 0-0 was the move-order of Sveshnikov-Gavrikov, Tallinn rpd 2002, analysed below under *7...d6 8 exd6 ♕xd6 9 0-0 g6 10 ♘a3 ♗g7 11 ♕e2 ♗e6 12 b3 cxb3 13 axb3 0-0 14 d4*.

B1)

7...d6 8 exd6 ♕xd6 *(D)*

8...e5 9 0-0 ♗xd6 can become dangerous for Black: 10 d3 cxd3 11 ♕xd3 ♗e6 12 ♖e1 f6 13 ♘d4 ♗c4 14 ♕h3 ♔f7 15 ♘d2 ♘xd4 16 cxd4 ♗e6 17 ♗b3 ♖e8 18 ♘e4 and White has too many threats, Adams-McShane, British League (4NCL) 1997/8.

9 0-0

9 ♘a3 ♕e6+ gives White nothing better than to swap queens and go for an equal endgame by 10 ♕e2, Sveshnikov-Yudasin, Kemerovo 1995.

9...g6

Or 9...♗g4, and now:

a) 10 ♖e1 ♘e5! 11 ♖xe5 ♗xf3 12 ♕e1 ♗d5 13 b3 e6 14 ♘a3 ♕d7 15 bxc4 ♘xc4 16 ♘xc4 ♗xc4 17 ♗b3 ♗xb3 18 axb3 ♗d6 19 ♖e2 0-0 20 d4 ∞ Tkachev-Bacrot, Cap d'Agde 2000.

b) 10 h3 ♗h5 11 ♕e2 e6 12 ♘a3 ♕f4 13 b3 cxb3 14 axb3 ♗d6 15 ♖e1 ♗xf3 16 ♕xf3 ♕xf3 17 gxf3 0-0 18 d4 ♗d5 19 ♘b5 ♗f4 20 ♗e4 ♗xc1 21 ♖axc1 ♖ad8 22 c4 ♘db4 23 c5!, Rozentalis-Greenfeld, Israeli Cht 1999. Now Black can't take on d4, because he would lose the b7-pawn. White's knight is coming to d6 and Black will have to sacrifice an exchange for it. Note the strategy of forcing Black to defend the c4-pawn by playing ♕e2 and ♘a3 before exchanging it off with b3.

10 ♘a3

White's move-order is flexible here. 10 ♕e2 and 10 ♖e1 are also possible.

Or 10 b3:

a) 10...♗g7 and then:

a1) 11 bxc4?! ♘xc4 12 d3 ♘b6 13 d4 0-0 14 ♘bd2 ♕c7 15 ♗a3 ♘d5 ∓ Dolmatov-A.Greenfeld, Lyons ECC 1994.

a2) 11 ♘a3 – *10 ♘a3 ♗g7 11 b3*.

b) 10...cxb3 11 axb3 &g7 allows White the additional option of 12 d4 0-0 13 &bd2.

10...&g7 *(D)*

11 b3

This is the most common move, but it is well worth carefully investigating the less tested alternatives for possible improvements:

a) 11 &e1 0-0 12 b3 &e6 13 &g5 &d5 14 &g4 cxb3 15 axb3 h6 16 &e4 &d7 17 &xd7 &xd7 18 d4 f5 was fine for Black in Nunn-Kramnik, Monaco Amber blindfold 1994.

b) 11 &e2 is logical, attacking the c4-pawn before liquidating it with b3, though it does run the risk of an early queen swap. There have been few practical tests to date. Black can try:

b1) 11...&e5 12 &xe5 &xe5 13 &xe5 &xe5 14 &e1 &f6 15 b3! (15 d4 cxd3 16 &xd3 0-0 17 &e4 ±) has the point that 15...&e6?! 16 bxc4 &xc4? fails to 17 &a4+ &f8 18 &xe6 &xa3 19 &xf6 +−.

b2) 11...&e6 12 &e4! 0-0 (12...f5!? 13 &xc6+ &xc6 14 &e1 0-0 15 &e5 &xe5 16 &xe5 f4!? 17 &c2 followed by 18 &d4 and then b3 and &a3 gives

White a clear advantage) 13 &e1 &d7 14 &f1 &ad8 15 &d3 cxd3! 16 &xe6 &xe6 17 &e1 &f5 18 g4 &xg4 19 &xd3 ± Harley-Munson, Bury St Edmunds 2002.

b3) 11...&e6 and then:

b31) 12 d4!? cxd3 13 &xd3 0-0 14 &b5 &d7 15 &d1 &d5 16 &e3 &xf3 17 &xf3 (17 gxf3!?) 17...&e5 18 &e2 &xd3 19 &xd3 &xd3 20 &xd3 &c4 21 &xa7 &xb2 22 &d7 ±.

b32) 12 b3 cxb3 13 axb3 0-0 14 d4 &g4. Note how the plan of playing &e2 and &a3 before b3 effectively gains White the tempo &e2 as Black has played ...&e6 and then ...&g4. Now:

b321) 15 h3 &xf3 16 &xf3 transposes to *11 b3 cxb3 12 axb3 0-0 13 d4 &g4 14 h3 &xf3 15 &xf3* – both sides have lost a tempo.

b322) 15 &e4 &e6! (one tactical justification of &e2 as an extra move is that after 15...f5 White can play 16 &c4! &xc4 17 &xc4+) 16 &c4 &d5 17 &d2 &f6 18 &d3 &xe2 19 &xe2 &e4 = Sveshnikov-Gavrikov, Tallinn rpd 2002. Black just escaped with equality here.

b323) 15 &c4! improves, as the extra move &e2 enables White to meet 15...&d5 with 16 &e4.

11...cxb3

11...&e6 12 &e2 – *11 &e2 &e6 12 b3*.

12 axb3 0-0 13 d4 &g4 *(D)*

Black prepares to break in the centre with ...e5. The immediate 13...e5 can be met by 14 dxe5 (14 &b5!? followed by &a3 – Lutz) 14...&xd1 15 &xd1 &xe5 16 &d4! ± Yudasin.

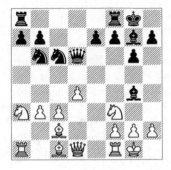

W

14 h3

White needs an improvement and this is one place to look for one:

a) 14 ♘c4 ♕d5! has the point 15 ♘e3 ♗xf3 16 ♘xd5? ♗xd1 17 ♘xb6 ♗xc2 ∓ (Yudasin).

b) 14 ♗e4 ♖ad8 (14...f5!? is more testing; e.g., 15 ♗d3 e5 16 ♘c4 ♕c7 17 ♘xb6 ♕xb6 18 ♗c4+ ♔h8 19 d5 {19 ♗a3 exd4!} 19...e4 ∞) 15 h3 ♗e6 16 ♖e1 ♗d5 17 ♗g5 ♗xe4 18 ♖xe4 ♖d7 19 ♕e2 ♘d5 20 ♘b5 ♕b8 21 c4 gives White the initiative, Sveshnikov-Rõtšagov, Åland 1997.

c) 14 ♖e1 has the point 14...♖fd8 15 h3 ♗xf3 16 ♕xf3 e5 17 dxe5 ♘xe5 (now Black cannot play ...♕xe5) 18 ♕xb7 – Dolmatov.

14...♗xf3 15 ♕xf3 e5 *(D)*

W

16 ♘b5

Instead:

a) 16 ♘c4?! ♘xc4 17 bxc4 exd4 18 ♗a3 ♕c7 19 ♗xf8 ♖xf8 (Yudasin) is a good exchange sacrifice for Black.

b) 16 dxe5 ♕xe5 is also good for Black.

16...♕d7

16...♕d5 is not good: 17 ♕e2 ♖ac8 18 c4 ♘xd4 19 ♘xd4 ♕xd4 20 ♗e3 ♕d7 21 ♖xa7 ♕c6 22 ♕f3 and White wins a pawn, Rozentalis-Konguvel, Koszalin 1998.

17 ♗a3 ♖fc8!

This threatens not only 18...exd4, but also 18...♘xd4. White has no good defence to this and must sacrifice a pawn.

18 dxe5 ♘xe5 19 ♕e2 a6 20 ♘d6 ♖xc3 21 ♖fd1

This was played in Rozentalis-Cu.Hansen, Esbjerg 2001. White has some compensation for the pawn, but Black is, of course, out of danger. Thus White needs to improve, and the best chance is probably either 14 ♖e1 or 11 ♕e2.

B2)

7...♕c7 8 ♕e2 g5 *(D)*

Black launches a spectacular attack on the defender of the e5-pawn. It is too late for Black to turn back since after 8...g6 9 0-0 ♗g7 10 ♖e1 0-0 11 ♘a3 (Harley-Somerset, Cambridge 2000) Black's c4-pawn is in trouble. Following 11...♘a5 12 b4, 12...♘c6 13 ♘xc4 ♘xb4 14 ♘xb6 ♘xc2 15 ♘xa8 ♕b8 16 ♗a3! ♘xe1 (16...♘xa3 17 d3! ±) 17 ♖xe1 ♖e8 18 ♘c4 ♕xa8 19 ♘g5 e6 20 ♕f4 +− is no good for Black, so he has to play 12...cxb3 13 axb3 ♘c6 14 d4, when White has gained time and space.

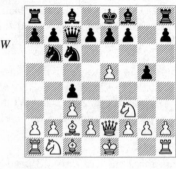

9 h3

Other options give Black good play:

a) 9 ♘a3?! g4 10 ♘b5 ♕b8 11 ♘g5 (11 ♘d6+? exd6 12 exd6+ ♗e7! ∓ Hodgson/Gallagher) 11...♘xe5 12 0-0 a6 13 ♘d4 h6 14 f4 hxg5 15 fxe5 ♗g7 16 ♖e1 d6 and Black must be better in this very messy position, Kazhgaleev-Nataf, French Cht (Montpellier) 2001.

b) 9 ♘xg5 ♕xe5 10 d4 (10 ♘xh7 ♗h6 and the knight is out of the game) 10...cxd3 11 ♗xd3 ♕xe2+ 12 ♗xe2 ♗g7 13 0-0 0-0 14 ♘a3 d5 15 ♘f3 e5 and Black is better, Macieja-Krasenkow, New Delhi FIDE 2000.

c) 9 e6 (White tries to spoil Black's centre, but Black's pawn-mass grants him good practical chances) 9...dxe6 10 ♘xg5 ♕e5 11 d4 (after 11 ♘e4 f5 12 ♘g3 ♕xe2+ 13 ♘xe2 ♗g7 14 ♘a3 0-0 15 0-0 ♗d7 Black has finished his development, Sveshnikov-Sakaev, St Petersburg 1997) 11...cxd3 12 ♗xd3 ♕xe2+ 13 ♗xe2 h6 14 ♘e4 e5 and then:

c1) 15 ♘a3 ♗f5 (or 15...f5 16 ♗h5+ ♔d8 17 ♘g3 e6 18 ♘c2 ♗d6 19 ♗d2 ♘c4 with an advantage, Ponomariov-Van Wely, Biel 2000) 16 ♘g3 (16 ♗f3 0-0-0 17 ♘c2 e6 18 ♗d2 ♗g6 and the f-pawn is ready to advance, Rozentalis-Hellers, Århus 1997) 16...♗g6 17 ♘c4 ♘d5 18 0-0 0-0-0 19 ♖e1 h5 20 h4 e6 leaves Black in control of the centre, Adams-Svidler, Groningen FIDE 1997.

c2) The latest improvement for White in this line is 15 0-0 ♗f5 16 ♘bd2 (supporting the e4-knight rather than retreating it immediately) 16...♗g6 17 a4 ♘d7 18 f3 f5 19 ♘f2 ♗g7 20 a5, Morozevich-Lautier, Cannes 2002. White has kept Black's initiative under control and has some chances to build up pressure against Black's weak pawns. Black is OK because of his strong centre, but the play is very complicated.

9...♗g7 10 0-0 ♘xe5 11 ♘xg5 d5 (D)

12 a4

Instead:

a) 12 ♗xh7 ♗f6 13 d4 cxd3 14 ♗xd3 ♘xd3 15 ♕xd3 and now Black should avoid 15...♕e5? 16 f4 ♕f5 17 ♕e2, when White manages to keep his extra pawn, Sermek-Tratar, Bled 2001. Instead, after 15...e5, we think that Black's bishop-pair and nice centre give him more than sufficient compensation for the pawn.

b) 12 b3 ♗d7 13 a4 cxb3 14 ♗xb3 ♗f5 15 a5 ♘bc4 16 d4 h6 17 dxe5 hxg5 18 ♗xg5 ♕xe5 (18...♗xe5 leads to a more complicated position that also seems to be fine for Black) 19 ♗xc4 dxc4 20 ♕xe5 ♗xe5 21 ♖e1 f6 22 f4 and this endgame promises equal chances, Rozentalis-Hraček, Bundesliga 1998/9.

12...h6 13 ♘f3 ♘bd7 14 ♖e1 0-0 15 ♘a3 a6 16 d4 cxd3 17 ♗xd3 ♘xd3

Pavasović-Yakovich, Dubai 2001 was agreed drawn here, but in the very next round, Sermek played on to win against Sveshnikov:

18 ♕xd3 *(D)*

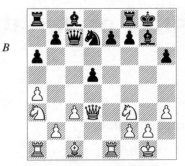

B

18...e6 19 ♗e3 b6

Rogozenko suggests 19...♘c5 as an improvement, when White is only marginally better.

20 ♕d2 ♔h7 21 ♗f4 e5 22 ♗g3 ♗b7 23 ♘d4 ♕d6?!

23...♖ae8 24 ♘f5 ♘c5 is better – Rogozenko.

24 ♘f5 ♕g6 25 ♘xg7 ♕xg7 26 ♘c4!

White has a clear advantage, Sermek-Sveshnikov, Dubai 2001.

Index of Variations

Chapter Guide

1: Alternatives to 2...e6, 2...d5 and 2...♘f6
1 e4 c5 2 c3 *15*

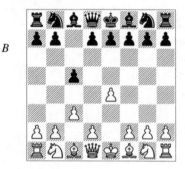

B

7: 2...♘f6: Sidelines
1 e4 c5 2 c3 ♘f6 3 e5 ♘d5 *116*

B

8: 2...♘f6 3 e5 ♘d5 4 d4 cxd4 5
♘**f3: 5...e6 and Other Moves**
1 e4 c5 2 c3 ♘f6 3 e5 ♘d5 4 d4 cxd4 5
♘f3 *132* **5...e6 6 cxd4** *133*

9: 2...♘f6 3 e5 ♘d5 4 d4 cxd4 5
♘**f3** ♘**c6 6** ♗**c4** ♘**b6 7** ♗**b3**
1 e4 c5 2 c3 ♘f6 3 e5 ♘d5 4 d4 cxd4 5
♘f3 ♘c6 *156* **6** ♗**c4** ♘**b6 7** ♗**b3** *156*

10: 2...♘f6 3 e5 ♘d5 4 ♘**f3**
1 e4 c5 2 c3 ♘f6 3 e5 ♘d5 4 ♘f3 *177*
4...♘c6 5 ♗**c4** ♘**b6 6** ♗**b3** *179*